THE CAMBRIDGE COMPANION TO
POSTMODERN THEOLOGY

Postmodernity allows for no absolutes and no essence. Yet theology is concerned with the absolute, the essential. How then does theology sit within postmodernity? Is postmodern theology possible, or is such a concept a contradiction in terms? Should theology bother about postmodernism or just get on with its own thing? Can it?

Theologians have responded in many different ways to the challenges posed by theories of postmodernity. In this introductory guide to a complex area, editor Kevin J. Vanhoozer addresses the issue head on in a lively survey of what "talk about God" might mean in a postmodern age, and vice versa. The book then offers examples of different types of contemporary theology in relation to postmodernity, while the second part examines the key Christian doctrines in postmodern perspective. Leading theologians contribute to this clear and informative Companion, which no student of theology should be without.

KEVIN J. VANHOOZER is Research Professor of Systematic Theology at Trinity Evangelical Divinity School, Illinois. Before that he taught for eight years at New College, University of Edinburgh, where he was Senior Lecturer in Theology and Religious Studies. He is the author of *Biblical Narrative in the Philosophy of Paul Ricoeur* (1990), *Is There a Meaning in this Text? The Bible, the Reader, and the Morality of Literary Knowledge* (1998), *First Theology: God, Scripture, and Hermeneutics* (2002), and *The Drama of Doctrine: A Canonical–Linguistic Approach to Theology* (2004). He was also the co-founder and co-chair for many years of the Systematic Theology group in the American Academy of Religion.

CAMBRIDGE COMPANIONS TO RELIGION

A series of companions to major topics and key figures in theology and religious studies. Each volume contains specially commissioned chapters by international scholars which provide an accessible and stimulating introduction to the subject for new readers and non-specialists.

Other titles in the series

Forthcoming

THE CAMBRIDGE COMPANION TO

POSTMODERN THEOLOGY

Editor

Kevin J. Vanhoozer

CAMBRIDGE
UNIVERSITY PRESS

PUBLISHED BY THE PRESS SYNDICATE OF THE UNIVERSITY OF CAMBRIDGE
The Pitt Building, Trumpington Street, Cambridge, United Kingdom

CAMBRIDGE UNIVERSITY PRESS
The Edinburgh Building, Cambridge, CB2 2RU, UK
40 West 20th Street, New York, NY 10011–4211, USA
477 Williamstown Road, Port Melbourne, VIC 3207, Australia
Ruiz de Alarcón 13, 28014 Madrid, Spain
Dock House, The Waterfront, Cape Town 8001, South Africa

http://www.cambridge.org

First published 2003
Reprinted 2004, 2005

Printed in the United Kingdom at the University Press, Cambridge

Typeface Severin 10/13 pt.   *System* LATEX 2_ε [TB]

A catalogue record for this book is available from the British Library

ISBN 0 521 79062 x hardback
ISBN 0 521 79395 5 paperback

Contents

Contributors

THOMAS A. CARLSON received his Ph.D. from the University of Chicago in 1995 and is Associate Professor in the Department of Religious Studies at the University of California, Santa Barbara, where he teaches courses in religion and modern philosophy, contemporary theory, and the history of Christian thought and culture. He is author of *Indiscretion: Finitude and the Naming of God* (1999), an investigation of negative and mystical theologies in light of deconstructive and phenomenological thought, and translator of several works by Jean-Luc Marion, including *God Without Being* (1991), *Reduction and Donation: Investigations of Husserl, Heidegger, and Phenomenology*, and *The Idol and Distance* (2001).

PHILIP CLAYTON holds a Ph.D. in both philosophy and religious studies from Yale University. Newly appointed to the Ingraham Chair at the Claremont School of Theology, he has taught previously at Haverford College, Williams College, and the California State University. Clayton has been guest professor at the Divinity School of Harvard University, and Humboldt Professor and Senior Fulbright Professor at the University of Munich. He is a past winner of the Templeton Book Prize for best monograph in the field of science and religion and a winner of the first annual Templeton Research Prize. His books include *The Problem of God in Modern Thought* (2000), *God and Contemporary Science* (1997), *Explanation from Physics to Theology: An Essay in Rationality and Religion* (1989), *Das Gottesproblem*, vol. 1: *Gott und Unendlichkeit in der neuzeitlichen Philosophie* (1996), and *The Emergence of Spirit* (2003).

DAVID S. CUNNINGHAM is Professor of Theology and Ethics at Seabury-Western Theological Seminary, Evanston, Illinois. His books include *Faithful Persuasion: In Aid of a Rhetoric of Christian Theology* (1991), *These Three Are One: The Practice of Trinitarian Theology* (1998), and *Reading is Believing: The Christian Faith Through Literature and Film* (2002). He was the lead editor of a Festschrift for Geoffrey Wainwright entitled *Ecumenical Theology in Worship, Doctrine, and Life* (1999). He serves as Co-Chair of the Christian Systematic Theology Group of the American Academy of Religion, is a founding member of the Ekklesia Project, and is currently an Alexander von Humboldt Fellow at the Albert-Ludwigs-Universität in Freiburg, Germany.

DAVID F. FORD is Regius Professor of Divinity at the University of Cambridge and Chairman of the Management Committee of the Centre for Advanced Religious and Theological Studies. He is a founder member of the Society for Scriptural Reasoning. His many publications include *Barth and God's Story* (1981), *Meaning and Truth in 2 Corinthians* (with Frances Young, 1987), *Theology: a Very Short Introduction* (1999), *Self and Salvation: Being Transformed* (1999), (ed.) *Modern Theologians: An Introduction to Christian Theology in the Twentieth Century* (1989; 1997), and *The Shape of Living (1997, 2002)*.

MARY McCLINTOCK FULKERSON is currently E. Rhodes & Leona B. Carpenter Associate Professor of Theology at Vanderbilt University Divinity School, after having taught for a number of years at Duke Divinity School and in Duke's Women's Studies Program. Her publications include *Changing the Subject: Women's Discourses and Feminist Theology* (1994) and numerous articles on gender, sexuality, and issues of theological authority and practice. Her current project is a book resulting from an ethnographic study of an interracial church entitled, *Traces of Redemption: Theology for a Worldly Church.*

STANLEY J. GRENZ is Distinguished Professor of Theology at Baylor University and Truett Seminary in Waco, Texas. He is the author of *The Social God and the Relational Self: A Trinitarian Theology of the Imago Dei* (2001), *Beyond Foundationalism: Shaping Theology in a Postmodern Context,* co-authored with John R. Franke (2001), and *Renewing the Center: Evangelical Theology in a Post-Theological Era* (2000). His earlier works include *A Primer on Postmodernism* (1996), *The Moral Quest: Foundations of Christian Ethics* (1997), *Theology for the Community of God* (1994, 2000), and *Twentieth Century Theology: God and the World in a Transitional Age,* co-authored with Roger E. Olson (1992). He is a consulting editor of *Christianity Today* and in 1999–2000 was a Luce Fellow in Theology.

DAVID RAY GRIFFIN is Professor of Philosophy of Religion and Theology at Claremont School of Theology and Claremont Graduate University, one of the directors of the Center for Process Studies, and the editor of the State University of New York Press Series in Constructive Postmodern Thought. His books include *The Reenchantment of Science: Postmodern Proposals* (1986), *God and Religion in the Postmodern World* (1987), *Evil Revisited* (1991), *Parapsychology, Philosophy, and Spirituality: A Postmodern Exploration* (1997), *Unsnarling the World-Knot: Consciousness, Freedom, and the Mind–Body Problem* (1998), *Religion and Scientific Naturalism: Overcoming the Conflicts* (2000), and *Reenchantment without Supernaturalism: A Process Philosophy of Religion* (2001).

GEORGE HUNSINGER is Hazel Thompson McCord Professor of Systematic Theology at Princeton Theological Seminary. An ordained Presbyterian minister, he is particularly interested in the theology of Karl Barth, and is the author of *How to Read Karl Barth: The Shape of His Theology* (1991) and *Disruptive Grace: Studies in the Theology of Karl Barth* (2000).

BRAD J. KALLENBERG is Assistant Professor of Religious Studies at the University of Dayton where he teaches courses in ethics and Protestant Christianity. He is author of *Ethics as Grammar: Changing the Postmodern Subject* (2001) and *Live to*

Tell: Evangelism for a Postmodern Age (2002), and co-editor of *Virtues and Practices in the Christian Tradition: Christian Ethics after MacIntyre* (1997, repr. 2003).

D. STEPHEN LONG is Associate Professor of Theology at Garrett-Evangelical Theological Seminary, where he teaches courses in theology and ethics. Prior to coming to Garrett-Evangelical he taught for three years at St. Joseph's University in Philadelphia. His most recent publications are *The Divine Economy: Theology and the Market* (2000) and *The Goodness of God: Theology, Church and Social Order* (2001). He is a founding member of the Ekklesia Project.

WALTER LOWE is Professor of Systematic Theology at the Candler School of Theology, Emory University. He has written *Mystery and the Unconscious: A Study in the Thought of Paul Ricoeur* (1977), *Evil and the Unconscious* (1983), and *Theology and Difference: The Wound of Reason* (1993).

NANCEY MURPHY is Professor of Christian Philosophy at Fuller Seminary, Pasadena, CA. She received the Ph.D. from University College Berkeley (philosophy of science) in 1980 and the Th.D. from the Graduate Theological Union (theology) in 1987. Her first book, *Theology in the Age of Scientific Reasoning* (1990), won the American Academy of Religion award for excellence and a Templeton Prize for books in science and theology. She is author of six other books and co-editor of six. Her research focuses on the role of modern and postmodern philosophy in shaping Christian theology and on relations between theology and science. She is a former chair of the Board of Directors of the Center for Theology and the Natural Sciences, Berkeley, CA.

DAN R. STIVER is Professor of Theology at Hardin-Simmons University, Abilene, Texas. His publications include *Theology after Ricoeur: New Directions in Hermeneutical Theology* (2001) and *The Philosophy of Religious Language: Sign, Symbol, and Story* (1996). He was editor of the *Review and Expositor* from 1994 to 1998.

KEVIN J. VANHOOZER taught for eight years at New College, University of Edinburgh, where he was Senior Lecturer in Theology and Religious Studies. He is currently Research Professor of Systematic Theology at Trinity Evangelical Divinity School, Illinois. He is the author *of Biblical Narrative in the Philosophy of Paul Ricoeur* (1990), *Is There a Meaning in this Text? The Bible, the Reader, and the Morality of Literary Knowledge* (1998), *First Theology: God, Scripture, and Hermeneutics* (2002), and *The Drama of Doctrine: A Canonical–Linguistic Approach to Theology* (forthcoming). He was also the co-founder and co-chair for many years of the Systematic Theology group in the American Academy of Religion.

GRAHAM WARD is Professor of Contextual Theology and Ethics at the University of Manchester. His books include *Barth, Derrida and the Language of Theology* (1995), *Cities of God* (2000), and *True Religion* (2002). He has edited *The Postmodern God* (1998), *The Certeau Reader* (1999), and the *Blackwell Companion to Postmodern Theology* (2001). He is senior executive editor of the journal *Literature and Theology*.

JOHN WEBSTER is Professor of Systematic Theology at the University of Aberdeen and formerly Lady Margaret Professor of Divinity at the University of Oxford. He is the author of *Barth's Ethics of Reconciliation* (1995), *Barth's Moral Theology* (1998), and *Barth* (2000), and he edited *The Cambridge Companion to Karl Barth* (2000). More recently he has written *Word and Church* (2001), *Holiness* (2002), and *Holy Scripture* (2003).

Preface

To call a theology "modern" is to situate it in a familiar narrative about the Enlightenment or to point out certain family resemblances (for example, critical, scientific) between the thinking of exegetes and theologians and their secular counterparts. No such consensus exists, however, with regard to the term "postmodern." Yet in the past twenty years or so postmodernity has become a concept that is as indispensable for understanding contemporary Western thought and culture as modernity has been for understanding the past three hundred years. For some, postmodernity marks the end of theology; for others, it is a new beginning. What is undeniable is that a number of theologians have now accepted this adjective as an accurate qualification of their approach to theology. Any genuine grasp of the present situation in theology, therefore, must come to grips with the various ways in which these theologians understand and appropriate "the postmodern."

Yet postmodernity is as essentially contested a concept as it is an indispensable one – a sure sign of its importance for society and the academy alike. No one discipline has a monopoly on its definition; indeed, "postmodern" turns up in contexts as diverse as art and architecture, on the one hand, and philosophy and cultural studies, on the other. Though its proponents typically resist hegemonic "metanarratives" that purport to offer universal theories which construe reality from a "God's-eye point of view," there is nonetheless something ambitious about the very concept of the postmodern. For to be postmodern is to signal one's dissatisfaction with at least some aspect of modernity. It is to harbor a revolutionary impulse: the impulse *to do things differently.*

Postmodernity is upsetting, intentionally so. Postmodern thinkers have overturned the tables of the knowledge-changers in the university, the temple of modernity, and have driven out the foundationalists. Or, to take an even older image: postmodern prophets have marched, Moses-like, into Egypt and demanded "Let my people go." Postmoderns have resisted their harsh modern taskmasters together with their requirement to make epistemological bricks out of the straw of logical propositions and the mud of universal human experience. Postmodernity is perhaps best construed as an "exodus" from the constraints of modernity, as a plea to release the other, as a demand to let particulars be themselves rather than having to conform to the structures and strictures of the prevailing ideological or political system. Whether this exodus from modernity leads to genuine liberation or to a new bondage remains, of course, a matter of dispute.

Part one presents and examines theologies that either call themselves postmodern or have been described as such. The chapters treat several varieties of postmodern theology (for example, postliberal, deconstructive) with a special view to explaining the way in which each type conceives the task, method, sources, and norms of theology. Each chapter shows how the adjective "postmodern" qualifies its particular brand. Part one thus represents an eightfold typological path, as it were, that leads to enlightenment, at least as far as the meaning of postmodern theology is concerned.

The essays in Part one hold a twofold interest for the student of contemporary theology: first, because they represent an impressive variety of approaches, a variety that presents the further challenge of specifying what, if anything, it is that constitutes their unity-in-diversity, what it is that justifies the common denominator "postmodern"; and second, because each essay makes a case, at least tacitly, on behalf of each type that it, more than the others, is the legitimate pretender to the postmodern throne.

Whereas the chapters in Part one approach theology via postmodernity, the essays in Part two do the reverse, approaching postmodernity from the vantage point of theology, which is to say, from the perspective of particular doctrines. Certain authors explore ways in which postmodern themes make creative contributions to the development of particular doctrines (for example, how might the postmodern critique of modern individualism yield resources for one's understanding of the church?). Other authors focus on the resources implicit in particular doctrines for engaging, and perhaps correcting, certain postmodern tendencies (for example, how might the doctrine of the Trinity allow us to think difference in terms other than conflict?). In this way, essays in Part two do not merely describe but *do* postmodern theology.

Readers will be interested to know that the image on the cover, "Christ II," was entered in a contest marking the 2000th anniversary of Jesus' birth. The image is in fact a "photomosaic" composed of hundreds of images of the Dead Sea Scrolls, a body of ancient Hebrew and Aramaic manuscripts written on papyrus and leather that date from 200 BC to AD 100. The scrolls include sections of the Old Testament as well as hymns, commentaries, and apocalyptic writings of the Qumran community. "Christ" is thus constructed of textual fragments – an apt commentary on Derrida's maxim,

"There is nothing outside textuality," and an apt metaphor for a volume on postmodern theology. After feasting on the present fragments contained herein, however, we may find, as with the fragments left over after the feeding of the 5,000, that our theological baskets, far from being empty, are in fact brim full.

KEVIN J. VANHOOZER

Part one

Types of postmodern theology

1 Theology and the condition of postmodernity: a report on knowledge (of God)

KEVIN J. VANHOOZER

PREFACE TO POSTMODERNITY: CONCEPT, CULTURE, OR CONDITION?

Those who attempt to define or to analyze the concept of postmodernity do so at their own peril. In the first place, postmoderns reject the notion that any description or definition is "neutral." Definitions may appear to bask in the glow of impartiality, but they invariably exclude something and hence are complicit, wittingly or not, in politics. A definition of postmodernity is as likely to say more about the person offering the definition than it is of "the postmodern." Second, postmoderns resist closed, tightly bounded "totalizing" accounts of such things as the "essence" of the postmodern. And third, according to David Tracy "there is no such phenomenon as postmodernity."[1] There are only postmodernities. Given these three points, the task of writing an introduction may seem to be well nigh impossible: "Abandon hope all ye who enter here!"

In fact, "postmodern" has become a gregarious adjective, and can often be seen in the company of such respectable terms as "literature," "philosophy," "architecture," "art," "history," "science," "cinema" – and, yes, even "biblical studies" and "theology." But what does the qualifier "postmodern" mean and how does it work? Does it carry the same force when linked to history as to theology, to art as to biblical studies? Typically, introductory studies of postmodernity take one of two routes: some follow its growth and trajectory in a single domain (for example, architecture, literature); others seek to give a theoretical account across a number of domains. With respect to the latter strategy, there is a further divergence: between theories that describe a process in the history of ideas, on the one hand, and socioeconomic processes, on the other.[2]

---

[1] David Tracy, "Fragments: The Spiritual Situation of Our Times," in John D. Caputo and Michael J. Scanlon, eds., *God, the Gift, and Postmodernism* (Bloomington: Indiana University Press, 1999), p. 170.
[2] These distinctions correspond more or less to those of Steven Connor who distinguishes postmodernity as a name for (1) developments in the arts and culture (2) the emergence of

In order to avoid employing such hierarchical binary oppositions as explanations "from above" and "from below," I shall resist describing post-modernity in either conceptual or cultural terms alone. I shall prefer, rather, to speak of the postmodern "condition" as something that is at once intel-lectual/theoretical and cultural/practical, a condition that affects modes of thought as well as modes of embodiment. Significantly, the first book to treat postmodernity as a distinct intellectual and cultural movement was Jean-François Lyotard's *The Postmodern Condition*, published in 1979.

A condition is something altogether different than a position. A posi-tion refers to one's location in space or, alternately, to one's opinion on a certain issue. The point is that a position, whether geographical or argu-mentative, can be plotted and specified more or less accurately. Positions are determinate – fixed, definite. A condition is altogether more diffuse, an environment in which one lives and moves and, in some sense, has one's being.

The postmodern condition. This phrase is susceptible of a number of possible meanings, of which three are especially relevant:

1 A set of circumstances that affect the existence or functioning of some-thing or other (for example, working conditions; living conditions).
2 A state of being or fitness. Athletes, for example, are typically in "good condition." Conversely, the term may be used to indicate some ailment or abnormality (for example, a heart condition). One challenge in de-scribing postmodernity is to judge which sense of condition applies: health (*salus*) or dire illness (*krisis*)?
3 A stipulation or requirement that must be fulfilled in order to do some-thing else (for example, condition of entry). What, then, is the passport into the postmodern? What conditions does postmodernity impose on individual and societies, believers and churches? Most urgently: does postmodernity present us with enabling conditions and hence with new opportunities and possibilities, or does postmodernity represent a dis-abling condition, a condition of *impossibility* say, for discovering truth or for talking about God?

What does it mean to do theology in the postmodern condition, to do theology under the conditions of postmodernity? This, the governing ques-tion of the present work, implies three others: (1) is there really such a thing as a distinctly and uniquely postmodern condition? (2) If so, just what kind

new forms of social and economic organization (3) a new theoretical discourse (see his "Postmodernism" in Michael Payne, ed., *A Dictionary of Cultural and Critical Theory* (Oxford: Blackwell, 1996), pp. 428–32.

of a condition is it? (3) Is postmodernity a condition from which Christian theology can, and should, recover, or does postmodernity represent a net gain for Christian faith? To be sure, one characteristic of the postmodern condition is a suspicion of simplistic either–or contrasts. The answer to this latter question, then, may be "both–and" or "neither–nor."

The purpose of this introduction is to set the stage for the essays that follow by surveying the cultural and intellectual contours of the postmodern. The first section begins with an examination of the so-called "postmodern turn," which is as much a turn *away from modernity* as a turn to something else. Who is in a position to report on the postmodern condition? No *one* voice taken in isolation is adequate. No single individual nor discipline is equipped to take the full measure of what I am calling the postmodern condition. As Best and Kellner note, different accounts of the postmodern turn can be given by the various disciplines. Accordingly, in what follows I shall conduct a series of "reports" on the postmodern condition from representatives from a variety of cultural and academic traditions. Yet Best and Kellner also contend that, despite these differences, there is indeed "a shared discourse of the postmodern, common perspectives, and defining features that coalesce into an emergent postmodern paradigm."[3] Accordingly, in the second section I suggest five complementary ways of characterizing the postmodern condition. No one of these descriptions, taken alone, is adequate, but together they make up a compelling composite picture, albeit one with blurred edges.

The third section puts theology in the picture in order to raise the explicit questions and issues addressed in subsequent chapters. How does postmodernity "condition" theology? For some, it means that theology need no longer do its work under the conditions of modernity. On this view, the postmodern condition results in the liberation of theology. For others, it means that theology must work under a new set of conditions, some of which may be as constraining, or as impossible, as their modern precursors. After exploring these possibilities, I shall go on to consider an alternative genealogy in which theologians tell quite a different story about the genesis of modernity and postmodernity alike. The moral of this counter-narrative is that postmodernity, instead of being a condition of theology, is actually a *theological* condition. I conclude with some thoughts on whether, and how, the postmodern condition ought to affect the mission of theology, and vice versa.

3 Steven Best and Douglas Kellner, *The Postmodern Turn* (New York: The Guilford Press, 1997), p. xi.

THE POSTMODERN CONDITION: AN INTERIM INTERDISCIPLINARY REPORT

To conduct a thorough and compelling paternity test for postmodernity is beyond the scope of the present chapter. Some account of its relation to modernity, however incomplete, is clearly necessary. However, like the French Revolution perhaps, there is no single causal explanation of what I am calling the postmodern condition. The modernity–postmodernity relation looks different when viewed in terms of the humanities, the social sciences, and the theoretical discourse of philosophy respectively. With this qualification in mind, we now turn to examine the onset and then the character of the postmodern condition.

The "postmodern turns"

The term "postmodern" signals some kind of relation to modernity, containing as it does the very word. Which part of the term is most significant: *post* or *modern*? This remains a point on which there is no little dispute. The other disputed point, of course, concerns the nature of "modernity" itself. Is modernity a *material* or an *ideological* condition? On this latter question, my own view is that it is both–and: neither simply a material nor simply an ideological condition, but both together. In other words, modernity and postmodernity are conditions that have both material and ideological aspects. It follows, then, that the work of sociologists and cultural historians, on the one hand, and philosophers, on the other, contribute something to an account of the transformation I am calling the postmodern turn.[4]

The "arts and humanities" turn

One of the earliest sightings of the term postmodern was in the field of architecture. "Modernist" architecture turned its back on traditional styles and concentrated on forms that served a structure's function, thus applying modernity's concern with instrumental reason to the shaping of physical space. The modernist building does not "mean" anything but simply serves its purpose. The postmodern turn in architecture consisted in the rejection of this ideal of universal form that expresses the "essence" of a given building. Charles Jencks, for example, argued that buildings, like texts, have both contexts and predecessors, and a building's style should be in dialogue as it

---

[4] Typically, introductions to postmodernity written by theologians tend to focus on changes in literary theory and epistemology. Insofar as theology concerns the interpretation of biblical texts and the knowledge of God, this is understandable. However, such reductionistic accounts are also more liable to underestimate the postmodern situation, which affects not only the intellectual in the academy, but the values and practices of everyday life as well (so Best and Kellner, *Postmodern Turn*, p. xi).

were with both.[5] Postmodern architects resist the illusion of "the universal perspective," preferring to allude to past styles, through a playful eclecticism, without being dominated by any one of them.

There was a similar reaction to the "modernist century" (approximately the 1850s to the 1950s) in the arts. One key feature of modernism is its belief in the autonomy of art; the artist was free to pursue purely aesthetic goals without having to worry about morality, religion, and politics. This belief in art for art's sake gradually led to a concern with the purely formal features of the work of art, which, in turn, led modern art to be highly self-conscious and self-referential, preoccupied with itself, accessible only to an elite. This was as true of Picasso's abstract expressionism as it was of Eliot's poetry and Schoenberg's serial music. Postmodern artists and writers renounce the belief in the autonomy of art and resist the modernist tendency toward abstraction and elitism. Postmodern artists and writers also tend to "quote" the historical tradition, to acknowledge their "concreteness" (viz., their location in history and culture), and to blur the boundary between "high" and "low" art.

The "culture and society" turn

From a different vantage point, the postmodern turn may be seen as a transformation of modern modes of social organization. "Modernity" in this context refers to social forces and institutional forms – secularization, industrialization, bureaucratization – that embody the Enlightenment ideals of rationality, individual autonomy, and progress. As a cultural and social phenomenon, modernity was "a secular movement that sought the demystification and desacralization of knowledge and social organization in order to liberate human beings from their chains."[6] Modern society is a triumphalistic exercise of instrumental rationality in the domain of the social. Once again, postmoderns reject the idea that there is one universal rational form.

The aim of "work" in modernity was to produce materials necessary for modern life: food, clothes, homes, cars. In modernity, there was a sharp dichotomy between the puritan work ethic and the hedonistic "leisure ethic" of self-expression and self-improvement which only a very few could afford to pursue. Society reaches a postmodern condition when "work" turns into art, that is, when more and more areas of life are assimilated into the logic of the marketplace, when the economy is increasingly geared to providing entertainment, and when the business of America is leisure. In a postindustrialist postmodern economy, goods are produced not to supply preexistent

---

5 See Charles Jencks, *The Language of Post-Modern Architecture* (New York: Rizzoli, 1977).
6 David Harvey, *The Condition of Postmodernity* (Oxford: Blackwell, 1990), p. 13.

needs, but to supply needs that are themselves created by advertizing and marketing strategies. What gets marketed is not an object so much as an image or a lifestyle.

The "philosophical and theoretical" turn

Modern thought was characterized by a drive for certitude, universality, and perhaps, above all, *mastery*.[7] In this respect, it is only fitting that the modern university rewards graduate students who have acquired specialized knowledge with a "Master's" degree. Newton showed that reason could master the mechanics of the natural world. Modernity, or the "Enlightenment Project," may be understood broadly as the attempt to bring critical rationality and scientific method to bear not only on the natural world but on humanity more generally conceived (for example, ethics, politics), and even "divinity" (for example, biblical criticism, philosophical theology).

Postmodern philosophers, many of them French intellectuals disillusioned after the Parisian university protests of May 1968, rebelled against the so-called "Enlightenment project" that sought universal human emancipation through the light of universal human reason, deployed through the powers of modern technology, science, and democracy. Postmodern thinkers rejected the idea that "reason" names a neutral and disinterested perspective from which to pursue truth and justice. Specifically, postmodern theory rejects the following modern postulates: (1) that reason is absolute and universal (2) that individuals are autonomous, able to transcend their place in history, class, and culture (3) that universal principles and procedures are objective whereas preferences are subjective.

There is continuing debate as to whether postmodernity represents a passage beyond or an intensification of modernity, taken either as a socio-economic or an intellectual condition. Is the postmodern a turn *away from* modernity or a *turning in* of modernity upon itself? To some extent, this question is inevitable, because postmodernity and modernity are joined at the hip, or at least as host and parasite, for the very meaning of postmodern depends on its difference from modernity. Nevertheless, some construe the postmodern as "most-modern," as the imploding of modernity, as the implicit paradox of modernity made explicit. On this view, postmodernity is simply modernity in its death-throes. Others see postmodernity as the emergence of new forms of experience, thought, and social organization.

---

[7] Cf. Gavin Hyman, who defines the modern as "the desire for an all-encompassing mastery of reality by rational and/or scientific means" (*The Predicament of Postmodern Theology: Radical Orthodoxy or Nihilist Textualism?* [Louisville: Westminster John Knox Press, 2001], p. 11).

I cannot settle these debates in this short space.[8] What does appear beyond dispute is that the latter half of the twentieth century has witnessed a series of cultural and intellectual developments that have unsettled a number of modern convictions. But those convictions have not been entirely dislodged. In that respect, postmodernity is not so much a clearly definable chronological period as it is a condition of history; it is not a specifiable moment on the timetable of history but a mood. Twenty-first-century Westerners now live "in parentheses" between the modern and the postmodern "in an interregnum period in which the competing regimes are engaged in an intense struggle for dominance."[9]

A report on knowledge and belief

One of the first and most important attempts to articulate the postmodern condition was François Lyotard's *The Postmodern Condition: A Report on Knowledge*.[10] Lyotard's report begins with an account of modern scientific knowledge. How do we account for its prestige? "Modern" designates "any science that legitimates itself with reference to a metadiscourse...making an explicit appeal to some grand narrative,"[11] for example, the Einsteinian or Darwinian paradigms. There are three conditions for modern knowledge: (1) the appeal to metanarratives as a foundationalist criterion of legitimacy, (2) the outgrowth of strategies of legitimation and exclusion, and (3) a desire for criteria of legitimacy in the moral as well as the epistemological domain. The key factor in Lyotard's analysis is the role of "metanarrative," a "master story" that serves as a comprehensive explanatory framework for everything else, "narratives which subordinate, organize and account for other narratives."[12] Modern discourses like science appeal to metanarratives that legitimate it by, for example, telling a story of how Enlightenment thinkers overcame ignorance and superstition thanks to critical methods, or how modern science has resulted in greater health and wealth for humanity.

Lyotard defines postmodernity in terms of a loss of faith in such grand narratives: the postmodern condition is one of "incredulity toward metanarratives." In Lyotard's words: "The grand narrative has lost its credibility...regardless of whether it is a speculative narrative or a narrative of

---

[8] For further discussion, see Paul Lakeland, *Postmodernity: Christian Identity in a Fragmented Age* (Minneapolis: Augsburg Fortress, 1997), pp. 12–13.

[9] Best and Kellner, *Postmodern Turn*, p. 32.

[10] Jean-François Lyotard, *The Postmodern Condition: A Report on Knowledge* (Minneapolis: University of Minnesota Press,1984 and Manchester: Manchester University Press, 1984). Lyotard's work was commissioned by the government of Quebec, which had requested a report on the state of "contemporary knowledge."

[11] Ibid., p. xxiii.   [12] Ibid., p. 30.

emancipation."[13] For example, postmoderns no longer accept the story that science tells to legitimate itself, namely, that it contributes to human freedom and well-being. Postmodernity, in short, cuts metanarratives down to size and sees them for what they are: *mere narratives.* Western science loses considerable prestige when viewed in terms of "the story white Europeans tell about the natural world." The mark of the postmodern condition of knowledge, then, is a move away from the authority of universal science toward narratives of local knowledge.

Eating from the postmodern tree of knowledge occasions a new "fall" and loss of innocence. No longer can we aspire to the knowledge of angels, much less a God's-eye point of view. How, then, are we to make judgments as to true and false, right and wrong? Lyotard acknowledges that the central issue of postmodernity is the possibility of ethics, that is, right action. Lyotard, for his part, is content to live with "little narratives." Yet there are many narratives, and this plurality is what makes the postmodern condition one of legitimation crisis: *whose story, whose interpretation, whose authority, whose criteria counts, and why?*[14]

Toward which metanarratives in particular are postmoderns incredulous?

Reason

Postmodernists reject the epistemological foundationalism that proclaims "come let us reason together" (on the basis of shared experience and shared logical categories). It is not that postmoderns are irrational. They do not reject "reason" but "Reason." They deny the notion of universal rationality; reason is rather a contextual and relative affair. What counts as rational is relative to the prevailing narrative in a society or institution. Postmodern rationality, we may say, is narration-based. Stated somewhat differently: reason is always *situated* within particular narratives, traditions, institutions, and practices. This situatedness *conditions* what people deem rational.

Postmoderns point out two other problems with modern epistemology: first, its referential view of language, where words unproblematically represent extralinguistic things and unproblematically express feelings and

---

[13] Ibid., p. 37; Best and Kellner criticize Lyotard for his tendency to identify modernity with Enlightenment thought. Stated somewhat differently: Lyotard offers a "docetic" interpretation of modernity that fails to engage with social and material reality (*Postmodern Turn,* p. 165).

[14] Perceptive readers, and analytic philosophers, will be quick to point out an apparent inconsistency: Lyotard dismisses metanarratives, but does he not present his own account in metanarrative terms, that is, as the "true" story of knowledge? We here encounter a common phenomenon in postmodern theorizing, namely, the appearance of performative self-contradiction.

values. Language is not a neutral tool but a social construction. Second, postmoderns resist the atomism and reductionism presupposed by science's working hypothesis that the real world of nature is physicalist and can be explained in terms of systems of causal laws, perhaps even by a single system, an all-encompassing explanatory framework or "unifying theory."

Truth

The above rejections combine to form a grand refusal of modernity's metaphysical project, namely, the project of mastering natural reality in a comprehensive conceptual scheme. "Postmodernists reject unifying, totalizing, and universal schemes in favor of new emphases on difference, plurality, fragmentation, and complexity."[15] Postmoderns are suspicious of truth claims, of "getting it right." Upon hearing the assertion that "that's the way things are," postmoderns are likely to respond, "that's the way things are for you." Truth on this view is a compelling story told by persons in positions of power in order to perpetuate their way of seeing and organizing the natural and social world. According to Michel Foucault, behind every discourse on truth there lurks rhetorical posturing: knowledge claims are violent impositions by powerful institutions; universal truth claims are simply masks for ideology and the will to power.

History

Postmoderns are also incredulous toward narratives that purport to recount universal history. Modern thinkers like nothing better than to tell stories about "universal history." From Kant to Hegel to Marx, modern thinkers have attempted to tell the story of humanity, usually in terms of the progress of the race. Postmodern historians reject the premise that history moves according to a unified linear logic. Discontinuity rather than continuity is the postmodern watchword. Furthermore, postmoderns are suspicious of claims to have got even local or partial histories correct. There is no more "one true story" of the past than there is of the present. Instead, histories – like philosophies – reveal more about the people who made them than they do about the way things actually are/were.

Self

It follows from the above that there is no one true way of recounting one's own history and thus no one true way of narrating one's own identity. But the self is decentered in other ways as well. Postmoderns reject the notion that the person is an autonomous individual with a rational

[15] Best and Kellner, *Postmodern Turn*, p. 255.

consciousness that transcends one's particular place in culture, language, history, and a gendered body. *Contra* Descartes, the self cannot even know its own mind. According to Paul Ricoeur, consciousness is not a given but a task, for we find ourselves always-already immersed in an embodied situation. Postmoderns do not believe in the metanarrative of the knowing subject. The postmodern self is not master of but subject to the material and social and linguistic conditions of a historical situation that precedes her.

Postmodern incredulity thus undoes H. Richard Niebuhr's three-stranded cord: "To be a self is to have a God, to have a God is to have a history, that is, events connected in a meaningful pattern; to have one God is to have one history."[16] In this respect, postmoderns agree with Nietzsche that "God" – which is to say, the supreme being of classical theism – has become unbelievable, as have the autonomous self and the meaning of history.

A report on language and life

The postmodern turn from metanarrative to narrative may also be viewed as a turn from subjectivity to language. Whereas Heidegger chided modernity for forgetting the question of being, postmodern thinkers contend that what has actually been forgotten is *language*. The knowing subject of modernity assumed that reason was universal, impervious to differences of culture and language. For moderns, language was a transparent medium that enabled consciousness to grasp reality. Postmoderns find this picture of the mind–world relation incredible. Not only do we not have nonlinguistic access to the way things are, but the way we speak and think is conditioned by the particular language in which we dwell. It is simply not the case that reality informs thought and that thought informs language.

"Language" refers not simply to English, French, Swahili, and so forth, but more specifically to the system of differences – the pattern of distinctions and connections – that a given vocabulary imposes on the flux of human experience. For example, a psychoanalyst uses a different set of categories to talk about dreams than does the neurologist, just as the sociologist uses a different set of categories to talk about the church than does the theologian.

Jacques Derrida has famously commented that "There is nothing outside the text."[17] This is not a comment about what there is in the world so much as a claim that what we know about things is linguistically, which is to say culturally and socially, constructed. Derrida elsewhere paraphrases his

---

[16] H. Richard Niebuhr, *The Meaning of Revelation* (New York: Macmillan, 1967), p. 59.
[17] Jacques Derrida, *Of Grammatology*, trans. Gayatri Chakravorty Spivak (Baltimore: Johns Hopkins University Press, 1976), p. 158.

point by adding, "there is nothing outside context."[18] By this Derrida means that it makes no sense to inquire into the meaning or truth of a sentence or text outside of a specific context. Moreover, every linguistic and conceptual structure is deconstructible (able to be disassembled, undone) because, for Derrida (and for structuralists and post-structuralists in general) language is a set of arbitrary distinctions. No one language carves up the world at its joints. Once one sees that languages are social constructions, it is difficult to continue believing in their universal reliability. *The postmodern condition thus pertains to one's awareness of the deconstructibility of all systems of meaning and truth.*

"Language" thus stands for the socially constructed order within which we think and move and have our being. Our speech and action are always-already situated, and hence conditioned, by one vocabulary or another. Post-modernity is thus a linguistic or textual condition in which human beings "suffer" language. This linguistic condition of postmodernity is at the same time a political condition because the differences inscribed in language privilege certain forms of social organization rather than others. Those who get to make the distinctions control the social imagination and thus hold the reins of social power. It is partially thanks to such insights that feminism may be deemed postmodern.

Given the centrality of narrative and language in accounts of the post-modern condition, it will come as no surprise to learn that some of the most important contributions to postmodern thinking have come from the domain of literary theory. Indeed, according to several French postmodern thinkers, literary theory has come virtually to displace philosophy, or, rather, philosophy has come to be seen as a species of rhetoric and literature. It was Nietzsche who denied facts in order to make room for interpretations. Indeed, for him, it is interpretation "all the way down." To the extent that the postmodern condition is linguistic and textual, those who inhabit it are sentenced to interpretation. Just as the meaning of a word does not come to rest in the thing to which it refers, so the meaning of a text lacks fixity due to the changing contexts in which it is read. The postmodern condition is therefore one of undecidable and unfinalizable interpretation.

THE POSTMODERN CONDITION: THE CONFLICT OF DESCRIPTIONS

To this point, we have traced the postmodern turn in a number of different areas: architecture, art, society, philosophy, and literary theory. Is

---

[18] Derrida, "Afterword," in *Limited Inc.* (Evanston: Northwestern University Press, 1988), p. 136.

there anything that can be said about the postmodern condition in general? I believe there is.

A new Copernican revolution

Copernicus decentered human vanity when he demonstrated that the sun did not revolve around the earth. Further decentering occurred when it became clear that our solar system is only one of many. The postmodern variation of this Copernican revolution is just as far-reaching: instead of history and culture revolving around reason, reason is now seen to orbit particular cultures and particular times in distinctive ways. The result is a further decentering of the human subject – a revolution not in cosmology, but in *consciousness.*

Other commentators go further, arguing that postmodernity affects not simply how we think about the world, but how we actually *experience* it. According to David Harvey, the postmodern condition refers to "a particular way of experiencing, interpreting, and being in the world."[19] Paul Lakeland agrees: postmodernity is a breakdown in the "givens" of modernity: "time, space, and order."[20] According to Kant, space and time are the two basic conditions for human experience, the environment for thinking, feeling, and doing. If the postmodern condition does indeed provoke a change in how we live space and time, it follows that the postmodern is nothing less than a revolution in human experience *simpliciter.*

Harvey views the postmodern condition "not so much as a set of ideas but as a historical condition," a new way of being-in-time/space, as it were.[21] For time and space have been flattened out. Time lacks the density of history; it has been compressed and accelerated in a post-industrial age whereby goods and services may be had twenty-four hours every day thanks to global communications and the internet. The internet and telecommunications have similarly compressed space, making distance of no consequence.[22] The first major consequence of this cultural acceleration has been "to accentuate volatility and ephemerality of fashions, products...ideas and ideologies, values and established practices."[23] Such a mode of experience is conducive to consumerism, less so to conservation. How can a culture where goods are disposable and services are instantaneous *preserve* anything of value? It is perhaps no coincidence that one of the key metaphors for what it is to be

---

[19] Harvey, *Condition of Postmodernity*, p. 53.   [20] Lakeland, *Postmodernity*, p. 2.
[21] Harvey, *Condition of Postmodernity*, p. viii. See ch. 15 for Harvey's analysis of time and space in the Enlightenment project of modernity.
[22] Graham Ward observes that "Surfing the net is the ultimate postmodern experience" ("Introduction, or, A Guide to Theological Thinking in Cyberspace," in Ward, ed., *The Postmodern God* (Oxford: Blackwell, 1997), p. xv).
[23] Harvey, *Condition of Postmodernity*, p. 285.

postmodern is the *nomad*. Heidegger got it only partially right when he said, "In language man dwells." Nomads do not dwell, but only pass through.

A protest against the "natural"

Postmoderns are latter-day philosophical "protestants" who resist the category of the natural, as in the "natural order," "natural law," or "natural sense." For "natural," postmoderns read "historical" or "political." Take, for example, something as apparently uncontroversial as a scheme of biological classification. Foucault cites a Borges story in which a Chinese encyclopaedia classifies animals according to the following categories: belonging to the Emperor, embalmed, tame, strays, having just broken the water pitcher, that from a long way off look like flies.[24] Well, why not? Why is this classification any less arbitrary than the Western convention of distinguishing creatures on the basis of whether they have backbones or not, or whether they reproduce by laying eggs or by giving birth? Foucault's point is that all classificatory schemes have their origin in specific historical "discourses" or formations of power-truth, and are as such culturally relative. The politics behind the "natural" may not be apparent in zoology, but it quickly comes to the fore in discussions about the nature of human sexuality or, for that matter, the family. The postmodern condition is one of "incredulity toward 'the natural,'" for the "natural" is but a historical narrative whose origins in narrative have been forgotten.

An iconoclastic purge

"Thou shalt not believe in absolutes." This postmodern imperative is allied to an iconoclastic urge. Lyotard not only finds it impossible to believe in metanarratives but accuses metanarratives of being "crimes against humanity."[25] Why? Because metanarratives – absolute truths – fund various forms of totalitarianism. "The ideology you shall always have with you." What is going on today – in religion, art, philosophy, and thinking in general – is a cleansing of the temples of knowledge of the last vestiges of conceptual idolatry.[26] The postmodern condition is one of life among the ruins of cast down idols, especially in the ruins of cast down -isms (for example, existentialism, structuralism, Marxism).[27] For postmodern iconoclasts do not abandon reason; they merely remove it from its pedestal and *situate*

---

[24] Foucault, *The Order of Things* (New York: Vintage Books, 1973), p. xv.

[25] In Lyotard, *The Postmodern Explained to Children: Correspondence 1982–1985* (Minneapolis: University of Minnesota Press, 1992).

[26] Cf. Jean-Luc Marion on the difference between the idol and the icon in *God without Being*, trans. Thomas Carlson (University of Chicago Press, 1991).

[27] See, in this regard, Bruce Ellis Benson, *Graven Ideologies: Nietzsche, Derrida & Marion on Modern Idolatry* (Downers Grove, IL: InterVarsity Press, 2002).

it. To locate an ideology or conceptual system in the rough and tumble of human history, culture, and politics is, of course, to demystify it. Henceforth there are "only human, all too human" -isms. Iconoclastic suspicion is a radicalization of Kant's attempt to determine the limits of reason. The result: a postmodern critique of *impure* reason.

A return of the repressed

The postmodern condition consists of more than negative gestures, more than shakes of the head and shrugs of the shoulder. In contrast with modernity, it also motions for the return of the repressed and for the embrace of the "other." Modern systems can only master reality by excluding what does not fit. That which falls outside our conceptual systems is thus deemed irrational or unscientific. This was the great paradox of the modern desire for mastery, "that in its quest for universal and totalizing comprehension, its system was obliged to *exclude* or *repress* that which lay outside it, thereby calling its universal and total comprehensiveness into question."[28] Common to several currents of postmodern thought is an anti-systematic impulse, "a predilection for the plural, the multiple, a valorization of everything that had been suppressed by earlier systematicity, everything that had been left out or relegated to the margins."[29]

Concern for the other is the major theme in the work of Emmanuel Levinas, for whom ethics – an infinite respect for the irreplaceable other – replaces epistemology as "first philosophy." Whereas modern systems tend violently to absorb the other – ideas or persons – into comprehensive schemes, Levinas contends that one's first responsibility is to let the other be rather than to cast the other in one's own image. One's obligations toward the other cannot be calculated. "Ethics" is not about moral systems or following rules; it is rather about respecting particularity and difference.

A recovery of "messianic" religion

One candidate for "most repressed other" in modernity is religion. At the very least, a strident secularism has kept religion out of the public square. The so-called fact–value distinction relegated faith to the margins of private preferences. Postmoderns have played Hamlet to modernity's Horatio, insisting: "There are more things in heaven and earth...than are dreamt of in our philosophy" (*Hamlet*, Act I, v). Postmoderns gesture not only in the direction of the other, but also toward the "beyond." In Graham Ward's words: "The emergence of the postmodern has fostered

---

[28] Hyman, *Predicament of Postmodern Theology*, p. 12.
[29] Robert Stam, *Film Theory: An Introduction* (Blackwell, 2000), p. 299.

post-secular thinking."[30] In particular, the postmodern condition has enabled the recovery of two neglected forms of religious discourse – the prophetic and the mystical – that seek, in different ways, to invoke the beyond: justice, the gift.

Even Derrida, in his later work, has begun to speak of something that is "beyond" deconstruction. Better: deconstructive analysis "is undertaken *in the name of something*, something affirmatively *un*-deconstructible."[31] This something, it turns out, is *justice*. Indeed, Derrida goes so far as to say that deconstruction *is* justice.[32] Everything depends, however, on his distinction between justice and law. "Law" refers to the formulas and structures that make up some judicial system. The law is deconstructible because it is constructed in the first place, historically instituted and constituted. In short, law is always *situated*, and hence prone to partiality. One deconstructs the law in the name of a justice to come, a justice beyond present human formulations. "Justice is what the deconstruction of the law means to bring about."[33] This is not to say that Derrida knows exactly what justice looks like. Indeed, justice for Derrida is the impossible, in the sense that it is incalculable on the basis of factors that are already present. Nevertheless, deconstruction is the desire that justice is "to come" (*à venir*).

Another religious theme that has received much attention of late is that of the gift. For Derrida, the gift is as "impossible" as justice. As soon as we give something to someone, we put that person in our debt, thus taking, not giving. The gift disappears in a web of calculation, interest, and measure. Such is the aporia of the gift, according to Derrida. It cannot be given without creating an economy – a system of calculation and exchange – of debt and gratitude. "It is reintroduced into the circle of an exchange and destroyed as a gift."[34] Can a gift be given in modern societies ruled by various forms of exchange? Morality and other forms of social convention work with a logic of equivalence; however, the true gift is always extravagant, exceeding what is strictly required. Can the gift be thought? Only an "expenditure without reserve," a giving that expects no reciprocity, a giving that forgets a gift has been given, would seem to measure up to Derrida's requirements for a true gift. Neither justice nor the gift is, strictly speaking, of this world; yet both are that for which postmoderns hope.

[30] Ward, "Introduction," p. xxii.

[31] John D. Caputo, *Deconstruction in a Nutshell: A Conversation with Jacques Derrida* (New York: Fordham University Press, 1997), p. 128.

[32] Derrida, "The Force of Law: 'The Mystical Foundation of Authority,' " in Drucilla Cornell, Michel Rosenfield, and David G. Carlson, eds., *Deconstruction and the Possibility of Justice* (New York: Routledge, 1992), pp. 68–91.

[33] Caputo, *Deconstruction in a Nutshell*, p. 131.

[34] Derrida, from "On the Gift: A Discussion between Jacques Derrida and Jean-Luc Marion," in Caputo and Scanlon, eds., *God, the Gift, and Postmodernism*, p. 59.

As with gifts, so with sacrifices. Abraham had to sacrifice his son, to give Isaac to God, without expecting anything back. Derrida writes that "God decides to *give back,* to give back life, to give back the beloved son, once he is assured that a gift outside of any economy, the gift of death...has been accomplished without any hope of exchange, reward, circulation, or communication."[35] Being responsible to the other involves a kind of death to self. Again, there are no rules for calculating responsibility, because I, and the other, and the situation are not anonymous variables in a moral equation but particular persons in singular situations. There are no logarithms for determining one's obligations. "Every other is wholly other" (*tout autre est tout autre*). This Derridean maxim effectively closes the gap between the ethical and the religious.

According to Caputo, Derrida's affirmation of the impossibility of justice, and the gift, is a gesture not of nihilistic despair but rather of faith: the desire for something *other* than what obtains in the present world order. Some such expectation of "the other to come" is inscribed in the very structure of deconstruction and what gives it its "messianic turn."[36] Postmodernity abolishes conceptual idolatry, one might say, in order to make room for faith. However, Derrida distinguishes the "messianic" from "messianism," where the latter stands for the belief that a particular Messiah has already come. The messianic, by contrast, has to do with what cannot (at present) be determined. The messianic is a structure of experience, apparently universal, that opens us to an unknown future. The faith of deconstruction is "through and through a messianic affirmation of the coming of the impossible."[37] The messianic is the unforeseeable, the beyond that is always desired but never attained. On this view, the postmodern condition is essentially, that is, structurally, messianic: constitutionally open to the coming of the other and the different. *Faith*, not reason – faith in a religionless (viz., messianic) religion – is thus endemic to the postmodern condition.

A refusal of Christian orthodoxy

There is a sixth possible construal which I will mention here but defer further discussion of it until we consider an alternative genealogy of modernity below. It amounts to the suggestion that the postmodern celebration of faith, not a historic faith but faith as a general condition, stems from a refusal of orthodox Christian doctrine.

---

[35] Derrida, *The Gift of Death* (University of Chicago Press, 1995), p. 96.
[36] Caputo, *Deconstruction in a Nutshell*, p. 159.
[37] Caputo, "Apostles of the Impossible: On God and the Gift in Derrida and Marion," in *God, the Gift, and Postmodernism*, p. 197.

THE POSTMODERN CONDITION OF THEOLOGY: A
REPORT ON KNOWLEDGE OF GOD

What, then, is the condition of postmodern theology? Again, the best
way to answer this is to contrast it with its modern counterpart.

Modern theology: correlationism

David Tracy states that modern theologies "were principally determined
not by the reality of God but by the *logos* of modernity."[38] Hans Frei's
diagnosis is similar: modern interpretive schemes eclipse the specificity
of biblical narrative, and with it, the singular *mythos* of Jesus Christ. In so
doing, thought Frei, modern theologians gain the whole world – the world
of academic respectability and cultural plausibility, in a word: *legitimation* –
yet lose their own souls. Paul Tillich's method of correlation, for instance, let
modern culture and thought forms set the agenda by asking the questions
which theology then answered. In Tillich's own work, the questions were
posed within an existentialist framework that predisposed him to interpret
the Bible in symbolic rather than historical terms. Tillich is illustrative of the
modern tendency to let some *logos* or other swallow up the biblical *mythos*.
Modern theological systems, like other -isms, are able only to think "more
of the same"; they leave the "other" unthought. In Tracy's words: "Theology
will never again be tameable by a system … For theology does not bespeak
a totality. Christian theology, at its best is the voice of the Other through all
those others who have tasted … the Infinity disclosed in the kenotic reality
of Jesus Christ."[39]

Postmodern typologies

The present work aims to describe various types of postmodern theology (Part one) and to give specific examples of these theologies at work (Part
two). Two previous studies have worked with fourfold typologies. In *Varieties of Postmodern Theology* the four types, and their key representatives,
are:

1   deconstructive or eliminative (Mark C. Taylor, Carl Raschke, Charles
     Winquist)
2   constructive or revisionary (David Ray Griffin)
3   liberationist (Harvey Cox, Cornel West)
4   conservative or restorationist (John Paul II).[40]

---

[38] David Tracy, *On Naming the Present: God, Hermeneutics and Church* (Maryknoll, NY: Orbis
     Books, 1994), p. 41.
[39] Tracy, "Theology and the Many Faces of Postmodernity," *Theology Today* 51 (1994), 114.
[40] Ed. by David Ray Griffin, William A. Beardslee, and Joe Holland (Albany: State University
     of New York Press, 1989).

Postmodern Theologies: The Challenge of Religious Diversity is organized similarly:

1   constructive (David Ray Griffin, David Tracy)
2   a/theological dissolutions (Thomas Altizer, Mark C. Taylor)
3   postliberal (George Lindbeck)
4   communal praxis (Gustavo Gutiérrez, James W. McClendon).[41]

By and large, the two lists overlap, with the exception that the "conserva-tive" option in the first book becomes the "postliberal" in the second, and the "liberationist" type is expanded into "communal praxis." The present work substitutes feminist for liberationist, preserves communal praxis as a dis-tinct type, and adds two new ones – radical orthodoxy and postmetaphysical theology – for a total of seven.

Does not even an expanded typology represent a singularly inappro-priate way to present postmodern theology? Is not classification a modern obsession? A postmodern typology will acknowledge both its non-necessary character and its rough edges. There are indeed many different ways that one could classify the contemporary theological scene (here we may recall the Borges story): theologians who prefer tweed to wool jackets; theologians who prefer jacket potatoes to wearing a coat and tie; theologians who live in California; theologians who wished they lived in California; theologians who live in California but wish they lived elsewhere, etc. In the final analy-sis, the typology presented herein must be considered both provisional and fallible. Yet, while it is less than absolute, it is not entirely arbitrary, for the positions were chosen on the basis of two leading criteria: first, that each type represents, if not a "school," than at least an approach of more than an individual theologian; second, that each approach believes itself to be responding to, rejecting, or passing through modernity, not inhabiting it.

The seven types represent various ways that theologians are negotiating the conditions of postmodernity. On some points, the seven are far apart. Some, for example, like reconstructive theology, believe that there is still room for metaphysics in postmodernity, though of a holistic rather than atomistic variety. Others, like postmetaphysical theology, contend that all forms of ontotheology must be left behind. Perhaps the most significant question concerns the nature of the postmodern condition: is it a stipula-tive condition, a requirement that must be met before theology can speak of God? Is postmodernity simply the latest extratextual framework into which theology must translate its discourse in order to be considered legitimate?

---

[41] Terrence W. Tilley, *Postmodern Theologies: The Challenge of Religious Diversity* (Maryknoll, NY: Orbis, 1995).

In exorcising the demon of individual rational autonomy from the subject of theology, how can we avoid other demons, some of them postmodern, from taking their place? Is postmodern theology simply a matter of exchanging one philosophical master for another, so that one now correlates with *postmodern* interests and concerns rather than modern ones? Or, alternatively, does doing theology under the conditions of postmodernity mean that philosophy and culture no longer set the agenda, that one need no longer correlate? In short: does postmodernity represent a new bondage or does it set the captives free?

Deconstructing postmodernity? An alternative genealogy

To consider types of postmodern theology is to focus on the postmodern as the condition of theology. There is, however, another way to construe the relation. For the return of the repressed includes the return of theology as a metadiscourse, as a "form of reflection that situates all other forms of reflection."[42] Theology returns, not as a modern science, but as a theo-drama that situates the human within the narrative of God's creative and redemptive activity. The suggestion, therefore, is to situate modernity and postmodernity alike within the story of what relates both what God is doing in the world through Jesus Christ and the Holy Spirit and what the world is doing in response. Postmodernity here appears as a properly *theological* condition.

Hans Urs von Balthasar provides an alternate genealogical account of modernity and, by implication, the postmodern. He locates the genesis of the "error" that was modernity in Duns Scotus' fateful departure from Aquinas' ontology. Scotus was the first theologian to adopt the Averroist reading of Aristotle that treated philosophy as the comprehensive science of being, where "being" is a univocal concept which applies both to the created and the uncreated.[43] The result of this move is twofold: ontologically, it denies God's transcendence; "being" is what the creature and the Creator now have in common. Epistemologically, it provides a magna carta for reason to undertake an independent study of all that has being without having recourse to revelation; the metaphysical project – the attempt to gain knowledge of being, including God, through reason – here achieves legitimacy.[44] The "God" thus known, however, is only a conceptual idol manufactured by human reason; and the "God" proclaimed dead or unbelievable by Nietzsche is,

---

[42] Nicholas M. Healy, *Church, World and the Christian Life: Practical–Prophetic Ecclesiology* (Cambridge University Press, 2000), p. 67.

[43] *The Glory of the Lord: A Theological Aesthetics*, vol. 5 *The Realm of Metaphysics in the Modern Age* (Edinburgh: T. & T. Clark, 1991).

[44] See Gavin Hyman, *The Predicament of Postmodern Theology*, ch. 2 for a fuller treatment of these themes.

likewise, only the construction of modern "ontotheology." On this account, then, the deconstructive or nihilist versions of postmodernity are actually the logical culmination of basically modern tendencies.

In reacting to modernity, postmodernity risks being defined, albeit negatively, by the same set of categories. For example, deconstructive postmoderns speak of "the death of God put into writing," yet the "God" they have in mind is the modern metaphysical construct. Christian orthodoxy, oriented toward God's revelation in Christ, tells a different story: "the triune life of God put into Word and writing." Some, though not all, of the chapters in Part two are exercises in such a counter-narration: they begin from Scripture and theology and go on to examine postmodernity in light of Christian doctrine rather than the other way around. Other chapters accept certain aspects of the postmodern condition, then go on to work out their significance for an understanding of a particular doctrine. Accordingly, the chapters in Part two display both the *postmodern* condition of theology and the *theological* condition of postmodernity.

CONCLUSION – THEOLOGY AND THE POSTMODERN MISSION

Missiologists Andrew Walls and Lamin Sanneh have argued that Christianity has always grown as a result of its encounter with the "other" in the history of church mission. Specifically, this growth takes place through the process of translating the faith into new languages and new cultures.[45] Walls says that "the attempt to transmit faith in Christ across linguistic and cultural frontiers revealed that Christ had meanings and significance never guessed before."[46] May we say something similar about the encounter of Christian faith and the "other" of postmodernity? Is postmodernity a "culture" into which the Gospel may be translated, or is it a condition from which the Gospel must be liberated? Perhaps the question is: who is on a mission to whom? Are postmoderns on a mission to save theology or are theologians

---

[45] Walls and Sanneh stress the translatability of the Gospel, which entails the recognition that no one culture has a monopoly on the form of language and life the Gospel may take. See Lamin Sanneh, *Translating the Message: The Missionary Impact on Culture* (Maryknoll, NY: Orbis, 1989); Andrew Walls, *The Missionary Movement in Christian History: Studies in the Transmission of Faith* (Maryknoll, NY: Orbis, 1996), esp. ch. 3. I recognize that these authors are primarily concerned with the history of "foreign" missions, that is, the history of the church in the west taking the Gospel into new geographical regions. I am extending their argument to the postmodern condition, considered as a culture, a move they may well wish to resist. Interestingly enough, however, Walls is aware of postmodern concerns about "difference" and comments that translation is "the art of the impossible" (p. 26). Christian confidence in translation rests on God's prior act of translation: the incarnation.

[46] Walls, *The Missionary Movement in Christian History*, p. xviii.

on a mission to save postmodernity? Again, it seems that we must reject the terms of this either–or. The term "mission" is nevertheless appropriate, for there is indeed a tacit purpose behind the postmodern turn.

Pride and sloth: postmodernity as *spiritual* condition

The mission of postmodernity, I suggest, has to do with bringing about not only new conditions of experience, but a new *shape of living*, to use David Ford's phrase.[47] Now the shape of life – the habitual patterns of thinking, of speech and of action – constitute the "spirit" of an individual or a culture. To the extent that culture and society are always exercising influence over the shape of our lives, it is no exaggeration to say that culture is a work of spiritual formation. The condition of postmodernity is neither simply philosophical nor simply socio-political, but *spiritual*, a condition in which belief and behavior come together in the shape of an embodied spirit.

But which spirit? What shape? Again, opinions differ. Critics of post-modernity would no doubt prefer speaking of spiritual deformation rather than formation. In the final analysis, perhaps both modernity and post-modernity fall short. Modernity cultivated autonomous knowing subjects and so cultivated shapes of life for which neither tradition nor community was a priority. If one had to associate the spirit of modernity with one of the seven deadly sins, surely it would be pride: pride in human reason, pride in human goodness, pride in human accomplishments. It is precisely at the prideful constructions of modernity – buildings, conceptual systems, po-litical regimes, theologies – that postmoderns direct their iconoclasm and ideology critique. Postmoderns aim to *situate* reason, reminding modern pretenders to a God's-eye point of view that they are in fact historically conditioned, culturally conditioned, and sexually gendered finite beings.

"Little children, keep yourselves from idols" (1 John 5:21). Are there idols peculiar to postmodernity? The preference for the creature over the Creator no doubt takes many forms. Human reason can lord it over divine revelation; human creativity can displace divine command. Yet the besetting temptation of the postmodern condition is not pride, I submit, but *sloth*. According to Dorothy Sayers, sloth is the sin "that believes in nothing, enjoys nothing, hates nothing, finds purpose in nothing, lives for nothing, and remains alive because there is nothing for which it will die."[48] *The question is whether certain forms of postmodernity act as corrosives to the*

---

[47] David F. Ford, *The Shape of Living: Spiritual Directions for Everyday Life* (Grand Rapids: Baker, 1997).

[48] Dorothy L. Sayers, *Christian Letters to a Post-Christian World: a Selection of Essays* (Grand Rapids: Eerdmans, 1969), p. 152.

conditions for the possibility of commitment, poisoning the will by depriving it of anything in which to believe ultimately.

Consider, for example, the postmodern stance toward the other. In modernity, the other (the weak, the foreign, the marginalized) was repressed, forced inside totalizing systems. In postmodernity, the other becomes the object of ethical concern. Or does it? Postmodern thinkers typically view the other as so different from anything our categories can name, so resistant to categorization, as to be unable to say anything positive about it. The other virtually dissolves. Lacking substance, the other, once again, becomes easy to ignore. For how can one care for or love that whose nature is unknown to us? Is it possible genuinely to love without knowing? Christianity too, of course, seeks to protect the "other," but it does so by *naming* the other: "neighbor."

Evangelism and discipleship: postmodernity as *sapiential* condition

It may be, then, that theology has a mission to postmodernity. Christians have an interest in promoting a particular shape of life, a particular spirituality, because they know something about the true end of humanity. They know it not because they discovered it but because they were told. The knowledge claim that Christians make about human nature and destiny is based neither on speculation nor observation, but upon apostolic testimony. It is not an apodictic truth, but a story: good news, a gospel. Ultimately what theology wants to say to postmoderns concerns wisdom: about living in accordance with the shape of the life of God displayed in the life of Jesus.

Can the Gospel, this message about the cross and resurrection of Jesus Christ, indeed be translated into the conditions of postmodernity? The Gospel was foolishness to the Greeks, and to the moderns. Will it fare better in postmodernity? "The devolution of Wisdom into Knowledge into Information may be the supreme source of degeneration in the postmodern society."[49] Let us sincerely hope that this will not be the case. We have learned from the postmoderns that knowledge is not disembodied. On this point, postmodernity and incarnational Christian faith are agreed. What is needed, therefore, is a translation of the Gospel that goes beyond conveying propositions – a translation that would *concretize* the Gospel in individual and communal shapes of living. Proclamations of the Gospel must be accompanied by performances that embody in new situations the wisdom and love of God embodied in the cross.

[49] Mary Midgley, *Wisdom, Information, and Wonder: What is Knowledge For?* (London: Routledge, 1991).

What shape will Christian wisdom take under the conditions of post-modernity? It is perhaps too soon to tell. But it should not be superficial, a mere surface phenomenon of culture. For Christian wisdom, embodied in the canonical Scriptures and the catholic tradition, is historically dense. In a situation where being is felt to be unbearably light, postmodern theology should seek to express ultimate significance – the weight of glory. It should strive for a shape of life that repeats differently the life of Jesus, a being-toward-resurrection where one's thoughts, feelings, and doings are conditioned not by the ephemeral processes of this world, where rust and moth corrupt, but by the narrative of the triune God, a story that plumbs the heights and the depths and which inserts us into the dramatic flow of evangelical reality.

Further reading
Best, Steven and Douglas Kellner, *The Postmodern Turn* (New York and London: Guilford Press, 1997).
Connor, Steven, *Postmodernist Culture: An Introduction to Theories of the Contemporary* (Oxford: Blackwell, 1989).
Griffin, David Ray, William A. Beardslee, and Joe Holland, *Varieties of Postmodern Theology* (Albany: State University of New York Press, 1989).
Harvey, David, *The Condition of Postmodernity* (Oxford: Blackwell, 1990).
Hassan, Ihab, *The Postmodern Turn: Essays in Postmodern Theory and Culture* (Columbus: Ohio State University press, 1987).
Hyman, Gavin, *The Predicament of Postmodern Theology: Radical Orthodoxy or Nihilist Textualism?* (Louisville: Westminster/John Know, 2001).
Kirk, J. Andrew and Kevin Vanhoozer, eds., *To Stake a Claim: Mission and the Western Crisis of Knowledge* (Maryknoll, NY: Orbis, 1999).
Lakeland, Paul, *Postmodernity: Christian Identity in a Fragmented Age* (Minneapolis: Augsburg Fortress, 1997).
Lyotard, Jean-François, *The Postmodern Condition: A Report on Knowledge* (Manchester: Manchester University Press, 1984).
Tilley, Terrence W., *Postmodern Theologies: The Challenge of Religious Diversity* (Maryknoll, NY: Orbis, 1995).
Ward, Graham, "Postmodern Theology," in David F. Ford, ed., *The Modern Theologians*, 2nd edn (Oxford: Blackwell, 1997), pp. 585–601.

2 Anglo-American postmodernity: a theology of communal practice

NANCEY MURPHY AND BRAD J. KALLENBERG

WHY WOULD ANYONE WANT TO THINK *THAT*?

We take Nicholas Lash, formerly Professor of Divinity at Cambridge University, as our first exemplar of postmodern theology in the Anglo-American tradition. Lash makes several claims that may strike the (modern) reader as strange. For one, he criticizes accounts of religious experience that assume such experience, at least in its richest and purest forms, to be experience *of God*. In contrast, he says, "on the account that I shall offer, our experience of God is by no means necessarily 'religious' in character nor, from the fact that a particular type of experience is appropriately characterized as 'religious,' may it be inferred that it is, in any special or privileged sense, experience of God."[1]

What is it, then, to know God? The word "God" is descriptive and not a proper name, and to believe in God is to believe that "there is something or other which has divine attributes." The important question, then, is not whether God *exists*, but how to speak of God without becoming inane. All attempts to speak about God express the speakers' deepest convictions about the character and outcome of that transformative (creative and redemptive) process in which they and others are engaged.[2] The outcome of this process will define what it is to be human. Thus, Lash says, "human persons are not what we initially, privately, and 'inwardly' are, but what we may (perhaps) together hope and struggle to become."[3]

So we are not persons yet, experience of God is not "religious" experience, and the question of God's existence is inappropriate. We have intentionally focused here on several of Lash's more surprising claims. To see why he would want to make them will require a narrative involving modern philosophy, its effects on modern theology, and a critique of that modern

---

[1] Nicholas Lash, *Theology on the Way to Emmaus* (London: SCM Press, 1986), p. 143. Cf. Lash, *Easter in Ordinary: Reflections on Human Experience and the Knowledge of God* (Charlottesville, VA: University Press of Virginia, 1988).
[2] Lash, *Theology on the Way to Emmaus*, pp. 158–66.   [3] Lash, *Easter in Ordinary*, p. 89.

way of thinking that Lash describes as not merely a mistaken philosophy but "a pathological deformation, a personal and cultural disease."[4]

CONSTRUCTING THE CARTESIAN THEATER

René Descartes (1596–1650) is called the father of modern philosophy and, as often happens to fathers when their children seek independence, is now blamed for most of the ills of modernity. We invoke Descartes's name often, but with the caveat that what matters most about Descartes's thought is those aspects that his followers found reason to adopt and develop.

Descartes is well known for his method of doubt: to question everything he had been taught and then attempt to reconstruct his world-view on the basis of any ideas found to be indubitable. Chief among these indubitables was the fact of his own thinking. Descartes's method was the beginnings of modern foundationalist epistemology. We focus here, instead, on Descartes's image of human nature. Descartes described himself as a thinking thing, distinct from and somehow "within" his body. Thinking is a process of focusing the mind's eye; but focusing on what? On ideas *in* his mind. Thus there arose the image of the "Cartesian theater": the real "I" is an observer "in" the mind, looking at mental representations of what is outside. Throughout his epistemological writings Descartes focused on the solitary knower: "I am here quite alone"; "I stayed all day shut up in a stove-heated room where I was completely free to converse with myself about my own thoughts."[5]

Stephen Toulmin and others provide a plausible account of why Descartes's quest for absolutely certain foundations seemed so important in his historical location: social and political life could no longer be based on the authorities of the past because these authorities' divergent claims had led Europe into the chaos of the Thirty Years War. The desire to find rational agreement beyond the bounds of religious and political parties led to a quest for knowledge that was general and timeless rather than local and timely – in other words, to the quest for universal theory.[6]

If we look not to politics but to science and the Catholic spiritual tradition we gain insight into the appeal of the image of the "Cartesian ego, sitting inside the skull and wondering whether it can make reliable contact with the world 'outside' the 'mind.'"[7] Descartes was undoubtedly familiar with

---

[4] Lash, *Theology on the Way to Emmaus*, p. 45.
[5] René Descartes, *Meditations on First Philosophy*, first meditation; *Discourse on Method*, part 2.
[6] Stephen Toulmin, *Cosmopolis: the Hidden Agenda of Modernity* (University of Chicago Press, 1990); cf. Jeffrey Stout, *The Flight from Authority* (University of Notre Dame Press, 1981).
[7] Lash's characterization, *Easter in Ordinary*, p. 64.

Augustine's musings on "the roomy chambers" of his memory where images and ideas are stored, and with Augustine's description of thinking as among "the things I do within, in that vast chamber."[8] But the physics and optics of Descartes's day made contact with anything outside the "chamber" seem problematic. The new "corpuscular" physics made it appear that all knowledge of the "outside world" needed to be transmitted by particles striking sensory surfaces, from which coded information could be sent to the brain and thence to the mind.[9] This picture set Descartes up for a pernicious sort of skepticism: how to know that this transmission process was reliable, or, more generally, how to know that any ideas in the theater accurately represented the outside world – if, indeed, there were an outside world. Wallace Matson describes this approach to philosophy as "inside-out," in contrast to outside-in philosophies, which begin with an account of the world and at the end explain the human mind and its knowledge in the terms of that account.[10]

Many of the prominent features of modern thought can be explained as consequences of this inside-out approach to philosophy. It explains the skepticism regarding sensory knowledge that preoccupied early modern philosophers. Descartes solved this problem by arguing that a good God would not allow him to be entirely deceived by his senses. It also explains the persistence of the "problem of other minds" – how do I know that there is an "I" inside other human bodies, that they are not mere robots? And if the very existence of other consciousnesses has been one of the intractable problems of modern philosophy, it is easy to see why Descartes and his followers would want an account of knowledge relying only on what the solitary individual can know for him- or herself. Thus, modernity has been a period preoccupied by anxiety about knowledge: how can I ever know that *any* of the contents of my mind actually represent the world outside? This thoroughgoing skepticism in all realms of knowledge is the ill that foundationalism in all its forms was intended to cure. Philosophy's job became, in the modern era, not the systematizing of all knowledge – about the natural world, human life and well-being, God – but rather the discipline whose job it was to assure that *any* sort of knowledge was possible by providing the foundations of science and ethics, as well as the prolegomena to theology.

The modern concern with language and with the problem of whether and how language *refers* to reality can be seen as another consequence

[8] Augustine, *Confessions*, book 10, chaps. 8–11.
[9] Theo C. Meyering, *Historical Roots of Cognitive Science* (Dordrecht: Kluwer, 1989).
[10] Wallace I. Matson, *A New History of Philosophy*, 2 vols. (San Diego, CA: Harcourt Brace Jovanovich, 1987), II, pp. 275–82.

of the image of the Cartesian theater. Richard Rorty describes Descartes's predicament as living behind the "veil of ideas."[11] But, if ideas represent reality, and words represent ideas, the question naturally arises whether *words* represent reality. Thus, when philosophers' attention shifts in the twentieth century from psychology to language (from ideas to words) the problem of the veil of ideas becomes the problem of the *veil of language*. Is there a real world to which our language refers (or to which our conceptual scheme corresponds) and is language transparent or opaque? Thus, modern philosophy of language has been preoccupied with questions of reference and representation: words get their meaning from the things in the world to which they refer, but how does reference *happen*? Postmodern thinkers of the sort represented here are content with the question: "Which description of reality is best?" But modern thinkers characteristically ask, "Look, we have descriptions; now, is there anything to which they correspond?" Their answers have produced a variety of realisms and anti-realisms. For example, in light of Immanuel Kant's (1724–1804) absolute distinction between things-as-they-appear (phenomena) and things-as-they-are-in-themselves (noumena), the frustration of not even being able to say that noumenal reality must *resemble* phenomena drove some to idealism (the view that all reality is mental). Twentieth-century positivist philosophers of science proposed an instrumentalist (as opposed to realist) view of scientific theories to avoid the question of *how* those theories represent the reality they (seemed to) postulate. Current versions of scientific realism argue that the practical success of science shows that its theoretical terms (such as "electron") do in fact refer to objects in the real world and that well-established theories provide approximate descriptions of the way things are.

The most common form of anti-realism today (still indebted to Kant) is what Nicholas Wolterstorff calls "interpretation–universalism": experience is always-already conceptualized. To peel away this interpretation from experience would not be to get at the pure given but to lose the only given we have – the interpreted given. "Prisoners, all of us, within the house of interpretation." But the supposition of a ready-made, structured world waiting to be interpreted may not even be intelligible – any attempt to think such a world is already an interpretation of it. So, better to conclude that things exist and are the way they are only relative to conceptual schemes.[12]

[11] Richard Rorty, *Philosophy and the Mirror of Nature* (Princeton University Press, 1979).
[12] Nicholas Wolterstorff, "Between the Pincers of Increased Diversity and Supposed Irrationality," in William J. Wainwright, ed., *God, Philosophy and Academic Culture: A Discussion Between Scholars in the AAR and the APA* (npp: The American Academy of Religion, 1996), p. 18.

It is important to see that both realisms and anti-realisms are attempting to answer the *same* knowledge question, namely: "Can we know whether our concepts correspond with reality?" In the case of anti-realism (here "interpretation–universalism"), the answer is "it is interpretation all the way down."

MODERN THEOLOGY IN THE CARTESIAN THEATER

Historian Claude Welch writes that "at the beginning of the nineteenth century the theological problem was, simply, 'How is theology possible?' This was a question of both rationale and method, and included, at least implicitly, the question whether theology is possible at all."[13] In this section we consider the role of Descartes's legacy in raising the question of the very possibility of theology. This will serve as background for recognizing recent developments in both theology and philosophy that move decisively beyond modern dilemmas.

Cartesian anxiety led to a quest for foundations for all academic disciplines. In theology it manifested itself in the development of *theological prolegomena* – attempts to answer the question how theology is possible, and especially how it can be shown to be universally valid. Earlier these endeavors were described as fundamental or philosophical or (most revealingly) foundational theology. Today, with foundationalism in disrepute, the same goal is pursued as "public theology."

If generalized epistemological anxiety is not sufficient to account for questioning the entire theological enterprise, we find further insights in the image of the Cartesian theater. Descartes's own approach to the problem of God set the stage for the majority who followed. Descartes cast about within his mind and found the idea of God. By means of complicated arguments (drawing on the scholastic philosophical resources he meant to leave behind) he managed to prove to his own satisfaction that his idea of God could only have been caused by a real God distinct from himself, and thus God exists.[14]

Yet Karl Barth has argued that this Cartesian "turn to the subject" has been fatal to theology: whenever Christianity is *founded* on human religious experience (as Friedrich Schleiermacher [1768–1834], the father of modern liberal theology, set out to do), the question will arise whether religion is a *purely* human phenomenon and thus God a mere projection (so Ludwig Feuerbach [1804–72]).[15] This argument has been summarized in the slogan

---

[13] Claude Welch, *Protestant Thought in the Nineteenth Century*, 2 vols. (New Haven: Yale University Press, 1972, 1985), I, p. 59.
[14] *Meditations on First Philosophy*, third meditation.
[15] E.g., Karl Barth, *Church Dogmatics*, vol. 1, part 2 (Edinburgh: T. & T. Clark, 1956), pp. 288–91.

that "a Schleiermacher will lead inevitably to a Feuerbach." We might rather say that an inside-out approach to theology will lead inevitably to religious skepticism.

But why turn to religious experience to support the theological structure? Because more traditional approaches faced comparable problems: historical–critical methods applied to the scriptural texts led to an image of the text as a *veil of words*. Hans Frei noted that, for moderns, the referent of the biblical texts came to be seen as the history lying *behind* the texts, and scholars thereafter argued over the extent to which the texts reveal or conceal what one needs to know in order to provide a foundation for theology (see chapter 3 below). Theologians of the fundamentalist movement solved the problem by positing an act of God: the Holy Spirit guarantees the inerrancy of the texts and their accurate representation of what lies behind them (just as, for Descartes, God had guaranteed accurate sensory representation of the external world).

Against this historical background we can see the significance of Lash's opposition not merely to the common notion that God is experienced by turning inward but, in Lash's words, to the entire "philosophical temper which finds it necessary and unproblematic to draw a global or metaphysical distinction between 'objective' facts ... and 'subjective' beliefs, impressions or attitudes."[16] With these words Lash echoes the most formidable opponent of the Cartesian theater: Ludwig Wittgenstein (1889–1951).

SHOWING THE FLY THE WAY OUT OF THE BOTTLE

Wittgenstein thought that Descartes's bifurcation of subject and object was particularly baneful philosophical confusion: "The idea of thinking as a process in the head, in a completely enclosed space, makes thinking something occult."[17] "One of the most dangerous ideas for a philosopher is, oddly enough, that we think with our heads or in our heads."[18] In order to counter such enchantments, he developed a therapeutic method of philosophy that attended to the "grammar" of ordinary language. In other words, Wittgenstein concerned himself with the patterns of ordinary language use within a given social matrix. This strategy undermines the very way the skeptic sets up the knowledge problem as one of ascertaining the correspondence between an *individual's* concepts and brute reality "out there."

---

[16] Lash, *Theology on the Way to Emmaus*, p. 174.
[17] Ludwig Wittgenstein, *Philosophical Grammar*, ed. Rush Rhees, trans. Anthony Kenny (Berkeley and Los Angeles: University of California Press, 1974), section 64.
[18] Ludwig Wittgenstein, *Zettel*, ed. G. E. M. Anscombe and G. H. von Wright, trans. G. E. M. Anscombe (Berkeley and Los Angeles: University of California Press, 1970), section 605.

Attending to the grammar of concepts – that is, to the linguistic practice of ordinary speakers (and here the plurality of "speakers" in every case is of utmost importance and yet all too frequently overlooked) – can prevent seeds of bafflement from taking root. At this point we might be tempted to ask whether Wittgenstein is not simply a behaviorist in disguise: "Aren't you at bottom really saying that everything except human behavior is a fiction?" Wittgenstein replied tersely to this question: "If I do speak of a fiction, then it is of a *grammatical* fiction."[19] His point is this: behaviorism looks at stimulus–response conditioning operating on the *individual*, whereas grammatical analysis comes to a full stop at the givenness of the whole hurly-burly of our social–linguistic world. In other words, what is real for humans is shown by the way human beings – in the plural – speak with one another. To pronounce upon matters that lie beyond the boundaries of language use can only breed confusion.

What troubled Wittgenstein was the pervasiveness of the urge to overcome the putative problem of skepticism by attempting to specify the correspondence between one's ideas "in here" and the world "out there." Kant dealt with the problem by making a sharp distinction between things-as-they-appear-to-us and (unknowable) things-as-they-are-in-themselves. While Kant himself thought that the mind that structured the phenomenal world was transculturally uniform, his work left open the possibility that persons or groups might operate with radically different cognitive frameworks – a possibility that only augmented skepticism. But Wittgenstein pressed Kant in a different direction. Crudely put, language played the part for Wittgenstein that the categorial framework played for Kant. And his careful exegesis of the hurly-burly of everyday speaking enabled Wittgenstein to *untangle* Cartesian skepticism. To recap, the problem for thinkers from Descartes onward has been knowing whether one's ideas corresponded with reality. Staring at my hand, I can wonder, "I don't know if this is a hand." But Wittgenstein can reply: "But do you know what the word 'hand' means? And don't say 'I know what it means now for me.' And isn't it an empirical fact – that *this* word is used like *this*?"[20]

Wittgenstein's celebrated demonstration of the impossibility of private language means that doubt can only go as deep as one's fluency in his or her native tongue. Moreover, one can never get a purchase on language to

[19] Ludwig Wittgenstein, *Philosophical Investigations*, ed. G. E. M. Anscombe and Rush Rhees, trans. G. E. M. Anscombe (New York: Macmillan, 1953), section 307.
[20] Ludwig Wittgenstein, *On Certainty*, ed. G. E. M. Anscombe and G. H. von Wright, trans. Denis Paul and G. E. M. Anscombe (New York, NY: Harper Torchbooks, 1972), section 306.

analyze it in general, for every description is done by means of language. Wittgenstein wryly observed:

> A French politician once said that it was a special characteristic of the French language that in French sentences words occurred in the sequence in which one thinks them.
>
> The idea that one language in contrast to others has a word order which corresponds to the order of thinking arises from the notion that thought is an essentially different process going on independently of the expression of the thoughts.[21]

We cannot treat the world in isolation from language because it is by means of language that we "treat" anything at all. Language is the means by which we understand both our world and ourselves: "It is in language that it is all done."[22]

Human inability to escape the inextricability of language and world enabled Wittgenstein to envision a realism that altogether avoided the problems of Cartesian skepticism. Wittgenstein asks: "How do I know that this color is red? It would be an answer to say 'I have learnt English.' "[23]

This strategy is not as trivial as it first appears. Imagine the skeptic standing in a downpour asking: "How do I *know* that I am wet?" For Wittgenstein, no puzzle surrounds the concept "know" that is not simultaneously solved by attention to the grammar of the word "wet." We learned the concept "wet" by being drilled by our mothers: "Come in out of the rain this instant! You're soaking wet!" Standing in the rain, wetting our beds, spilling on our shirts, falling down in puddles, and the like, comprise a complicated form of life in which young English speakers are socialized into correct usage of the term "wet." Thus, the adult who speaks the word in the context of a steady rain *already* correctly uses the concept, which is to say, coherent with the way the rest of the linguistic community uses the term. This habitual reflex for correct usage is what we mean, at bottom, by retorting to the skeptic, "*You're* all wet!"

The philosopher's temptation is always to use words in illegitimate or ungrammatical ways. The skeptic overlooks the ordinary use of words like "know" when asking "how do I know I'm wet?" Philosophy of religion suffers from similar confusion and requires a similar therapy: believers insist, and atheists deny, that "God exists." But the grammar of "exists" shows that the sentence engenders confusion. We ordinarily say, "For how long has this institution existed?", "When did dinosaurs cease to exist?", and "Sadly,

---

[21] Wittgenstein, *Philosophical Grammar*, section 66.
[22] Ibid., section 95.   [23] Ibid., section 381.

racism still exists in the world today." In each case, it makes sense to speak of something's coming into existence and passing out of existence – a mode of reality that Christian believers rightly say does not apply to God. If the grammar of "exists" means that the word applies to the furniture of the universe, then we ought to agree with the atheist that God does not "exist." As Kierkegaard put it, "God does not exist, He is eternal."[24]

A similar analysis could be made of the grammar of the word "God." What does the word "God" mean? The word becomes meaningful by its use in a complicated form of life: we pray to God, we witness about God, we confess our sins to God, and so on. If practice gives the word its sense, then the word "God" spoken from within an atheistic form of life and the word "God" spoken by Christian believers are simply homonyms. It is no wonder that the theist–atheist debate has been interminable.

What astonished Wittgenstein is the (largely unnoticed) agreement in our form of life that enables linguistic practices to become matters of habit. We pucker at lemons, coo at babies, cry when we skin a knee, and pale when our friend skins a knee. Wittgenstein calls these behaviors "primitive reactions" in order to emphasize their givenness for the functioning of language. One way (and only one way) to think of the connection between primitive reactions and language use is to imagine vocables as going proxy for these other behaviors.

> How do words *refer* to sensations? ... Here is one possibility: words are connected with the primitive, the natural, expressions of the sensation and used in their place. A child has hurt himself and he cries; and then adults talk to him and teach him exclamations and, later, sentences. They teach the child new pain-behavior.
>
> "So you are saying that the word 'pain' really means crying?" – On the contrary: the verbal expression of pain replaces crying and does not describe it.[25]

Wittgenstein's point is that language does not *refer*, or *picture*, or *correspond to*, some nonlinguistic reality; there is no way for us to imagine that to which language corresponds ("a state of affairs," "the world," "reality," etc.) except in terms of the very language that this "reality" is supposed to be considered in isolation of. Rather, learning a language is an irreducibly social enterprise by which a child is trained into a communal mode of living. Thus Wittgenstein likened language to a series of games that require partners for playing: "In a conversation: One person throws a ball; the other does

---

[24] Søren Kierkegaard, *Concluding Unscientific Postscript*, intro. and notes by Walter Lowrie, trans. David F. Swenson (Princeton University Press, 1941), p. 296.

[25] Wittgenstein, *Philosophical Investigations*, section 244. See also section 257.

not know: whether he is supposed to throw it back, or throw it to a third person, or leave it on the ground, or pick it up and put it in his pocket, etc."[26]

Wittgenstein saw an interdependent relation among primitive reactions, socially constituted forms of life, and language use. Agreement in primitive reactions constitutes a community's form of life, which, in turn, conditions the shape of its language-games, which, in turn, shapes the way the community conceives the world, which, in turn, shapes the primitive reactions shared by its members.[27]

Such an arrangement has suggested to some the need for a wholesale conversion to a very different way of thinking. At the very center of this conversion would be a deep humility that confesses grave human limits; we cannot pretend to achieve a translinguistic God's-eye view from which to judge the putative correspondence between ideas and words or between words and states of affairs. We receive our community's linguistic practices, and the form of life internally related to these practices, as a gift that enables communication – *but only within grammatical limits*. How humiliating! Surely we can do better than that! But perhaps we cannot recover from Babel after all.

For Wittgenstein, our human inability to extract language from world or world from language meant that the picture of the Cartesian theater, which so neatly separated subjects from objects, only muddies the water. In contrast, clarity begins with an acknowledgment of the irreducibly social character of human experience and the intrinsic relation of human experience to the real world: "What has to be accepted, the given, is – so one could say – *forms of life*."[28]

For theologians after Wittgenstein, there is much work to do in order to free religious believers from the Cartesian bottle. To take up our former examples, what distinguishes human persons is not the possession of a little "I" inside the mind, but the practice of telling stories and having our stories told to and by one another.[29] Thus, we are not persons yet, but persons-on-the-way as our stories unfold. Moreover, as Lash warns, "religious experience" is neither private nor self-identifying nor self-authenticating. What counts as "religious" experience can only be so identified and described once the communal gift of language is already largely in place. By the same token, if naming appears to be the paradigmatic case of the Cartesian ego acting

[26] Ludwig Wittgenstein, *Culture and Value*, ed. G. H. von Wright and Heikki Nyman, trans. Peter Winch (Oxford: Blackwell, 1980), p. 74e.
[27] See Brad J. Kallenberg, *Ethics as Grammar: Changing the Postmodern Subject* (University of Notre Dame Press, 2001), pp. 203–15.
[28] Wittgenstein, *Philosophical Investigations*, p. 226e.
[29] Lash, *Theology on the Way to Emmaus*, p. 73.

in isolation, Lash cannot imagine the word "God" functioning simply as a label. Rather, "God" acts as a proxy for a whole host of stories that manifest God's publicly knowable character. (What can "*YHWH yireh*" mean but a shorthand account of Genesis 22?) Finally, the question of God's existence is inappropriate because the grammar of "God" does not admit questions of existence, for that puts matters too hypothetically. As Wittgenstein commented to Drury: "Can you imagine St. Augustine saying that the existence of God was 'highly probable'?"[30]

It is frequently objected that Wittgenstein's work yields a fideism that undermines theology's ability to do serious work. In surprising contrast, Wittgenstein thought that it was *Descartes*'s legacy that threatened to distort theology: "if you believe, say, Spinoza or Kant, this interferes with what you believe in religion; but if you believe me, nothing of the sort."[31]

From Wittgenstein's stance, first-order religious claims mean what they mean within the given form of life. Referring explicitly to theology, Wittgenstein remarked: "How words are understood is not told by words alone,"[32] rather, it is *praxis* that gives words their sense.[33] But this does not mean that religious claims are insulated from criticism. On the contrary, theology performs both critical and constructive tasks. By attending to the grammar of religious discourse, theologians discipline the tendency of believers' words toward self-delusion and over-simplification. Moreover, theological grammarians coach believers in the proper use of first-order language in a way that enables them to see the pattern of God's presence in the realm of the ordinary. In Lash's words:

> It is the task of those who bear the burden of theological
> responsibility to show, quite concretely, in particular circumstances,
> *how* it is that the question of human identity, significance and destiny
> may be construed as the question of God; to show how it is that the
> *coincidence* of these questions, as the content of specifically Christian
> hope, is clarified, defined and illuminated by the life, teaching, death
> and resurrection of Jesus the Christ.[34]

CLOSING THE OMEGA

So then, modern theology operates within the conceptual confines of the Cartesian theater, crafting a theology that is simultaneously *individualistic*

---

[30] M. O'C. Drury, "Some Notes on Conversations with Wittgenstein," in Rush Rhees, ed., *Recollections of Wittgenstein* (Oxford: Oxford University Press, 1984), p. 105.
[31] Cited in Fergus Kerr, *Theology after Wittgenstein* (Oxford: Blackwell, 1986), p. 32.
[32] Wittgenstein, *Zettel*, section 144.   [33] Wittgenstein, *Culture and Value*, p. 85e.
[34] Lash, *Theology on the Way to Emmaus*, p. 17.

(in that religion is founded upon my experience here and now) and *totalizing* (in that human nature is presumed to be everywhere uniform). Postmodern theology inhabits a different space altogether, for if the language by which religious experience is enabled and described is not of an individual's own making, then religion itself has an irreducibly social and historical component. Investigation into religious reality is never more profound than when the faithful historical *community* is its object. Thus Lash asks: "What kind of community is it that might be realistically and concretely envisaged as the symbolic or sacramental expression of eschatological hope, of a hope that is effectively critical of all idolatrous absolutization of particular places and times, nations and destinies, projects and policies?"[35] If Lash has been prodded by Wittgenstein to change the very *questions* he inherited from modern theologians, John Howard Yoder can be seen to occupy a similar space in so far as he transforms their *answers*.

Yoder was a walking set of contradictions: a Mennonite theologian[36] who studied under Barth and ended his career teaching at the University of Notre Dame; a proactive pacifist who tirelessly advanced the "modest proposal" that Christians refrain from killing each other as the first step toward abolishing war; a sectarian (by Ernst Troeltsch's standards) who advocated strong social action (Yoder himself both served Mennonite relief and mission agencies throughout Europe and Algeria as well as spent twenty years working in various capacities for the World Council of Churches); a church historian who is as much postmodern as he is pre-modern by virtue of his affirmation that Jesus' life and teachings, including the prohibition of killing, are normative for us today.

Yoder entered the fray of contemporary theology through the door of church history and focused his energies on the historical reality of the community that worships Jesus. Yoder understood the unbroken historical continuity of that community not only as permission to say "this is that" (i.e., this church today is that church back then), but also as that which validates this community's present moral judgment (by virtue of the present Christian community's approximation to the first-century church's discourse and form of life). Yoder was thus suspicious of the modern obsession to find foundations for ethics and theology in theoretical demonstrations of first *principles* since this overlooks the obvious prior condition: "There had to be a human social fabric, in which people's relationships were mediated

---

[35] Ibid., p. 191.
[36] Yoder resisted the term "Mennonite theologian," preferring instead to view himself as a theologian of the church catholic.

by communication, through various kinds of signals but most evidently in words."[37]

In the absence of theoretical foundations, Yoder suggested that ethics must begin with "a phenomenology of moral life" – that is, with a description of the moral life of an actual community. Ironically, such a description is, in fact, *less* biased than accounts of putative first principles, because community life is subject to criteria that philosophical discussions are not: the viability of a historical community depends on the ongoing felicity of its communications. Thus, "for the society to be viable, most of this communication has to be 'true' most of the time; i.e. it has to provide a reliable basis for structuring our common life, counting on each other and not being routinely disappointed." This social matrix is simply the given beyond which ethics cannot go. "The fabric exists, and functions more or less well, before anyone asks for an accounting about why it works. The 'accounting' that we can do is therefore not 'validation' but *a posteriori* elucidation."[38]

For Yoder, then, Christian ethics could not be separated from theology since both involve explication of the Gospel as it has been embodied in the form of life of the believing community since the New Testament. Jesus matters for contemporary believers because Jesus mattered for the original lot. Yet Yoder is not advocating a naive biblicism that might be offered in place of other reductive methodologies. He explained: "Precisely because of my commitment to a community which in turn is committed to canonical accountability, I saw no way to squeeze such accountability into such a straitjacket [as biblicism]."[39] In contrast: "Skepticism about methodological reductivism and respect for the 'thick' reading of any real history, in which the Bible belongs, go naturally hand in hand."[40] Consequently, Yoder understood there to be a dialectical relationship between canon and community.

On the one hand, the canon shapes the community. Faithfulness to the cruciform pattern established by the story of Jesus is the chief aim of those for whom the biblical texts are taken to be Scripture. The biblical texts have been read in various ways – as literature, as science, as fiction, etc. – but those for whom the biblical texts are canonical read them *as Scripture* and thus submit themselves to interrogation *by* the text rather than become the interrogators *of* the text. Yoder's "precritical"[41] reading strategy enabled him

[37] Yoder, "Walk and Word: The Alternatives to Methodologism," in Stanley Hauerwas, Nancey Murphy, and Mark Nation, eds., *Theology without Foundations: Religious Practice and the Future of Theological Truth* (Nashville, TN: Abingdon Press, 1994), p. 79.
[38] Ibid., p. 80.   [39] Ibid., p. 87.   [40] Ibid., p. 88.
[41] See Hans Frei, *The Eclipse of Biblical Narrative: a Study in Eighteenth- and Nineteenth-Century Hermeneutics* (New Haven, CT: Yale University Press, 1974).

to be well informed of historical–critical debates over the textual minutiae (such as are incorporated into the copious footnotes of *The Politics of Jesus*[42]) yet remain untroubled by historical–critical challenges that take the Bible as an object of study rather than the lens through which the world is brought into focus.

On the other hand, community life is determinative for the proper reading of Scripture. Before we can know how the Scripture ought to be read, Yoder wants us to get clear on who is the "we" doing the reading. Thus in "The Otherness of the Church" he insists on the enduring distinctive identity of the church over and against the world by recounting the narrative of Christian history both prior to and after the church's (lamentable) Constantinianization.[43] Similarly, Yoder writes that Jesus' "original revolution" was the establishment of the church as the social embodiment of a radical pacifist alternative to secular strategies for living together.[44] When *this* community rightly reads Scripture, its reading takes the form of an ecumenical conversation that is sometimes reforming and other times prophetic, and only insiders have a sense of timing that is developed finely enough to tell the difference.

Modernity, wrote Stephen Toulmin, is a giant Ω-shaped detour.[45] If Toulmin's metaphor is apt, then we should not be surprised to discover that postmodern philosophy shares much in common with its premodern cousins (a thesis not pursued here) and that postmodern theology finds a kinship with premodern theology. While Lash has crafted his theology with an eye toward Wittgenstein, Yoder's theology resonates with Anglo-American postmodern thought even though he explicitly eschewed philosophy in favor of close reading of the historical Christian community. In our view, both Lash and Yoder disclose the way forward for theologians who have grown lonely under the bewitchment of Cartesian solipsism.

AN EMERGING THEOLOGY OF COMMUNAL PRACTICE

As writers born and raised in the modern world, we had to resist the temptation to begin this chapter with a theoretical definition of the general philosophical characteristics of Anglo-American postmodern theology. We began instead with examples and historical narrative. At this point, though,

[42] 2nd edn (Grand Rapids, MI and Carlisle, UK: Eerdmans and Paternoster Press, 1994).
[43] John Howard Yoder, "The Otherness of the Church," in Michael G. Cartwright, ed., *The Royal Priesthood: Essays Ecclesiological and Ecumenical* (Grand Rapids, MI: Eerdmans, 1994), pp. 53–64.
[44] John Howard Yoder, *The Original Revolution* (Scottdale, PA: Herald Press, 1971), pp. 148–82.
[45] Toulmin, *Cosmopolis*, p. 167.

an overview is in order. We suggested an understanding of "post"-modern as that which dissolves longstanding modern dilemmas by escaping the bewitchment of pictures or images that have shaped them. We concentrated here on the image of the Cartesian theater because we see it as most powerful, but there are others: knowledge as a building, language itself as a picture (representation) of a world divorced from it, physical reality as a series of levels of complex wholes all reducing without remainder to their simplest parts.[46]

In the centuries since Descartes a cosmopolitan European philosophical community has become divided – one now has to specify "Anglo-American" or "Continental" tradition – but this is a distinction of style rather than geography. A number of Anglo-American philosophers, since the mid-twentieth century, have contributed to the dissolution of modern problems. We can mention here only some of the most significant. Gilbert Ryle[47] and Richard Rorty[48] have joined Wittgenstein in his critique of the Cartesian mind. W. V. O. Quine provided a picture of knowledge as a web or net to replace Descartes's building image.[49] J. L. Austin showed how the social and practical aspects of language take precedence over reference and representation.[50] Thomas Kuhn emphasized the role of communal practice in science.[51] Alasdair MacIntyre emphasized the social embodiment and historical rootedness of all human reasoning, both theoretical and moral.[52]

We count as postmodern, then, theologians who either explicitly appropriate these philosophical developments or who have arrived at similar positions by alternate routes. Some representatives: David Burrell and Rowan Williams, obviously indebted to Wittgenstein; the Yale School and its fellow travelers, who acknowledge debts to Wittgenstein, Austin, and Quine; James Wm. McClendon, Jr. and Stanley Hauerwas, who acknowledge debts to Austin and Wittgenstein but, as did Yoder, arrived at similar conclusions by disparate routes.

Despite risk of over-simplification, we can describe all of these as sharing a concept of mind that is irreducibly linguistic in texture and thus already actively entangled with reality. There is no general problem of knowledge or

---

[46] Nancey Murphy and James Wm. McClendon, Jr., "Distinguishing Modern and Postmodern Theologies," *Modern Theology* 5 (1989), 191–214.
[47] Gilbert Ryle, *The Concept of Mind* (University of Chicago, 1949).
[48] Rorty, *Philosophy and the Mirror of Nature*.
[49] W. V. O. Quine, "Two Dogmas of Empiricism," *Philosophical Review* 60:1 (1951), 20–43.
[50] J. L. Austin, *How to do Things with Words*, ed. J. O. Urmson and G. J. Warnock (Oxford: Clarendon Press, 1962).
[51] Thomas S. Kuhn, *The Structure of Scientific Revolutions*, 2nd edn (University of Chicago Press, 1970).
[52] Alasdair MacIntyre, *Whose Justice? Which Rationality?* (University of Notre Dame Press, 1988).

reference or representation. Rather, there are specific problems of meaning and knowledge and practice germane to various disciplines at particular points in their development. Theology has its own particular epistemological and linguistic and practical problems. Theologians do not have to wait for an adequate philosophical foundation before they begin; they are already a part of a tradition of inquiry and thus the task is not to begin from scratch but to pick up where their predecessors left off.

So for postmodern theologians there is no general question of whether or how theology is possible – many do it before breakfast! There is no need to answer the question, "does the word 'God' refer?" The question is instead, "what is our God really like?" There is no need for them to begin with the question, "is Christianity true?" The question is rather, "are there good reasons to *be* a Christian, to engage in this form of life?" and this is as much a moral question as an epistemological one.

But why be postmodern? We have emphasized the role of pictures in shaping the thought of an historical era. Is one picture (the old one) not as good as another? An answer to this question requires some reflection on how philosophical change comes about. We suggest that pictures generate philosophical theories and programs. But sometimes the philosophical programs run into obstacles; the theories succumb to repeated critique (for example, foundationalism). When a new picture is offered (for example, Quine's web), it not only provides an alternative and a fresh set of resources, but also shows why the older program failed, and was bound to fail, exactly where it did. So there is no going back.

Further reading

Kallenberg, Brad J., *Ethics as Grammar: Changing the Postmodern Subject* (University of Notre Dame Press, 2001).

Kerr, Fergus, *Theology after Wittgenstein* (Oxford: Blackwell, 1986).

Lash, Nicholas, *Theology on the Way to Emmaus* (London: SCM, 1986).

Murphy, Nancey, *Beyond Liberalism and Fundamentalism* (Philadelphia: Trinity Press International, 1996).

   Anglo-American Postmodernity: Philosophical Perspectives on Science, Religion, and Ethics (Boulder, CO: Westview Press, 1997).

Placher, William C., *Unapologetic Theology* (Louisville, KY: Westminster/John Knox Press, 1989).

Rorty, Richard, *Philosophy and the Mirror of Nature* (Princeton University Press, 1979).

Toulmin, Stephen, *Cosmopolis: The Hidden Agenda of Modernity* (University of Chicago Press, 1990).

Wittgenstein, Ludwig, *Philosophical Investigations*, trans. G. E. M. Anscombe (New York: Macmillan, 1958).

Yoder, John Howard, *The Politics of Jesus*, 2nd edn (Grand Rapids: Eerdmans, 1994).

3 Postliberal theology

GEORGE HUNSINGER

If postliberal theology depends on the existence of something called the "Yale School," then postliberal theology is in trouble. It is in trouble, because the so-called Yale School enjoys little basis in reality, being largely the invention of theological journalism. At best it represents a loose coalition of interests, united more by what it opposes or envisions than by any common theological program.

One indicator that the Yale School is mostly a fiction is that no two lists of who allegedly belongs to it are the same. Everyone agrees that the short list includes Hans Frei and George Lindbeck, both of whom taught at Yale over roughly the same period, more or less from the 1950s to the 1980s. After that, however, the nominees vary widely, though they can perhaps be divided into three categories: Frei's and Lindbeck's Yale colleagues, their Yale-related contemporaries, and their students. Does the Yale School include Brevard Childs, David Kelsey, and Paul Holmer? All were colleagues, and all have been nominated; but why other colleagues should be excluded, like Nils Dahl, Wayne Meeks, Gene Outka, or even Robert Clyde Johnson, is not clear. Does it include Stanley Hauerwas, a frequently mentioned contender, not on the Yale faculty, but with a Yale Ph.D.? Does it include William Placher, Bruce Marshall, Ronald Thiemann, Kathryn Tanner, David Yeago, Joseph DiNoia, James Buckley, or myself, to mention only a few? Who knows? We all did our doctoral work at Yale, which at least seems to have placed us in the running. Prima facie, however, one is looking at a fairly diverse bunch. Are there unifying interests or themes?

If we stick for a moment with Frei's and Lindbeck's students, certain tendencies are perhaps discernible, but only with varying degrees of convergence, divergence, and incompatibility. One axis might run, say, between "neo-confessionalists" and "neo-secularists." Roughly speaking, the former would tend to move from the traditional to the modern, from received confessional theologies to theological method, or from ecclesial commitments to secular disciplines, whereas the latter would move more in the opposite direction, from the methodological to the confessional, or from the secular to the ecclesial, with a complex range of options in between. The only real commonality would be somehow to negotiate these interests. Another axis would represent ecumenical interests that traverse the familiar confessions or communions, representing yet also criss-crossing the Reformed, the Lutheran (mostly evangelical-Catholic in tendency), the Anglican, and the Roman Catholic traditions. Not least, but perhaps crucially, another axis might span, or exemplify, a neglected difference between "postliberal" and "neoliberal" positions. That difference, however, in some sense, is arguably the difference between Frei and Lindbeck themselves.

Besides the lack of a common program, the main reason why there is no Yale School is that little-noticed differences exist between the two defining principals. Though not absolute, they are by no means negligible. Frei was oriented toward Barth; Lindbeck, toward Aquinas and Luther. Frei's method of relating theology to other disciplines fell most naturally into thought-forms reminiscent of Barth (Gospel/Law); Lindbeck's method, by contrast, into thought-forms indebted to Luther (Law/Gospel). The logic of Frei's theology tended to move from the particular to the general, from the ecclesial to the secular, and from the confessional to the methodological; the logic of Lindbeck's theology moved more or less in the opposite direction, from the general to the particular, from the secular to the ecclesial, and from the methodological to the confessional.[1] The two theologians also differed on questions of truth. Although both were "nonfoundationalists" sympathetic to Wittgenstein, holding that cognitive and pragmatic aspects of truth should be seen as inseparable, Frei did not follow his colleague in making the one a function of the other. As opposed to Lindbeck's pragmatism that made truth depend strongly on use, Frei quietly aligned himself instead with a less pragmatist position that he called "moderate propositionalism."[2] Nor did Frei think, as did his colleague, that doctrines qua doctrines were merely regulative (as opposed to being also constitutive).[3] The former theologian

---

[1] For similar (and much more detailed) reflections on how the two Yale theologians follow contrasting procedures in their methodologies, see Mike Higton, "Frei's Christology and Lindbeck's Cultural–linguistic Theory," *Scottish Journal of Theology* 50 (1997), 83–95.

[2] See Hans W. Frei, "Epilogue: George Lindbeck and *The Nature of Doctrine*," in Bruce D. Marshall, ed., *Theology and Dialogue*, (University of Notre Dame Press, 1990), pp. 140–41.

[3] See for example Frei, *Types of Christian Theology* (New Haven: Yale University Press, 1992), pp. 124–25. In this passage Frei discusses the historic Chalcedonian Definition. Note that he does not distinguish sharply between "first-order" and "second-order" discourse, but more mildly between first-level and second-level functions. Most importantly, Frei does not regard the second-level function as merely regulative. On the contrary, he takes it for granted that this grammatical level also makes truth claims, functioning in a way that is conceptually "descriptive" or "redescriptive." See also p. 42.

was thus somewhat less latitudinarian than the latter.[4] Frei stood for "generous orthodoxy"; Lindbeck, for "orthodox generosity."

Consequently, with respect to truth and method in theology, Frei may be seen as more directly "postliberal"; Lindbeck, as slightly more "neoliberal." "Postliberalism," as used here, would be that form of tradition-based rationality in theology for which questions of truth and method are strongly dependent on questions of meaning, and for which questions of meaning are determined by the intratextual subject matter of Scripture. Postliberalism bids for a paradigm shift in which liberalism and evangelicalism are overlapped, dismantled, and reconstituted on a new and different plane. Neoliberalism, by contrast, would be more nearly a revisionist extension within the established liberal paradigm. It does not so much depart from as perpetuate the liberal/evangelical split characteristic of modernity itself.

The neoliberal elements in Lindbeck's thought can be seen in his "cultural–linguistic" theory. This theory is really three theories in one: a theory of religion, a theory of doctrine, and a theory of truth. The theory of religion is "cultural"; the theory of doctrine, "regulative," and the theory of truth, "pragmatist." Whereas the theory of religion is possibly postliberal, the theories of doctrine and truth are more properly neoliberal. For Lindbeck as for modern liberal theology, both "doctrine" and "truth" are so defined as to make them significantly non-cognitive. Any conceivable propositional content in theological language is relativized. Although the strategies of relativization are different, the modern liberal aversion to propositional content is much the same.

Modern liberal theology tends to regard received church doctrines as propositional, but truth as "experiential–expressive." It proceeds, in effect, to turn its non-cognitive theory of religious truth against received doctrines so that propositional content is at once relativized and made dependent, in meaning and truth, on logically independent interpretative schemes (for example, ontology, metaphysics, analytical philosophy, historicism, naturalism, social theory, depth psychology, etc.). Once Christian doctrinal content has been relativized, reinterpreted, or reduced by independent disciplines functioning as interpretative schemes, practical content is typically promoted as the remaining element of religious significance.

Lindbeck's "cultural–linguistic" theory is "neoliberal" insofar as it achieves much the same outcome by other means. Whereas liberalism

---

[4] For an example of Lindbeck's "latitudinarianism," see his essay "Atonement and the Hermeneutics of Intratextual Social Embodiment," in Timothy R. Phillips and Dennis L. Okholm, eds., *The Nature of Confession: Evangelicals and Postliberals in Conversation* (Downers Grove, IL: InterVarsity Press, 1996), pp. 221–40. He finds a way of validating both Anselm and Abelard on the atonement.

relativizes doctrine's propositional content by reinterpretation, neoliberalism does so by redefinition (the "rule theory"). Whereas liberalism promotes religion's practical content by way of a theory of religious truth that is "experiential–expressive," neoliberalism does so by means of a new theory of truth that is more pragmatic. The neoliberal critique does not break with the liberal paradigm. Although it substitutes pragmatism for expressivism, it tends to perpetuate the liberal aversion to propositionalism. Neither liberalism nor neoliberalism can quite do justice, from a properly postliberal point of view, to the truth claims of Christian discourse.

The first use of the term "postliberal," in the relevant sense, occurred in Hans Frei's doctoral dissertation.[5] Although in that work it merely indicated the two basic phases of Barth's development (from liberal to postliberal), the stage was set for thinking about "postliberalism" as a theological option in its own right. At least three aspects in Barth's break with liberalism, as Frei analyzed it, turned out to be portents of the future: critical realism (dialectic and analogy), the primacy of God, and Christocentricity. A suggestive convergence emerges at this point between Barth and Lindbeck. If one were to correlate Barth's postliberalism with the latter's cultural–linguistic theory, the results might be: a theory of truth determined by critical realism, a theory of doctrine determined by divine primacy, and a theory of religion determined by Christocentrism. Although on this reading postliberalism would not be confined to the "Yale School," that School would represent a partial mediation and independent development of richer, more definitive postliberal theologies such as are found in figures like Hans Urs von Balthasar and Karl Barth. In what follows, some ideas of Frei and Lindbeck will be examined in relation to such larger programs as they bear on the emergent themes: truth, doctrine, religion.[6]

POSTLIBERALISM: TRUTH AS DETERMINED BY CRITICAL REALISM

Lindbeck's typology of the nature and function of theological language is, arguably, something like comparing two apples and a banana. "Cognitive propositionalism" and "experiential expressivism" are the same sort of thing, but the "cultural linguistic theory" is not.[7] When the latter is

---

5 Hans W. Frei, "The Doctrine of Revelation in the Thought of Karl Barth, 1909 to 1922: The Nature of Barth's Break with Liberalism," unpublished dissertation (Yale University, 1956), pp. 430–34, 513, 536.
6 Since these are obviously enormous topics, what follows can be no more than a sketch.
7 See Lindbeck, *The Nature of Doctrine: Religion and Theology in a Postliberal Age* (Philadelphia: Westminster, 1984), pp. 30–45.

unpacked, the relevant aspect is, as suggested, a pragmatist theory of truth, more nearly neoliberal than postliberal in inspiration.

My own work has involved a sympathetic reworking of the Lindbeck typology to direct it more plausibly along postliberal lines.[8] Although differing from Lindbeck at the theoretical level, the revised typology is by no means incompatible with much of Lindbeck's actual writing since *The Nature of Doctrine*. In any case, the new typology was constructed, in part, to rescue Barth's postliberalism from the invisibility to which the Lindbeck proposal seemed otherwise to consign it. (A typology that cannot really account for figures like Barth and von Balthasar, in such matters, would seem to have something against it.)

The revised typology redesignates cognitive propositionalism as "literalism," and amends experiential expressivism to simply "expressivism." From a postliberal point of view, the real problem with the former is not that it is either "cognitive" or "propositional," but just *how* it is so. Regardless of whether biblical narrative or language about God is in view, literalism sees the mode of textual reference as strongly univocal in ways that postliberalism would regard as untenable.[9]

Postliberalism, on the other hand, would largely agree with Lindbeck's analysis of expressivism, but it need not restrict what religious language is supposedly "expressing" only to non-cognitive religious experiences. (Some of Lindbeck's early expressivist critics thought they could dispatch his entire typology merely because of this restriction.) The logic of expressivism does not change when it is expanded, as the revision allows, to include the covert linguistic expression of social or political power relations (for example, "patriarchy"). The manifest content of religious language is still equivocal in its mode of reference; its surface content must still be unmasked and reinterpreted for its real cognitive content, which is always latent, and always unavailable apart from the use of some logically independent conceptual scheme (or combination of schemes). Since neither biblical language about events nor language about God can be taken "literally," the only alternative, supposedly, is to take it "metaphorically" or "symbolically," as if the meaning of these terms were obvious, uncontested or context-neutral.[10] In any case,

---

[8] See George Hunsinger, "Beyond Literalism and Expressivism: Karl Barth's Hermeneutical Realism," in *Disruptive Grace: Studies in the Theology of Karl Barth* (Grand Rapids: Eerdmans, 2000), pp. 210–25.

[9] A good representative of this type would be Carl F. H. Henry. See for example his essay "Is the Bible Literally True?" in *God, Revelation, and Authority*, vol. 4 (Waco, TX: Word, 1979), pp. 103–28.

[10] The revised typology makes it clear that "literalism" and "realism" both have their own contextually determined definitions of these terms, and that the respective definitions across the typology are at strong variance with one another. Consequently, a mere appeal to "metaphor" solves nothing.

the mode of reference with respect to the manifest content (about God or events) is always strongly equivocal.[11]

"Realism," according to the revised typology, is the distinctively postliberal option. Where literalism sees the mode of reference for theological language as univocal, and expressivism as equivocal, postliberalism sees it as analogical. Analogy (in Barth's case often combined with dialectical modes of expression) allows for significant elements of both similarity and dissimilarity between word and object, text and referent, whether the textual referent is God or historical events or some combination of the two. Analogical modes of reference are, by definition, neither univocal nor equivocal, but they are nonetheless communally standardized and propositionally valid in ways that Lindbeck's pragmatism disallows.[12]

With respect to language about God, by opting for analogical modes of reference, postliberalism merely retrieves patristic and medieval insights that were often eclipsed during modernity by the polarized clash between liberalism and fundamentalism. "God is light," wrote Irenaeus in a remarkably pithy comment, "but he is unlike any light that we know."[13] God's cognitive availability through divine revelation allows us, Irenaeus believed, to predicate descriptions of God that are as true as we can make them, while God's irreducible ineffability nonetheless renders even our best predications profoundly inadequate. Because only God is properly light, all other light is necessarily improper and dependent, and yet our only conceptual access to the light which God is depends inexorably on that light which is not God. Whether postliberalism thinks this matter through with someone like Barth in terms of the actualism of grace, or with someone like von Balthasar in terms of the Roman Catholic understanding of the *sacramentum mundi*, the false polarizations of modernity are overcome. Instead of divine availability at the expense of irreducible transcendence (literalism), or divine transcendence at the expense of real availability (expressivism), postliberal critical realism recovers the historic ecumenical conviction of divine availability to true predication in the midst of transcendent ineffability.

The Yale emphasis on narrative may be placed in this context. By coupling Barth's distinctive sensitivity to biblical narrative (*Geschichte*) with

---

[11] A good example of this type would be Paul Tillich, though the progeny in academic religious studies are legion. See, for example, his essays in *Theology and Culture* (New York: Oxford University Press, 1964), pp. 3–75.

[12] I suspect that literalism and expressivism would each have its own distinctive way of accommodating what is valid in Lindbeck's pragmatism. For a discussion of how pragmatic factors can be accommodated by realism, without ceasing to be realism, see Hunsinger, "Truth as Self-Involving: Barth and Lindbeck," in *Disruptive Grace*, pp. 305–18.

[13] Irenaeus, *Against Heresies* II.13.4 in A. Roberts and J. Donaldson, eds., *The Ante-Nicene Fathers*, vol. 1 (Grand Rapids: Eerdmans, 1987), p. 374 (translation slightly revised).

Auerbach's figural analysis of literary realism, Frei gained both a critical and a constructive vantage point. In *The Eclipse of Biblical Narrative*,[14] he developed an influential criticism of modern biblical hermeneutics; and in *The Identity of Jesus Christ*,[15] he constructed rudiments of a narrative Christology. In his later work he shifted away from making formal claims about how the narrative genre logically depicted Jesus' unsubstitutable identity as the Savior to more sociological or historical claims about how the church, on the whole, has read the Gospel narratives in this way.[16]

At least three issues of importance for the future of postliberal theology arose from Frei's hermeneutical work: first, the relationship between intratextuality and extratextuality; second, the postcritical interpretation of biblical narratives; and finally, how to understand the overall unity of the biblical witness. For Frei, intratextuality was related to extratextuality as meaning was related to truth, and everything depended, he insisted, on keeping the two logically distinct. His ambiguous phrasing, however, sometimes created the impression that "what the narratives are about" (the identity of Jesus Christ) was merely intratextual and nothing more. What Frei meant is surely captured, however, by Francis Watson, who has defined "intratextual realism" as "the irreducibly textual mediation of realities that nonetheless precede and transcend their textual embodiment."[17] The problem of extratextual truth was something that Barth wanted to solve by reconceiving the true referent and then appealing to the actualism of grace alone.[18] The meaning and truth of biblical narratives, he believed, did not depend strongly on historical veracity narrowly conceived. Whether or to what extent postliberalism ought to follow him is a matter that will continue to be vigorously discussed.[19]

What postcritical biblical interpretation might mean is again something that finds its richest range of examples in the towering postliberal figure of

---

[14] Frei, *The Eclipse of Biblical Narrative: A Study in Eighteenth- and Nineteenth-Century Hermeneutics* (New Haven, CT: Yale University Press, 1974).

[15] Frei, *The Identity of Jesus Christ: The Hermeneutical Bases of Dogmatic Theology* (Philadelphia: Fortress, 1975).

[16] See Frei, "The 'Literal Reading' of Biblical Narrative in the Christian Tradition: Does It Stretch or Will It Break?" in *Theology and Narrative: Selected Essays* (New York: Oxford University Press, 1993), pp. 117–52.

[17] Francis Watson, *Text, Church and World* (Grand Rapids: T. & T. Clark, 1994), p. 286. Watson's book is an excellent example of recent postliberal hermeneutics.

[18] On Barth's reconceiving the narrative referent, see Hunsinger, "Beyond Literalism and Expressivism," in *Disruptive Grace*, pp. 212–15. On his appeal to the actualism of grace, see pp. 219–21. See also George Hunsinger, *How to Read Karl Barth: The Shape of His Theology* (New York: Oxford University Press, 1991), p. 289 n. 1.

[19] With respect to Frei and his modifications of Barth, especially regarding the precise status of historical investigation into Christ's resurrection, see my discussion in the "Afterword" to *Theology and Narrative*, pp. 265–68.

Karl Barth. As Rudolf Smend has suggested, Barth is the proper successor of Wellhausen and modern biblical criticism.[20] Barth presupposes the full validity of biblical criticism, in principle, without being hamstrung by it. It frees us, he believed, from naive realism (literalist univocity) without heavily determining (as often supposed by literalists and expressivists alike) the larger questions of meaning and truth. Those questions are still logically inseparable from the direct wording of the biblical texts, he maintained, to which we can never pay thoughtful enough and close enough attention. Although in hindsight some of Barth's exegesis may seem excessive or overly imaginative, it would surely be ungenerous not to acknowledge his enormous contribution in this area,[21] one that, along with von Balthasar's, has scarcely begun to be tapped and assessed.[22]

Frei knew that the category of narrative was insufficient to account for the unity of Scripture, even though, with Barth, he regarded narrative as central to that unity.[23] More recent postliberal proposals have appealed, among other things, to the shape of the canon, to narrationally structured symbolic worlds, or to authorial discourse.[24] This is obviously a very large area, and one that can barely be touched upon here. If one further comment on Barth may be permitted, however, it would be this. He did not think that the unity of Scripture depended finally on any such proposals as those just mentioned. That his work was done prior to the advent of redactional criticism may not be so great a liability as some would suggest. He knew enough about the diversity of Scripture to realize that no large-scale efforts at conceptual harmonization were likely to succeed. Instead he proposed a postliberal strategy of juxtaposition, at once ordered and yet also flexible, centered on the particularity not of a system but a name.[25] That the one living Jesus Christ is himself the unity of Scripture, requiring dialectical explication without the aid of a single unifying scheme (or set of schemes), is an option whose promise postliberalism has yet to explore.

[20] Rudolf Smend, "Nachkritische Schriftauslegung" in *Parrhesia: Karl Barth zum achtzigsten Geburtstag* (Zurich: EVZ-Verlag, 1966), pp. 215–37.
[21] For an initial appreciation, see for example James A. Wharton, "Karl Barth as Exegete and His Influence on Biblical Interpretation," *Union Seminary Quarterly Review* 28 (1972), 5–13.
[22] For a discussion of postcritical exegesis in von Balthasar, see Brian McNeil, "The Exegete as Iconographer: Balthasar and the Gospels," in John Riches, ed., *The Analogy of Beauty* (Edinburgh: T. & T. Clark, 1986), pp. 134–46.
[23] Frei, "Remarks in Connection with a Theological Proposal," in *Theology and Narrative*, pp. 31–32.
[24] For a useful survey see Lindbeck, "Postcritical Canonical Interpretation: Three Modes of Retrieval," in Christopher Seitz and Kathryn Greene-McCreight, eds., *Theological Exegesis: Essays in Honor of Brevard S. Childs* (Grand Rapids: Eerdmans, 1999), pp. 26–51.
[25] For a brief account of the juxtapositional strategy, see my essay "Karl Barth's Christology: Its Basic Chalcedonian Character," in *Disruptive Grace*, pp. 131–47.

POSTLIBERALISM: DOCTRINE AS DETERMINED BY THE PRIMACY OF GOD

Lindbeck's "rule theory" of doctrine has not had many takers, nor is it likely to do so. Lindbeck acknowledges the oddity of his proposal: "It may seem odd to suggest that the Nicaenum in its role as a communal doctrine does not make first-order truth claims, and yet this is what I shall contend."[26] One reason for the demurral is that not even Wittgenstein dichotomized first-order and second-order discourse as Lindbeck does. Frei is much closer to Wittgenstein when he assumes that a proposition's "second-level" doctrinal usage can be both regulative and assertive at the same time (more or less the usual ecumenical position). Another reason is that Lindbeck seems to have misread Lonergan on the Nicene Creed. As Stephen Williams has shown, Lonergan, on whose account Lindbeck leans heavily, does not see the Nicaenum as merely regulative.[27] Finally, as a means of accounting for continuing ecumenical disagreement (the motive Lindbeck gives for his idea), the rule theory seems like too much of a tour de force. The best hopes for ecumenical rapprochement, it would seem, lie not in one side capitulating to the other (the only option Lindbeck mentions besides his own), nor in minimizing intractable differences, but rather in pushing forward, in mutual repentance, to more complex and multidimensional doctrinal formulations that can critically appropriate what is valid in opposing views (*Aufhebung*).

Lindbeck's rule theory has the merit of calling attention, however, to the peculiar axiomatic status of certain propositions (implicit or explicit) in Christian discourse. These axioms, whether regulative, assertive or both, are often at variance with the reigning plausibility structures of modernity. Theologians who operate within those plausibility structures, like David Tracy or James Gustafson, have resorted to accusing Lindbeck, and with him the whole postliberal enterprise, of something called "fideism." Evangelical conservatives, for their part, have voiced similar anxieties about "relativism." Although these charges are not always backed by careful definition and analysis, they do signal a certain widespread uneasiness with postliberal epistemologies. What might be said in reply?

This is again a very large topic that can be dealt with only in very broad strokes. The philosophical discussion of nonfoundationalism after Wittgenstein has sometimes moved in directions favorable to postliberalism.[28] The

---

[26] Lindbeck, *The Nature of Doctrine*, p. 19.
[27] Stephen Williams, "Lindbeck's Regulative Christology," *Modern Theology* 4 (1988), 173–86.
[28] For a good, brief introduction to "nonfoundationalism," written with theological interests in mind, see William C. Placher, *Unapologetic Theology: A Christian Voice in a Pluralistic Conversation* (Louisville, KY: Westminster/John Knox Press, 1989), pp. 24–36. For a more technical discussion, see John Thiel, *Nonfoundationalism* (Minneapolis: Fortress/Augsburg, 1994).

theological epistemologies of Barth and von Balthasar, which at first seemed odd to many, do not seem quite so strange in light of recent philosophical developments. Alasdair MacIntyre, for example, has developed an account of tradition-based rationality. He argues strongly against the possibility of neutrality in assessing the claims of rival large-scale traditions; and he explains how, by means of empathy, imagination, and insight, their adherents can nonetheless understand, disagree with, and learn from one another. The rational possibility of a paradigm shift, of switching from one large-scale commitment to another, is sensitively discussed. It is, however, the illusion of a view from nowhere – of "a tradition-independent rational universality" – that is apparently behind such (foundationalist) epistemological anxieties as "fideism" and "relativism."[29] The illusion of a neutral standpoint must be left behind, because when it comes to the large-scale traditions that govern existential commitments, there is no circumventing (for anyone) the risks of faith.

Between postliberal theology and contemporary epistemology, the parallels, which are just beginning to be explored, can be suggestive. Von Balthasar's religious epistemology converges, for example, with Hilary Putnam's "internal realism." According to Victoria S. Harrison, five key similarities stand out.[30] (1) All knowledge begins in a set of antecedent beliefs about the world; no knowledge can exist without some prior belief. (2) Because objectivity is always relative to a conceptual scheme, objectivity is not the same as neutrality. "The objects really exist, but ... one requires a conceptual scheme appropriate to identifying the object in question."[31] (3) Because method depends strongly on the object of knowledge, no one method is valid for all forms of inquiry. (4) Rationality is analogical, not identical, across the intellectual disciplines. (5) Some subjective belief-stance is the precondition for obtaining knowledge in any field. In short, like MacIntyre, Putnam contends that there is no neutral conception of rationality to which we can appeal, a belief shared by postliberal theology – over against modern theology in its standard liberal and evangelical forms.

In *Types of Christian Theology*, Hans Frei reflected on the kind of relationship proper to theology and other disciplines. He rejected various modern options in favor of postliberalism. Neither assigning logical priority to secular disciplines nor seeing them in co-equal mutual correlation with Christian theology was adequate. Secular disciplines were to be

---

[29] Alasdair MacIntyre, *Whose Justice? Which Rationality?* (University of Notre Dame Press, 1988), pp. 335, 352–53.

[30] Victoria S. Harrison, "Putnam's Internal Realism and von Balthasar's Epistemology," *International Journal for Philosophy of Religion* 44 (1998), 67–92, esp. 82.

[31] Ibid., p. 85.

subordinated to "Christian self-description" (as Frei called it), and used only on an ad hoc basis, for purposes of description rather than large-scale explanation. Although the reasons Frei gave for subordination were largely pragmatist in orientation (Christian theology is a practical discipline of communal self-description), more substantive, if underdeveloped, reasons seem also to have been in force. In carrying out the theological enterprise, Frei urged that Christian categories take logical priority over other disciplines.[32] This advice was apparently the direct methodological outcome of what he had discovered in his dissertation about "God's priority" as a major theme in Barth's break with liberalism. "Theology arises," he noted, "because the Church is accountable to God for its discourse about God."[33]

Two applications of Frei's methodological advice are instructive. The interdisciplinary proposal developed by Deborah van Deusen Hunsinger is perhaps the most explicit account to date of the postliberal grammar embedded in Frei's typology. Theology and psychology, she proposes, are not properly related by granting priority to psychology, or by co-equal mutual correlation, or by "integration." "Integration" is not a theoretical desideratum, but a skill to be developed by the ecclesial practitioner (in the context of pastoral counseling). The grammar governing the relevant interdisciplinary relations is provided by the Chalcedonian pattern. Theology and psychology are related in practice by a pattern of inseparable unity ("without separation or division"), irreducible distinction ("without confusion or change"),[34] and asymmetrical ordering (the logical precedence of theology over psychology). It is especially van Deusen Hunsinger's asymmetrical ordering principle that gives postliberal methodological expression to the priority of God.[35]

Theology and philosophy are two disciplines related by much the same postliberal grammar (though more implicitly) in Bruce Marshall's recent work, yet with much greater emphasis, as is perhaps appropriate to the case, not only on theology's priority, but also on its assimilative power. By contrast to the familiar methodological practices of modernity, which have correlated, subordinated, assimilated, or curtailed Christian theological content to some grand secular philosophy (for example, Kant, Hegel, Marx, Heidegger, Bloch, Whitehead, Ricoeur, Jung, Hayek, Fukuyama, Irigaray,

---

[32] Frei, *Types of Christian Theology*, esp. pp. 38–46, 78–83. [33] Ibid., p. 39.

[34] Note that by allowing each discipline its own genuine relative autonomy ("without confusion or change"), and by focussing mostly on ad hoc modes of relation, postliberalism blocks the methodological imperialism associated with a movement like radical orthodoxy.

[35] Deborah van Deusen Hunsinger, *Theology and Pastoral Counseling: A New Interdisciplinary Approach* (Grand Rapids: Eerdmans, 1995).

Derrida – the list is endless),³⁶ Marshall offers something refreshingly different. He not only tackles some of the toughest minds in contemporary philosophy (Frege, Tarski, Davidson), but shows an unerring postliberal touch. Arguing on Trinitarian grounds that the Christian way of identifying God ought to have unrestricted primacy when it comes to the justification of belief, he proposes a Trinitarian way of reshaping the concept of truth. Whatever the disputes about the details, Marshall admirably demonstrates what Frei meant by making ad hoc, descriptive use a secular discipline without losing proper theological control.³⁷

POSTLIBERALISM: RELIGION AS DETERMINED BY CHRISTOCENTRISM

The hallmark of a properly postliberal approach to religion is that it speaks on the basis of explicit religious commitment. In line with its nonfoundationalist leanings in epistemology, it sees modern attempts to speak on the basis of neutrality as illusory; because neutrality is finally a nonneutral commitment, and what is worse, one that typically leads to distortions in its interpretations of religion. Although postliberalism does not eschew the search for adequate descriptive categories that will illumine what "religion" is, it will favor descriptions that are formal enough to include all the relevant phenomena, yet open-textured enough to allow for religious disagreement and irreducible difference. It will acknowledge that actual religious commitment has too often been a source of arrogance, bigotry and violence while yet seeking for resources within the tradition from which it speaks for combating such deplorable evils.

For postliberalism, no one strategy is mandatory for negotiating between formal description and explicit commitment. The only requirement would be somehow to do justice to both (and evaluation would pertain to how well both requirements are met). At the descriptive end of the spectrum, Paul J. Griffiths has proposed that religions are distinguished by three main properties: comprehensiveness, unsurpassability, and centrality. A religion will offer a "comprehensive" account of the world, one that somehow provides a framework for interpreting all aspects of experience. It will be "unsurpassable" in the sense that, for its actual adherents, no other account

---

³⁶ Insofar as radical orthodoxy merely reverses this relation, it remains trapped within the bounds of modernity.

³⁷ Bruce D. Marshall, *Trinity and Truth* (Cambridge University Press, 2000). Note that, although Marshall contends that a sentence's meaning depends on its truth (pp. 90–96), he also states that "whether a sentence is true depends, in part, on what it means" (pp. 97–98). In the relevant sense, his views comport with "postliberal theology" as defined at the outset of this chapter.

can replace or subsume it. And it will be "central," because it will be vitally related to the deepest questions of human existence (ultimate loyalty, lifestyle, morality, death, etc.).[38] What is of interest here is not the relative adequacy of this account, but rather the kind of account that it is. It is the kind which makes clear that religions are inherently exclusive in the sense that one can not adhere to more than one at the same time.[39] Griffiths – perhaps the most outstanding Christian representative of a postliberal approach to religious pluralism – goes on to correlate his formal proposal with a keen appreciation for von Balthasar's way of relating Christology to religious plurality.[40]

Griffiths owes an obvious debt to Lindbeck's influential "cultural–linguistic" theory of religion. Like Griffiths, Lindbeck also moves mostly from formal, phenomenal analysis to considerations of explicit religious (Christian) commitment. Religion, he argues, is not primarily a matter of assent to religious truths; nor is it primarily a matter of particular symbolic forms (whether linguistic or not) that somehow codify and transmit deep, prelinguistic "religious" experiences. Rather, as Clifford Geertz has pointed out, religion is more like a cultural system that one linguistically inhabits, and within which one is shaped into a form of life, so that becoming religious is something like learning a language.[41]

Lindbeck's theory of religion has been effective in its argument against expressivist interpretations of religious truth. Although language and experience may well be related dialectically, many have found it to be plausible, as Lindbeck argues, that from a cultural–linguistic point of view, experience is more nearly shaped by language than the reverse.[42] Griffiths offers a valuable corrective to Lindbeck however by allowing a stronger place for cognitive–propositional elements:

> But the uncomfortable fact remains that religious world-views do have
> explicit truth-claims associated with them; that these truth-claims are
> in many cases simply incompatible with one another; and that the
> incompatibility of truth-claims, coupled with significant differences in
> stated religious goals, leaves us absolutely no good reason to believe
> either that all religions are aimed at the same goal or that all conflicts
> between religious truth-claims are merely apparent.[43]

---

[38] Paul J. Griffiths, "The Properly Christian Response to Religious Plurality," *Anglican Theological Review* 79 (1997), 3–26.

[39] The problem of syncretism would complicate though not invalidate this account.

[40] See Griffiths, "One Jesus, Many Christs?" *Pro Ecclesia* 7 (1998), 152–71, esp. 165–68.

[41] Lindbeck, *The Nature of Doctrine*, pp. 31–42.   [42] Ibid., pp. 36–37.

[43] Paul Griffiths and Delmas Lewis, "On Grading Religions, Seeking Truth, and Being Nice to People – a Reply to Professor Hick," *Religious Studies* 19 (1983), 75–80, esp. 79.

Although Lindbeck need not disagree with any of this, his aversion to propositionalism leads him to minimize the ways in which religions may actually involve incompatible truth claims.[44]

Within postliberal approaches to religion, an unresolved tension exists between those who proceed from descriptive formality to commitment and those who move more in the opposite direction from explicit commitment to formality. The former, like Lindbeck and Joseph A. DiNoia,[45] strive toward a winsome irenicism that would minimize conflict; the latter, like von Balthasar and Barth, tend more readily toward tough-minded polemic and critique; Griffiths stands somewhere near the midpoint. All, however, would uphold the basic Christian conviction, which they regard as logically non-negotiable, that salvation is through Christ alone; and all attempt to reconcile the *solus Christus* with the salvation of non-Christians.

Griffiths distinguishes the Christian response to religious pluralism into a-priori and a-posteriori aspects. Since Barth represents perhaps the strongest a-priori (as well as polemical) response within postliberalism, his views may be briefly noted to round out the spectrum.[46] Barth was concerned not primarily with religious pluralism, but with "religionism" as a modern Christian heresy. Liberal theology had made experiential–expressive "religion" into the criterion of revelation rather than the reverse, a move that represented a fatal anthropocentrism at the expense of Christology. Following Luther,[47] Barth then went on to depict religion as a form of faithlessness and therefore sin. As a perennial human phenomenon

---

[44] To sum up: Lindbeck is "neoliberal" insofar as he displays what I have called the liberal aversion to propositionalism. This aversion clearly shows up in his theory of truth and his theory of doctrine, and to some degree also in his theory of religion. He is nonetheless "postliberal" in several respects. First, by criticizing both literalism and expressivism, he attempts to move beyond these sterile alternatives. Second, he approaches the idea of analogical reference, holding that Christian theological language, when used properly in practice, does make truth claims and impart true knowledge of God, even though we cannot specify the *modus significandi*. Third, he does not believe that all conflicts between religious truth claims are merely apparent (though he wishes to maximize that possibility). His insight into religion as a cultural–linguistic system, his break with foundationalism, and his emphasis on the incommensurability of different religions – most recently on the irreducible particularity of Israel – are all enormously important contributions. Finally, he enlivens postliberalism's ecumenicity, not least by tilting toward von Balthasar in a way that counterbalances Frei's interest in Barth.

[45] Joseph A. DiNoia, *The Diversity of Religions: A Christian Perspective* (Washington, DC: Catholic University of America Press, 1992).

[46] For an excellent discussion, see Garrett Green, "Challenging the Religious Studies Canon: Karl Barth's Theory of Religion," *The Journal of Religion* 75 (1995), 473–86. Excellent also is Joseph A. DiNoia, "Religion and the Religions," in John Webster, ed., *The Cambridge Companion to Karl Barth* (Cambridge University Press, 2000).

[47] Luther (not Barth or Bonhoeffer) was the first theologian to interpret Paul's polemic against "the law" as a polemic against "religion." See Martin Luther, *Lectures on Galatians 1535*, in *Luther's Works*, vol. 27, ed. Jaroslav Pelikan (St. Louis: Concordia Publishing House, 1964), pp. 87–90.

(not least within the church), religion was always both inevitable and futile. Since it could not deliver what it promised, it resulted in "a sterile cycle of religious affirmation, crisis, and breakdown, followed by the outbreak of new religious movements condemned to repeat the process."[48] Only in the sense that one could speak of a "justified sinner" was it possible to speak of "the true religion." Where someone like Lindbeck offered a formal analysis for how one religion might be exclusively true ("categorial adequacy"), Barth's argument was substantive: "On the question of truth or error among the religions only one thing is decisive... *the name of Jesus Christ.*"[49] A richer elaboration of both formal and substantive considerations, a more fully informed analysis of both a-priori and a-posteriori elements, as represented most promisingly by Griffiths, sets an important agenda for the future of postliberalism's approach to religious pluralism.

Finally, a comment from Lesslie Newbigin will serve to round out the picture of how postliberalism views religion from a standpoint determined by Christocentrism. Newbigin provides a response to the categories of exclusivism, inclusivism and pluralism that dominate much contemporary discussion. Postliberals would not locate themselves within any of these categories.

> It has become customary to classify views on the relation of
> Christianity to the world religions as either pluralist, exclusivist, or
> inclusivist... [My] position is *exclusivist* in the sense that it affirms the
> unique truth of the revelation in Jesus Christ, but it is not exclusivist
> in the sense of denying the possibility of the salvation of the
> non-Christian. It is *inclusivist* in the sense that it refuses to limit the
> saving grace of God to the members of the Christian church, but it
> rejects the inclusivism which regards the non-Christian religions as
> vehicles of salvation. It is *pluralist* in the sense of acknowledging the
> gracious work of God in the lives of all human beings, but it rejects a
> pluralism which denies the uniqueness and decisiveness of what God
> has done in Jesus Christ.[50]

Newbigin here represents what Frei meant by "generous orthodoxy." In a way typical of postliberal theology, he combines a high Christology with an open soteriology. The biblical witness to Jesus Christ as the world's unique

---

[48] Barth as summarized by Green, "Barth's Theory of Religion," 481.
[49] Barth, *Church Dogmatics*, vol. I, part 2 (Edinburgh: T. & T. Clark, 1956), pp. 280–361, on p. 343 (following Green's translation, "Barth's Theory," 482).
[50] Lesslie Newbigin, *The Gospel in a Pluralistic Society* (Grand Rapids: Eerdmans, 1989), pp. 182–83 (italics added).

and indispensable Savior, he believes, still allows (and even requires) certain questions to remain open in hope.

CONCLUSION

Although Frei, Lindbeck, and the "Yale School" gave strong impetus to postliberal theology, postliberal theology involves far more than the Yale School. It includes not only perhaps the two greatest theologians of the twentieth century (Barth and von Balthasar) and at least one great missiologist (Newbigin), but also a number of promising younger theologians whose work is just starting to bear fruit. They can be recognized by a common set of goals, interests and commitments, especially their ecumenical interests and their desire to move beyond modernity's liberal/evangelical impasse. As made newly possible in our culture by the rise of nonfoundationalism, they have begun to rethink old questions like the truth of theological language, interdisciplinary relations, and religious pluralism. They are the tribe Lindbeck hopes will increase.

Further reading
Frei, Hans W., *Types of Christian Theology* (New Haven: Yale University Press, 1992).
Griffiths, Paul J., "The Properly Christian Response to Religious Plurality," *Anglican Theological Review* 79 (1997), 3–26.
Lindbeck, George, *The Nature of Doctrine: Religion and Theology in a Postliberal Age* (Philadelphia: Westminster, 1985).
Marshall, Bruce D., *Trinity and Truth* (Cambridge University Press, 2000).
Van Deusen Hunsinger, Deborah, *Theology and Pastoral Counseling* (Grand Rapids: Eerdmans, 1995).
Watson, Francis, *Text, Church and World* (Edinburgh: T. & T. Clark, 1994).

4 Postmetaphysical theology
THOMAS A. CARLSON

Aiming to be neither "postmodern" nor "premodern" nor indeed "modern," the "postmetaphysical" theology associated with French thinker Jean-Luc Marion (b. 1946) responds to a Christian God and Father who, as absolute love or charity, and according to that charity's "essential anachronism,"[1] would remain beyond all historical or cultural determination even while abandoning himself fully to history in the Christ. From such a perspective, Marion's theology seeks to free the self-revelation of the Christian God from every precondition or determination of human thought and language – and above all from the thought and language of "Being" that have dominated Western metaphysics and its "ontotheological" conception of God as a "supreme being."

In his critique of metaphysics as "ontotheology," Marion is indebted primarily to Martin Heidegger (1889–1976), and in an eventual critique of Heidegger himself, Marion will draw on the post-Heideggerian thought of Emmanuel Levinas (1905–1995), but Marion's core theological vision is shaped most decisively by the "divine-names" theology and "mystical" theology found in the late fifth- or early sixth-century writings of Dionysius the Areopagite (or the "Pseudo-Dionysius"). In the Dionysian appeal to an inconceivable and ineffable "Good beyond Being," Marion locates an extra-metaphysical "God without Being." The "without" in this theology of "God without Being" does not mean to indicate that God is not or does not exist,[2] but rather that any divine existence or nonexistence that human thought might ever imagine falls infinitely short of the divine generosity that stands at the heart of revelation. The highest name for God, Marion insists, is not to be found in the metaphysical predication of Being or essence but rather in the theological praise of goodness or love, for while finite creatures must first be in order to love, God loves "before Being," and through that love alone God's goodness gives all – including the Being of beings itself. If the

---

[1] Jean-Luc Marion, *God without Being*, trans. Thomas A. Carlson (University of Chicago Press, 1991), p. xxii.
[2] Ibid., p. xix.

God of metaphysics is a God who must be or exist in such a way that human thought might comprehend or even prove, according to some rational concept, that and what God is, the God of Marion's Christian faith is a God who generously gives himself not to be proved rationally or comprehended conceptually but rather received in the love of contemplation and prayer, the life of liturgy. On the basis of this faith, Marion articulates his God "without Being" in order "to bring out the absolute freedom of God with regard to all determinations, including, first of all, the basic condition that renders all other conditions possible and even necessary – for us, humans – the fact of Being."[3]

As assumed and perpetuated by the history of metaphysics, Marion argues, the primacy of Being involves a misguided attempt to determine and comprehend God according to the measure of human concepts, and this attempt reaches its summit in the modern Western philosophy of the subject. Hence, Marion's theological project will demand a twofold critique: first, a critique of all metaphysics, where God is persistently reduced to the proportions of some concept (from Plato's form of the good and the Plotinian One to Descartes's *causa sui* and Leibniz' principle of sufficient reason); second, correlatively, a critique of specifically modern metaphysics, where the appearance of God (as of all beings) is conceived only on the prior basis of a subjectivity that would define or measure the Being of beings (from Descartes's *cogito* through Hegel's absolute subjectivity even into Nietzsche's will to power and Heidegger's *Dasein*). Marion's theological critique of "ontotheological" conceptions of God within the history of metaphysics, therefore, will be tied intimately to a critique of ontotheological conceptions of human subjectivity in the modern context.[4]

Marion structures his theological critique of metaphysics according to the poles of the "idol" and the "icon," which, within Marion's quasi-phenomenological treatment, define two distinct modes of visibility for the divine, or two ways of apprehending the divine.[5] In the idol, the divine

---

3 Ibid., p. xx.
4 In his masterful study of Descartes, *On Descartes's Metaphysical Prism*, trans. Jeffrey L. Kosky (University of Chicago Press, 1999), Marion has worked out very fully the interplay between the ontotheology of God (as *causa*) and the ontotheology of the subject (in the *ego cogito*) within the foundations of modern philosophy.
5 Idol and icon are phenomenological categories insofar as they signal nothing other than modes of visibility for the divine, or modes of apprehension of the divine; at the same time, however, "the icon has a theological status, the reference of the visible face to the intention that envisages, culminating in the reference of the Christ to the Father: for the formula *eikōn tou theou aoratou* concerns first the Christ. It would remain to specify in what measure this attribution has a normative value, far from constituting just one application of the icon among others," in *God without Being*, pp. 23–24. On the complex relation between phenomenology and theology in Marion, see my chapter "The Naming of God and the Possibility of Impossibility: Marion and Derrida between the Theology and Phenomenology

comes into visibility only according to the prior conditions and limits of the human subject's intentional consciousness; therefore, within the idolatrous mode, my vision of the divine proves to be an indirect or invisible mirror of my own thinking, thus obfuscating the definitive otherness and incomprehensibility of the divine. In the icon, by contrast (and here Marion's debt to Levinas runs deep), the visibility of the divine would irreducibly precede and therefore exceed the conditions and limits of any intentional consciousness; in the iconic mode of vision, therefore, I do not constitute the divine in its visibility, but rather, through a radical reversal of intentionality, I am first envisaged and thereby constituted by a divinity whose otherness exceeds my intention and comprehension.

Marion's critique of metaphysics as an "ontotheology" will be based on his assertion that the "God" of ontotheology amounts to a "conceptual" idol in which some well-defined and therefore limited concept of "God," some predication of God's essence made present to the mind, is taken to be equivalent with God himself; such a concept and predication, which really constitute only an invisible mirror of purely human thought, blocks the fundamental sense in which the God of faith would exceed the limits of any definition, predication, essence, or presence. Growing equally out of ontotheological thinking, both "atheism" and the so-called "proofs" for God's existence would simply mark two sides of the same error; in both cases, the "success" of one's position (whether it be negating or affirming) is immediately a failure, since it would depend on the clarity and precision with which one defines the essence of a God who by definition exceeds all definition or essence. If God is by definition indefinable, or essentially beyond essence, then both the negation of God and the affirmation of God on the basis of any conceptual delimitation of essence would prove bound to failure because bound to an idolatry that mistakes human concepts for God himself.

To understand this metaphysical reduction of God to the limits of a concept, one must understand, with Heidegger, the "ontotheological constitution" of metaphysics, wherein theology (special metaphysics) and ontology (general metaphysics) relate to one another according to an ambiguity in the conception of "ground." In metaphysical thinking, as Heidegger argues in his 1957 essay on "The Onto-theo-logical Constitution of Metaphysics,"[6] Being (*Sein*) is understood to ground every being (*Seiende*) in its Being,

of the Gift," in *Indiscretion: Finitude and the Naming of God* (University of Chicago Press, 1999); and John D. Caputo's essay, "Apostles of the Impossible: On God and the Gift in Derrida and Marion," in Caputo and Scanlon, eds., *God, the Gift, and Postmodernism* (Bloomington: Indiana University Press, 1999).

[6] Martin Heidegger, "The Onto-theo-logical Constitution of Metaphysics," in Joan Stambaugh (trans.), *Identity and Difference* (New York: Harper and Row), 1969.

while at the same time the highest being, God understood as self-causing cause, is understood to account for beings as a whole.[7] When theology and ontology are tied in this manner, Heidegger insists, the fundamental difference between Being and beings (the "ontological difference") is forgotten or covered over. Within such forgetting, the highest questions finally concern only the representation of beings, and the highest among such representations would be that of God as supreme being, the self-causing cause of all other beings: "The Being of beings is represented fundamentally, in the sense of ground, only as *causa sui*. This is the metaphysical concept of God."[8] As Marion will argue, when thus restricted to the concept of cause and thereby made to obey the logic of efficiency, God becomes an idol who meets the measure and serves the needs of human thinking. As later in Leibniz' "principle of sufficient reason," where the *causa sui* would find its full metaphysical status, God here merely serves as "the principle of our comprehension of all beings."[9]

When made in this way to answer the requirements and conditions of conceptual thinking, the metaphysical God ceases to be the God of a living religious practice or of a truly Christian faith. In this direction, Marion accepts and extends Blaise Pascal's famous distinction between the God of the philosophers and the God of Abraham, Isaac, and Jacob – or between the God of understanding and the God of will.[10] Following Pascal (and Augustine), Marion argues – against metaphysics – that the real obstacle within the human relation to God is not weakness of understanding but arrogance of the will;[11] we move toward God not in conceiving him more clearly but in loving him more fully – through the religious and liturgical life that metaphysical concepts do not suffice to sustain or even to provoke. Indeed, as Heidegger indicates, since humanity "can neither pray nor sacrifice" to the God of the philosophers, "the god-less thinking which must abandon the God of philosophy, God as *causa sui*, is . . . perhaps closer to the divine God."[12]

At this point within Marion's theological project, the "death of God" announced by Friedrich Nietzsche (1844–1900) comes to play a productive role. If the godless thinking to which Heidegger appeals might open a path to

---

[7] Heidegger, "Onto-theo-logical Constitution," pp. 70–71.

[8] Heidegger, quoted in Marion, *God without Being*, p. 35.

[9] Marion, *L'Idole et la distance* (Paris: Grasset), 1977, p. 31.

[10] See Pascal's "Memorial," in *Pensées*, trans. A. J. Krailsheimer (New York: Penguin, 1966).

[11] On the historical situation of this issue, see Marion, "The Idea of God," in Daniel Garber and Michael Ayers, eds., *The Cambridge History of Seventeenth-Century Philosophy*, vol. 1 (Cambridge University Press, 1998), esp. p. 292; on its phenomenological implications, see Marion, *Étant donné: Essai d'une phénoménologie de la donation* (Paris: Presses Universitaires de France, 1997), pp. 419–23.

[12] Heidegger, quoted in Marion, *God without Being*, p. 35.

some more divine God, then the "death of God," by destroying all metaphysical concepts of God, might hold real theological promise. A confrontation with the death of God, Marion suggests, can help us to take seriously "that the 'God' of ontotheology is strictly equivalent to an idol, one that presents the Being of beings as the latter are thought metaphysically."[13] And if God can "begin to grab hold of us" only to the degree that "we claim to advance outside of ontotheology,"[14] then Nietzsche's critique of metaphysics, by pointing beyond ontotheology, may open us to the hold of God. From a perspective that takes Nietzsche seriously, then, while nonetheless assuming the absolute primacy of Christian revelation, Marion can interpret the Nietzschean "death of God" as a failure of metaphysical concepts or idols of God and, in the light of such a failure, the apparent absence or withdrawal of God in modern thought can be taken to mark God's very presence or advent. From this perspective, the presence or advent of God should now, as ever, remain the function of an absence that no concept could ever present.

Marion frames this theological coincidence of presence and absence, advent and withdrawal, according to the logic of paternal "distance," which he develops both through a reading of such moderns as Nietzsche (and Hölderlin) and through the reading of biblical thought and the writings of Dionysius. The logic of such distance allows Marion to articulate, in biblical and Christian terms, the sense in which "the withdrawal of the divine would perhaps constitute his ultimate figure of revelation,"[15] and thus the sense in which our ignorance of God even in modern thought and culture could well signal God's most overwhelming presence. Plenitude and poverty would coincide, for Marion, in the self-revelation of a God whom no one sees without dying – or better, in the self-revelation of a God whose love surpasses understanding. Such a love would be exercised primordially through the paternal distance wherein separation alone allows for filial relation. Hence, the love in which poverty and overabundance coincide, the love in which relation implies separation, must be approached in Christological and Trinitarian terms, for "poverty coincides with overabundance, in the divine, because God admits – this is what the Spirit makes us see – the distance of a Son."[16]

This Christological and Trinitarian coincidence of poverty and overabundance, gift and abandon, this paternal distance in which love advances through withdrawal and withdraws through advance, is precisely what metaphysical concepts of God, in their attempt to grasp and make present to the comprehension of thought, simply cannot see. By showing too much (a God made present in the presence of a thinking that comprehends), the concepts produced by metaphysics would show too little, inasmuch as God

---

[13] *L'Idole*, p. 37.   [14] Ibid., p. 37.   [15] Ibid., p. 114.   [16] Ibid., p. 146.

by definition exceeds all definition, or inasmuch as God's fullest presence is given to human thought only as absence. The modern destruction of these concepts, therefore, which can leave an apparent void, in fact opens anew a space for thinking and speaking the incomprehensible and ineffable love of the Father.

However, while Marion relies both on a Nietzschean twilight of the idols and on a Heideggerian critique of ontotheology, that reliance has its crucial limits, since Marion will detect a persistent idolatry in both these thinkers: in the first, through the subjection of all gods to the will to power; and in the second through the subjection of God to the conditions of Being and hence to the being for whom Being is an issue, human existence as *Dasein*.

If a Nietzschean twilight of the idols helps clear away the overly limited concepts of "God" produced by metaphysics, it does so only by understanding those concepts as expressions of the "will to power"; in this sense, while pointing beyond metaphysical idolatry, the twilight of the idols remains itself idolatrous. When Nietzsche announces and celebrates the possible birth of new gods in the wake of the metaphysical God's death, those new gods also express only the will to power and so in fact recapitulate the metaphysical idolatry beyond which Nietzsche may be pointing. "The 'God' who dies," Marion finally argues, "remains still too close, metaphysically, for his death not to be idolatrous, and for the new face that succeeds him not to establish another idol, still metaphysical – that of the will to power."[17] Thus, if Nietzsche falls among the most powerful of those modern thinkers who help us to understand the question of divine manifestation in terms of withdrawal or absence, he does not yet go far enough.

In similar fashion, according to Marion's theological perspective, Heidegger both succeeds and fails in pointing us beyond the idolatry of ontotheology. If the ontotheology of modern thought amounts to idolatry because it would, from Descartes (1596–1650) through Nietzsche, subject the appearance of God to the limits of a thinking or willing subject, the Heideggerian thinking that seeks to pass beyond ontotheology's supreme being still maintains its own idolatry – in the subjection of God's appearance to the conditions of Being and to the priority of *Dasein* as that being for whom Being is an issue. As Marion emphasizes, Heidegger insists already at the time of *Being and Time* (1927), in his lecture "Phenomenology and Theology,"[18] that "the analytic of *Dasein* precedes and determines the conditions of that being that is affected by the Christian event – 'christianness.' In a word, the analytic of *Dasein* indicates, ontologically, a pre-Christian

---

[17] Ibid., p. 102.
[18] "Phenomenology and Theology," in *The Piety of Thinking*, trans. James G. Hart and John C. Maraldo (Bloomington: Indiana University Press, 1976).

content and datum whose 'christianness' marks only an ontic corrective";[19] this means that, within the Heideggerian framework, "the invariant of *Dasein* appears more essential to man than the ontic variant introduced by faith. Man can eventually become a believer only inasmuch as he exists first as *Dasein*." From this perspective, "God could never appear within the field of questioning thought except under the mediating conditions first of 'christianness,' and then of *Dasein*."[20] Since God here can play only an ontic role in modifying the ontologically prior *Dasein*, God is reduced to a "supreme" being who is really not very supreme – since in order to operate at all he must operate within conditions set first by finite Being-in-the-world. A similar logic of subjection would be found in the later Heidegger, where the appearance of God would emerge only within the "worlding of the world" (in the fourfold of earth and sky, mortals and divinities) or within the "truth of Being," whose openness alone permits, first, the "essence of the sacred" and, then, "the essence of divinity" in whose light alone "can it be thought and said what the name 'God' must name."[21] As already in 1927, so in these later contexts, the subjection of God to the worldhood of the world or to the truth of Being marks also a subjection of God to that finite *Dasein* for whom alone world or Being ever open.

Marion's theological critique both of metaphysics and of its Heideggerian overcoming, therefore, will require an attack on the modern subject who not only appears clearly in Descartes's *cogito* and persists in Nietzsche's will to power but remains active also in Heidegger's *Dasein*. By contrast to the autarchic subject who dominates modern philosophy even into Heidegger, Marion's theological subject, born in relation to the iconic revelation of the Father, is modeled on the passivity of Christic subjectivity itself.

This theological subject, whose structure and temporality will be echoed in Marion's later phenomenological model of subjectivity,[22] comes to birth in – or indeed as – a response to the goodness, charity, or love given primordially in the distance of the Father, who reveals himself not according to the conditions of what any subject might need or be able to conceive but rather on his own terms: as himself, of himself, and starting from himself alone – unconditionally and inconceivably. If the subject is not to be idolatrous, it must be constituted fundamentally in relation to the call of God's

[19] *L'Idole*, p. 267. [20] Ibid., p. 267.
[21] Heidegger, quoted in Ibid., p. 268; see also Marion, *God without Being*, pp. 70–72.
[22] For a brief introduction to this phenomenological model, developed within a discussion of Heidegger's *Dasein*, see Marion's "L'Interlogué," in Eduardo Cadava, Peter Connor, and Jean-Luc Nancy, eds., *Who Comes After the Subject?* (New York: Routledge, 1991). For a more thorough development, see *Reduction and Givenness* (pp. 192–202) and, especially, *Etant donné* (all of Book V, "L'Adonné").

unconditional and inconceivable love, which is revealed, without Being, beyond all foresight or calculation, according to the horizon of "the gift" that is given within, or as, paternal distance.

This gift of revelation in distance, which embodies a love beyond Being, is signaled already, Marion argues, in the fact of language itself, for "the very essence of language, comprehending and anticipating us by its overflow, comes to us, in distance, as a fact – that is to say, a given, a gift. As an animal endowed with languages, man, in those languages, perceives distance."[23] Coming to birth in response to a gift that I am not originally present to intend (language as always already given), I live that response in and through my reception and repetition of the gift itself – by answering to it and through it; called (in the vocative or the accusative) even before I am (as conscious and self-conscious, in the nominative), I am always already responding, late, to the gift that gives me to myself. Ever in delay with respect to this originary gift of language, I can never master or contain that gift in and through my use of it.

This means, for Marion, that my linguistic response to the incomprehensible distance signaled by the gift of language can never capture the essence of that distance or master that gift by means of predication or its claims to knowledge. "The unthinkable," Marion argues, "speaks even before we think we hear it; the anteriority of distance holds out to us a language that both precedes and inverts our predication."[24] Ever late in responding to the gift of language that first gives me to myself, I will never comprehend the essence of that gift or, therefore, bring it fully to presence in predication. This precedence of language over the comprehension and predication of essence comes to expression most notably for Marion in what he identifies as "the gift of the Name": "more essential than the predication that we can (not) employ concerning the unthinkable, there occurs the giving of the Name."[25] One can understand this gift of the Name both in relation to human subjectivity generally and, more specifically, in relation to the Name of God and the Christological reception of that Name.

At the level of human subjectivity generally, the logic of the name signals the logic of language as gift in the following manner:

> The name that I bear (that by which I call myself, name myself and identify myself) simply reproduces after the fact the name which others first called me (that to which I answer, by which I am known and mistaken, and which has been imposed on me). Therefore, the experience of the proper name – received or given – never ends up

[23] *L'Idole*, p. 242. [24] Ibid., p. 198. [25] Ibid., p. 198.

fixing the essence of the individual in presence, but always marks that, in principle, the individual does not coincide with its essence, or its presence exceeds its essence.[26]

The name as gift does not capture a definite essence through predication but rather signals a presence that would exceed any predicative definition of essence; indeed, the "proper" name applies to the subject only "improperly" and thereby signals, at bottom, the fundamental anonymity of the subject's presence. If this is the case for the human subject, Marion reasons, it would be all the more so for God: "thus, supposing that praise attributes a name to a possible God, one should conclude that it does not name him properly or essentially, nor that it names him in presence, but that it marks his absence, anonymity, and withdrawal – exactly as every name dissimulates every individual, whom it merely indicates without ever manifesting."[27]

If Marion can interpret the name as that which indicates without manifesting, or as that which refers without predicating, if he can thus interpret the name as a mark of absence, anonymity, and withdrawal, the ground or inspiration for this interpretation is biblical and Christological, for "the gift of the Name" refers first to the unnameable Name of Exodus 3:14, which would itself be given ultimately in the Christic revelation where, as according to Dionysius, the transcendent God is "hidden even amidst the revelation."[28] Interpreting the gift of the Name in and through the incarnate Word, Marion argues that this unnameable Name, the revelation of the hidden as hidden, "comes to us as the unthinkable within the thinkable, because the unthinkable *in person* delivers it to us."[29] The personal presence of the unthinkable – the Word incarnate, the Christ as icon of the invisible Father – thus becomes the ground for understanding all human subjectivity.

Indeed, out of a fundamental passivity, the human subject receives language – and above all the Name – as a gift; emerging only in response to that gift, the subject lives in a "Christic mode" of humanity characterized by a linguistic "dispossession of meaning."[30] In other words, the subject who receives language as immemorial gift can never – through the predicative discourse of conceiving and Being – master the sheer givenness of language itself. Beyond Being and its knowledge, and hence beyond their language, would stand the generosity of divine Goodness and the praise of such Goodness – which requires an essentially non-predicative, or "hymnic" discourse

---

[26] Marion, "In the Name," trans. Jeffrey L. Kosky, in Caputo and Scanlon, eds., *God, the Gift, and Postmodernism*, p. 29.

[27] Ibid., p. 29.

[28] Pseudo-Dionysius, Third Letter, in *Pseudo-Dionysius: The Complete Works*, trans. Colm Luibheid (New York: Paulist Press, 1987).

[29] *L'Idole*, p. 187.   [30] Ibid., pp. 188, 189.

that Marion will locate in the praise of prayer. While such discourse would have its Christian center in the *Credo* and in the *Pater Noster,* it could not, in principle, be contained within the determinate content of any one prayer; only an immeasurably multiform discourse of prayerful praise could answer rightly to the bottomless anonymity of the inconceivable "Good beyond Being" whose generosity is signaled in the gift of the unnameable Name.

In sum, the theological discourse of praise that would remain fundamentally non-predicative follows the Christic logic of life, death, and resurrection. Just as the Word receives his Name from the Father in distance and submits his will to the Father's will even unto death, so does the theological subject receive its language in such a way that any possession of meaning through predication would be lost, and predicative discourse would "die" through negation and silence. But, just as Christic death gives way to resurrection, so does the bottomless silence of the theological subject give way to infinite proclamations of praise.

The most important source for Marion's theological understanding of language here is the divine-names theology and the mystical theology of Dionysius (or, in French, "Denys"), who, according to both Hans Urs von Balthasar and Maximus Confessor, "tends to substitute for the *saying* of predicative language another verb, *humnein,* to praise."[31] The move from a predicative to a hymnic form of language is at bottom, for Marion, a move in the direction of prayer, which, as Aristotle suggests, would be "a *logos* but neither true nor false"[32] – that is, a form of language that surpasses the categorical and metaphysical alternative between affirmation and negation, a language that signals the "third way" of a "de-nomination" that, by naming and un-naming at once, points beyond both naming and un-naming. An understanding of this "third way" is essential to an understanding of Marion's approach to the whole question of "negative theology."

Contrary to many misreadings, both of Marion and of Dionysius, Marion rightly argues that Dionysius' mystical theology exceeds the alternative between affirmative (or "kataphatic") and negative (or "apophatic") theologies – both of which, if based in categorical statements on the essence of God, would amount to idolatry. Linguistic negation captures God no more adequately than linguistic affirmation, and hence, Marion insists, the real contribution of the negative moment in Dionysian theology would be to offer "a beyond of the two truth-values of categorical predication."[33] Associated most appropriately with the "mystical," such a beyond would signal a third mode of theological language articulated through Dionysius' use of "hyper-" terms (God is "beyond Being" or "hyper-essential" as *hyperousios,*

---

[31] Ibid., p. 232.   [32] Aristotle, quoted in ibid., p. 232.   [33] Ibid., p. 192.

"beyond Good" or "super-Good" as *hyperagathos*, etc.); these "hyper-" terms, Marion argues, aim to indicate the manner in which God, as cause of all, is both immanent to all and transcendent over all – and hence the manner in which God can receive the name of every being even as he stands beyond any name or being. Beyond both every affirmation and every negation and hence neither darkness nor light, neither error nor truth, the Dionysian God would exceed the metaphysical choice between presence and absence and thereby disrupt any straightforward "metaphysics of presence."

As a language that points beyond the metaphysical alternative between affirmation and negation, the language of the Dionysian "hyper-" terms would be for Marion the only language appropriate to the core Christological truth that God, beyond presence and absence, advances in his withdrawal and withdraws in his advance. If the discourse of praise responds to this Christological truth, it does so in the measure that it states nothing positively or negatively about the nature or essence of God, but rather directs itself endlessly toward God in a linguistic movement of love or desire. The endless profusion of divine names would enact the desire of the theological subject in face of God's inexhaustible anonymity. Before such anonymity, the subject can praise God only under the "index of inadequation" that preserves the insurmountable gap between our language and the God to whom it would refer.[34] Acknowledging this gap by praising God only "as" Trinity, "as" Goodness, etc., without claiming thereby to capture God's essence in any way, the movement from predication to praise would signal a shift from the theoretical to the pragmatic, or from the metaphysical to the liturgical.

The force of this pragmatic, liturgical use of language emerges clearly for Marion in Baptism, where, "far from attributing to God a name that is intelligible to us, we enter into his unpronounceable Name, with the additional result that we receive our own. The Name above all names therefore de-nominates God perfectly, by excepting him from predication, so as to include us in it and allow us to name it on the basis of its essential anonymity."[35] Called in Baptism by a name that is given to us before we comprehend it, we receive that call through the response in which we would name in return, endlessly, the unnameable Name that we praise liturgically.

The Christological truth of language, then, is enacted liturgically in such a way that we receive the gift of our name, or of language more broadly, only in the responsive repetition of that gift, wherein we would name and rename infinitely the Name beyond all names. This Christological truth is, for Marion, the truth of the icon itself, and hence of iconic subjectivity, where the thinking and speaking I is overwhelmed by an inconceivable

---

[34] See ibid., p. 233.   [35] "In the Name," p. 38.

generosity that precedes and awakens that very thinking and speaking. Both the revelation of the icon and the subjectivity to which that revelation gives birth would, in Marion's thinking, exceed the idolatry of metaphysics in its ontotheological constitution, for the subject created in the image of an incomprehensible God is itself incomprehensible and uncomprehending. The "de-nomination" of Dionysius, then, would lead not to a metaphysics of presence, whether in the ontotheology of God or in the ontotheology of a self-grounding and self-transparent subject, but rather to "a *theology of absence* – where the name is given as having no name, as not giving the essence, and having nothing but this absence to make manifest...But if essence and presence, and therefore a fortiori ground and the concept of Being, are missing from this name, one can no longer speak of onto-theology or metaphysics or a 'Greek' horizon."[36]

The degree to which Marion succeeds in articulating a "postmetaphysical" or "extrametaphysical" theology depends directly on the degree to which the Dionysian model of language that he develops does actually yield such a theology of absence, or more specifically the degree to which "the name" in such theology is or can be given "as having no name, as not giving essence, as having nothing but this absence to make manifest." On this question, the most notable challenge to Marion has been raised by Jacques Derrida (to whom Marion is actually responding in his essay "In the Name"). The disagreements between Marion and Derrida here are complex, and they surely cannot be resolved in the present space, but their outlines and implications can briefly be sketched.[37]

With regard to Dionysian theology and Marion's use of it, Derrida remains suspicious about the degree or manner in which the Dionysian God proves in fact "beyond" Being and, correlatively, about the degree or manner in which the theological discourse of "praise" in Dionysian contexts can in fact remain "non-predicative." Both of these suspicions will bear, in turn, on the central question of the "gift" in theological contexts.

Derrida's central suspicion regarding the negative or "apophatic" language of Dionysian theology is that such language, through the use of the very "hyper-" terms that Marion emphasizes, remains *within* the thought of Being or essence, for such language intends, precisely, to indicate truly, without idolatry, the manner in which God actually *is* – even if somehow

---

[36] Ibid., p. 37.

[37] The debate between Marion and Derrida over the interpretation of Dionysian theology is summarized in chapter 6 of my *Indiscretion: Finitude and the Naming of God*; Marion and Derrida subsequently conducted a public debate over these issues, in English, at Villanova University (September, 1997), and the transcript of that debate – as well as commentary and analysis by John Caputo – are now available in Caputo and Scanlon, eds., *God, the Gift, and Postmodernism*.

beyond or above Being as we might conceive it. Distinguishing his own thought of *différance* from any "negative theology" such as that of Dionysius, Derrida indicates that the two would differ "in the measure to which 'negative theology' seems to reserve, beyond all positive predication, beyond all negation, even beyond Being, some hyperessentiality, a being beyond Being."[38] Derrida here argues that the "hyper-" terms of Dionysius, which seek to pass beyond affirmation and negation alike, do so not to indicate a liberation of God from Being but rather to indicate the excellence of God's Being, the incomparable mode in which God *is*. If Dionysian language can seem to yield a theology of absence, that absence is in fact a function of the superabundant presence of the God whose Being exceeds that of all finite beings. Following the classic Neoplatonic distinction, Dionysian negation with regard to the divine is a negation not according to lack or absence, but according to an excess of presence. Negation aims to save God's presence, not to deny it, or to place it in undecidability – and in this sense the negative movement in Dionysian language remains "economic": it gives up finite language about God only in order to save God's infinite presence.[39]

At this level, Derrida suspects that Dionysian theology, attempting to speak the name of God as beyond all names, or attempting to think the God beyond all thought, would in fact remain faithful to an "ontotheological" economy that seeks to speak and think truly of God and his Being, an economy that aims to avoid speaking and thinking in such a way as to hide God's unconditional truth behind the limited and thus false "idols" of our human language and concepts:

> It is a matter of holding the promise of saying the truth at any price, of testifying, of rendering oneself to the truth of the name, to the thing itself such as it must be named by the name, *that is, beyond the name*. The thing, save the name ... In that way it also belongs, without fulfilling, to the space of the philosophical or onto-theological promise that it seems to break ... to say God such as he is, beyond his images, beyond this idol that being can still be, beyond what is said, seen, or known of him; to respond to the true name of God, to the name to which God responds and corresponds beyond the name that we know him by or hear. It is to this end that the negative procedure refuses, denies, rejects all the inadequate attributions. It does so in the name of a truth.[40]

[38] Jacques Derrida, "How to Avoid Speaking," in Harold Coward and Toby Foshay, eds., *Derrida and Negative Theology* (Albany: State University of New York Press, 1992), p. 77.

[39] On this, see Caputo's analysis in "Apostles of the Impossible," pp. 195–97.

[40] Derrida, "Sauf le Nom," in Thomas Dutoit, ed., *On the Name* (Stanford University Press, 1995), p. 69.

If Dionysian theology constitutes a language that uses affirmation and negation in order to pass, by means of hypernegation, beyond affirmation and
negation, if it would thereby refer infinitely to the divine while insisting on
the irreducible inadequation between all human language and the divine,
it would do so only to indicate the superabundant presence of God's superessential Being – and despite the various levels of negation, that presence
itself is never in doubt. Indeed, the assumption of presence is the very starting point for such theology, at least to the degree that it will not, on the
basis of the endlessly referential movement of its language, entertain the
possibility that "one *can just as well* conclude that the referent – everything
save the name – is or is not indispensable"; while Derrida would bet that
"all history of negative theology … plays itself out in this brief and slight
axiom,"[41] he suspects that Dionysius and Marion alike presuppose a referent that – however absent it may seem – nevertheless remains a necessary
and overfull presence. God, then, is not beyond Being, but rather God *is*
in the most excessive, inconceivable, and ineffable mode. Dionysian language would endlessly signal its own inadequacy only in order to indicate
this truth of God's Being beyond all Being, and in this measure the God of
apophatic theology does not simply stand free of the truth sought, within
ontotheology, under the name of Being.

At the same time, as with so many other topics, on the topic of negative
theology Derrida is always speaking in several voices at once. Hence, while
raising the suspicion that Dionysian theology remains ontotheological in
the sense just indicated, Derrida will also emphasize the ways in which
apophatic theologies can unsettle the ontotheological tradition to which
they may seem to belong. If, on the one hand, faithful to an ontotheological
economy that aims to speak the truth of God, apophatic theologies also, on
the other hand, in their most unsettling negativity, can represent a threat
or a danger for any tradition: "Placing the thesis in parenthesis or in quotation marks ruins each ontological or theological proposition, in truth each
philosopheme as such. In this sense, the principle of negative theology, in a
movement of internal rebellion, radically contests the tradition from which
it seems to come."[42] Derrida here signals an important ambiguity within any
tradition of apophatic or negative theology. At once dependent on and destructive of the self-identity of its tradition, the apophatic movement would
mark "one of the most remarkable manifestations" of the "self-difference" of
all traditions.[43] Since the negative, apophatic movement in theology needs
the determinate content of the affirmative, kataphatic language it would
aim to unsettle or destroy, the tradition whose definition depends on such

[41] Ibid., p. 60.   [42] Ibid., p. 67.   [43] Ibid., p. 71.

kataphatic language would need both to include the apophatic (in order to avoid idolatry) and to keep the apophatic in check (in order to maintain the tradition's self-identity). Like a parasite, the apophatic would live in or upon a tradition that could neither fully include nor fully exclude it.

The question of tradition here, tied closely to the question of "hyper-essentiality" and its economy, also relates directly to the question of "non-predicative" discourse. As seen above, through the analysis of prayer (*euchē*) and praise (*humnein*) in Dionysius, Marion develops a theory of non-predicative discourse as the sole discourse that might suit the God who, because beyond Being, would elude all predication. To the degree that God's essence cannot be defined, theological language cannot predicate anything of God but only praise God in his incomprehensibility and ineffability. For this reason and in this sense, Marion argues, the function of theological language would not be theoretical, philosophical, or metaphysical, but rather pragmatic, *theo*-logical and liturgical. Liturgical language would not comprehend God within fixed metaphysical concepts but rather praise God through the ongoing performance of prayer.

Resisting what he takes to be an overly quick passage from praise to prayer here, Derrida wonders whether the former does not, in fact, necessarily, remain a predicative form of discourse. If one might imagine prayer to constitute some form of pure address or appeal, a form of pure call to the other in which neither the identity of that other nor the content of the call would need to be determined, could one say the same about praise? Derrida suspects that praise in fact does preserve "the style and the structure of a predicative discourse. It says something about someone."[44] If prayer might perform an appeal to some other who can or even must remain beyond determination, praise can seem, through its content, to determine its addressee – if only to distinguish that addressee from other possible addressees, other possible recipients of praise. In Dionysius and Marion alike, Derrida suggests, such a determination would function to distinguish Christian theology from all other possible discourses surrounding the unknowable and ineffable: "How can one deny that the encomium qualifies God and *determines* prayer, *determines* the other, Him to whom it addresses itself, refers, invoking Him even as the source of prayer? How can one deny that, in this movement of determination (which is no longer the pure address of the prayer to the other), the nomination of the *trinitary* and superessential God distinguishes Dionysius' *Christian* prayer from all other prayer?"[45] If prayer might be taken to address itself *to* an indeterminate other, precisely in its otherness and indetermination, praise would not simply address itself

44 "How to Avoid Speaking," p. 137.   45 Ibid., p. 111.

to an other but rather speak *of* that other, in distinction from other possible others; hence, however inadequate the language that praises God *as* Trinity and superessential goodness, that language nonetheless remains invested in a determinacy and determination that are not empty; it concerns the economy within which an incomprehensible God might nonetheless be recognized and kept as, among other things, Christian. The theoretical question regarding predicative and non-predicative forms of language thus pertains here also to very practical issues like the foundation and maintenance of an identifiably Christian community and tradition, and these issues, in turn, would have serious implications in ecclesiastical and political directions.[46]

Furthermore, and finally, such determination would be significant not only to the foundation and maintenance of an identifiable community and tradition – and hence to the ecclesiastical and political implications of Marion's theology – but also to the core theological question of the "gift." In analyses of the gift that have been very widely discussed, Derrida hypothesizes that "the gift" stands as a paradoxical figure of "the impossible." That is, if the basic scheme of the gift is that wherein someone gives something to someone, and if the gift must by definition be given "without return," then to meet any condition of the gift would in fact be to annul it as gift, for the recognition or identification of giver, recipient, or gift itself would inscribe the gift within some economic circle (the giver's sense of investment or self-satisfaction, the recipient's sense of gratitude or debt, the forms of calculation that can enter from either side, etc.). To remain without return, the gift would need somehow to stand beyond any horizon of economic calculation or expectation, and hence outside of any memory and irreducible to any present presence; somewhere between absolute surprise and radical forgetting, it would have to appear without appearing "as such" – which for Derrida suggests a phenomenological "impossibility" that is the very condition of the gift.

Contrary to common misreadings, Derrida does not claim that the gift is simply or straightforwardly impossible, or that "there is no gift," but rather that "if there is a gift" (and Derrida consistently approaches the gift in the hypothetical), the gift would mark a figure of *the* impossible – which implies a distinction between "that about which one simply cannot speak" and, by contrast, "that about which one can no longer speak, but which one

---

[46] On concern over the ecclesiastical and political implications of Marion's theology, see, for example, John Caputo, *The Prayers and Tears of Jacques Derrida* (Bloomington: Indiana University Press, 1997), p. 47. Derrida likewise wants to remain vigilant to the interplay between the theological and the political. On the question of hierarchy and politics in relation to Dionysius and Marion, see "How to avoid Speaking," p. 134, n. 9.

can no longer silence."[47] *The* impossible here articulates a double bind: it engenders thought, language, and desire surrounding that which thought, language, and desire can never grasp "as such." Indeed, the very *possibility* of thought, language, and desire would require their relation to this figure of the impossible, since their full and actual conversion into "philosophy, science, and the order of presence" would annul them *as possible*. Like the impossible possibility of death in Heidegger, the impossible in Derrida ever *remains* to be thought, spoken, and desired: "Perhaps there is naming, language, thought, desire, or intention only there where there is movement still for thinking, desiring, naming that which gives itself neither to be known, experienced, or lived – in the sense in which presence, existence, determination regulate the economy of knowing, experiencing, and living."[48] *The* impossible in Derrida (the naming of God, death, justice, the coming of the Messiah, etc.) maintains the irreducible openness of futurity; it always remains to come, and hence remains, in its "not yet," always possible.

The core difference, then, between the positions marked by Marion and Derrida, is perhaps this: for Marion, the impossibility of naming God results from the fact that God's presence is always already overwhelmingly given, while, for Derrida, the impossibility of naming God might have more to do with the endless deferral of such presence by the differential trace of language that cannot be inscribed within the circular closure of any economy.

The danger of Dionysian hyperessentialism and the persistence of predication in the forms of praise directed to Marion's Dionysian God would appear, for Derrida, in the economic closure of a gift whose source is after all identified as the Father, and whose recipient is indeed a son indebted to that Father. Of Marion's theology, it seems right to insist, as Derrida does, that the call of the originary gift that first gives birth to a subject is made to "conform to the call of the father, to the call that returns to the father and that, in truth, would speak the truth of the father, even the name of the father, and finally the father inasmuch as he gives the name."[49] In this direction, the identity of the father, the truth of the father, and the return of the call to the father in his truth can indeed seem to inscribe the gift within the closure of some economic circle. It seems less certain, however, that this charge holds, as Derrida believes, in relation to Marion's phenomenology of the call.[50] For if the gift in Marion's theology is undoubtedly and necessarily the gift through which, as sons, we are called by – and answer endlessly to – the unnameable Name of the Father, the gift of the call in

---

[47] Derrida, *Given Time: I. Counterfeit Money*, trans. Peggy Kamuf (University of Chicago Press, 1992), p. 147.
[48] Ibid., p. 29.   [49] Ibid., p. 52.   [50] As I have argued in *Indiscretion*, pp. 207–8.

Marion's phenomenology must, in its very origin and by phenomenological necessity, remain indeterminate, unknown, and anonymous; indeed it must do so to a degree that the theological gift could not without losing its identity as theological and Christian. To precisely this degree, one can wonder whether, when Marion's theology aims to "give pure giving to be thought,"[51] it must not aim finally to transgress its own bounds, according to which the giver of all gifts is confessed, praised, and hence identified as God the Father. If the purest giving is that whose source no thought or language could identify, then perhaps theology itself must yield to a thinking in which, as in Marion's phenomenology, the source of givenness can and must remain without any name or identity whatsoever – be it that of the *causa* (as in metaphysics), that of Being (as in Heidegger), that of the Other (as in Levinas), that of self-affection (as in Michel Henry), or, finally, that of the Father himself.

Further reading

Caputo, John D., "Apostles of the Impossible: On God and the Gift in Derrida and Marion," in Caputo and Michael J. Scanlon, eds., *God, the Gift, and Postmodernism* (Bloomington: Indiana University Press, 1999).

Carlson, Thomas A., *Indiscretion: Finitude and the Naming of God* (University of Chicago Press, 1999).

Derrida, Jacques, *On the Name*, ed. Thomas Dutoit (Stanford University Press, 1995).
"How to Avoid Speaking: Denials," in Harold Coward and Toby Foshay, eds., *Derrida and Negative Theology* (Albany: State University of New York Press, 1992).

Heidegger, Martin, "The Onto-Theo-logical Constitution of Metaphysics," trans. Joan Stambaugh, in *Identity and Difference* (New York: Harper and Row, 1969).
"Phenomenology and Theology," in James G. Hart and John C. Maraldo, eds., *The Piety of Thinking* (Bloomington: Indiana University Press, 1976).

Marion, Jean-Luc, *God without Being*, trans. Thomas A. Carlson (University of Chicago Press, 1991).
"The Saturated Phenomenon," trans. Thomas A. Carlson, *Philosophy Today* (Spring 1993), 103–24.
"Metaphysics and Phenomenology: A Relief for Theology," trans. Thomas A. Carlson, *Critical Inquiry* 20 (1994), 572–91.
"The Idea of God," trans. Thomas A. Carlson and Daniel Garber, in Daniel Garber and Michael Ayers, eds., *The Cambridge History of Seventeenth-Century Philosophy*, vol. 1 (Cambridge University Press, 1998).

---

[51] As Marion indicates: "To give pure giving to be thought – that, in retrospect it seems to me, is what is at stake in *God without Being*," in *God without Being*, p. xxv.

5 Deconstructive theology

GRAHAM WARD

In 1982 a group of American theologians, schooled in philosophy of religion (particularly the death-of-God thinking from Hegel and Nietzsche and the linguistic turn taken by Wittgenstein and Heidegger) encountered the work of Jacques Derrida and saw the potential of deconstruction for furthering their project of announcing the end of theology. A book emerged, *Deconstruction and Theology*,[1] edited by Thomas Altizer, featuring essays by the most prominent of them: Thomas J. J. Altizer, Mark C. Taylor, Robert Scharlemann, Charles Winquist, Max Meyer, and Carl Raschke. In the same year Mark C. Taylor published his full length study *Deconstructing Theology*, to be followed in a collection under his editorship *Deconstruction in Context* in 1986. Of course, Derrida's work (along with Paul de Man's) was taking the American literary world by storm from the mid seventies when English translations of his work began to appear. And the influence of Derrida's thinking on those schooled in hermeneutics, and primed for the next move that might be made following Gadamer's *Truth and Method*, was beginning to be felt earlier than 1982.

Carl Raschke was one of the first to register the importance of Derrida's thought. Back in the summer of 1977 he was busy reading the late Heidegger and thinking through the relationship between the semantic emphasis of hermeneutics and the semiotic emphasis of pragmatists like C. S. Peirce. Raschke was working on a book that was to be published in 1979, *The Alchemy of the Word: Language and the End of Theology*.[2] The chapter in which Derrida appears involves a discussion on transcendence that examines the work of Wittgenstein, Peirce, and Ricoeur. Finally, he arrives at Derrida's distinctive contribution to this tradition. Derrida's critiques of logocentrism and presence, his account of *différance*, provide the *apparatus criticus* "for making the appropriate gestures toward conceiving language as transcendence, which is at once an epochal break with the metaphysics

---

[1] (New York: Crossroad, 1982).   [2] (Missoula: Scholars Press, 1979).

of certainty."[3] And yet, at this point, Derrida disappears from Raschke's argument, in favor of a discussion of writings by late Heidegger and the way Martin Buber's dialogicalism can supplement their thinking. It is as if in the late seventies the importance of deconstruction for theology is not fully grasped. Certainly Raschke's account of the importance of Derrida's thinking is slightly awry. The comment about Derrida's notion of "language as transcendence" seems to suggest that Raschke believed Derrida was a linguistic idealist. This is a very literal interpretation of one of Derrida's most famous statements: "there is nothing outside the text." Derrida later criticized those who interpreted him along these lines. It is not language but undecidability or aporia – what he termed at one point "arche-*différance*" – that governs, acting as not a transcendent but a quasi-transcendent. But more of that later. Theologians were beginning to grapple with this latest in the linguistic turn and, by the early eighties, as more of Derrida's project was translated and more secondary material emerged, there was better understanding. Other American theologians, like John D. Caputo, began to pick up the scent of something new.

Before pursuing this trail, and adding to it those theologians who began, in the late eighties, to appropriate Derrida's work for Jewish studies and more postliberal/conservative Christian theological projects, let us pause and ask what it was that Derrida's notion of "deconstruction" promised. Fundamentally, as is evident in Raschke's early work, it was an account of language. The death-of-God theologians, whose project emerged in the mid 1960s with the publication of a volume[4] edited by Thomas J. J. Altizer and William Hamilton wrote out of an anti-metaphysical sensibility. Liberal Christian theology under the influence of Tillich and Reinhold Niebuhr had increasingly become interested in metaphor, myth, and symbol, and the death-of-God theologians (including Raschke) developed this linguistic and narratological concern into an emphasis upon the inability of theological discourse to speak constatively about dogmatic, transcendental certainties. Rejecting transcendentalism, accepting the Kantian distinction between the phenomenal and the noumenal, affirming a certain reading of Hegel that, in Jesus Christ, God as transcendent Being poured himself into the immanent created orders without remainder, and insisting then that Wittgenstein was right that one could only speak of things in this world, they emphasized the need to expunge theological discourse of metaphysical claims.

Derrida's work provided these death-of-God theologians with an anti-metaphysical account of language. Language pointed to itself, not to any

---

3 Ibid., p. 24.
4 *Radical Theology and the Death of God* (Harmondsworth: Penguin, 1968).

realms or personages, revelations or hierarchies above, beyond or outside the secular world it constructed. Furthermore, this semiotic account of language pointed up the metaphoricity of all acts of communication. The movement of signs, the translation of a sign from one context into another, the very iteration that signs needed to be conventionally accepted as signifying – disrupted and rendered ultimately ambivalent all semantic or referential intention. Fundamentally, this was the analysis of meaning that "deconstruction" furnished: that a communicated message, like a letter, never simply arrived at the address to which it was posted. The world was a fable spun by words with an endless potential for being misread, misunderstood, and misinterpreted; words which were excessive to the bureaucratic demands for order, system, definition, and transparency. Words possessed alchemical power (again[5]) – and several of the death-of-God theologians spoke mellifluously of the poetic, the creative, the virtual worlds of language. Dogmatic theological claims could, then, be deconstructed to open up the dynamic potential of semiosis (the endless slippage of meaning and interpretation), the phantasmagoric cosmologies it suggested and the new liberations it promised. "Christian atheism," "atheology," "erring" became positive terms in a new appeal to a transfigurative power and the development of a secular incarnational aesthetics. This religious aesthetics was given phenomenological bolstering through an interpretation of Kant's understanding of the sublime as that which was unpresentable. A mystic unpresentability circumcised representation itself. Deconstructive "theology" was concerned with thinking through the traces of this scarification in language and its implications.

To understand what exactly was new about Derrida's approach to language, we need to return to one of the founding fathers of semiotics, to Ferdinand de Saussure's understanding of the nature and operation of language. As I have argued elsewhere, Saussure's thinking also develops within a broadly Kantian framework.[6] His concern lies not with the relationship between words and the world to which they may or may not hook up. He is not interested in demonstrating or denigrating any correspondence view of language: this word corresponds in some way to that object "out there." The "out there," like Kant's "thing in itself" is not available to think. Instead,

---

[5] By "again" I mean here that there has been a tradition up to Paracelsus in the seventeenth century of believing words possessed intrinsic power over the objects they named, and that the natural world could be bent to the will of the one who knew how to unlock this power. Kabbalistic mysticism, for example, taught that the world was made out of letters by God. Sir Philip Sidney, the sixteenth-century poet and Elizabethan courtier, in his book *Defense of Poesie* expressed the common belief that poetic language could return things to how they were before the Fall.

[6] See Ward, *Barth, Derrida and The Language of Theology* (Cambridge University Press, 1995).

Saussure's attention is drawn to a system of associations and differentials among the signs composing any speech act. As such, he is concerned with the signifier/signified relationship – that is, with how names signify. The signifed is not any object in the world, but the thought or concept of an object. Though Saussure examines both the synchronic and the diachronic aspects of language, it is the synchronic, the time-frozen moment of a speech act, to which structural linguistics attends.

With Derrida's work the emphasis is on what we might call the "economy of the signifier" – the fact that the signification of any word is caught up in the forward pull of the signifiers that follow or supplement it. The chain of signifiers moves on toward an open future, and so that which the signifiers communicate is always deferred. Deconstruction is an examination of an endemic deferral of meaning within language. As an account of the pragmatics of writing and speaking, unlike either Saussure or Wittgenstein, Derrida is concerned with temporality – the effects of time. Signs not only are caught up in nets of identities and differences, as Saussure's work indicated or families of resemblance, as Wittgenstein observed, they are also part of economies or movements that defer their signification. This observation is axiomatic for Derrida's understanding of *différance*. *Différance* names that operation of differing and deferring which takes places among signs and which brings about a continual displacement or dissemination of meaning, and hence the supplementary nature of signification.

This turning of attention toward temporality, to what Paul de Man, in developing his understanding of allegory, called "the rhetorics of time"[7] betrays Heidegger's impact upon what came to be known as "post-structuralism." The rhetorics of time critique movements beyond language and putative engagements with either the presence or the absence of meaning inferred to lie ultimately on the other side of words. For Derrida, encounters with presence and absence necessitate illegitimate transcendental moves toward atemporality. These moves cannot be made within language; and outside of language is nothing we can speak about. His post-structural emphasis upon the rhetorics of time forestalls and questions the possibility of such a move toward transcendental a priori. To the freeze-framing attention paid to names/labels, by structural linguistics, is added then an attention to verbs, to economies, to deferrals, withdrawals, tracings, practices, teleologies, and eschatologies. Derrida's examination of the "middle-voice" with respect to *différance* illustrates this: though a noun, *différance* names a verbal event or activity that cannot be determined either as passive or active. In grammar

---

7 See de Man, *Blindness and Insight: Essays in the Rhetoric of Contemporary Criticism* (London: Methuen, 1983).

the "middle voice" is a verb that takes the passive form but is in fact bearing an active sense.

All discourse is haunted, for Derrida, by this other scene – that which frames language, that which exceeds and keeps its signification from being finalized. And the finalization of meaning – its accomplishment as a perfected act of communication – is the fantasy language dreams. For linguistic signs are established through convention, that is, iteration; and iteration is the very principle that forestalls language ever being used simply to say. The meaning of a term is endless disseminated over every context within which it is repeated. As such, deconstruction has a certain syntax that posits and denies. Derrida rehearses this syntax in several pithy phrases: "religion without religion," "community without community," "the impossible possibility of…" (friendship or justice). The formula is "*x* without *x*." *Différance*, dissemination and supplementarity constitute the process of the deconstruction (which appears negative unless we hear in it also the more positive French phrase *de construction*) of meaning.

All discourse, therefore, performs for Derrida the allegory of *différance*. Allegory names that continual negotiation with what is other and outside the text. In this negotiation language deconstructs its own saying in the same way that allegorical discourse is always inhabited by another sense, another meaning. Saying one thing in terms of another is frequently how allegory is defined. Saying is always deconstructive because it operates in terms of semantic slippage and deferral, in terms of not-saying. In this respect, all acts of communication betray a similarity to negative theology: they all in saying something *avoid* saying something. Both allegory and negative theology, then, are self-consciously deconstructive; they are discourses in which the mimetic economy is conscious of itself. As discourses they perform the kenosis or emptying of meaning that *différance* names.

For the death-of-God theologians this kenotic movement that Derrida identifies at the heart of language is fundamentally important for the connection they wish to make between Christ as the Word of God and the kenosis of Christ in both his incarnation and crucifixion. Luther, the Pietists, Hegel, and then several German Protestant theologians throughout the nineteenth century had developed the doctrine of kenosis.[8] Thomas J. J. Altizer, in his book *Christian Atheism*, traces some of this development and endorses

---

[8] The doctrine of kenosis can be located much earlier in Christian thinking – in Origen, for example. But deconstructive theology is, by and large, a Protestant project. Because Altizer associates the death-of-God with kenosis he does not go back any further than Luther. Origen and Nyssa relate kenosis to both crucifixion and resurrection, for example. John D. Caputo is a Catholic by background. It is significant that his work puts little emphasis upon the doctrine of kenosis. He has been exercised more by the relationship between deconstruction and negative theology.

a certain reading of Hegel's treatment of kenosis: that in Christ the transcendence of God became an immanent process in the world. The impassibility of God became the Spirit of Christ in the community. God died to his own transcendence. Deconstructive theology fused this understanding of the kenosis of Christ with Derridean deconstruction. The Word of Christ was disseminated throughout all words; the Spirit of Christ was the economy of *différance* itself – set to bring about new liberating kingdoms, new forms of Christian *jouissance*.

To some extent, Derrida could be left behind at this point, or rather discussions of whether their interpretations of Derrida were good ones were seen as irrelevant to those developing a deconstructive a/theology. It did not matter that Derrida himself seemed to draw a distinction between the economy of *différance* and negative theology. The doctrine of kenosis has some important affinities with negative theology, but, after all, on Derrida's own terms there could be no definitive interpretation of his work. It could only be and would always be misread. But, just when debates between secular and religious deconstructionists were beginning to emerge, Derrida himself began increasingly to write about theological discourse. More precisely, he began a series of explorations that led in two directions. On the one hand, he began to examine with more critical depth the distinction he had drawn earlier between *différance* and negative theology. On the other, he began to consider the relation between the movement of *différance* in, as, and through time and the movement of the spirit through history (as teleology, Messianism, and eschatology). From the early eighties onwards, developing the few cryptic contents in his essay "Différance" and his book *Positions* (translated in 1981), Derrida began explicitly to discuss Messianism ("D'un ton apocalyptique adopté naguère en philosophie") and God-talk ("Comment ne pas parler: dénégations"). This new departure in his writing effectively took deconstruction out of the hands of literary theorists and gave it to theologians (both Jewish and Christian). Susan Handelman's book *The Slayers of Moses: The Emergence of Rabbinic Interpretation in Modern Literary Theory*[9] pointed toward the new direction deconstruction was taking. This new development was excellently rehearsed and analyzed in Kevin Hart's book *The Trespass of the Sign: Deconstruction, Theology and Philosophy*.[10]

We will examine these explorations, and what impact they might have on theological discourse which accepts deconstruction as a description of an ongoing transferential process, in due course. But, as these more explicit theological investigations by Derrida were being published and attention began

[9] (Albany: State University of New York Press, 1982).
[10] (Cambridge University Press, 1989).

to focus on deconstruction and negative theology, Derrida's work was being appropriated by theologians who were more postliberal, even conservative – a far cry from the death-of-God theologians who had gravitated to Derrida's earlier work. These explicitly Christian theologians, more so than the death-of-God group, were working within an acceptance of the traditionally held tenets of the faith. They recognized in deconstruction something that was profoundly theological rather than atheological: not a tool for bringing theology to an end, but a description of an operation intrinsic to the theological task itself. For, insofar as theology has always been aware that the knowledge it produces facilitates an understanding of the human condition and the world we live in more than a knowledge of God-in-Godself, and insofar as it has therefore had to be critical about its own discourse – whether through the paradoxes of negative theology, the investigation into the nature of analogy, or the employment of a dialectical method of critiques – and confess its ignorances, then to that extent the task of theology with respect to thinking through the ongoing relationship with what is other and transcends the created order has *always* been deconstructive.

The question arises whether deconstruction could ever have been thought at all, had not theological discourse pointed the way. In fact, as early as 1977 the conservative Catholic theologian Jean-Luc Marion had used Derrida's thinking in his theological milestone, *L'Idole et la distance*,[11] but Marion was not known outside of France at this time. Throughout the late eighties and early nineties connections between the work of Karl Barth and Jacques Derrida were being examined with a view to employing Derrida's analysis of *différance* in a constructive theological project. Early work appeared in essays by Richard Roberts, David Klemm, and Walter Lowe. Books appeared: Richard Roberts, *Theology on its Way? Essays on Karl Barth*;[12] Stephen Webb, *Re-figuring Theology: The Rhetoric of Karl Barth*;[13] and Walter Lowe, *Theology and Difference: The Wound of Reason*.[14] These studies drew associations between Karl Barth's early, dialectical work and Derrida's notion of deconstruction. They were followed by two studies relating the whole of Barth's project to Derrida's economy of *différance*: my own *Barth, Derrida and the Language of Theology* and Isolde Andrews, *Deconstructing Barth: A Study of Complementary Methods in Karl Barth and Jacques Derrida*.[15] All these projects drew upon Derrida's own writings without wishing to suggest that Derrida himself was a theologian or to synthesize Christian doctrine with Derrida's philosophy of language. Derrida's thinking, for this theological approach, could be used therapeutically: to

---

[11] (Paris: Grasset, 1977).   [12] (Edinburgh: T. & T. Clark, 1991).
[13] (Albany: State University of New York Press, 1991).
[14] (Bloomington: Indiana University Press, 1993).   [15] (New York: Peter Lang, 1996).

elucidate a logic of signification that Barth himself seemed aware of in his own deliberations on the theological project. If the triune God was other than the world that God created and yet also implicated in operating within that world, then Derrida's descriptions of a quasi-transcendental economy of signification might illuminate the nature of theological discourse itself. For theological discourse always and only functions within a generative revelation, given in Christ. But it can never appropriate this transcendental operation of revelation as such. It can only employ those resources for signification handed down to theologians by the tradition and the particular historical and cultural discourses that contextualize any work. So these theologians argued, refusing to accept that Derrida's work put an end to transcendence, presence, and meaning. In fact, they saw Derrida's work as playing between and deconstructing the dualisms of immanence and transcendence, presence and absence, meaning and slippage.

By the late nineties there were two main theological approaches to deconstruction and theology, besides a group who wished to point up some comparisons between Derrida and Buddhism.[16] The two approaches were represented in two books that appeared in 1997: John D. Caputo, *The Prayers and Tears of Jacques Derrida*[17] which, while drawing attention to the way *différance* was not the foundation for a Christology, described Derrida's project as an enquiry into *homo religiosis*; and William S. Johnson, *The Mystery of God: Karl Barth and the Postmodern Foundations of Theology*[18] which drew a comparison between deconstruction's opening up of aporia and the theological appeal, in emphasizing the mystery of God, to its own lack of metaphysical foundations.

At this point let me return to some investigations I left hanging in my exposition of Derrida's analysis of messianism and God-talk. As we have seen, all discourse performs for Derrida the allegory of *différance* and in doing so installs a quasi-transcendental principle. It is the nature of this quasi-transcendental that needs investigating. My colleagues John Milbank and Catherine Pickstock have both criticized Derrida for composing a transcendental argument for nihilism.[19] A transcendental argument is understood philosophically as providing an account for that which "is the condition for the possibility of." We can put this interpretation of Derrida's transcendental argument in this syllogistic form:

---

[16] For an example of this work see Toby Forshay, ed., *Derrida and Negative Theology* (Albany: State University of New York Press, 1992).

[17] (Bloomington: Indiana University Press, 1997).

[18] (Louisville: Westminster John Knox Press, 1997).

[19] See Milbank, *Theology and Social Theory* (Oxford: Blackwell, 1990) and Pickstock, *After Writing: The Liturgical Consummation of Philosophy* (Oxford: Blackwell, 1997).

1 language is concerned with the communication of meaning;
2 that communication of meaning is always caught in the time-lag of re-presentation and so meaning is never self-present, it is always deferred;
3 therefore the condition for the possibility of language as the communication of meaning is an impossibility, a transcendental absence or lack it cannot convert.

On this transcendental argument, then, deconstruction might be employed by a theological project to draw attention to the operations of the linguistic sign, but it cannot be "theologized" per se because then the *nihil* would be the condition for naming God. Certainly the deconstructive theologians of the death-of-God school *do* understand nothingness or emptiness or the unpresentable as the transcendental condition for the generation of all form, including God-talk. The question remains whether this is a correct interpretation of deconstruction, such that any theology founded upon is going to subscribe to a metaphysical nihilism.

I submit that here is the critical point theology has reached with respect to its appropriation of Derrida's thinking on deconstruction. While some American philosophers of religion continue to see Derrida as an important conversation partner, the theological voices have become more concerned with the implications of Derrida's project as a whole. At Villanova, in 1999, when Derrida met with several theologians focusing upon the conference theme "Questioning God," he seemed to endorse that he was constructing a transcendental argument to "out transcendentalize Levinas' transcendentalism."[20] This shocked those who had interpreted Derrida as voicing an anti-metaphysical position. But what kind of a transcendentalist thinker is he? The deferral of meaning in *différance* allows us to witness transferential relations between phenomena given in time. But what are the consequences – ethical, political, theological, philosophical – of this endless deferral? Derrida asks, "is there a proper story for this thing [deconstruction]? I think it consists only of transference, and a thinking through of transference, in all the sense that this word acquires in more than one language, and first of all that of the transference between language."[21] The implications of this "thinking through of transference," I suggest, form the current center of discussion for the theologians.

Three positions on the kind of "transference" *différance* involves are evident. First, as I have sketched, Derrida's work installs a transcendental nothingness outside the text that is the condition for the possibility

---

[20] See the round-table discussion in John D. Caputo, ed., *Questioning God* (Bloomington: Indiana University Press, 2001).
[21] Ibid., pp. 14–15.

of language; a language that continually refers back to and is haunted by this transcending ground. Or, secondly, Derrida's project points to a quasi-transcendental, a non-origin, which cannot be named either nihilism or plenitude. It is simultaneously the ground for all possibility and the undermining of all possibility; a continual source of failure and a perpetual source of hope. It is not a transcendental condition for, or cause of, anything. Derrida (on the logic of his own thinking) cannot make *différance* either a constitutive or a regulative ideal, for he cannot define its nature. So *différance* is both a formal principle (and therefore regulative) for the economy of the sign, but not necessarily existing outside that economy and yet predicated on an excess, or what he calls the *khora*, "a gulf and chaos," outside or beyond (and therefore constitutive). "There is *khora* but the *khora* does not exist... [I]n its so enigmatic uniqueness, [it] lets itself be called or causes itself to be named without answering, without giving itself to be seen, conceived, determined."[22] We have then undecidability. This undecidability is both a formless absence and yet creative; a nothing that also evokes a future possibility, a hope, a promise. The future is endlessly coming; the hope is then never arrived at. It is always only arriving. For some this undecidability, being neither positive nor negative, makes open-endedness the possibility for change, negotiation, and the ongoing democratic process. For others, and this is the third of the three positions I am outlining, this undecidability as the final non-answer of every examination of meaning establishes in effect an absurd world-view, comparable to the world of Camus' Sysiphus. For, while making *différance* a quasi-transcendental it seems to transcendentalize aporia – the undecidable. That is, the utterly ambivalent then becomes the condition for the possibility of language and the meaning of any action. There is endless "movement," as with Sysiphus' task, but it will only inscribe a failure. *Différance* on such a reading is a form of what Hegel would call the bad infinite. If this third position is correct, then we are close again to a nihilism, for, while decisions can be made and acted upon, decisions as such are rendered local, pragmatic, and, fundamentally, arbitrary. Derrida's most recent work on the ethical and political implications of his work would then flounder. The difference between the nihilisms of the first and the third positions is that in the first position the nihilism is a negative ontological condition – the nothing becomes something that might be a ground (even a non-foundational ground) or origin. In the nihilism of the third position the nothing is not an origin but a consequence of the arbitrariness and relativism of communication in the infinite deferral of meaning.

[22] "*Khora*," in Thomas Dutoit, ed., *On the Name*, trans. David Wood (Stanford University Press, 1995), p. 97.

We might catalogue these positions as follows: (1) Derrida is a nihilist because nothing is the transcendental ground for signification, which renders all things meaningless. (2) Derrida is not a nihilist. On the contrary, his work examines a deconstructive operation that can be used constructively to draw attention to the marginalized, the excluded, the politics, and the finitude of any defined position. Meaning is deferred, not erased, and therefore open to a promise. (3) Derrida is not a straightforward nihilist. He does not transcendentalize the nihil and render everything meaningless. The transcendentalizing of indeterminacy does not result in everything being meaningless. But endless deferral of meaning, while not erasing meaning, does render it local and ephemeral, which in effect suggests an absurd world-view in which human beings are embroiled in endless wrestling with accidental meaningfulness and endemic misunderstanding.

Let us now go further and attempt to examine which of these three positions perhaps best describes the kind of transcendental argument informing deconstruction. I suggest we return to those descriptions of the operation of deconstruction most extolled by the death-of-God theologians and those intrigued by the relationship between *différance* and negative theology. Derrida: " 'God' 'is' the name of this bottomless collapse, of this endless desertification of language. But the trace of this negative operation is inscribed in and on and as the event (what comes, what there is and which is always singular, what finds in this kenosis the most decisive condition for its coming or its upsurging)."[23] Derrida appeals here to a certain kenotic operation fundamental to that syntagma of deferral, "*x* without *x*" – without apparently realizing that kenosis can only be understood theologically in terms of Christ's work with respect to Trinitarian operations. He examines the apophatic writings of Angelus Silesius. His language, miming Silesius', is freighted with negativity: "bottomless collapse," "endless desertification."

For those wanting to take up Derrida's work as a therapeutic tool for examining theological discourse, Derrida's explicit writings on negative theology may not be the most productive place for investigation. For he takes up and mimes the negativity in a way that needs to be counter-balanced by his accounts of deconstruction as the "promise" and the "yes, yes." Derrida's discourse on and within negative theology can too easily be dismissed as nihilistic if attention is only paid to the constative statements that can be extracted from this work. Respect for the very brio of the discourse – its abrasiveness, its elusiveness, the rhetorics of its polyphonic performance – is necessary. For example, there is a staging of at least two voices in his essay

[23] "Sauf le nom," in *On the Name*, pp. 55–56.

"Sauf le nom." Since the voices are not named, only several pronominal in-
terjections of "I" located, the voices cannot be numbered. One voice corrects,
sometimes questions, sometimes develops the thought of the voice preced-
ing it, so that, where statements suggest a passing "over to the other edge"[24]
into a total alterity or an absolute outside, other statements insist that the
"event remains at once in and on language, then, within and at the surface."[25]
That is, there is no pure outside. The outside is already operating within.
And in the movement to absolute surrender there is a recognition that
"everything would remain intact…after the passage of a via negativa."[26]
So, while rehearsing Silesius' "bottomless collapse," what Derrida points to
in this essay is the way the "collapse" never comes. The edge of the absolutely external is never crossed. So we never fully make that passage into
the desert. We never have access to the abyss as such. Language can never
complete the kenotic process. The desertification is a form of playing within
God, not a movement over the edge into that which is wholly other. "Negative
theology then can only present itself as one of the most playful forms of
the creature's participation in this divine play."[27] The other in difference
is quasi-transcendental and that is why it is inscribed "in and on and as"
the event of writing, finding in the surrender of fixed and stable reference
"this kenosis [which is] the most decisive condition for its coming and its
upsurging."[28]

What Derrida draws us toward here is thinking about language in terms
of creation and participation. He does not use the metaphor of incarnation,
but the economy of discourse transgresses construals of inside and outside,
immanent and transcendent, in a way analogous to the Christian understanding of the incarnate Word and the God who is not simply for us, but
also with us and working through us. Conceived in this way, kenosis becomes
the allegory of deconstruction while deconstruction becomes the allegory
of all signifying economies. Kenosis is the condition for the possibility of
deconstruction; the condition for the possibility of naming. Kenosis installs
aporia, the ambiguity or metaphoricity that prevents language from strictly
being denotational. Kenosis prevents language from being the transparent
medium for identities and identification. The aporia that results remains
irreducible, for the kenosis here (unlike in the Christian doctrine of kenosis)
is endless. But Derrida stresses that it is "Aporia, rather than antimony…
insofar as it is neither an 'apparent or illusory' antimony, nor a dialectical
contradiction in the Hegelian or Marxist sense, nor even a 'transcendental
illusion in a dialectic of the Kantian type,' but instead an interminable

---

[24] Ibid., p. 70.   [25] Ibid., p. 58.   [26] Ibid., p. 74.
[27] Ibid., p. 75.   [28] Ibid., p. 56.

experience."[29] He goes on to say that there is no experience of aporia as such: "the aporia can never simply be endured as such. The ultimate aporia is the impossibility of the aporia as such. The reservoir of this statement seems to me incalculable."[30] It is in this sense that one has to understand Derrida's infamous statement "il n'y a pas de hors-texte" ("There is nothing outside text"). With respect to the discourse of negative theology, there are not then "fissures opened by our language" that are not simultaneously bound and constructed by that language. To accept the independent existence of the fissures as such is to become blind to one's own use of metaphor. Aporia is only evidenced and produced in the dissemination and exchange of signs. This is his quasi-transcendence, which seems to me to articulate the third of our three positions. It is not nihilist in any straightforward way, as is Heidegger's *Abgrund* of the Nothing, for example.

Ultimately, for Derrida, indeterminacy is all philosophy can think. *Pace* Aristotle, philosophy cannot give us God, only the endlessly dissemination of the signifier "God." Derrida outlines, by working on, the very limits of what philosophy can think. The world as philosophically examined is agnostic. To live in or endure this indeterminacy is to experience life as a ship moving across a dark, unending ocean:

> [S]earchlights without a coast... sweep across the dark sky, shut down or disappear at regular intervals and harbor the invisible in their very light. We no longer even know against what dangers of abysses we are forewarned. We avoid one, only to be thrown into one of the others. We no longer even know whether these watchmen are guiding us towards another destination, nor even if the destination remains promised or determined.[31]

This is the absurd world-view made manifest by Derrida's secular thinking, in which rafts of illumination travel like star ships through the folds of a dark infinity. A world in which transferential relations, amphibolous regulative relations as Kant calls them, are necessarily instituted, like friendships, to conceal the madness of a semiosis which renders all things meaningless. And yet, as Derrida understands, this too is only one picture; and to decide upon this cosmology would be too determinative of what *différance* gives us to think. So elsewhere another conflicting metaphorics comes into play: "love in friendship, lovence beyond love and friendship following their determined figures, beyond all this book's trajectories of reading, beyond all ages, cultures and traditions of loving."[32]

---

[29] Derrida, *Aporias*, trans. Thomas Dutoit (Stanford: Stanford University Press, 1993), p. 16.
[30] Ibid., p. 78.   [31] Ibid., p. 81.   [32] Ibid., p. 69.

Derrida's world seeks to maintain the integrity of secular thinking and even certain enlightenment ideals: freedom, equality, democracy by consensus. It also seeks to maintain an ethics of integrity based upon philosophical thinking sticking with what is permissible within its own domains, even though the basis for that thinking is aporia as such, even though what ensues is the impossible possibility of enlightenment ideals and the integrity of every discourse with respect to them. But what happens when we refuse philosophy's secular autonomy? What happens when a theologian, whose world-view could not accept Derrida's, undertakes, with help from Derrida, the task of "the thinking through of transferences"?

Derrida is no theologian, and when he employs theological vocabulary (like kenosis, like "Word") he does not think the language through with any theological sophistication. His treatment of negative theology, for example, is philosophical and decontextual; it is not in terms of the tradition or the grammar of the faith as practiced by Pseudo-Denys, Eckhart, and Silesius. The Word is equated with logocentrism (the full, realized presence of meaning) and with the transcendental signifier that stabilizes and gives identity to all things. There is no recognition or understanding of the relationship of the Word to the Triune Godhead and creation. Furthermore, he shows little understanding of "presence" as it is understood theologically. He reads presence as modernity reads presence – as immediate, direct truth, as self-authenticating meaning, as the full realisation in this moment of time (the now) of identity. Derrida does not understand presence as grace. He does not understand the mediatorial operation of the Word and the Spirit within creation, a creation that is not finished, and a Word which is not yet complete. The presence of God in grace is not the violence of the moment – but the unfolding of the divine maintenance and sustenance of the world. Taking the incarnation seriously is not being translated out of the world into immediate contact with God; it is recognising the movement of God in what has been gifted for us in the world. Incarnation cannot admit the inadequacy of mediation and representation; for it is itself implicated in and both sanctions and sanctifies mediation and representation. To accept the antimony is gnostic.

Christian theological anthropology begins with human beings *made in the image of* and, as such, we are the creators and purveyors of image-making. This was the basis for John Damascene's great defense of icons: "For what reason, then, do we adore one another, except because we have been made in the image of God . . . But, furthermore, who can make a copy of the invisible, incorporeal, uncircumscribed, and unportrayable God? However, through the bowels of his mercy God for our salvation was made man in truth, not in appearance of man...but really made man in substance."[33] Christ, the incarnation of the Word of God, is a quasi-transcendental as such, by which I mean that Christ as the revelation of God operates both econom- ically (in the world) and transcendentally (beyond the world in Trinitarian relations with the Godhead). Christ's coming wounds our words with the trace of that which is "invisible, incorporeal, uncircumscribed, and unpor- trayable." Our naming and language-making – that proceed from our being *made in the image of* – undergo an emptying, as the Word operates in and through our words. But this kenosis is of Christ, a consequence of Christ's own emptying of his own transcendental divinity. It does not introduce a bad infinite, for it is not endless. The kenosis proceeds from and returns to God. The kenotic economy of Christ works in, through, and beyond this world, installing not absence but resurrection of life. Our words are reori- ented to the truth that is in Christ. Given this premise, Derrida's analysis of quasi-transcendental operations might well be helpful. Derrida writes about what "takes place, what comes to pass with the aporia"[34] of *différance*:

> the absolute arrivant does not yet have a name or an identity. It is not an invader or an occupier, nor is it a colonizer, even if it can also become one... Since the arrivant does not have an identity yet, its place of arrival is also de-identified: one does not yet know or one no longer knows which is the country, the place, the nation, the family, the language, and the home in general that welcomes the absolute arrivant... It even exceeds the order of any determinable promise... because...the absolute arrivant makes possible everything to which I have just said it cannot be reduced, starting with the humanity of man.[35]

It is not simply that Christ is *différance* or Christ names *différance* or Christ and the operation of the Spirit inform the economy of *différance*. But it might be possible to think theologically after Derrida by acknowledging that Christ is neither a proper name that we know how to employ (and know what we mean by employing it) nor an identity we can delineate and turn into a template. After all, as Thomas Aquinas well knew: "God is not known to us in His nature, but is made known to us from His operations or effects...This name God is an appellative name, and not a proper name."[36] Augustine defines the nature of the anthropology that ensues, and opens the way for a further negotiation with the "thinking through of transferences":

[33] *St. John of Damascus, Writings*, ed. and trans. F. H.Chase (Washington: Catholic University of America Press, 1958) pp. 370–71.
[34] Derrida, *Aporias*, p. 32.   [35] Ibid., pp. 34–35.
[36] *Summa Theologiae*, Pt. 1 q 13 articles 8 & 9.

"God, by deferring hope, stretches our desire...This is our life, that by longing we should be exercised."[37] It is here that we can begin to investigate another relationship between deconstruction, installed by an economy of deferral, and theology – an exercise in longing for God or participating in God's longing for us. This is not a Derridean project, but what Derrida has done provides us with a way of reading the signs that might enrich an understanding of, even as it reiterates, the Christian tradition. Christian theology has always been parasitic in this way. It is exactly by undertaking such a work that the deconstructive world-view can be redeemed.

Further reading

Caputo, John D., *The Prayers and Tears of Jacques Derrida* (Bloomington: Indiana University Press, 1997).

Hart, Kevin, *The Trespass of the Sign: Deconstruction, Theology and Philosophy* (Cambridge University Press, 1989).

Lowe, Walter, *Theology and Difference: The Wound of Reason* (Bloomington: Indiana University Press, 1993).

Ward, Graham, *Barth, Derrida and the Language of Theology* (Cambridge University Press, 1995).

---

[37] *De doctrina christiana* 4.6.

6 Reconstructive theology

DAVID RAY GRIFFIN

Reconstructive postmodern theology derives its philosophical bearings from the movement in which Alfred North Whitehead is the central figure, with William James and Charles Hartshorne being, respectively, the most important antecedent and subsequent members. Although theology based on this movement has widely been known as "process theology," not all process theology is properly called postmodern. Process theology *is* reconstructive postmodern theology insofar as it thematizes the contrast between the modern and the postmodern, emphasizes the distinctively postmodern notions in Whiteheadian philosophy, employs these notions for deconstruction of classical and modern concepts and for ensuing reconstruction, and relates the resulting position to other forms of postmodern thought. Although this form of postmodern thought has generally been called "constructive," as in the title of the State University of New York Press Series in Constructive Postmodern Thought, the term "reconstructive" makes clearer that a prior deconstruction of received concepts is presupposed.

ORIGINS

Although the term "postmodern" was not used by Whitehead himself, the notion is implicit in his 1925 book, *Science and the Modern World*, in which he says that recent developments in both physics and philosophy have superseded some of the scientific and philosophical ideas that were foundational for the modern world. Whitehead's most explicit statement about the end of the modern epoch occurs in a discussion of William James' 1904 essay "Does Consciousness Exist?," the crux of which Whitehead takes to be the denial that consciousness is a stuff that is essentially different from the stuff of which the physical world is composed. Whitehead suggests that, just as Descartes, with his formulation of a dualism between matter and mind, can (with some exaggeration) be regarded as the thinker who inaugurated the modern period, James, with his challenge to Cartesian dualism, can (with similar exaggeration) be regarded as having inaugurated "a new stage in philosophy." Viewing this challenge together with that offered to "scientific materialism" by physics in the same period, Whitehead suggests that this "double challenge marks the end of a period which lasted for about two hundred and fifty years."[1] Having described the scientific and philosophical thought of that period as distinctively modern, Whitehead thereby implied that his own philosophy, which sought to unite the philosophical implications of relativity and quantum physics with the Jamesian rejection of dualism, was distinctively postmodern, but without using the term.

The term itself was applied to Whitehead's philosophy in a 1964 essay by John Cobb entitled "From Crisis Theology to the Post-Modern World," which dealt with the emerging discussion of the "death of God."[2] Arguing that the dominant modern mentality, which equates the real with the objects of sensory perception, excludes the possible causality and even reality of God, thereby leading to relativism and nihilism, Cobb portrayed Whitehead's philosophy as distinctively postmodern by virtue of the fact that his epistemology rejected the primacy of sense perception, that his ontology replaced material substances with events having intrinsic value and internal relations, and that he developed these ideas by reflecting on problems in modern science. In *God and the World* in 1967 and "The Possibility of Theism Today" in 1968, Cobb restated his argument that Whitehead provides a postmodern vision in which theology is again possible.[3] These writings provided the stimulus for my decision in 1972, as co-editor of a volume on Cobb's theology (which did not actually appear until 1977), to orient my introductory essay around the notion that Cobb was providing a "postmodern theology for a new Christian existence."[4] In Cobb's 1975 book, *Christ in a Pluralistic Age*, he enlarged his use of the term "postmodern," employing it to refer to a pluralistic method and mind-set that goes beyond the idea of a single truth without falling into complete relativism.[5]

Cobb was not the only one who was thinking of Whitehead's philosophy as postmodern. In the same year as Cobb's seminal essay (1964), Floyd

---

[1] A. N. Whitehead, *Science and the Modern World* (New York: Free Press, 1967), p. 143.

[2] John B. Cobb, Jr., "From Crisis Theology to the Post-Modern World," *Centennial Review* 8 (Spring 1964), 209–20; reprinted in Thomas J. J. Altizer, ed., *Toward a New Christianity: Readings in the Death of God Theology* (New York: Harcourt, Brace and World, 1967) and several other anthologies.

[3] Cobb, *God and the World* (Philadelphia: Westminster Press, 1967), pp. 135, 138; "The Possibility of Theism Today," in Edward H. Madden, Robert Handy, and Marvin Farber, eds., *The Idea of God: Philosophical Perspectives* (New York: Charles C. Thomas, 1968), pp. 98–123.

[4] Griffin, "Post-Modern Theology for a New Christian Existence," in David Ray Griffin and Thomas J. J. Altizer, eds., *John Cobb's Theology in Process* (Philadelphia: Westminster, 1977), pp. 5–24.

[5] Cobb, *Christ in a Pluralistic Age* (Philadelphia: Westminster, 1975), pp. 15, 25–27.

Matson, who was also influenced by Whitehead, advocated a "postmodern science," by which he meant one that overcame mechanistic, reductionistic, and behaviorist approaches.[6] In 1973, a "postmodern science" was advocated at greater length and with more explication of Whitehead's position by Harold Schilling.[7] In that same year, Charles Altieri argued that it is Whitehead's philosophy, even more than Heidegger's, that best explains the connection between fact and value suggested by a number of American poets considered by Altieri to be distinctively postmodern.[8] In a 1976 book subtitled *Resources for the Post-Modern World*, Frederick Ferré, besides following Schilling in speaking of the need for the kind of "postmodern science" provided by Whitehead, also suggested that Christian process theology presents a "postmodern version of Christianity" that could help overcome the ecological crisis engendered by modernity.[9]

While at Cambridge University in 1980, I gave a lecture, in the form of a response to *The Myth of God Incarnate*,[10] entitled "Myth, Incarnation, and the Need for a Postmodern Theology." Arguing that we need "a postmodern outlook [that] would preserve the unquestionable advances made by the tenets of modernity, but relativize some of them by placing them within the context of a more inclusive understanding, somewhat as Newtonian physics is included in but somewhat modified by twentieth-century physics," I added that "Cambridge's own Alfred North Whitehead has provided a philosophic vision that can be called postmodern and does make possible the kind of theology that is necessary in our time."[11] Three years later I founded the Center for a Postmodern World (in Santa Barbara, California). Its invited lecturers and 1987 conference, "Toward a Postmodern World," provided most of the material for the three books that launched the State University of New York Press Series in Constructive Postmodern Thought.[12] Through the influence of this center and book series, a circle of reconstructive postmodern thinkers was formed, some of whom are involved in distinctively Christian thinking, including – besides Cobb, Ferré,

[6] Floyd W. Matson, *The Broken Image: Man, Science and Society* (1964; Garden City: Doubleday, 1966), pp. vi, 139, 228.
[7] Harold K. Schilling, *The New Consciousness in Science and Religion* (Philadelphia: United Church Press, 1973), pp. 44–47, 73–74, 91, 183, 244–53.
[8] Charles Altieri, "From Symbolist Thought to Immanence: the Ground of Postmodern American Poetics," *Boundary* 2:1 (1973), 605–42.
[9] Frederick Ferré, *Shaping the Future: Resources for the Post-Modern World* (New York: Harper & Row, 1976), pp. 100, 106–7.
[10] John Hick, ed., *The Myth of God Incarnate* (London: SCM Press, 1977).
[11] Griffin, "Myth, Incarnation, and the Need for a Postmodern Theology," unpublished MS (available at the Center for Process Studies), p. 34.
[12] *The Reenchantment of Science: Postmodern Proposals* and *Spirituality and Society: Postmodern Visions*, both of which I edited, and *God and Religion in the Postmodern World*, which contains my own essays (all published in 1988 by the State University of New York Press).

and myself – New Testament scholar William Beardslee, biologist Charles Birch, economist Herman Daly, and feminist Catherine Keller.

Having long considered 1964 the year in which the term postmodern began to be applied to the Whiteheadian approach, I subsequently learned that this application had actually been made as early as 1944, when John Herman Randall, Jr., writing of the emergence of " 'postmodern' naturalistic philosophies," referred to Whitehead as "one of the pioneers" of this movement.[13] The great advantage of this postmodern naturalism, according to Randall, is that by rejecting the modern, mechanistic, reductionistic type of naturalism, it overcomes the modern conflict of scientific naturalism with moral, aesthetic, and religious values – a description that accords completely with the stated purpose of Whitehead's philosophy.[14] In any case, whether the use of the term "postmodern" to refer to a Whiteheadian approach is said to have begun in 1944 or 1964, it is ironic that some critics, understanding the term in light of meanings it took on in the 1980s, have considered the Whiteheadian use of the term opportunistic. It is noteworthy that, in a 1995 volume on "early postmodernism" in which Altieri's 1973 article was reprinted,[15] the editor's introduction draws attention to the great difference between this early "postmodernism" and the type of thought with which the name later became associated. The task of the present chapter, in any event, is to explain not only what the Whiteheadian type of postmodern theology says, but also why its advocates consider it genuinely postmodern.

THE QUESTIONS OF METAPHYSICS
AND RATIONALITY

The fact that reconstructive postmodern theology is based on a metaphysical type of philosophy makes it distinctive, given the fact that "metaphysics" is one of the things that most other forms of postmodernism believe we now are, or should be, beyond. This difference is to some extent terminological, in that many of the "definitions" of metaphysics that are presupposed in this widespread rejection do not apply to Whitehead's thought. Many postmodernists, for example, presuppose the Kantian conception, according to which metaphysics is the attempt to talk about things beyond all possible experience, whereas Whitehead understands it as the endeavor

---

[13] John Herman Randall, Jr., "The Nature of Naturalism," Yervant H. Krikorian, ed., *Naturalism and the Human Spirit* (New York: Columbia University Press, 1944), esp. pp. 367–69.

[14] Whitehead, *Science and the Modern World*, pp. vii, 156, 185; *Process and Reality: an Essay in Cosmology*, corrected edn, ed. David Ray Griffin and Donald W. Sherburne (New York: Free Press, 1978), p. 15.

[15] Paul A. Bové, ed., *Early Postmodernism: Foundational Essays* (Durham, NC: Duke University, 1995).

to construct a coherent scheme of ideas "in terms of which every element of our experience can be interpreted," adding that the "elucidation of immediate experience is the sole justification for any thought."[16] Sometimes metaphysics is understood as an approach that necessarily does violence to experience for the sake of a tidy system, but Whitehead, who praised the intellectual life of William James for being one long "protest against the dismissal of experience in the interest of system,"[17] insisted repeatedly on the need to consider the "whole of the evidence" and *every* type of experience, insisting that "[n]othing can be omitted."[18] Thinkers influenced by Heidegger sometimes portray metaphysics as necessarily committed to the domination of nature, but Whitehead's metaphysical analysis leads him to say that our experience of actuality is "a value experience. Its basic expression is – Have a care, here is something that matters!"[19] Still another reason for rejecting metaphysical systems is that they claim to attain certainty, but Whitehead regards a metaphysical system as a tentative hypothesis, an "experimental adventure," adding that "the merest hint of dogmatic certainty as to finality of statement is an exhibition of folly."[20] Closely related is the widespread assumption that metaphysics is necessarily "foundationalist" in the sense now widely discredited, according to which the philosopher begins with a few indubitable basic beliefs, from which all other beliefs are deduced. But Whitehead explicitly rejected the idea "that metaphysical thought started from principles which were individually clear, distinct, and certain."[21]

However, although many of the apparent differences between Whiteheadians and other types of postmodernists can be dismissed in these ways, a real difference remains. Reconstructive postmodernism is oriented around the conviction that we must and can reconcile religion and reason, which in our time largely means religion and science. Whitehead, in fact, said that philosophy's most important task is to show how religion and the sciences (natural and social) can be integrated into a coherent world-view.[22] Many other postmodernists, by contrast, reject *any* attempt at a comprehensive account of things, whether the attempt be called a metanarrative, metaphysics, or something else, considering all such attempts to be ideological efforts to impose one's will on others. But Whiteheadian postmodernists, while recognizing that every such attempt will involve distortions due to

[16] Whitehead, *Process and Reality*, pp. 3, 4.
[17] Whitehead, *Modes of Thought* (New York: Free Press, 1968), p. 3.
[18] *Science and the Modern World*, pp. vii, 187; *Adventures of Ideas* (New York: Free Press, 1967), p. 226.
[19] *Modes of Thought*, p. 116.   [20] *Process and Reality*, pp. 8, 9, xiv.
[21] Whitehead, *The Function of Reason* (Boston: Beacon Press, 1958), p. 49.
[22] *Process and Reality*, p. 15.

ignorance and bias, deny that the very effort to engage in comprehensive thinking necessarily involves hegemonial intentions.[23] They argue, furthermore, that the human need for stories or narratives orienting us to reality as a whole cannot be removed by declaration.[24]

The differences here involve fundamentally different ideas about modernity's fatal flaw. While these other postmodernists see modernity as afflicted by rationalistic pretensions, Whitehead regards modernity as an essentially *anti*-rational enterprise. This point depends on the idea that the ideas that we inevitably presume in practice should be taken as the ultimate criteria for rational thought. "Rationalism," says Whitehead, "is the search for the coherence of such presumptions."[25] A precedent-setting instance of modern anti-rationalism was Hume's acknowledgment that in living he necessarily presupposed various ideas, such as a real world and causal influence, that could find no place in his philosophy. Whitehead argues that, rather than resting content with a philosophical theory that had to be supplemented by an appeal to "practice," Hume should have revised his philosophy until it included all the inevitable presuppositions of practice.[26] The reason that it is anti-rational to deny in theory ideas that are necessarily presupposed in practice is that one thereby violates the first rule of reason, the law of noncontradiction, because one is simultaneously denying (explicitly) and affirming (implicitly) the idea in question.

OVERCOMING PROBLEMATIC MODERN ASSUMPTIONS

From the reconstructive postmodern perspective, it lies at the heart of the task of postmodern thinking to overcome the assumptions that led to the modern dualism between the ideas affirmed in theory and those presupposed in practice. The crucial assumptions are taken to be the *sensationist view of perception*, according to which our sensory organs provide our only means of perceiving things beyond ourselves, and the *mechanistic view of nature*, according to which the ultimate units of nature are devoid of all experience, intrinsic value, internal purpose, and internal relations. It is

[23] Cobb, "Introduction" to *Postmodernism and Public Policy: Reframing Religion, Culture, Education, Sexuality, Class, Race, Politics, and the Economy* (Albany: State University of New York Press, 2002).
[24] William A. Beardslee, "Christ in the Postmodern Age: Reflections inspired by Jean-François Lyotard," in David Ray Griffin, William A. Beardslee, and Joe Holland, eds., *Varieties of Postmodern Theology* (Albany: State University of New York Press, 1989), pp. 63–80; "Stories in the Postmodern World: Orienting and Disorienting," in Griffin, ed., *Sacred Interconnections: Postmodern Spirituality, Political Economy, and Art* (Albany: State University of New York Press, 1990), pp. 163–76.
[25] *Process and Reality*, p. 153.   [26] Ibid., p. 13.

these correlative ideas that led to the modern divorce of theoretical from practical reason and thereby to the Humean–Kantian conviction that metaphysics, which would show how the two sets of ideas can be integrated into a self-consistent world-view, is impossible.

The sensationist theory of perception is responsible for many of the problems, including those involving causation, a real world, and a real past. With regard to causation, Hume famously pointed out that, although we have usually thought of causation as involving some sort of *necessary connection* between the cause and the effect, because the "cause" is thought to exert *real influence* on the "effect," sensory data provide no basis for this idea, so that causation, to be an empirical concept, must be redefined to mean simply *constant correlation* between two types of events. Although Hume continued to presuppose in practice that causation involves real influence – that his wine glass moved to his lips because he used his hand to lift it – he said that qua philosopher he could not employ that meaning.

Hume even said that he as philosopher could not affirm the reality of the world. He could not help, he pointed out, being a realist in everyday life, necessarily presupposing that he lived in a world with other people and things, such as tables and food. According to his analysis of perception, however, he did not perceive such things but only sense data, such as colors and shapes. As a philosopher, therefore, he had to be a solipsist, doubting the existence of an external world, even though in practice, including the practice of using a pen to record his skeptical ideas on paper, he had no doubts. At the outset of the twentieth century, George Santayana showed that the Humean brand of empiricism leads not simply to solipsism but to "solipsism of the present moment."[27] Because sense perception reveals only various data immediately present to our consciousness, we must be agnostic about the reality of the past and therefore of time.

Empiricist philosophy was said, accordingly, to be unable to support four of the most fundamental presuppositions of the empirical sciences – the reality of causal influence, time, the past, and even the world as such. Having no basis for saying that causal relations observed in the past will hold true in the future, this kind of empiricist philosophy obviously could not justify the principle of induction. Much postmodernism has drawn the conclusion that science, generally taken to be the paradigm of rationality, is itself rationally groundless.

The sensationist version of empiricism leads to the same conclusion about normative values. Philosophers had traditionally affirmed the existence of logical, aesthetic, and moral norms. Sensory perception, however,

[27] George Santayana, *Skepticism and Animal Faith* (New York: Dover, 1955), pp. 14–15.

can provide no access to such norms. Early modern philosophers, such as John Locke and Francis Hutcheson, said that we know such norms because they were divinely revealed or implanted in our minds. But late modernity, having rejected supernatural explanations, concluded that all such norms are our own creations. Most forms of postmodernism have emphasized the implications of this conclusion, saying that we must regard even our most basic moral convictions as local conventions with no rational grounding – even while continuing to presuppose, in the very act of writing such things, that various moral norms, such as the idea that we should not repress "difference" and oppress the "other," are universally valid. The apparent necessity to presuppose various ideas even while criticizing them is sometimes justified by referring to them as "transcendental illusions" in the Kantian sense.

Whiteheadian postmodernism, rather than accepting the inevitability of such contradictions, follows James' "radical empiricism" in rejecting the sensationist view of perception. At the heart of Whitehead's epistemology is his deconstruction of sensory perception, showing that it is a hybrid composed of two pure modes of perception. Hume and most subsequent philosophy noticed only "perception in the mode of presentational immediacy," in which sense data are immediately present to the mind. If this were our only mode of perception, we would indeed be doomed to solipsism of the present moment. But this mode of perception, Whitehead argues at great length – much of *Process and Reality* and virtually all of *Symbolism*[28] are devoted to this point – is derivative from a more fundamental mode, "perception in the mode of causal efficacy," through which we directly perceive other actualities as exerting causal efficacy upon ourselves – which explains why we know that other actualities exist and that causation is more than constant conjunction. One example of this mode of perception, which Whitehead also calls "prehension," is the prehension of our own sensory organs as causing us to have certain experiences, as when we are aware that we are seeing a tree *by means of* our eyes. Such prehension, while presupposed in sensory perception, is itself nonsensory.

Another example of this nonsensory perception is our prehension of prior moments of our own experience, through which we know the reality of the past and thereby of time. This point depends on a third idea deconstructed by Whitehead – the idea, common to modern and premodern Western thought (although rejected long ago by Buddhists), that enduring individuals are "substances," with a "substance" understood to be both actual and not analyzable into entities that are more fully actual. According to Whitehead's alternative account, an individual that endures through time,

---

[28] *Symbolism: Its Meaning and Effect* (1927; New York: G. P. Putnam's Sons, 1959).

such as an electron, a living cell, or a human soul, is analyzable into momentary actual entities, which he calls "actual occasions." To remember a
previous moment of one's own experience, therefore, is to prehend an actual
entity that is numerically different from the actual occasion that is one's
present experience.[29] Modern and premodern thought, by regarding the
soul or mind as numerically one through time, had blinded philosophers to
our primary experiential basis for the idea of time.

The significance of these explanations of the origin of our basic categories, such as actuality (which combines the Kantian categories of "existence" and "substance"), time, and causality, would be hard to overstate,
given the fact that Kant's "Copernican revolution," which lies behind most
forms of idealism, phenomenology, structuralism, and postmodernism, was
based on the need to explain such categories while assuming, with Hume,
the sensationist doctrine of perception. Equally important to the distinction
between Whitehead-based and Kant-based forms of postmodernism is the
fact that Whitehead, by insisting on the reality of nonsensory perception, allows our apparent awareness of normative values to be accepted as genuine.
Our moral and aesthetic discourse, accordingly, can be regarded as *cognitive*, capable of being true or false (or somewhere in between). This point is
fundamental to the respective strategies for overcoming modern scientism.
Whereas Kantian forms of postmodernism, such as Richard Rorty's, put
moral and aesthetic discourse on the same level with scientific discourse by
denying that either type tells us about reality, Whiteheadian postmodernism
achieves parity by showing how both types can express real, if partial, truths
about the nature of things – partial truths it is the cultural role of philosophy
to harmonize.

Whereas the sensationist view of perception led to contradictions between theory and practice with regard to realism, causation, the past, time,
and norms, the mechanistic view of nature leads to such a contradiction
with regard to freedom. Early modernity reconciled human freedom with
this view of nature by means of a Cartesian soul, different in kind from the
stuff of which the body is composed. The relation of such a soul to its body
could be explained, however, only by means of a Supernatural Coordinator
(as Descartes, Malebranche, and Reid all agreed). The late modern demise
of supernaturalism, accordingly, entailed the transmutation of Cartesian
dualism into a full-fledged materialism, in which the soul, mind, or self
is taken to be merely a property or epiphenomenon of the body's brain,
not an entity with any agency of its own. Whatever the "self" is, it has no
power of *self*-determination. Freedom must be denied (or redefined to make

---

[29] Whitehead, *Adventures of Ideas*, pp. 220–21.

it compatible with determinism, which amounts to the same thing). Some late modern philosophers explicitly admit that they must continue to pre-suppose freedom in practice while not being able to make sense of it in theory.[30] Much postmodernism accentuates this contradiction, proclaiming in unnuanced ways the "disappearance of the (centered) self" while exhorting us to use our freedom to overcome oppressive views and practices.

Whiteheadian postmodernism, instead of accepting materialism or anti-realism or returning to early modern dualism, rejects the mechanistic view of nature at the root of these stances. Its alternative view – again, antici-pated by James[31] – is panexperientialism, according to which experience and thereby spontaneity, intrinsic value, and internal relations go all the way down to the most primitive units of nature. Besides calling all actual entities actual occasions, accordingly, Whitehead also calls them "occasions of experience." On the basis of this panexperientialism, the unanswerable questions faced by materialists as well as dualists – *where* and *how* did things with experience, spontaneity, intrinsic value, and internal relations emerge out of bits of matter wholly devoid of these? – need not be asked. Evolution involves real emergence, but it is the emergence of higher types of spontaneous experience out of lower types.

All such doctrines, usually under the name "panpsychism," are widely rejected as patently absurd. Such rejections often rest on characterizations that do not apply to Whiteheadian–Hartshornean panexperientialism. Critics rightly say, for example, that it would be absurd to attribute any free-dom and thereby any experience to sticks and stones. But it is essential to this doctrine, the more complete name of which is "panexperientialism with or-ganizational duality,"[32] to distinguish between aggregational organizations, which as such have no experience or spontaneity, and "compound individ-uals," which do.[33] Even after becoming aware of this distinction, however, modern thinkers tend to consider panexperientialism to be self-evidently false, which suggests that one of modernity's most basic assumptions is being challenged. The same is true of the Jamesian–Whiteheadian endorse-ment of nonsensory perception, as evidenced by the fact that most admiring

[30] John Searle, *Minds, Brains, and Science* (London: British Broadcasting Corporation, 1984), pp. 85–86, 92–98.
[31] Marcus P. Ford, *William James's Philosophy: a New Perspective* (Amherst: University of Massachusetts Press, 1982); "William James," in David Ray Griffin, John B. Cobb, Jr., Marcus P. Ford, and Pete A. Y. Gunter, *Founders of Constructive Postmodern Philosophy: Peirce, James, Bergson, Whitehead, and Hartshorne* (Albany: State University of New York Press, 1993), pp. 89–132.
[32] Griffin, "Introduction" to *Reenchantment without Supernaturalism: a Process Philosophy of Religion* (Ithaca, NY: Cornell University Press, 2001).
[33] Griffin, *Unsnarling the World-Knot: Consciousness, Freedom, and the Mind–Body Problem* (Berkeley: University of California Press, 1998), chs. 7, 9.

treatments of James' thought virtually ignore the fact that he endorsed the reality of telepathy and devoted much of his time to psychical research.[34] In any case, these distinctively postmodern views about being and perceiving, besides solving various philosophical problems, also provide the basis for a distinctive type of postmodernism.

FURTHER COMPARISON WITH THE DOMINANT IMAGE OF POSTMODERNISM

The term "postmodernism" is commonly associated with a wide variety of ideas that together constitute what can be called the "dominant image of postmodernism." Whiteheadian postmodernism exemplifies this dominant image in many respects. It rejects foundationalism and with it the quest for certainty; it accepts the need to deconstruct a wide range of received ideas, including the ontotheological idea of God, the substantial self, and history as having a predetermined end; and it seeks to foster pluralism and diversity, both human and ecological.

However, the reconstructive type of postmodernism also differs from the dominant image of postmodernism in many respects. Some of these differences are implicit in the very fact that this approach is metaphysical. For example, whereas most postmodernists speak derisively of the "correspondence theory of truth" and the idea of language as "referential," reconstructive postmodernists defend these notions, partly by pointing out that their denials lead to what Karl-Otto Apel and Jürgen Habermas call "performative contradictions,"[35] partly by showing how Whitehead's philosophy, with its panexperientialist ontology and nonsensationist view of perception, overcomes the standard objections.[36] Closely related is the fact that reconstructive postmodernism, while rejecting foundationalism, also rejects a complete relativism of both truth and value.[37] Central to avoiding relativism with regard to truth is the acceptance of the inevitable presuppositions of practice, which some of us call "hard-core commonsense notions," as universally valid criteria of adequacy.[38] The avoidance of complete

---

[34] Marcus Ford, "William James"; "James's Psychical Research and its Philosophical Implications," *Transactions of the Charles S. Peirce Society* 34 (1998), 605–26.

[35] Martin Jay, "The Debate over Performative Contradiction: Habermas versus the Poststructuralists," Jay, *Force Fields: Between Intellectual History and Cultural Critique* (New York: Routledge, 1993), pp. 25–37.

[36] Cobb, "Alfred North Whitehead," in Griffin et al., *Founders*, pp. 165–95, esp. 181–87; Griffin, *Reenchantment without Supernaturalism*, ch. 9.

[37] Cobb, *Postmodernism and Public Policy*, ch. 2.

[38] Griffin, "Introduction," *Founders*, pp. 1–42, esp. 23–29; *Unsnarling*, ch. 2, "Confusion about Common Sense."

relativism with regard to normative values is based partly on the fact that the nonsensationist doctrine of perception allows for a direct (albeit not infallible) perception of such values. The idea that such norms or values somehow exist so as to be prehendable, however, requires another topic, the existence of God – a subject that brings us to distinctively theological doctrines.

POSTMODERN CHRISTIAN DOCTRINES

Conservative-to-fundamentalist theologians have said that modern liberal theology has become increasingly vacuous. Although reconstructive postmodern theologians agree, they argue that the problem with modern liberalism was not its liberal world-view and method, according to which supernaturalism is rejected and the truth of religious beliefs is to be based on experience and reason rather than the authority of Scripture and tradition, but its acceptance of the modern assumptions discussed earlier. If those assumptions are accepted, so that reason is equated with *modern* reason, there is no disputing those postmodernists who believe it impossible for a theology to be both reasonable and robust.[39] By rejecting those assumptions, however, a postmodern liberal theology can develop robust Christian doctrines.

At the heart of this theology is its naturalistic theism. This theism is naturalistic not in the sense of equating God with the world, or otherwise denying distinct agency to God, but simply in the sense of rejecting supernaturalism, understood as belief in a divine being that can interrupt the world's normal causal principles. This rejection is rooted in its view of the relation of God to being itself, which it renames "creativity" to reflect the fact that that which all beings embody is not passive stuff but dynamic energy. Creativity, more precisely, is each actual occasion's twofold power to exercise a modicum of self-determination (final causation) and then to exert influence (efficient causation) on future events. Traditional theism, with its (ontotheological) equation of God with being itself, said that this twofold power is essentially embodied in God alone. Because any power possessed by creatures is a gift, the normal causal patterns among creatures could be interrupted at any time. This position was fully enunciated only with the postbiblical development of the doctrine of creation *ex nihilo*. Whiteheadian postmodern theologians return to the view, common to Plato, the Bible, and

39 Jeffrey Stout, *The Flight from Authority: Religion, Morality, and the Quest for Autonomy* (University of Notre Dame Press, 1981), pp. 118, 140, 146.

most Christian thinkers prior to the end of the second century, that our universe was created by God's bringing a particular type of order out of chaos.[40]

The necessity for this type of creation, involving a long evolutionary process, is explained in terms of the idea that creative power is essentially embodied in a world of finite actualities as well as in the divine actuality. The divine power, accordingly, is necessarily persuasive. It could not be coercive in the sense of unilaterally determining what happens in the world. This view provides the basis for a theodicy that defends the perfect goodness of our creator without minimizing the evil of our world.[41] The distinction between God and creativity provides, in fact, the basis for a robust doctrine of demonic evil, with the basic idea being that God's creation of human beings brought into existence a level of worldly creativity that not only could become diametrically opposed to the divine creativity, but also could do so with sufficient power to threaten divine purposes.[42] This view of the God–world relation also reconciles theism with the scientific community's naturalistic assumption that no events, however extraordinary, involve violations of the world's basic causal principles.[43]

The naturalism of this theism does not, however, prevent it from endorsing the assumption of Christian faith that God acts variably in the world, so that some events are "acts of God" in a special sense. The key idea here is that although divine action is formally the same in every event, it can differ radically in content, effectiveness, and, at the human level, the role it plays in the constitution of the self. On the basis of these ideas, reconstructive postmodern theologians have entered into the traditional discussion of how God was literally incarnate in Jesus, arguing for a position that overcomes the standard dichotomy of regarding Jesus as wholly "different in kind" or merely "different in degree" from other human beings.[44] They have also argued that this type of naturalism, with its variable divine

[40] Griffin, "Creation out of Nothing, Creation out of Chaos, and the Problem of Evil," in Stephen T. Davis, ed., *Encountering Evil*, 2nd edn (Philadelphia: Westminster/John Knox, 2001); Catherine Keller, *The Face of the Deep: A Theology of Becoming* (New York: Routledge, 2003).

[41] Griffin, "Creation out of Nothing"; *God, Power, and Evil: a Process Theodicy* (Philadelphia: Westminster, 1976); *Evil Revisited: Responses and Reconsiderations* (Albany: State University of New York Press, 1991).

[42] Marjorie Suchocki, *The Fall to Violence: Original Sin in Relational Theology* (New York: Continuum 1994); Griffin, *Evil Revisited*, pp. 31–33; "Why Demonic Power Exists: Understanding the Church's Enemy" and "Overcoming the Demonic: the Church's Mission," *Lexington Theological Review* 28 (1993), 223–60.

[43] Griffin, *Religion and Scientific Naturalism: Overcoming the Conflicts* (Albany: State University of New York Press, 2000).

[44] Cobb, *Christ in a Pluralistic Age*, chs. 7–10; *Postmodernism and Public Policy*, ch. 1.

influence, can, unlike neo-Darwinism, illuminate both the directionality and apparent jumps in the evolutionary process.[45] This form of liberal theology has thereby provided far more robust doctrines of divine creation and incarnation than found in *modern* liberal theologies.

This return to traditional concerns regarding divine creation and incarnation is sometimes accompanied by a return to ontological wrestling with the Christian idea of God as Trinitarian.[46] Such thinking, besides providing the basis for Christological reflection, has also been employed to relate Christian faith to other religions, especially insofar as the resulting Trinitarianism involves the distinction between God and creativity (or being itself), because this distinction provides for a form of religious pluralism that is quite different from that formulated by John Hick. Opposing the traditional Christian view that theistic religious experience, which has been dominant in Christianity, is basically veridical but nontheistic religious experience, which has been especially prevalent in Buddhism and Hinduism, is basically mistaken, Hick suggests that we think of ultimate reality in itself as a noumenal reality to which no substantive attributes can be assigned, which implies that both views are equally mistaken. Whiteheadian theologians, by contrast, are able to consider theistic and nontheistic religious experiences equally veridical. Rather than accepting Hick's assumption that all religions are oriented toward the same ultimate reality, they regard God as the *personal* ultimate and creativity as the *impersonal* ultimate. Doctrines based on theistic religious experience refer to the former, while doctrines based on nontheistic religious experience refer to the latter.[47]

This more pluralistic view of ideas about ultimate reality is correlated with a more pluralistic idea of salvation. Rather than holding, with Hick, that the various religions promote basically the same kind of salvation, Whiteheadians argue that different religions promote different types of salvation, a view that is now becoming more widespread.[48] Salvation as these theologians portray it in their own Christian thinking involves several dimensions. Whereas process theologians have always conceived of salvation as involving two dimensions – salvation as present liberation/wholeness

---

[45] Griffin, *Religion and Scientific Naturalism*, ch. 8.
[46] Joseph A. Bracken, SJ, and Marjorie Hewitt Suchocki (eds.), *Trinity in Process: a Relational Theology of God* (New York: Continuum, 1997).
[47] Cobb, *Beyond Dialogue: Toward a Mutual Transformation of Buddhism and Christianity* (Philadelphia: Fortress, 1982); *Transforming Christianity and the World: A Way beyond Absolutism and Relativism*, ed. Paul F. Knitter (Maryknoll, NY: Orbis, 1999); Griffin, *Reenchantment without Supernaturalism*, ch. 7.
[48] S. Mark Heim, *Salvations: Truth and Difference in Religion* (Maryknoll, NY: Orbis, 1995).

and as everlasting preservation in the divine experience (called by White-head "the consequent nature of God") – postmodern process theologians add two more dimensions: salvation as the reign of divine (rather than demonic) values on earth[49] and salvation as eventual sanctification in a life after death.[50] The affirmation of life after death is possible for this position, in spite of its rejection of supernaturalism and appeals to author-ity, because its rejection of sensationism, combined with its rejection of brain–mind identism, allows it to take seriously the empirical evidence for life after death.[51] It is this feature of reconstructive postmodern theology that is probably most important for its intention to provide a form of liberal theology that, by being sufficiently robust to be widely acceptable in the churches, can overcome modernity's liberal–conservative antithesis.[52]

THEOLOGY AND ETHICS

Equally important to its advocates is the desire to overcome the mod-ern separation, opposed by the various types of liberation theology, between theology and ethics. "A postmodern theology," it declares, "must be a liber-ation theology," which means, among other things, that doctrines of God, sin, and salvation must be articulated with "reference to the concrete sins from which God is presumably trying to save us."[53] One of these sins is certainly modern society's treatment of the earth, which has resulted in a global ecological crisis. Partly because of its panexperientialism, according to which individuals at all levels have intrinsic value and are internally re-lated to individuals at all other levels, Whiteheadian postmodern theology has devoted great attention to this issue from the time the human threat to the environment came into general consciousness.[54] Charles Birch's term

---

[49] Cobb, *Postmodernism and Public Policy*, ch. 1; Griffin, "Overcoming the Demonic."

[50] Cobb, *Christ in a Pluralistic Age*, chs. 11–16; "The Resurrection of the Soul," *Harvard Theo-logical Review* 80 (1987), 213–27; Griffin, *God and Religion*, ch. 6; *Evil Revisited*, pp. 34–40; *Reenchantment without Supernaturalism*, ch. 6.

[51] Griffin, *Parapsychology, Philosophy, and Spirituality: a Postmodern Exploration* (Albany: State University of New York Press, 1997); *Religion and Scientific Naturalism*, ch. 7.

[52] Cobb, *Christ in a Pluralistic Age*, pp. 15, 27; Griffin, *God and Religion*, pp. 2, 6; "Liberal but not Modern: Overcoming the Liberal–Conservative Antithesis," *Lexington Theological Quarterly* 28 (1993), 201–22.

[53] Griffin, "Postmodern Theology as Liberation Theology: a Response to Harvey Cox," Griffin, Beardslee, and Holland, *Varieties of Postmodern Theology*, pp. 81–94, at 81.

[54] Cobb, *Is it too Late? a Theology of Ecology* (Beverly Hills, CA: Bruce, 1972); Griffin, "White-head's Contributions to a Theology of Nature," *Bucknell Review* 20 (1972), 3–24; Charles Birch and Cobb, *The Liberation of Life: from the Cell to the Community* (Cambridge Univer-sity Press, 1981); Birch, *Confronting the Future* (1976; rev. edn, New York: Penguin Books, 1993); *Regaining Compassion for Humanity and Nature* (Kensington: New South Wales University Press, 1993); Jay B. McDaniel, *Of God and Pelicans: a Theology for the Reverence of Life* (Louisville: Westminster/John Knox, 1989).

for this perspective is, in fact, the "postmodern ecological world-view."[55] This term points to one of the most significant differences from Kant-based types of postmodernism, which, rather than overcoming the human alienation from nature fostered by modern dualism, intensify this alienation by portraying nature as simply a human construct.[56]

A closely related sin taken with utmost seriousness by postmodern process theologians is patriarchy, with Cobb suggesting that "[c]ulturally and intellectually, the most important movement of the twentieth century may prove to have been feminism."[57] Unlike those postmodernists who see the source of our problems as having arisen about four hundred years ago, Catherine Keller points out that feminists date it about four *thousand* years ago, when androcentric history began in earnest. She maintains, nevertheless, that feminism is a *conditio sine qua non* of any genuinely postmodern world.[58] As illustrated by Keller's writings and the recent endorsement of process theology by Carol Christ,[59] there are many features of this type of postmodern theology – including its rejection of divine power as unilateral determination, its emphasis on divine responsiveness, and its emphasis on internal relations, all of which cut against portraying the divine and the human in stereotypically masculine terms – that provide ontological support for cultural feminism, especially ecofeminism.

Closely related to this theology's support for both ecological and feminist liberation is its dedication to liberating the planet from modern economism, with its ideology of unending economic growth. Far from promoting the common good, this ideology, which has replaced nationalism as the global religion,[60] has undermined communities, destroyed the environment, and increased the gap between rich and poor.[61] Indeed, argues Cobb, it is through modern political and economic theory that modern thought, with its dualism and individualism, has had its most significant and harmful influence on our present situation.[62] A postmodern economic theory would be based on the (Whiteheadian) idea of "persons-in-community," with the

55 Birch, *On Purpose* (Kensington: New South Wales University Press, 1990), pp. xvi, 73–85, 114–37.
56 Cobb, *Postmodernism and Public Policy*, ch. 5.   57 Ibid., ch. 4.
58 Keller, "Toward a Postpatriarchal Postmodernity," in Griffin, ed., *Spirituality and Society*, pp. 63–80, at 64, 74.
59 Carol P. Christ, *Rebirth of the Goddess: Finding Meaning in Feminist Spirituality* (Reading, MA: Addison-Wesley, 1997), pp. 104–7.
60 Cobb, *The Earthist Challenge to Economism: a Theological Critique of the World Bank* (London: Macmillan, 1999), pp. 13–27.
61 Herman E. Daly, "The Steady-State Economy: Postmodern Alternative to Growthmania," in Griffin, ed., *Spirituality and Society*, pp. 107–22; Daly and Cobb, *For the Common Good: Redirecting the Economy Toward Community, the Environment, and a Sustainable Future*, 2nd edn (Boston: Beacon, 1994).
62 Cobb, *Postmodernism and Public Policy*, ch. 5.

community to which we are internally related being at least the entire living world.[63]

This theology also seeks liberation from the global political order distinctive of modernity. One feature of this order that has been opposed is its militarism, which now includes nuclearism.[64] But the more general feature of the modern world order is the system of sovereign states, rooted in the Peace of Westphalia of 1648 and early modern political theorists such as Hugo Grotius and Thomas Hobbes. This international anarchy not only provides the permitting cause of militarism, it is argued, but also prevents solutions to four other problems equally interlocked with the global economy: the global ecological crisis, global apartheid, massive human rights abuses, and the undermining of national and local democracies.[65] The transcendence of this order with a postmodern world would require the creation of democracy at the global level. The Christian rationale for global democracy is that it is a necessary condition for a world ruled by divine rather than demonic values, for which Christians pray every time we repeat the Lord's prayer.[66]

Further reading

Bracken, Joseph A. and Marjorie Hewitt Suchocki, eds., *Trinity in Process: A Relational Theology of God* (New York: Continuum, 1997).

Cobb, John B., Jr., *Christ in a Pluralistic Age* (Philadelphia: Westminster, 1975).

Griffin, David Ray, *God and Religion in the Postmodern World* (State University of New York Press, 1988).

Keller, Catherine and Anne Daniell, eds., *Process and Difference: Between Cosmological and Poststructuralist Postmodernisms* (Albany: State University of New York Press, 2002).

Whitehead, Alfred North, *Process and Reality: an Essay in Cosmology*, corr. edn, eds. David Ray Griffin and Donald W. Sherburne (New York: Free Press, 1978).

---

[63] Cobb, "From Individualism to Persons in Community: a Postmodern Economic Theory," Griffin, ed., *Sacred Interconnections*, pp. 123–42; *Postmodernism and Public Policy*, ch. 5; Daly and Cobb, *For the Common Good*, ch. 8.

[64] Keller, "Warriors, Women, and the Nuclear Complex: Toward a Postnuclear Postmodernity," in Griffin, ed., *Sacred Interconnections*, pp. 63–82; Griffin, "Peace and the Postmodern Paradigm," *Spirituality and Society*, pp. 143–54; "Imperialism, Nuclearism, and Postmodern Theism," *God and Religion*, 127–45.

[65] Griffin, *Beyond Plutocracy, Imperialism, and Terrorism: the Need for Global Democracy* (forthcoming).

[66] Griffin, "Overcoming the Demonic," 257–59.

7 Feminist theology

MARY McCLINTOCK FULKERSON

Even with all their diversity, feminist, womanist, and *mujerista* theologies have one thing in common: they make the liberation of women central to the theological task.[1] This is not to say that there is complete consensus concerning the ends of such liberation. For example, feminists who argue that the flourishing of women is achieved by resistance to sexism are criticized by those who claim that such patterns unduly privilege the category of gender. Despite these conflicts, however, feminist, womanist, and *mujerista* theologians have historically shared a general liberation hermeneutic, marked, at least in part, by commitments around identity.[2] Rather than positioning themselves as generic "theology," these works emerged out of situations of oppression for marginalized groups that initiated critical assessments of existing social, ecclesial, and theological structures. The result has been liberative interpretive practices crafted from new combinations of the tradition and contemporary resources.[3]

Postmodernism enters this theological discourse by providing resources designed to advance such liberative ends.[4] The primary litmus for any postmodernism will be its contribution to analyses of the complexities of gender,

---

[1] Despite some uses, "feminist" is not generic for any theology about women. "Womanist" refers to African American women's use of Alice Walker's notion of the distinct experiences of black feminists. *Mujerista* theologies work from the lived experience of US Latinas. Postmodernism helps with these issues, as I will explain later.

[2] "Marked" theology has a qualifier. "Unmarked" references are judged to be generic and universal (even if they are not). That "she" or "womankind" can (still) not be generic indicates its "marked" status. People "of color" are marked – judged to be the people who have "race," while white people are without race, unmarked, and thus the norm. These statuses reflect a group's power.

[3] For the liberation hermeneutical circle see Juan Segundo, SJ, *The Liberation of Theology*, trans. John Dury (Maryknoll, NY: Orbis, 1976), p. 8; Elisabeth Schüssler Fiorenza, *Bread Not Stone: The Challenge of Feminist Biblical Interpretation* (Boston: Beacon Press, 1984), pp. 43–63.

[4] Dick Hebdige observes that being undefinable makes "pomo" a buzzword. However, the multiplicity of its referents ("the décor of a room ... fashion ... the attack on the 'metaphysics of presence' ... broad societal and economic shifts into a 'media,' 'consumer' or 'multinational' phase," etc.) is not damning: "the more complexly and contradictorily nuanced a word is, the more likely it is to have formed the focus for historically significant debates," Dick Hebdige,

race, sexual, and class oppressions.[5] What is "post" about such resources is their refusal of some of the "modern" habits in theology, but only those that inhibit exploration of these conditions of oppression. Feminist, womanist, and *mujerista* theological concerns with power, conflict, and desire dictate that certain critiques of modernism are not particularly useful. For example, theologies that focus on the distinctiveness of Christian identity to correct perceived destabilizing effects of modern historical–critical theologies are unpopular with liberation feminists.[6] The concern with the organic, communal linguistic holism of Christian identity in postliberal theologies associated with George Lindbeck is not conducive to attention to power, conflict, and desire, the inevitable ingredients in the struggles addressed by feminist, womanist and *mujerista* theologies.[7] The metaphors of language learning and grammar in his cultural–linguistic model are pale tools at best for deciphering the disorderly social realities of oppression/liberation.

What we do find in liberation-focused feminist theologies are appropriations of philosophical forms of postmodernism, such as Foucaldian critiques of the modern subject and modern notions of power, Lacanian/psychoanalytic accounts of the desiring subject, and post-structuralist/deconstructionist thought, all of which articulate refusals of unified and totalizing modern accounts of reason. While those forms associated with post-structuralism and deconstruction draw criticism for being unstable, increasingly feminists have seen interesting possibilities in these destabilizations.

Three themes have emerged amongst postmodern feminist thinking that are useful to feminist theologies: (1) the instability of the subject, (2) the force of the "unsayable, the unrepresentable as it constitutes and ruptures all that is said," as one theological student of postmodernism puts it, and (3) the liberative implications of these ideas when applied to the category

---

"Staking out the Posts," in *Hiding in the Light: On Images and Things* (London and New York: Routledge), pp. 181–82. Since a comprehensive definition would be impossible, I will merely attend to the elements of postmodernism useful to feminist theology.

5 Not every form of "postmodernism" appears in feminist, womanist, and *mujerista* theological thinking. A helpful account of different post-structuralisms and postmodernisms is Scott Lash, *Post-Structuralist and Post-Modernist Sociology* (Brookfield, Vermont: Edward Elgar Publishing, 1991).

6 Figures like George Lindbeck, James W. McClendon, and Stanley Hauerwas do not identify as "postmodern," but are so designated by being critics of modern theology.

7 One account of postmodern theology includes only one feature (critiques of representational–expressivist language theories) found in feminist postmodernisms, but without its necessary connection to themes of power, desire and the irruption of the "outside." See Nancey Murphy and James Wm. McClendon, Jr. "Distinguishing Modern and Postmodern Theologies," *Modern Theology* 5 (1989), 191–214.

of gender.[8] Exploring these will produce a fuller picture of postmodernism, as well as its implications for theological discourse.

BACKGROUND DEVELOPMENTS

A brief rehearsal of developments in US feminist thinking brings the postmodern themes into view. Throughout the second wave of US feminism (1960s–1980s) both secular and religious feminisms depended upon a common sense notion of woman as a unified, historical subject. Since women had been ignored, rendered invisible, and marginalized throughout history, feminist work of this period was designed to correct these problems. It typically took the forms of historical retrieval, efforts at political, social and economic enfranchisement, and scrutiny of the formerly invisible domains of domesticity, sexuality, sexual violence, and reproduction.

Key to much of this thinking was recognition of the constructed nature of gender in the production of masculinity and femininity. What was taken to be liberating about the concept "gender" was the idea that social identity is a construction used to locate persons in relation to power; it gave feminists leverage to counter the biologistic and determinist accounts of maleness and femaleness that locate men and women "naturally." If this social defining and locating was taken to be mere convention, it could be changed; insofar as it was to the disadvantage of women, it could be argued that it was morally problematic.

No sooner had this second wave begun than complaints emerged that its primary subject, woman, was modeled after a white, middle-class, heterosexual woman. Secular and religious thinkers alike, Audrey Lorde, bell hooks, Ntozake Shange, Alice Walker, Katie Cannon, and Delores Williams among others, focused attention on such issues. Important ethical–political implications resulted from these conversations, such as the discovery that when the focus is women of color, reproductive issues other than access to abortion surface, such as sterilization abuse.[9] As a consequence, the experiences and wisdoms of African American, Latina, Asian American, lesbian, and other groups of women gradually became standard additions to feminist conversations.[10]

---

[8] Graham Ward, "Postmodern Theology," in David F. Ford, ed., *The Modern Theologians: An Introduction to Christian Theology in the Twentieth Century*, 2nd edn (Cambridge, MA: Blackwell Publishers, 1997), p. 588.
[9] Angela Yvonne Davis, *Women, Culture, & Politics* (New York: Random House, 1989).
[10] While this is false as a story of "latecomers" to the issues of feminism – women of color had been organizing and "doing theology" concurrently with whitefeminists – it is an oft-told tale that does refer to the (limited) discourse of the academy.

Some features of this scenario can be found in the theologies of Mary Daly, Sallie McFague, Rosemary Radford Ruether, Letty Russell, (early) Elisabeth Schüssler Fiorenza, Judith Plaskow, and other of the groundbreaking feminist theologians of the twentieth century.[11] These writers assumed a natural biological subject, woman, who had been erased from history, oppressed by a misogynist Christian tradition and society. Their work recovered women agents, critiqued their religious traditions, and formed constructive imaginative alternatives for liberation. These theologies were by and large about liberation from multiple forms of oppression, understood as social sin. Although often construed as the primary sin, sexism was not their only concern; racism, class exploitation, and increasingly heterosexism were key to the concerns of feminist theologies.

Paralleling the critiques brought against non-religious feminist thinking, the works of womanist theologians, such as Delores Williams, Katie Cannon, Jacquelyne Grant, and *mujerista* theologians, such as Ada Maria Isasi-Díaz, Yolanda Tarango, and other non-Western and non-hetero women's theologies helped this process along by challenging the implicit universal woman assumed by feminist theologies. As a result, no feminist theologian could omit reference to the additional problems of race, class, and sexuality by the later years of the second wave, even as in most cases these problems were add-ons to gender.[12]

In addition to the multiple voices complicating secular and religious feminism, a crucial shift occurred in secular feminist thinking in the transition from the 1980s to the 1990s that has called into question the identity politics of most feminisms. Identity politics is a frame of thinking characteristic of many progressive movements. It assumes that one's identity is defined by a marker of social advantage/disadvantage. For feminist identity politics, the primary marker is gender. Thus difference between women is dealt with by multiplying the markers of disadvantage; "woman" is a plurality of subjects, each specified by an identity marker added on to gender. This account is challenged by the discovery that gender is not a constant, self-identical marker. Some women, Aristotelian slaves, for example, simply had no gender, because to have the status of a "woman" in ancient Greece

---

[11] I am limiting my account to Christian and Jewish, but mainly Christian. Beverly Harrison, Margaret Farley, Carter Heyward, Carol Meyers, Ross Kraemer, and Bernadette Brooten did key restorative work for women in Judaism.

[12] Whitefeminists Susan B. Thistlethwaite and Sharon Welch took issues of race/gender head on. See Thistlethwaite, *Sex, Race and God: Christian Feminism in Black and White* (New York: Crossroads, 1989) and Welch, *A Feminist Ethic of Risk*, rev. edn (Minneapolis: Fortress Press, 2000). Appeal to "women" is not outdated; it is a necessary practice. Postmodernist exploration is a new form of investigation, not the erasure of references to men and women.

one had to be a free woman married to a man (defined as free citizen).[13] Gender, then, is not one thing, but is co-constituted by other relations of power.

The shift away from gender as a stable grid of analysis is further complicated by the work of Judith Butler, among others. Pluralizing woman (or genders) to account for differences is for Butler not enough. As long as the construction of gender leaves sex intact, critical analysis is incomplete. Feminism can no longer assume that sex is simply a fixed, anatomical feature of human identity, yielding the (natural) binary man and woman. Nor is sexual identity an inner truth of subjectivity. In fact, Butler argued, a Foucaldian discursive power regime maintains a tight but constructed causal connection between (binary) sex, gender, and properly directed desire for the opposite sex. The constant reiteration or performance of this regime of sex/gender/desire and not the natural outworking of innate identity and desire reproduces heterosexual subjects. Feminist reiteration of "woman," then, effectively "others" or occludes any other subject possibilities.[14] Just this effect leads some to reject homosexuality, based upon the argument that it is a concept that mirrors heterosexuality rather than contesting it. The result is "queer theory," a project designating alternatives to heterosexuality that are not bound to notions of fixed sexual identities.[15]

This brief account of developments in feminist theory is incomplete and oversimplified. The methods and assumptions of the great variety of feminisms, early and more recent, still circulate and overlap. However, the move to theorization of subjects that began in the 1990s has created a distinctive set of explorations. Importantly, such efforts attempt to move feminism beyond the additive strategies of the first decades of second-wave feminism. These theoretical explorations expose the problematic character of considering race, gender, class, sexuality, and other markers as definitional for separate identities, thereby facilitating inquiries into how race, gender, class, sexuality, etc. are co-constitutive of *all* subjects. No subjects, then, are simply a compilation of additive identities, but are rather produced by differently configured contextual systems and practices.

These challenges to the naturally gendered subject correspond to theoretical conversations on postmodernism outside of feminism that critique

---

[13] Elisabeth Spelman, *Inessential Woman: Problems of Exclusion in Feminist Thought* (Boston: Beacon Press, 1988).

[14] Judith Butler, *Gender Trouble: Feminism and the Subversion of Identity* (New York: Routledge, 1990).

[15] See Eve K. Sedgwick, *Epistemology of the Closet* (Berkeley, CA: University of California Press, 1990); Kathy Rudy, *Sex and the Church: Gender, Homosexuality and the Transformation of Christian Ethics* (Boston: Beacon Press, 1997), pp. 92–107; Laurel Schneider, "Queer Theory," in A. K. M. Adam, ed., *Handbook of Postmodern Biblical Interpretation*, pp. 206–12.

the modern subject. And, while such connections still evoke for some the fear of the loss of "woman," for many feminist thinkers destabilization of the unified subject is about the advance of one of its primary concerns, i.e., the connection of gender to multiple regimes of power. Thus its usefulness to liberative ventures is secured.[16]

THE INSTABILITY OF THE FEMINIST THEOLOGICAL SUBJECT

The challenges to the naturally gendered subject from secular feminist postmodernism raise the first theme for feminist theological appropriation of postmodernism, i.e., the instability of the gendered subject. Before proceeding, however, it bears remarking that theologians' use of work like Butler's is not a complete departure from what feminist theologians were already doing. From the beginning, feminist theology was a refusal of a certain kind of modern subject, for example, the unmarked falsely generic (male) subject that dominated theology. Thus, something like a destabilizing of the male subject is going on in the work of foremothers Ruether, Russell, Daly, and McFague. Womanists and *mujeristas* contested the "modern" unmarked woman of whitefeminists. However, the difference between these earlier models and postmodern feminist theologies is the fact that the latter call into question the unified natural woman subject. With this questioning come new ways of thinking about the relation of gender (and other markers) and power to language, including the expansion of the destabilizing factors to include desire and the unconscious, visceral register of subjectivity.[17]

One important avenue into the complexities of subjectivity is the vehicle of language, particularly with theories about the undecidability of meaning.[18] Questioning representational and expressivist theories of language, recent feminist theologies appropriate post-structuralist accounts to unmask the unfixed, political nature of signifying. In one way these accounts add to the rich work of feminist theologians on symbols, metaphors and models; in another they are at odds with these models, because they are based upon philosophical assumptions that there is no deeper "real

---

[16] For Butler's rebuttal to the fear that post-structuralism reduces reality to language, see *Bodies That Matter: On the Discursive Limits of "Sex"* (New York: Routledge, 1993).

[17] "Visceral" invokes feminist concern with bodies and the prelinguistic domain of disgust, fear and loathing which constitutes and disrupts experience. Lacanian-based views are related to psychosexual development. For its role in social change, see postmodern political theorist William Connolly, *Why I am Not a Secularist* (Minneapolis: University of Minnesota Press, 1999), pp. 1–29.

[18] Post-structuralisms differ; some concern language with Saussure as forebear (Derrida), others are connected with language, but focus more on desire (Lacan, Foucault).

meaning" to be gotten. Postmodern accounts of language, such as post-structuralism, are alternatives to modern representational theories. Post-structuralism has roots in structuralist thinking which understands language as a function of relations rather than positive references. Linguist Ferdinand de Saussure said that signs are constituted in linguistic systems within which meaning is produced by differences (from phonemic differences, like "bat" and "cat," to semantic differences, as in "woman" and "man").[19] While **post**-structuralism moves beyond Saussure's structures, which seem to close meaning, the benefit of both is to highlight the conventional nature of signifying: signs do not match up with things, but direct one to other signs and require analyzes of the effects of meaning, especially the exclusions, as post-structuralists insist.

Rebecca Chopp's *The Power to Speak: Feminism, Language, God*, for example, does feminist theology by exploring language as constitutive of the social–symbolic order.[20] Theology cannot be treated apart from the political. Since all language is unstable and connected to desire and power, theological referents must be traced to the social–political discourses of the systems that constitute women. Chopp's work traces out the semiotic processes of the closed monotheistic patriarchal ordering of society and the oppressive relations it sustains, revealing how accounts of language which allow "God" or divine authority to function as guarantor of a closed system of theological meaning obscure the relations of power and interest. The post-structuralist bent of her theory directs Chopp to the openings and fissures that appear in any structure. At those fissures, those who occupy the "margins" are potential sources for new emancipatory discourses, not because of their inner truths or natures, but because of their positionality. As a disruption of the dominant ordering logic of man/woman, then, specific women's practices create breaks in asymmetrical gender systems. Rather than look for the "real feminist meaning" of a Christian symbol, Chopp reappropriates the Christian theme of "Word" in a post-structuralist mode. The Word is a "perfectly open sign" a reminder to feminist, womanist, and other theologies of the danger of "monotheistic ordering" and constant need for new emancipatory discourses. Chopp offers a newly constructive recognition of the life-giving character of ordinary women's practices.

My *Changing the Subject: Women's Discourses and Feminist Theology* argues that post-structuralism connected to power analysis can open to view

---

[19] Ferdinand de Saussure's notion of the sign as arbitrary was crucial to the development of post-structuralism, of which Jacques Derrida's critique of the metaphysics of presence is exemplary. For their similarities, see Philip Lewis, "The Poststructuralist Condition," *Diacritics* 12 (1982), 2–22. Also Jane Tompkins, "A Short Course in Poststructuralism," *College English* 50 (November, 1988).

[20] Rebecca Chopp, *The Power to Speak: Feminism, Language, God* (New York: Crossroad, 1989).

subjects that are missed by feminist theology, with its modern accounts of language, gender and power.[21] Different and intersecting discursive regimes produce different subjects called "women." Replacing an assumed natural "woman" with the concept of "subject position" allows thinking about the subject "woman" as "positioned" or located and produced by different cultural conventions, religious traditions, and access to resources. These regimes create different forms of "subjection" (Foucault), but also new significations that become openings for change. Poor, white Pentecostal women are positioned differently than white, middle-class Presbyterian women or progressive academic feminists. Pressures from economic marginalization and anti-institutional, performance-centered religious traditions combine such that even the complementary gendering Pentecostals share with middle-class Presbyterian women produces a different subject position. Resistance to the subjections of their location for both will have a different look from the discursive strategies of a feminist like Mary Daly of the professional managerial class, whose (early) radical parodic anti-theology proclaims the death of God the Father. Taking subject positions seriously means that the feminist account of the sexist character of the Bible and particular gendered configurations like "father God" in the tradition have to be further complicated in relation to the differences in women's social locations. Important questions emerge from post-structuralism that go beyond the destabilizing of the fixed subject, including the need to question fixed texts and fixed notions of what is liberative in theological thinking.

There is no "real" woman subject lurking behind the discursive constructions of my account of these subject positions – something they all have in common – and that is the point. However, there is more than multivalent signifying processes to be identified in the destabilizing forces that constitute subjects. Desire and the unconscious are crucial elements in the destabilization of subjects, and a number of feminist theologians agree with Chopp that such figures as Kristeva help develop analyzes of the complex interplay of language, desire, and power.

Important theological writing appropriating the work of French feminists Julia Kristeva, Luce Irigaray, and Hélène Cixous, draws out the implications of the unconscious and its repressions for the formation of the subject. The crucial background figure for French feminism is Jacques Lacan, a French psychoanalyst who uses post-structuralism to reinterpret Freud. Lacan makes it possible for feminists to understand the primacy of the phallus as a function of a hegemonic signifying order that is inextricably tied to

---

[21] Mary McClintock Fulkerson, *Changing the Subject: Women's Discourses and Feminist Theology* (Minneapolis: Fortress Press, 1994).

desire and lack. They then explore the difference sexual difference makes in its constitutive relation to language. In an important collection of essays, *Transfigurations: Theology and the French Feminists*, authors explore the relation between theology and the instability constituted by these prelinguistic domains of psychosexual experience. Through these domains French feminists expand the postmodern concern with the other – that which is "outside" the dominant systems – frequently identifying "woman" as the repressed other, a theme with strong resonance for theologians. Despite debates over the possible essentialism of these thinkers, the exploration of the crucial role of the visceral dimensions of coming to be a subject is an undeniable contribution. Not only is language associated with repression and with women's bodies, the addition of the visceral recognizes that fear and revulsion constitute the spectrum of corporeal responsiveness and thus are inextricably connected to human "knowledge" of the other. Kristeva's concept of the "abject," for example, refers to the dimension of that lack in all subjects that invokes intolerable connections with death and animality, from taboos against food and bodily sexual acts to that of human waste.[22] Nowhere is this contribution clearer than in its pertinence to issues of violence, as seen in use of Kristeva to explore women and violence by such authors as Martha Reineke, Amy Hollywood, and Elizabeth Grosz.[23]

THE RUPTURING "OUTSIDE"

The constitutive character of language in several of these accounts should not be confused with a kind of causal determinism (as Butler is quick to point out.)[24] It is important to distinguish between social constructionism, where feminists are saying that a complementary view of gender causally defines women as emotional, nurturing, and so forth, and a postmodern (or post-structuralist) view. The latter view, and thus the difference, is indicated in my second theme, the role of the unsayable and the unrepresentable in constituting and rupturing all that is said. This theme is prefigured by the feminist concern with the unconscious; it is helpful to explain it in relation to a post-structuralist account of signifying.

---

[22] Julia Kristeva, *Powers of Horror: An Essay on Abjection*, trans. Leon S. Roudiez (New York: Columbia University Press, 1982.)

[23] Martha Reineke, *Sacrificed Lives: Kristeva on Women and Violence* (Bloomington: Indiana University Press, 1997); Amy Hollywood, "Violence and Subjectivity: Wuthering Heights, Julia Kristeva, and Feminist Theology," in C. W. Maggie Kim, Susan M. St. Ville, and Susan M. Simonaitis, eds., *Transfigurations: Theology and the French Feminists* (Minneapolis: Fortress, 1993), pp. 81–108; Elizabeth Grosz, *Sexual Subversions: Three French Feminists* (Sydney: Allen & Unwin, 1989).

[24] Butler, *Bodies That Matter: On the Discursive Limits of "Sex"* (New York: Routledge, 1993).

Signifying does not refer to a fixed, external reality in post-structuralism. What gives a term positive meaning is a contrast – a differential that is necessary to the meaning but cannot itself be said. This "outside" operates as a foundation of sorts by holding concrete meaning in place and becomes a kind of "metaphor for understanding or intelligibility itself," as Jane Tompkins puts it.[25] For example, if "man" gets its meaning from its contrast with "woman," as opposed to a match with an extradiscursive body, then "woman" is "not-man" and functions as a sort of "outside" that holds up or constitutes the boundary of maleness. Many theorists think of that "outside" as a politically repressed or occluded reality that is necessary to the "said," just as homosexuality is the necessary "outside" to heteronormativity.

On such a view a position cannot be attained that breaks free of the exclusionary gesture.[26] Any production of meaning depends upon "outside" (rejected) meanings for its unity. There is a bind here that distinguishes this form of postmodernism from the second wave notion that gender is a construction. As liberating as it has been, the construction of gender can imply an analytic and causally defining agency that is free from the web of exclusion. Post-structuralists would say this view renders invisible the "unsayable," the "outside" that a construction itself depends upon. The point here is to recognize a bondage-like dimension to discourse. Post-structuralism forces the admission that no place is free from the exclusionary. Once again, it reminds feminist theologians of the unavoidable political effects of feminist discourse.[27]

The first two themes of postmodernism in feminist theology lead to the third. The destabilized subject complicated by language, desire, and power, is not an entity, a substance, but a relation or sets of relations. Identity is always forged out of differences, and the notion of differences is not confined to signs. Signs depend upon an "outside," an excluded or the unsayable. Systems and social–symbolic orders do as well. It is a short step from construing the semantic and phonetic difference that supports a contrast to thinking of the "outside" as the other, or marginalized populations. The other or outside is not only excluded, but threatens always to "disrupt" the unity that conceals it, as Graham Ward puts it, particularly when the force of the unconscious and its desires come into play. Thus the two themes

[25] Tompkins, "Short Course," p. 739.
[26] See Mary McClintock Fulkerson, "Contesting the Gendered Subject: A Feminist Account of the *Imago Dei*," in Rebecca S. Chopp and Sheila Greeve Davaney, eds., *Horizons in Feminist Theology: Identity, Tradition, and Norms* (Minneapolis: Fortress Press, 1997), pp. 103–7.
[27] Serene Jones, "Bounded Openness: Postmodernism, Feminism, and the Church Today," *Interpretation* 55 (2001), 52–54.

conspire to raise the question of gender anew. If "woman" cannot be a sign that exists outside of relation, constituted by an outside, how might feminist discourse itself operate with a form of othering?

FEMINIST THEOLOGY AND GENDER (TROUBLE?)

As the work of secular feminists such as Butler portends, the central unifying term of feminism, "woman," is troubled and disrupted by the themes of postmodernism. To make "woman" the central figure of these liberation theologies not only invokes the binary man–woman and the heterosexual regime of sex and desire, but also calls gender, the central marker of identity for feminist theology, into question. Clearly some feminist theologies take this seriously. However, more work is needed. Ellen Armour's coinage of "whitefeminism" is a crucial reminder that the "outside" of the focus on gender is (still) the notion of race.[28] If gender can be the marker of one's identity, one is presumably without race. To have gender as one's primary identity sets up a center, an essential woman, that locates other women at the margin. Extending Derrida's "difference" with Irigaray's sexual difference, Armour shows ways in which race is continually elided in the feminist theological invocation of woman. Just as Butler is right that "woman" sets into play the heterosexist regime of sex-gender-desire, the feminist gender regime is linked to a system of racial othering as well. Feminist theology, then, is founded on an other that disrupts the unity, "woman," when we can be made to see the (invisible) marker of race privilege.

While neither the need to speak of "woman" nor the usefulness of gender will disappear, such practices need supplementation by notions of gender that do not stand alone.[29] A number of redefinitions from feminist theories appear promising on this: from Butler's notion of gender as performance, the notion of many genders (extending Spelman), "'woman' as a position within a set of power relationships" (Diana Fuss), to a revised Sartrean social collectivity where gender is "material effects and collectivized habits" (Iris Young). Susan Friedman speaks of a new "geographics of identity," where the move away from fixedness is captured in images of spatialization, ranging, and moving. Thus are added borderland and hybrid

---

[28] Ellen T. Armour, *Deconstruction, Feminist Theology, and the Problem of Difference: Subverting the Race/Gender Divide* (University of Chicago Press, 1999). Even feminist theologies, such as my own, which appropriate postmodernism are critiqued.

[29] Sharon Welch sees a constructive function in whitefeminists' appeal to their experience for women of color. "Sporting Power: American Feminism, French Feminisms, and an Ethic of Conflict" in *Transfigurations*, pp. 171–98.

to images of subject position.[30] Donna Haraway's important work on the un-decidability of the human and nonhuman is pursued by feminist theologian Elaine Graham, who investigates religion and cyborg identity.[31] While the constructive redefining will surely continue, minimally, a definition must achieve something like Lisa Disch's definition: gender is a "social process of differentiation that assigns meaning to categories such as race, ethnicity, nationality and class from their interrelationship – even if they seem to be standing alone."[32] Important work by feminist Jewish thinkers on sexual-ized figuring of "the Jew" suggests that religion, too, is a key category in this configuration.[33] In short, to continue to define gender only as binary sex-differentiation is to be fooled by a process of power.

With the postmodern challenges to gender come clarifications of an ambiguity that plagues accounts of feminist theology and the "embarrassed etc.," as Butler would put it, of the additional list of identity theologies such as womanist and *mujerista* theologies, among others. By virtue of the ex-clusions surfaced in these postmodern themes, the possibility that feminist theology can stand for all theologies by and about women is called into question in a new way. This chapter focuses predominantly on (Christian) feminists who write explicitly with postmodernist themes; they have turned out to be whitefeminists whose work, particularly insofar as it stays focused on unraced gender, needs more disruption. By definition, theologians such as Ada Maria Isasi-Díaz, Delores Williams, and other feminists of color are constantly positioned by whitefeminism as add-ons. Consequently they write as destabilizers (even postmoderns?) insofar as they are always need-ing to position their accounts as "not white."[34] Turning the tables on the false generic of whitefeminism, some suggestive proposals image the func-tion of inclusiveness through terms associated with women of color. Karen Baker-Fletcher, for example, uses the term "sisterist" to incorporate her womanism into a term for solidarity with women of other religions, eth-nicity, race, and sexual orientation. Out of her work on the construction of

---

[30] Susan Stanford Friedman, *Mappings: Feminism and the Cultural Geographies of Encounter* (Princeton University Press, 1998).

[31] Elaine Graham, "Becoming Divine in a Cyberfeminist Age," *Information, Communication & Society* 2:4 (1999), 419–38.

[32] Lecture. See Disch's "On Friendship in Dark Times," in Bonnie Honig, ed., *Feminist Interpretations of Hannah Arendt* (University Park, PA: Pennsylvania State University Press, 1995).

[33] Daniel Boyarin, Jay Geller, Susannah Heschel, Ellen Umansky, Naomi Seidman, Ann Pelle-grini, Laura Levitt, among others.

[34] This does not rule out other forms of exclusion in their writing. But for reasons why Third World peoples should avoid postmodernism see Leonardo Boff, "Modernity/Postmodernity," in Virginia Fabella and R. S. Sugirtharajah, eds., *Dictionary of Third World Theologies* (Maryknoll: Orbis Books, 2000), pp. 146–48.

whiteness, Thandeka speaks of a day in the future when the universal term will be people "of color."[35]

Future strategies must offer new ways to think gender/race/class/religion/sexuality together even as strategic practices in which naturalized language about "real" singular identities continues, too.[36] The benefit will be deepened understanding of the conditions that constrain us all, even in different ways. Just as the attention to women of color in the first wave brought to awareness the very different stakes of social policies for white, middle-class women and African American women, the postmodern interrogations allow the deeply embedded, invisible complicities to surface. But they also yield new ways to live and flourish in ambiguous zones that cannot be simply labeled "liberated" or "oppressed."[37] Ironically this postmodern reminder of the exclusionary effects of all discourse might reveal undeniable connections in a way that does not claim a homogenizing and false common sisterhood.

GROWING EDGES

Feminist, womanist and *mujerista* work also expands postmodernist thinking by connecting discourse analysis with the economic and the political. Elizabeth Bounds' work on community uses Raymond Williams and Habermas to relate critiques of modernity to critiques of global capitalism. She shows how theological/ethical proposals for community that fail to recognize attendant material relations reinforce the homogeneity of the professional managerial class and invite nostalgia. Bounds finds resources in feminist and womanist proposals even as she presses them to do more.[38]

Another effort prefers the postmodernism of Italian philosopher Gianni Vattimo over Derrida as an antidote to the metaphysics of presence. Marta Frascati-Lochhead commends Vattimo-style nihilism because it serves as an index of the end of metaphysics and to prefigure emancipation. Such

---

[35] Karen Baker-Fletcher, *Sisters of Dust, Sisters of Spirit: Womanist Wordings on God and Creation* (Minneapolis: Fortress Press, 1998), pp. 8–11. Thandeka, *Learning to be White: Money, Race, and God in America* (New York: Continuum, 1999).

[36] All theories "falsify" reality – necessarily – in order to advance a practice. Anthony Appiah shows how language about individual agency (unified subjects) might be wrong in terms of theory about social structures (subjected subject positions), but "right" in another region of reality. See "Tolerable Falsehoods: Agency and the Interests of Theory," in Jonathan Arac and Barbara Johnson, eds., *Consequences of Theory* (Baltimore, MD: Johns Hopkins University Press, 1991), pp. 63–90.

[37] Along with Baker-Fletcher, Sharon Welch is adept at reconceiving the opposition liberation–oppression. See her *Sweet Dreams in America: Making Ethics and Spirituality Work* (New York: Routledge, 1999).

[38] Elizabeth M. Bounds, *Coming Together/Coming Apart: Religion, Community, and Modernity* (New York: Routledge, 1997).

freedom responds to modernity's global capitalism and the reduction of Being to exchange value. Partially begun by feminist Christianity, the response is complete only when Christianity accepts its own mortality – destabilization as kenosis, the end of the self-emptying God of caritas. Both Bounds and Frascati-Lochhead's projects initiate a necessary inquiry into the ways in which language and gender are connected to power that is material. The impact of global technological communication on theological discourse, that is, the social relations effected by the economic as well as the political and cultural, is a destabilized reality that requires continued theological attention.[39]

Another feminist theology treats postmodernism as a phenomenon of material relations, but also looks at relations of power in the erotic of Christian discourse. Marcella Althaus-Reid's *Indecent Theology* advocates a new "body-paradigm" that comes not "from the European Other, but from Argentinean women lemon vendors, who embrace in their lives the economic and sexual connotations of the survivors of the destruction of the Grand narrative of Latin America."[40] She destabilizes theological meanings by connecting them to the desperate poverty of Latina women and also by exposing what liberationists have overlooked, the sexual nature of the Christian tradition. Appropriating postmodern refusals of origins and faithfulness as repetition, indecent theology "undresses and uncovers sexuality and economy at the same time." It refuses gender binaries, employing queer theory to expose problems like homosocial consent in the work of liberation theologians, designed to perpetuate patriarchy and homophobia. Performing her analysis throughout the text, Althaus-Reid maintains that the irruption of the obscene (Lacan) in indecent theology allows this alienation to appear but with emancipatory possibilities. To do otherwise continues the expropriation of the suffering of the people, turning it into a product that contains reality. Decent theology, then, is like going to bed with God without having real sex.

BUT IS IT THEOLOGY?

Accounting for the theological character of this work is a task dependent upon the operative definition of theology. For certain views of revelation feminist, womanist and *mujerista* work is simply unintelligible. For theology that interprets historical liberation as manifestation of God's reality,

---

[39] Marta Frascati-Lochhead, *Kenosis and Feminist Theology: The Challenge of Gianni Vattimo* (Albany: State University of New York Press, 1998).

[40] Marcella Althaus-Reid, *Indecent Theology: Theological Per/versions in Sex, Gender and Politics* (New York: Routledge, 2002).

however, feminist theological uses of postmodernism make important con-tributions, a few of which bear mention. First there is crafting of constructive traditional theological concerns in light of postmodern themes. Defining doctrine as the mapping of Christian life and scripts for its performance Serene Jones takes up classic Reformed doctrines in light of feminist theo-retical proposals.[41] Of particular interest is her feminist reading of sanctifi-cation and justification juxtaposed with strategic essentialism, a pragmatic resolution of the essentialist–constructivist debate. While refusing to col-lapse the two, the juxtaposition proves disclosive and constructive. The Christian's experience of being loved/supported by God outside of any nat-ural identity combined with the need to critique concrete identities when they are deforming – her reading of sanctification/justification – is analo-gous to the feminist need for strategic (normative) accounts of "woman" along with the refusal of any and all deforming "identity politics." Jones' comparisons begin work rarely seen when the primary interest is what the-ology might learn from secular feminist theory.What might each gain from the other?

Kathryn Tanner uses postmodern versions of culture theory to rethink a feminist theological doctrine of tradition. Theorists Raymond Williams, Stuart Hall, Foucault, Laclau, and Mouffe have moved beyond orthodox Marxism to appreciate the political character of culture. Assuming post-structuralist views on the instability of cultural meanings, they expose the fluidity of culture, its temporary stabilizations and its relation to power. For feminist theologians, these theories aid the construction of a theolog-ical politics of culture. This means recognition of the unfixed character of the Christian tradition and its complex connections with constellations of power. Sensibilities to the race, gender, sexual and class resonances of creedal statements, biblical stories, Jesus icons, etc., entail recognition that they are always conjoined with particular cultural elements and institu-tions, thus can stimulate reconfiguration of new combinations. In the the-ory jargon, feminists can dis-articulate meanings that appear harmful and rearticulate them with other cultural elements to yield liberative effects of meaning.[42] Not only does the tradition become richer with this theoriza-tion, the inadequacy of authorizing present practice by simple appeal to "the past" or "the tradition" is exposed.

A feminist philosopher of religion shows that French feminists are im-portant not only for recovering the unconscious, but to rethink explicitly

---

[41] Serene Jones, *Feminist Theory and Christian Theology: Cartographies of Grace* (Minneapolis: Fortress, 2000).

[42] Kathryn Tanner, "Social Theory Concerning the 'New Social Movements' and the Practice of Feminist Theology," in Chopp and Davaney, eds., *Horizons in Feminist Theology*, pp. 179–97.

theological concerns. Grace Jantzen's work with Irigaray constructs a feminist philosophy of religion based upon natality, shifting from patriarchal obsession with death to life.[43] She deconstructs the foundationalism in much philosophy of religion and theology, ably exposing the poverty of its cognitive focus by a contrast with the bounty of natality. With Irigary's concept of the sensible transcendental and becoming divine, Jantzen also moves theological thinking out of the problematic binary trap in which feminist theology had been caught: either there is transcendence and revelation, preserving theological discourse from criticism and stabilizing masculinist religion, or the feminist is suspected of being Feuerbachian, posing religion as projection and thereby "playing God." The potential in Jantzen for reconceiving the transcendence/immanence binary is a vital and constructive trajectory for feminist theology.

Jantzen's work also contributes to movement out of the oppositional thinking that can come with liberation movements by creating fresh sensibilities of flourishing. From new imagic paradigms of natality, to the creative use of jazz, improvisation, and sporting power by Sharon Welch, to queering of Christian identities by feminist ethicist Kathy Rudy, and the complexities of the feminized sexualization of "Jew" for Jewish feminist identities by Ann Pellegrini, postmodernism is generating important ways of honoring and imagining agencies that can slip outside the reach of systems.[44]

Many other issues remain to be surfaced and developed in feminist, womanist and *mujerista* theologies as a result of postmodern thought. Those raised in this essay are connected to efforts to think the practice of liberation more fully and imaginatively. Various forms of instability termed "postmodern" – the instability of signs, discourses, desire, subjects, cultural clusters, and political/economic configurations – serve to expand our grasp of the conditions of oppression and its alleviation. Oddly, the potential threat to religious faith suggested by the destabilizing effects of these theories has not materialized. I suspect the continued vitality of such theologies is the need to keep claims particular and partial in religious practices of resistance and emancipation, as Sharon Welch observes. Clearly these theologies continue to oppose forms of theological universalism and absolutism, which are taken to be homogenizing rather than protective of the truth of faith, and they flourish. Perhaps, then, the "intrinsic relativism of a feminist theology of liberation" does not undermine a kind of truth but is its very possibility.[45]

43 Grace Jantzen, *Becoming Divine: Toward a Feminist Philosophy of Religion* (Bloomington: Indiana University Press, 1999).
44 Welch, *Sweet Dreams*; cf. Rudy, *Sex and the Church*.
45 Sharon Welch, *Communities of Resistance and Solidarity: A Feminist Theology of Liberation* (Maryknoll, NY: Orbis Books, 1985), pp. 84–87.

Another way to think about the usefulness of postmodern themes for feminist, womanist, and *mujerista* theologies is their convergence around the question of the other. Identifying historic forms of excluding and effacing the other, these theologies create an ethics of the other. However since these exclusions produce a "saming" of the other, it is an ethic that opens us to receive from the other.[46] What may be the gamble of these theologies is that this turn to the other, accompanied by vigilant refusal of unending gestures of exclusion, has great resonances with much in the religious tradition of Christianity and Judaism. As such, this turn must be distinguished from the "turn to the subject," the reduction of theology to anthropology.[47] With its liberative-inflected instabilities, postmodern feminist, womanist, and *mujerista* turns to the other may signal a fundamentally theo/a-centric move.[48] In traditional terms, the condition for the ontological courage they invoke must be ascribed to the Eternal itself.

Further reading

Armour, Ellen, "Questioning 'Woman' in Feminist/Womanist Theology: Irigaray, Ruether, and Daly," in C. W. Maggie Kim, Susan M. St. Ville, and Susan M. Simonaitis, eds., *Transfigurations: Theology and the French Feminists* (Minneapolis: Fortress Press, 1993), pp. 143–69.

Chopp, Rebecca and Sheila Greeve Davaney, eds., *Horizons in Feminist Theology: Identity, Tradition, and Norms* (Minneapolis: Fortress Press, 1997).

Kim, C. W. Maggie, Susan M. St. Ville, and Susan M. Simonaitis, eds., *Transfigurations: Theology and the French Feminists* (Minneapolis: Fortress Press, 1993).

Haraway, Donna, " 'Gender' for a Marxist Dictionary: The Sexual Politics of a Word," in *Simians, Cyborgs, and Women: The Reinvention of Nature* (New York: Routledge, 1991), pp. 127–48.

Peskowitz, Miriam and Laura Levitt, eds., *Judaism Since Gender* (New York: Routledge, 1997).

Tolbert, Mary Ann, "Gender" in A. K. M. Adam, ed. *Handbook of Postmodern Biblical Interpretation* (St. Louis: Chalice Press, 2000), pp. 99–105.

Weigman, Robyn, *American Anatomies: Theorizing Race and Gender* (Durham, NC: Duke University Press), 1995.

---

[46] David Tracy, "Many Faces of Postmodernity," *Theology Today* 51 (1994), 108.

[47] Joerg Rieger, *God and the Excluded: Visions and Blindspots in Contemporary Theology* (Minneapolis: Augsburg/Fortress, 2001), pp. 99–127.

[48] A compromise attempt at gendered language for God.

8 Radical orthodoxy

D. STEPHEN LONG

The volume *Radical Orthodoxy* bears the subtitle "A New Theology." This could easily mislead readers, preventing them from understanding radical orthodoxy. It is not a "new" theology. If it were to present itself as such, it would merely take the form of one more "modern" theology, which radical orthodoxy is not. Although it could qualifiedly be labeled postmodern, radical orthodoxy is neither a newer nor improved version of modern theology, for an interminable "newness" characterizes modernity. As Gianni Vattimo tells us: "if we say that we are at a later point than modernity, and if we treat this fact as in some way decisively important, then this presupposes an acceptance of what more specifically characterizes the point of view of modernity itself, namely the idea of history with its two corollary notions of progress and overcoming."[1] Through overcoming the past, modernity progresses toward the new. Precisely because radical orthodoxy is not a "modern" theology it does not overcome the past – not even a modernity that can never be past – or progress toward the novel.

"Modern" theology looks for *new* categories within which to present a theological essence, usually understood in terms of a "mystery" that transcends the "new" categories used for its expression. Like modernity itself, modern theology is "progressive"; moving from the old toward the new, which never quite arrives. Thus modern theology is caught within a dialectic of presence and absence. It moves from what it lacks – the promised but absent "new" – toward what it hopes for – the presence of the new. In this movement the past is continually dissolved into an absent future, which promises to render the past and all its sacrifices meaningful. Progress becomes our fate and ethics is tied to a sacrificial economy. We are taught to sacrifice particular interests and commitments for the sake of the future arrival of the new. Postmodernity places this modern progress in question. Like postmodernity, radical orthodoxy seeks to escape the constraints of modern progress.

---

[1] Gianni Vattimo, *End of Modernity* (Baltimore: John Hopkins University Press, 1988), p. 4.

If the term "*post*modernity" is to be used in terms other than that already laid down by the modern, then it must use the term "post" with circumspection. Postmodernity is not what comes after the new; it is the "dissolution of the category of the new."[2] It seeks to turn us out of a progressive orientation toward the new that gives the illusion of movement when it in fact stands still, identically repeating the movement from absence to a deferred presence interminably; for this is the "end" of modernity. Like *post*modernity, *radical* orthodoxy is not the next stage of development in a progressive movement. It does not seek to serve the end of modernity. Thus it will be misunderstood if it is viewed as a "novel" theology. Instead it remembers the roots that nurture a Christian ontology, practical philosophy, and aesthetics in order to move us outside modernity's interminable end. This remembering of our theological roots turns the modern back upon itself to expose what it has forgotten, what it could never fully abandon, and yet what it cannot account for – the theological.

MODERN TRANSCENDENTALISM: FORGETTING THEOLOGY AND POSTMODERN RECOVERY

The modern tries unsuccessfully to sever itself from its theological roots through transcendentalism, which is not the same as transcendence. In fact, transcendentalism loses the significance of transcendence and constructs an immanent world where all knowledge is deemed possible based on what the human subject qua human subject already possesses. The philosopher Immanuel Kant defined transcendentalism. He wrote: "I call transcendental all knowledge which is occupied not so much with objects as with our mode of knowing objects insofar as this knowledge is supposed to be possible a priori."[3] Modernity is the construction of a space and time where the conditions for the possibility of knowing (the transcendental) are given not in "things" but in our ability to transcend such objects by way of a critical reflective standpoint that assumes a "secure" subjective presence. Through this transcendental standpoint, objects of knowledge are given meaning. Ontology, ethics, and aesthetics are structured by the secure presence of the transcendental standpoint and not the sensuality of "objects" themselves.

Once this transcendentalism becomes the basis for ontology, ethics, and aesthetics, "God" becomes irrelevant for the practical matters of everyday existence. "God" provides little beyond safeguarding an already secure presence. "God" is at most a supporting framework that props up transcendentalism by way of providing a secure ground for a transcendental standpoint.

[2] Ibid.
[3] Immanuel Kant, *Critique of Pure Reason* (New York: St. Martin's Press, 1965), p. 59.

This is called "ontotheology," and it defines the space within which "God" can be conceived within Western metaphysics. "Ontotheology" is the answer Martin Heidegger gave to the question, "How did God get into philosophy?" The answer was onto-theo-logic. It is a logic which names "that particular thinking which everywhere tries to fathom and comprehend Existence as such but within the totality of Being as ground (Logos)."[4] This "Being as ground" can only think "God" as *causa sui*, the self-caused cause. The space to think "God" becomes determined by an efficient causality.

Once "God" is forced into this space, then it is easy either to establish a barricade that polices "God" as an ineffable sublimity (Kant) or, once we recognize that being needs no ground, to forget "God" altogether (Nietzsche). When "God" becomes "policed" by transcendentalism then theology is forced beyond philosophy, politics, ethics, and economics. They become possible solely on the basis of the secure presence the transcendental standpoint provides, which is a thoroughly "natural" being that derives from no theological supplementation.

Because of their indebtedness to modern transcendentalism, many modern philosophers think of reality apart from any orthodox theological language. They do this not because they work out of an anti-dogmatic perspective, but because they are dogmatically certain what the a-priori conditions for knowledge are. This secure standpoint is referred to as a "metaphysics of presence." Behind the possibility of modern philosophy, politics, ethics, and economics lurks this "metaphysics of presence."

Modern transcendentalism attempts the severing of philosophy, politics, ethics, and economics from its theological roots by grounding them in a metaphysics of presence, which becomes more certain to us than knowledge of God. What becomes certain is our own transcendental standpoint and "God" is to be thought according to that a-priori certainty. Modern transcendentalism severs discourse from its theological roots not merely by forgetting God, but by thinking God in such a way that God does not matter. But it never quite achieves its task.[5] A postmodern philosophy and aesthetics recognizes the failure of the modern repression of these roots, it even expresses surprise that these roots continue to nurture life at the end of modernity. As Luce Irigaray comments: "It seems we are unable to eliminate or suppress the phenomenon of religion. It reemerges in different forms, some of them perverse: sectarianism, theoretical or political

---

[4] Martin Heidegger, *Essays in Metaphysics: Identity and Difference* (New York: Philosophical Library Inc., 1960), p. 52.

[5] For a more extended conversation as to how modernity seeks to think God such that God can be thought yet in such a way that God does not matter, see D. Stephen Long, *The Goodness of God* (Grand Rapids: Brazos Press, 2001).

dogmatism, religiosity."[6] For postmodernity, religion is not simply a primitive form of life supplanted by a more rational politics and ethics. Religion continues to appear in some guise, usually through some form of sacrificial economy.

RADICAL ORTHODOXY: FOR AND AGAINST POSTMODERNITY

Because modern transcendentalism rendered a world where God was irrelevant, radical orthodoxy finds a momentary ally in postmodern deconstruction. No secure presence based upon a critical reflective standpoint remains stable. It can always be deconstructed. The ontotheology that was used to secure that presence is transcended; God can be thought outside the space it defined. But the alliance between postmodernity and radical orthodoxy can be at most momentary, for, like modern philosophers, most postmodern thinkers cannot find their way back to the roots to remember them. The roots have for them no "proper name." In fact, these roots *are not*. All that is present is the gap between meaning and being which can be identified at most as *différance* or as the *khora*, that blind spot behind God's back which escapes his gaze.[7]

Many postmodern philosophers find orthodox Christian theology colluding with modern transcendentalism. Both are charged with perpetuating a metaphysics of presence through conceiving God as *causa sui*. But radical orthodoxy suggests that the collusion may not be between Christian orthodoxy and modern transcendentalism, but between modern transcendentalism and postmodernity. For the "secure" presence that modernity initiated (at least with Descartes) was based on the premise of a thoroughgoing absence. A dialectic of absence–presence defines both modernity and postmodernity. Moreover, postmodernity itself too easily becomes one more form of transcendentalism where philosophers remain captured by a dogmatic knowledge of the conditions for the possibility of knowledge; for these philosophers *say* to us what they say they cannot speak. They know the nothing behind God's back with a certainty that simply makes absence in(de)finitely present. This "space" that escapes God's gaze and is called the *khora* is used in postmodern philosophy to deconstruct any secure presence. For this space behind God's back can be nothing other than nothingness itself. For this reason, John Milbank "deliberately treats the writings of Nietzsche, Heidegger, Deleuze, Lyotard, Foucault, and Derrida as elaborations of

---

[6] Iragaray, *Sexes and Genealogies* (New York, Columbia University Press, 1993) p. 75.
[7] See Derrida's "How to Avoid Speaking," in Graham Ward, ed., *The Postmodern God: A Theological Reader* (Oxford: Blackwell, 1997), pp. 167–90.

a single nihilistic philosophy."[8] This single nihilistic philosophy supposedly assumes no metaphysical foundations. But Milbank argues that it assumes something quite similar to a metaphysical foundation – an ontological violence.

Ontological violence cannot be accounted for within the conditions postmodern thinkers establish. They argue that all truth is contingent upon language and that therefore it is not metaphysically secure, but narratively dependent. Yet an original ontological violence functions in their work more like a transcendental condition for the possibility of knowledge than a contingent form of knowledge narratively defined. Ontological violence is as metaphysical as the modern standpoint postmodernity deconstructed. Once this is recognized it allows theology to outnarrate postmodernity's effort to "overcome" metaphysics. For the compelling beauty of radical orthodoxy is its discovery that Christian orthodoxy assumes an ontology of peaceableness that both modernity and postmodernity cannot recognize because they assume an original ontological violence as the transcendental condition for the possibility of (an always elusive) meaning.

WHAT IS RADICAL ORTHODOXY?

Radical orthodoxy cannot be understood without some prior knowledge of the debates within and between modern and postmodern philosophy. Radical orthodoxy is a theology that enters into that fray by remembering orthodox Christian claims and showing how they bear on those debates. It emerged out of John Milbank's dissatisfaction with modern theology's acceptance of its fate (implicit and explicit) as innocuous and irrelevant because it allowed theology to be positioned by philosophical transcendentalism. Milbank first saw the seeds of this while studying the work of Hans Urs von Balthasar and Jacques Derrida under the tutelage of Rowan Williams.[9] By thinking through both von Balthasar's and Derrida's critique of modern secularism, Milbank developed a theological insight that neither von Balthasar nor Derrida alone could have developed. Theology did not merely give "facts" meaning that were themselves known without theology. For, once transcendentalism is no longer given a privileged dogmatic status, then theological language must be viewed as constitutive of the real as any form of modern philosophy (including sociology). After abandoning theology's position of humility before modern transcendentalism, radical orthodoxy remembers the Christological filling of space and time

---

[8] Milbank, *Theology and Social Theory* (Oxford: Blackwell, 1990), p. 279.
[9] For a fuller discussion of this see Jeff Sharlet's "Theologians Seek to Reclaim the World With God and Postmodernism," in *The Chronicle of Higher Education*, June 23, 2000, pp. A20–A22.

such that metaphysics can be truly overcome and the space and time of the modern and postmodern is revealed for what it is – choreographed spontaneity. Theologians and philosophers are then freed to develop a Christian practical philosophy and ontology that will be more mediating of other discourses (politics, economics, ethics) than other forms of orthodox theology with which radical orthodoxy has some sympathy, such as the theology of Karl Barth and Hans Urs von Balthasar. While radical orthodoxy is more interested in mediating other discourses via theology, it claims to be less accommodating to the modern spirit than even those theologies that eschewed mediation altogether. Radical orthodoxy cannot develop theology solely by professing basic Christian dogma; it develops theological doctrine always at the same time that it discusses politics, economics, and ethics. It is *radical* not only in re-membering the *roots* (radix), but also in re-membering the intrinsic and necessary connection between theology and politics, and this calls into question modern politics, culture, art, science, and philosophy.

RADICAL ORTHODOXY'S TURN: CHRISTOLOGICAL FILLING OF SPACE AND TIME

Radical orthodoxy finds in "Jesus Christ" the proper name that makes possible a difference, which is not tied to the violent metaphysics of *différance*. The space within which postmodernity operates is the same space within which the modern operated. That space can be characterized by the form Immanuel Kant gave to it in his third critique, the critique of judgment. Kant both gave us the transcendental conditions within which modern epistemology imprisoned knowledge and he showed us the limitations of that imprisonment. In his first critique Kant launched a second "Copernican revolution" by supposing that rather than our knowledge conforming to things, things conform to our knowledge. This meant that we could no longer know things as they are, but only things as they appear to us and are synthesized into concepts by us. But this left little space for theology as a rational pursuit; theology was at best a-rational. Knowledge of God was still possible, but it was a matter of pure faith, faith separate from and devoid of reason. "I critiqued reason," suggested Kant, "in order to make room for faith." But the room made for faith was a space where nothing reasonable could be said about God. Thus, while theology could still be practiced through faith alone, through revelations inaccessible to reason, or through private personal experiences, theology could not reasonably be employed in any decisive political, philosophical, or ethical sense.

132 D. Stephen Long

The space for theology was a pure supernatural space. That space was brought into play as making possible a modern aesthetics; for in his third critique Kant defined the sublime based on the gap between the presentation of the infinite and the inability to represent that presence conceptually. The form that emerged from the contradiction between the always inadequate conceptual representation of the infinite and the infinite itself produced both the pleasure and pain of the beautiful. As Lyotard noted, the modern is characterized by a "nostalgia" for this nonrepresentable presence. Modern aesthetics seeks to recover an original presence that can never be recovered. Postmodernity still operates within that same "beautiful" (and tragic) space, but without the possibility of nostalgia; for that which "presents" itself always does so in terms of a space that contained an original supplement. Therefore no return to the original is possible; there is no origin. What presents itself only does so at the exact time that the presentation is deferred, erased, i.e., as it embraces or is embraced by death.

In radical orthodoxy, the Christological filling of space means that Jesus is the "theological sublime."[10] The resurrected Jesus takes the place modern and postmodern aesthetics give to tragedy or death. Whereas in modernity and postmodernity the sublime is fundamentally tragic and therefore predicated upon an ontological violence, in radical orthodoxy the sublime assumes an ontological priority of peaceableness. Radical orthodoxy finds in Jesus the beginning and filling of space such that the distinction between an infinite presence and a finite representation does not assume a gap that entails conflict. The father need not die at our hands for the sons to survive. The *logos* need not negate the source from which it is begotten for it to be heard. As Milbank puts it, Jesus is "the most comprehensive possible context: not just the space within which all transactions between time and eternity transpire, but also the beginning of all this space, the culmination of this space, the growth of this space and all the goings in and out within this space."[11] In other words, Jesus is "very God and very Man." Jesus is the form within which creation and redemption occur, and there is "nothing" outside this space upon which creation can be formed. As Rowan Williams notes, this means that God's creative power is not "power over."[12] There is nothing over which God would need to exercise power. God does not create by containing a threatening chaos. God creates through pure gift of God's own self. "Jesus" names the gift that makes both creation and redemption possible.

---

[10] See Frederick Bauerschmidt, "The Theological Sublime," in John Milbank, Catherine Pickstock, and Graham Ward, eds., *Radical Orthodoxy* (London: Routledge, 1999), pp. 201–20.

[11] Milbank, *The Word Made Strange* (Oxford: Blackwell, 1997), p. 150.

[12] Rowan Williams, *On Christian Theology* (Oxford: Blackwell, 2000), p. 68.

"Jesus" does not simply name the attempt to copy an original image. He is not the presence of the absent Father inscribed in time. If Jesus names this attempt at copying, theology would be open to being deconstructed by postmodern *différance*. For such an attempt always requires a "supplement at the origin" (the engraving of speech in writing) whereby *différance* can do its work deferring the possibility of an originary presence because of the supplement that attempts to copy it. But the postmodern critique of Christianity wrongly assumes it depends on such a metaphysics of presence. An orthodox Christology discloses the error. For as Frederick Bauerschmidt notes (drawing on the work of Hans Urs von Balthasar), "the form of revelation does not present itself as an independent image of God, standing over against what is imaged, but as a unique hypostatic union between archetype and image. The sublime archetype is in the form; one might say that the form is the 'real presence' of the archetype."[13] When the form of the hypostatic union receives its proper place within the doctrine of the Trinity, Christian theology not only overcomes a metaphysics of presence, it also avoids the nihilistic postmodern strategy to overcome presence through its constant deferral. It heals us from thinking we must acquiesce to ontological violence.

OVERCOMING METAPHYSICS

Postmodernity recognizes the illness in modernity but it cannot "overcome" it. As Graham Ward so aptly explains it, postmodern efforts to overcome the violence of metaphysics are like someone standing in a box, holding on to its sides, and trying to jump out.[14] Postmodernity cannot overcome the end of modernity but seems fated to replay that ending again and again. Radical orthodoxy bears witness that "only theology overcomes metaphysics."

Does it matter whether theology or postmodern philosophy overcomes metaphysics?[15] What difference does this make? Radical orthodoxy's "labyrinthine" prose tempts some to read it only as an academic parlor game used for inconsequential power struggles in high-brow university religion and philosophy departments. But this is a mistake. In radical orthodoxy,

[13] Bauerschmidt, "The Theological Sublime," p. 208.
[14] See Graham Ward, "Introduction or A Guide to Theological Thinking in Cyberspace," in *The Postmodern God* (Oxford: Blackwell, 1997), pp. xv–xlvii.
[15] By "metaphysics" something specific is intended here. What is not meant is that theology must overcome every account of philosophy or ontology. The "metaphysics" that must be "overcome" is the philosophical discipline that developed after Suarez and led to ontotheology. The best account of this can be found in Jean-Luc Marion's essay, "Metaphysics and Phenomenology," in Graham Ward, ed., *The Postmodern God*, pp. 279–98.

theology *matters*. The secularism that "defined and constructed" the world for several centuries "suspended matter" over a void. As the matter begins to dissolve within the "cyberspace" of that void, the significance of matter itself is called into question, placed under erasure. The editors of *Radical Orthodoxy* write: "Speaking with a microphoned and digitally simulated voice, secularism proclaims – uneasily, or else increasingly unashamedly – its own lack of values and lack of meaning. In its cyberspaces and theme-parks it promotes a materialism which is soulless, aggressive, nonchalant and nihilistic."[16] A soulless matter is a matter without form, a matter without shape that dissolves into the pure potentiality of power and death. Our new cyber-reality, the "ultimate in the secularization of the divine," may be the conclusion of modernity. "Nothing is produced, though everything is marketed."[17] Matter no longer matters for it has no form. Before we are lost and given over to the language of gigabytes, ram, cyber, net-surfing, etc., radical orthodoxy reminds us that there was (and hopefully still is) another language that matters – Trinity, Jesus, hypostatic union, resurrection, church, Holy Spirit, *creatio ex nihilo*, transubstantiation. Turning the secular toward its repressed theological premises may heal us from the death secularism invites us to, even in its "religious" and "spiritual" guises. Overcoming metaphysics matters because, if it can be accomplished, we might find healing from the choreographed politics and economics sustained by and in that metaphysics, a metaphysics that like Heidegger's crossing out of being assumes death. Postmodernity cannot heal; it only prolongs death and makes it the meaning of life. But theology can *turn* the violence of metaphysics and the secular back to what has been forgotten – theology or, more importantly, God.

Radical orthodoxy begins by questioning the dualism between reason and revelation, faith and nature. It does not seek some privileged space for theology separate from reason and philosophy. Radical orthodoxy does not overcome modernity through negation and progress; modernity is "overcome" through a "turning" (*Verwindung*) that undoes any secure division between faith and reason, theology and philosophy. This is accomplished by rereading five key philosophical themes present in the past two centuries: "the linguisticality of reason, the ontological difference, the priority of existence over essence, the priority of dialogue, and the sensuality of all human thought."[18] Rather than fleeing from these philosophical themes and finding some safe theological object that philosophy cannot touch,

[16] Milbank, Pickstock, and Ward, eds., *Radical Orthodoxy*, p. 1.
[17] Ward, *The Postmodern God*, p. xvii.
[18] Milbank, Pickstock, and Ward, eds., *Radical Orthodoxy*, pp. 6 and 23.

radical orthodoxy works through them, showing how they need and assume theological supplementation.

Linguisticality of reason

The "linguistic turn" in modern philosophy is well known. Heidegger's recognition that language is the chamber within which being is disclosed, Wittgenstein's analysis of language-games, and Derrida's statement – "there is nothing outside the text" – move rational analysis from ostensive definition and subject/object representation to a recovery of "the prose of the world." The linguistic turn makes possible an ontology not indebted to the conception of "substances" that are secure without language such that language has only an ornamental role. Theologians need not fear this linguistic turn; for the Word has always been central in Christian theology. But the linguistic turn can collude with modern transcendentalist thought, assuming that linguistic mediation of reality embodies something such as Kantian categories giving the subject an a-priori access to what she can and cannot think. This renders the *linguistic* mediation itself dependent upon some prior nonlinguistic reality, whether that be the ontological difference of Heidegger or Derrida's sacrificial economy. This would be an incomplete linguistic turn. In contrast to this incomplete linguistic turn, radical orthodoxy advocates a more radical linguisticality that assumes language truly discloses being.[19] Milbank notes:

> for the Anglo-Saxon linguistic obsession, whether Wittgensteinian
> or Derridean, the stress is that we are inevitably located inside
> words, conventions and traditions. Sometimes the danger here is of
> textualising aridity, of formality and smug self-reference. Moreover,
> a notion that we are "trapped" inside language can re-affirm
> transcendentalist knowable limits to finitude, and in consequence,
> encourage an over-agnostic construal of analogical discourse about
> God.

While the linguistic turn can be a form of transcendentalism, Milbank does not find that phenomenology's "primary intuition" provides an adequate alternative. Husserl's "primary intuition" claimed that things present themselves to us in their corporeality as they are.[20] But because this functions primarily as an act of cognition, Milbank argues that it "ignores linguistic, cultural and historical mediation" and "is irredeemably apolitical." Radical orthodoxy offers an alternative to both linguistic transcendentalism and a phenomenological original intuition.

---

[19] See Milbank, "Intensities," *Modern Theology* 15 (1999), 474–75.
[20] See Marion, "Metaphysics and Phenomenology," p. 285.

for radical orthodoxy's mediating perspective, linguistic expression and intuitive experience are inseparable. We see in making, make in seeing, and this constitutes one main point of Catherine Pickstock's liturgical turn. Since God is not an item in the world to which we might turn, he is only first there for us in our turning to him. And yet we only turn to him when he reaches us; herein lies the mystery of liturgy – liturgy which for theology is more fundamental than *either* language *or* experience, and yet is both linguistic and experiential.[21]

The linguisticality of reason does not assume a prior space of ontological difference where being is only disclosed against the backdrop of the erasure of Being. Death is no gift, and neither speaking nor writing is construed as possible only within a sacrificial economy of death. The liturgical turn is more thoroughly linguistic because it assumes that our speaking participates via analogy in God's eternal plenitude. We do not know the limits of language a priori.

Ontological difference

This does not assume that language is of divine origin. The liturgical turn perpetuates Christian orthodoxy's claim that language is of human origin.[22] This avoids the assumption that language itself mediates God to the creation such that any Christological mediation offered through the church would be unnecessary. Language itself does not give us access to God any more than does experience qua experience. To assume otherwise would require positing God as the *causa sui* within which we can think God because we can first think ourselves. At its most basic, this is the problem of ontotheology. We cannot think God without thinking of being understood univocally predicated of both God and creation. Heidegger challenged ontotheology with his recovery of the ontological difference.

What is ontological difference? Heidegger thought that Western philosophy had forgotten the question of being. By thinking of knowledge in terms of subject and objects, philosophy neglected a more fundamental difference – the difference between Being and beings. By "beings" (*essents*) were intended everyday "things" such as "tools, people, Bach's fugues, the earth itself."[23] The "being" (*essent*) of these things seems determinate, easily identifiable. We can point to something and say "that *is* it." But, when we attempt to speak of the being that would be common to all these things, it

---

[21] Milbank, "The Programme of Radical Orthodoxy," pp. 10–11 (unpublished version). This essay can now be found in *Radical Orthodoxy? A Catholic Inquiry*, ed. Laurence Hemming (Aldershot: Ashgate, 2000); these extracts appearing on p. 43.

[22] Milbank, *Word Made Strange*, p. 84.

[23] Heidegger, *Introduction to Metaphysics* (New Haven: Yale University Press, 1959), p. 75.

does not seem to be so determinate. What is the "is" that all these things are? "It" is not so easy to define. This common "Being" seems to be "empty and indeterminate." And yet we could not know "beings" if it were not for Being. As Heidegger puts it, "the much vaunted essent can only disclose itself as such insofar as we already understand being in its essence." If we did not know the difference between Being and not-being, none of these *essents* could be for us.

Our being is caught in the midst of a necessary contradiction. Being is for us both determinate and indeterminate and our being is possible only through this contradiction. "We find ourselves standing in the very middle of this contradiction," writes Heidegger, and this is "more real" than "dogs, cats, etc." Therefore, he concluded, "Because the understanding of being resides first and foremost in a vague and indefinite meaning, and yet remains certain and definite, because accordingly the understanding of being with all its rank, remains obscure, confused and hidden, it must be elucidated, disentangled and torn from its concealment." In other words – beings appear only as they are disclosed against the backdrop of the crossing out of Being.

Derrida called Heidegger's placing of being under erasure the "last writing," that is to say it is the end of metaphysics. He also called it the first writing because this is where thought escapes metaphysical closure. In the difference between being and Being we escape the assumption that being is secured because Being is *causa sui*. Derrida sees in Heidegger the end of metaphysics, an end that overcomes a long history and tradition that began with Plato and extends itself through Christianity. This tradition has come to an end with Heidegger because now, rather than a secure presence, difference allows being to appear. Ontotheology is overcome.

But radical orthodoxy denies that Platonism, Aristotelianism, or medieval Christian theology depend on this ontotheology; for, *contra* Heidegger and Derrida, modernity does not fulfill but invents this metaphysics, and postmodernity remains trapped within it. In contrast to it, Plato, Aristotle, and Aquinas offered a different "ontological difference" that did not assume God as *causa sui* or a necessary metaphysical violence as the condition for the appearance of being. Plato's good beyond being was not ontotheological. Likewise, Aristotle's metaphysics assumed an "aporetic oscillation" between "every being" and "first being." Thomas Aquinas assumed a "real distinction" between essence and existence in created beings that required analogical discourse in order to explain the relationship between God and creation. God's essence is God's existence. But a "real distinction" exists between creaturely essence and existence. Thus being cannot be univocally predicated of God and creatures. When Scotus argued for a "formal distinction" between essence and existence, it made possible thinking God and creation within a univocal account of being; the kind of ontology that ontotheology requires. Ontotheology first occurs with Suarez who thinks being "without reference to any non-material or absolute beings" and then thinks God as *causa sui* "univocally conceived as of the same type as a finite cause."[24] Prior to thinking being and God in these terms, Christian theologians were able to conceive of God as "the hidden manifestness of Being in beings" without assuming that beings appear only as Being is placed under erasure. Thus they were able to think "ontological difference" without the sacrificial economy within which both Heidegger and Derrida continue to think of it. They did this by thinking in terms of "analogy and participation."

Postmodernity does not finally escape modernity's ontology because postmodern discourse cannot refer beings to an "ungraspable infinite" but can only seek a "graspable immanent security." This becomes a "choreographed" space where the difference within which beings appear is really a sameness dependent upon meaninglessness and death. That it is "choreographed" refers to two key themes of postmodernity – the *khora* and the "graph" (*gramma* or trace). Drawing upon Plato's Timaeus, many postmodern thinkers refer to the space within which language (graph) appears as the *khora*. It is a "specular surface" upon which discourse and subjectivity can occur.[25] It is the "rhythmic pulsion" that is not yet language but makes language possible.[26] Or, as John Caputo puts it, "Khora is neither an intelligible form nor one more sensible thing, but rather, that in which sensible things are inscribed." *Khora* names the space in which things appear. It has a feminine, womb-like character. It is intended to critique Western patriarchal assumptions. Thus Caputo states: "philosophy tends to stick to the father (*eidos*) and its legitimate son (*cosmos*) as if the father begets the son without the help of a woman – a bad biology to which the whole history of theology gives ample witness."[27] But does this specular space accomplish its purpose? Catherine Pickstock thinks it fails.

In her *After Writing*, Pickstock contrasts a liturgical city to a choreographed, unliturgical, immanentist city. The former is the ecclesial city where the enactment of the Eucharist makes possible a "coincidence between sign and body" that the deferral of meaning in the choreographed immanent city cannot acknowledge. The choreographed city only appears to offer a difference. The graphing of difference upon an empty *khora*

[24] Milbank, "Only Theology Overcomes Metaphysics," in *Word Made Strange*, p. 41.
[25] Iragaray, *Speculum of the Other Woman* (Ithaca, NY: Cornell University Press, 1985), p. 143.
[26] *The Kristeva Reader*, ed., Toril Moi (New York: Columbia University Press, 1986), p. 93.
[27] Jacques Derrida and John D. Caputo, *Deconstruction in a Nutshell*, (New York: Fordham University Press, 1997), pp. 84, 92.

produces an infinite sameness that not only defers meaning; it is meaningless. It is the meaninglessness of death.[28] In opposition to the "choreographed spontaneity" of modernity, radical orthodoxy refers being to a "Christian thought" where "between one unknown and the other there is here no representational knowledge, no 'metaphysics,' but only a mode of ascent which receives something of the infinite source so long as it goes on receiving it, so constituting, not a once and for all theory (or account of the ontological difference) but an endlessly repeated-as-always-different theoretical claim which is nothing other than all the biographies of every ascent, and the history of human ascent as such."[29] Thinking being in terms of this infinite/finite ratio gives matter a depth it does not possess by itself. It moves us beyond thinking being solely in terms of an indefinite immanent scale where each thing emerges solely by its distance from other things, and calls that gap the unnamable "*khora.*"

Existence over essence

Radical orthodoxy does not assume we arrive at essences only by abstracting from existence. The question of existence answers the question *an sit* – does it exist? The question of essence answers the question *quid est* – what is it? The quiddity or essence of things is not discovered by abstracting from things as they exist. The "forms" of things requires an "intimation" of the infinite, but this intimation takes place in and through desire that arises only in and through existing things. Knowledge of the essence of something requires "sensuality." Drawing upon St. Augustine's understanding of knowledge as rooted in desire, radical orthodoxy reads the eroticism of our existence as iconic. Desire directs us to God.

> Here, in Augustine, "will" or "desire" indicates that aspect of our being (indeed of all created beings) which somehow already has something and yet does not have it. In this way "will" names not, as for Pelagius or later in Western tradition, *a faculty*, but simply that problematic site where inner is also outer, active is also passive, present is also past and future, and knowing is also loving. And what justifies such a remaining with the problematic (which otherwise would betoken a purely philosophic skepticism) is precisely the incomprehensible faith in the world as created out of nothing: that is to say, as "other" from God and yet constituted only out of God.[30]

---

[28] Catherine Pickstock, *After Writing: On The Liturgical Consummation of Philosophy* (Oxford: Blackwell, 1998), p. 3.

[29] Milbank, "Only Theology Overcomes Metaphysics," p. 45.

[30] Milbank, Pickstock, and Ward, eds., *Radical Orthodoxy*, p. 11.

God creates "*ex nihilo*" and the *nihil* is not an "is"; it is not some eternal space or *khora* which provides existence with a "ground" outside of God. God creates that which is not God, but God creates it. Thus our being must be understood analogically in relationship to God's being. Existence does not then reveal a thing's essence. There is no coincidence between creaturely existence and essence; the meaning of existence is not present solely in the existent itself. The existent can only be adequately known by its ratio to the infinite. In this ratio its essence is discovered. Such knowledge takes its form from Christology, from the hypostatic union.

> Just as with Christ, we *see* only his human nature, and his divine nature is manifested in the unique narrative pattern of his life which has the integrity of the divine *person* and *logos*, so also all we *see* in human beings are animals, but it is the beauty of their unique form of life, their strange "political" blending of solitude and sociality which display, in human personhood a human nature. Hence it is only our faint anticipation and then echo of a divine redeemed humanity, intelligently erotic, erotically intelligent, which *at all* distinguishes us as more than animal, more than *nihilistic*.[31]

We discover a thing's essence not by looking behind it, nor by recognizing its relationship to a "nihilated" being. We discover a thing's essence in its bodiliness. Knowledge is sensual.

Priority of dialogue

That knowledge is bodily does not imply that it is individual or purely subjective; for bodies themselves are not constituted by an interiority. Radical orthodoxy resonates (for a moment) with the philosopher Emmanuel Levinas' argument that grounds human subjectivity in exteriority. Our subjectivity does not arise from a transcendental apperception of unity that occurs interior to a subject. Subjectivity arises from the ethical demand "the other" places upon us. Only in dialogue with others do we become subjects. But, for Levinas, we always arrive too late to meet the demands of this alterity, and arriving too late requires that ethics remain sacrificial. I become "hostage" to the demands of the other that I can never fulfill. However, this moral economy must also work in reverse. The other becomes hostage as well. We all become hostages to each other, and our first concern must be the good of the other through the sacrifice of my (and his or her) good.

Jacques Derrida likewise finds all ethical obligation to occur within a sacrificial economy. His statement – "there is nothing outside the

---

[31] Milbank, "The Theological Critique of Philosophy," in Milbank, Pickstock, and Ward, eds., *Radical Orthodoxy*, p. 31.

text" – operates within a space defined by this (modern) sacrificial economy. He draws upon the myth of Theuth in Plato's *Phaedrus* to explain
what he means. Theuth is an inventor who shows his inventions to the god
Thamus, especially his invention of writing. This invention, Theuth argues,
will help people remember. But Thamus disagrees. Far from helping people
remember, writing will only make them forget. "They will rely on writing
to bring things to their remembrance by external signs instead of on their
own internal resources."[32] People will no longer need to remember because
writing will store memories within texts. The act of writing absents the presence of memories from subjects who can now only recollect those memories
from texts. The author will no longer be necessary, only the text. Writing,
therefore, entails death. The minute someone writes, she makes possible a
difference between the memory present in herself and the memory present
in the text. The former is no longer necessary. Writing is dying.

Thamus suggests that orality preserves the presence of memory, but
writing destroys it. But Derrida suggests that nothing takes place outside
the difference present in writing, not even orality itself. Writing here is
not just text, it is the condition within which all life operates, including
the ethical obligations others brings to us. Not even God as present in the
face of the other removes us from this transcendental condition for ethical
obligations. Commenting on Levinas' account of alterity, Derrida remarks:
"In effect either there is only the same, which can no longer even appear
and be said, nor even exercise violence (pure infinity or finitude); or indeed
there is the same and the other, then the other cannot be the other – of the
same – except by being the same (as itself: ego) and the same cannot be
the same (as itself: ego) except by being the other's other: alter ego."[33] In
other words, if everything is the same – a pure infinity or a pure finitude –
one could not recognize the difference through which the "face" makes us
ethically responsible. But if, on the other hand, there is a difference that
I can acknowledge, it requires both "the same and the other." If that is
the case then the other can never be simply other unless it is the other of
the same. This entails a "transcendental violence" where the other appears
only through my ability to see the other as the same as me. For Derrida,
"these necessities are violence itself or rather the transcendent origin of
an irreducible violence."[34] And that means that the possibility of ethical
responsibility depends upon a "transcendental violence" or an "economy of
violence."

[32] Plato, *Phaedrus* (London: Penguin Books, 1973), p. 96.
[33] Derrida, "Violence and Metaphysics," in *Writing and Difference* (University of Chicago Press,
1978), p. 128.
[34] Ibid.

What then do we do to avoid this necessary violence? "Discourse therefore, if it is originally violence, can only do itself violence, can only negate
itself in order to affirm itself, make war upon the war which institutes it
without ever being able to reappropriate this negativity, to the extent that it
is discourse." And this would be "the least possible violence" for "one never
escapes the economy of war."[35] This leads Derrida to "the gift of death."

For both Levinas and Derrida, we cannot meet the demands of the
other for the Other who meets us in the face of the other asks of us an
infinite responsibility that can only finally be fulfilled when we sacrifice
ourselves and our particular loves, giving without expecting return. But
this ethical demand prevents us from encountering specific neighbors in
their corporeality. For Derrida, fulfilling the obligations of such concrete
persons would be a betrayal of the infinite responsibility the Other demands
of us. Derrida developed this notion of infinite responsibility in his *The
Gift of Death*. He states: "What binds me to singularities, to this one or
that one, male or female, rather than that one or this one, remains fully
unjustifiable (this is Abraham's hyper-ethical sacrifice), as unjustifiable as
the infinite sacrifice which I make at each moment."[36] To fulfill the demand
of any particular neighbor is to refuse the infinite responsibility that the
Other asks of me in the face of my neighbor. Only when I am willing, like
Abraham, to sacrifice Isaac without hope of return can I truly be ethical. As
Derrida puts it: "The absoluteness of duty and responsibility presume that
one denounce, refute and transcend at the same time, all duty, responsibility,
and every human law."[37] Once again we find that postmodernity does not
move decisively beyond Kantianism. Both determine ethical obligations in
terms of a sacrificial economy. Only by sacrificing my own particular desire
can I meet an ethical obligation. We remain trapped within a sacrificial
economy. A theological turn is needed.

Far from ontologizing violence and making tragedy the eternal word,
radical orthodoxy develops ethics through the possibility of the redemption
of evil and the restoration of all things in God. This redemption must be
witnessed to even now such that a sacrificial economy must not be val-
orized in ontology, aesthetics, ethics, politics, or economics. The Christian
interpretation of the story of Abraham bears witness to this. According
to Hebrews, Abraham looked to the other "city" whose foundation is God
(Hebrews 11:10). This gaze frees him from the "fear of death" and the "life-
long bondage" of the fleshly city (Hebrews 2:15). It does so because of the

35 Ibid., pp. 138 and 148.
36 Derrida, *The Gift of Death* (University of Chicago Press, 1995), p. 71. See also D. Stephen
    Long, *Divine Economy: Theology and the Market* (London: Routledge, 2000), p. 145.
37 Derrida, *The Gift of Death*, p. 66.

promised return, a promise given to him and Sara, which meant that he could in faith offer up Isaac. This offering was not a valorization of sacrifice or the assumption that life is composed of eternal grief and joy. Abraham's offering was based on his consideration that "God was able to raise men even from the dead" (Hebrews 11:19). It could only be done because of the promise of return, a return that undoes the sacrificial economy precisely because no single other can stand as my "sacrifice." A finite death does not open up infinitude, and the withdrawal of infinitude does not make possible the finite. Instead, the finite is possible only through its analogical relation to, and participation in, the infinite. This means there is always a promise of return. This promised return, this resurrection, is the end of sacrifice. This makes possible a truly dialogical account of subjectivity, which does not assume that only through my death or the other's can I fulfill the obligations with which God meets me in my neighbor.

Sensuality of Knowledge

That subjectivity is constituted dialogically assumes that knowledge is mediated through the desire of and for bodies – social, political, individual. Knowledge of God is erotic. But this is not a sexualized male–female (or male–male, female–female) erotics. It is an erotics that refuses to "take the human to be a measure of the Christic."[38] It thinks the materiality of the body through its eschatological in-formation. As Graham Ward argues, the allegorical displacements Jesus' body undergoes from circumcision to crucifixion to extension via the Eucharist and church produce an erotic attraction that overcomes the limits that often constrain either a homo- or heterosexual desire. This desire does not arise out of a lack. It is not a desire for the body qua body. "The physical body is displaced – for it is not the physical body as such which is the source of the attraction but the glorification of the physical body made possible by viewing him through God as God."[39] Jesus' body becomes iconic, capable of producing a desire for God not based on lack, but on the fullness of God indwelling Jesus' glorified body.

Just as knowledge of God is mediated via an eschatologically in-formed materiality, so it is mediated via the ecclesial body. On the road to Emmaus, two disciples travel with the resurrected Jesus and do not recognize him until he breaks bread with him, but then Jesus vanishes. The disciples then proclaim the resurrection. Jesus' resurrected body is not an object capable of fetishization for Jesus absents himself – even in the text – and this makes possible the witness of the church.[40] The church becomes his

[38] Milbank, Pickstock, and Ward, eds., *Radical Orthodoxy*, p. 163.
[39] Ibid., p. 166.   [40] Ibid., p. 174.

body – extended in space and time. As William Cavanaugh argues, this ecclesial body is the true political body. The state can only be a "simulacrum" thereof. It is the instantiation of an ontological violence that assumes the social body is produced through the "assimilation of things in nature to me." A counter-ontology and politics is discovered in the ecclesial body where the defining act is the Eucharist, which "assimilates me into God's body."[41] The sensuality of our knowledge entails a particular ordering of desire through these social bodies so that we might participate in God's goodness.

CONCLUSION

What is radical orthodoxy? It is a theologic that mediates politics, ethics, philosophy, and aesthetics without becoming correlationist and accommodating the modern spirit. It is postmodern only in that it turns the philosophical advantages toward which postmodernity points, and completes them theologically. It is the return of Christian orthodoxy, but with a historical and linguistic difference that makes possible theological work in politics, economics, and ethics. It is a Christian metaphysic that does not begin with transcendentalist assumptions that predicate knowledge of God upon a secure knowledge of ourselves. Instead it assumes that participation in the church makes possible a theological knowledge that must then mediate all other forms of knowledge. But this mediation must take place within the terms in which it has been received – as gift. Radical orthodoxy can then avoid the false pathos of humility that characterizes modern theology, but it need not refuse to learn from the ways in which this gift of knowledge has not always been embodied in the life of the church and in Christian tradition. It is radical in that it is also capable of calling the church itself back to its roots at the same time that it seeks to bear witness to those roots to all of humanity. As Rowan Williams puts it:

> To belong to the community of Christian belief at all is to assume that the pattern of relation between persons and between humanity and God which is displayed as gift and possibility in the Church is open to humanity at large, and to act on that assumption in respect both of the internal structures and of the external polity of the Church.[42]

Such a gift and possibility requires theology to be nothing less than "orthodox" in order to maintain the priority of God's gift in Jesus Christ as the form that makes possible creation and redemption. *Creatio ex nihilo*, the full divinity and humanity of Christ, the importance of the hypostatic

---

[41] Ibid., p. 194   [42] Williams, *On Christian Theology*, p. 20.

union, orthodox Trinitarianism, and an insistence on the church as the body of Christ all seek to maintain this giftedness. Such an orthodoxy is radical in that it must constantly mediate all forms of knowledge through the certainty of this gift. Ontology, ethics, aesthetics, politics, economics gain their real intelligibility when understood in terms of this radical gift. In turn, we understand the gift itself more fully.

Further reading

Hemming, Laurence, ed., *Radical Orthodoxy? A Catholic Inquiry* (Aldershot: Ashgate, 2000).

Milbank, John, *The Word Made Strange: Theology, Language, Culture* (Oxford: Blackwell, 1997).

Milbank, John, Catherine Pickstock, and Graham Ward, eds., *Radical Orthodoxy: A New Theology* (London: Routledge, 1999).

Pickstock, Catherine, *After Writing: On the Liturgical Consummation of Philosophy* (Oxford, Blackwell, 1998).

Part two

Christian doctrine in postmodern perspective

9 Scripture and tradition

KEVIN J. VANHOOZER

One way of telling the story of modernity and postmodernity is by charting the relationship, often volatile and sometimes violent, between Scripture and tradition. At stake is the nature and *locus* of divine authority: does it reside in the canon or in the community?

In one sense, the postmodern condition would seem to be a swing back to the authority of tradition, in particular, to the authority of interpretative traditions. On the other hand, the postmodern situation brings to light certain reductionistic tendencies in thinking about language and literature. Some look to the later Wittgenstein as indicating a new way of thinking about language. Interestingly, Wittgenstein's emphasis on language use correlated to forms of life brings back the very Scripture/tradition dynamic in a postmodern key. For what is tradition if not a form of life to know and glorify God? And what is Scripture if not a certain use of language to name God?

SCRIPTURE AND TRADITION IN MODERNITY: FROM REFORMATION TO ENLIGHTENMENT

Protestantism: the eclipse of tradition?

From one perspective, the Reformation was a victory of the Scripture principle over ecclesial tradition. The reality, however, is more complex, for the Reformers did not object to the use of the church fathers or deny that the Bible ought to be interpreted in the context of the life of the ongoing church. What they rejected was rather the elevation of noncanonical, and hence human, traditions that were thought to supplement the revelation given in Scripture.[1] The Reformers' so-called "Scripture principle" identified the Bible as God's word in human speech, while the notion of the priesthood of

---

[1] Heiko Oberman has argued that the issue of the Reformation was not Scripture versus tradition so much as the struggle between two opposing concepts of "tradition." Tradition I is Oberman's term for the early church's belief that the content of apostolic Scripture and apostolic tradition coincide. On this view, church tradition was simply a way of making sense of Scripture, the Word of God written: "The history of obedience interpretation is the Tradition of the Church" (Oberman, *Forerunners of the Reformation* [New York: Holt,

all believers handed Scripture to the laity and encouraged them to interpret it for themselves.

William Abraham depicts Luther and Calvin as "canonical foundationalists" who treat biblical texts as so many deposits of propositional truth. For the Reformers, Scripture became the secure basis for belief. Abraham laments Scripture's slide from its position as ecclesial canon, a means of grace and a matter of soteriology, to its role in modern theology as a doctrinal criterion, a means of adjudication and a matter of epistemology.

According to Abraham, the significance of the Reformers' principle of *sola scriptura* extends far beyond the question of Scripture and tradition. Indeed, it precipitated "a massive epistemological crisis for the whole of Western culture."[2] Failure to agree on the meaning of Scripture rendered its function as epistemic norm inoperative, thus leading not only to a conflict of interpretations and a plethora of denominations but also to the wars of religion in the sixteenth to seventeenth centuries. And, in an ironic twist of events, the conflict of biblical interpretations paved the way for the independent foundationalist strategies of philosophers like Descartes and John Locke.[3]

On Abraham's account, the Reformers bequeathed the so-called "Cartesian anxiety" to the West, namely, the obsession with the question of how to ground one's proposals in the context of debates between rival authorities. Descartes thus appears as a secularized version of the Reformers' quest for a normative stand-point outside tradition. In Descartes's case, the result was a universal method of knowing that would lead all rational thinkers to an apprehension of universal truths. Differences of opinion could thus be settled by argument rather than by aggression, by syllogism rather than the sword.

Whereas the Reformation individual appealed to the illumination of the Holy Spirit, a source of light available only to some, the modern individual appeals to the illumination of reason, a source of light available, at least in principle, to all. While it is probably an exaggeration to speak of the eclipse of tradition in Protestant theology, it is fair to say that, in the wake of the Reformation, tradition played the role of moon to Scripture's sun: what light, and authority, tradition bears it does so by virtue of reflecting what shines forth from Scripture.

Rinehart, and Winston, 1966] p. 54). Tradition II, by contrast, was a later development which posited a second, supplementary source of revelation outside Scripture.

[2] William Abraham, *Canon and Criterion in Christian Theology: From the Fathers to Feminism* (Oxford: Clarendon Press, 1998), p. 163.

[3] Abraham's argument is here largely indebted to Richard Popkin's *The History of Skepticism from Erasmus to Spinoza* (Berekley, CA: University of California Press, 1979).

Biblical criticism: the eclipse of Scripture

Enlightenment thinkers typically preferred to view the world by the light of reason rather than Scripture. Indeed, the modern biblical critic is perhaps the paradigmatic autonomous rational individual who heeds Kant's call, issued in his essay "What is Enlightenment," to "Dare to use your own reason."

To study the Bible in the modern university meant employing the same critical methodologies used to study any other ancient text. Since the eighteenth century, biblical critics have by and large bracketed out the concerns of faith. Critics typically tend to treat the biblical text as evidence for something other than what God was doing in Israel and Jesus Christ – evidence used to reconstruct the original situation and "what actually happened" or the history of the text's composition. Some critics treat the text as evidence of the religion of ancient Israel, "what they actually believed." On this view, the text is a witness not to the object of faith (viz., God, salvation history) but to faith, to some human religious experience which has come to verbal expression in the Bible. Most significantly, modern biblical scholarship showed that the biblical texts themselves had histories.

Hans Frei has convincingly documented the devastating effect of the critical method on the theological interpretation of Scripture.[4] For precritical readers, biblical narrative just was the story of the real world. The biblical text was the framework with which to interpret history. Biblical criticism reverses this relationship: henceforth, the Bible must be interpreted in the context of the natural, scientifically explicable world. The result is the eclipse of the very notion of "Scripture."

In the first place, the critical approach denies the unity of the Old and New Testaments, opting instead to focus on historical discontinuity and theological diversity. Secondly, the presumption of naturalism inclines critics to explain the events to which biblical narratives refer in terms other than those in which they are presented. Jesus does not therefore enact the identity of God, as the texts claim, but must be understood in the light of some other context, for example, as a wandering sage in the context of Palestinian Judaism or, alternately, as a symbol for new being-in-the-world in the context of existential philosophy. What gets lost, says Frei, is the literal sense of biblical narrative, for which the meaning and referent of the text is a matter of what it says/shows.

It is with modern liberal theology, rather than with the Reformation, that we see the real overthrowing of authoritative Scripture and ecclesial

---

[4] Hans Frei, *The Eclipse of Biblical Narrative* (New Haven: Yale University Press, 1974).

tradition. For, unlike the Reformers, many modern theologians were prepared to reject the ancient creeds – even the apostolic tradition of the NT itself – in their haste to revise Christian faith in order to correlate it with modern learning and concerns. The Enlightenment represents the triumph of *logos* over *mythos*, the end of mythological thinking about God and about the way in which God acts in the world.

Modernity is less a child than a distorted image of the Reformation. The reasons for the Reformers' skepticism of ecclesial tradition were not those of Enlightenment thinkers. While there may be a formal parallel of sorts (i.e., each rejects the authority of interpretative traditions), material differences remain: the Reformers located authority in a self-revelation of the triune God; Enlightenment thinkers located authority in a rational self. While it is therefore too simplistic to draw a straight line from Luther's protest "Here I stand" to Kant's "Dare to use your own reason," what remains indisputable is that the net result of modernity was the demystification of both Scripture and tradition: the former was treated "like any other book" and the latter "like any other prejudice."

AFTER MODERNITY: THE CRITIQUE OF "CRITICISM" AND THE VINDICATION OF TRADITION

The most fundamental difference between modern and postmodern biblical studies has to do with the status of the critic herself, the autonomous knowing subject. In modernity, the subject sovereignly and disinterestedly uses method to reach knowledge and truth. In postmodernity, the priority is for subjects to acknowledge their own situatedness and interestedness.

Tradition rehabilitated and become rationality: hermeneutics

Hans-Georg Gadamer declared in *Truth and Method* that modernity's search for the right method was itself the problem.[5] The truth of art and literature gets communicated in ways that cannot be scientifically verified. Indeed, the task of understanding is less epistemological than ontological: it is all about human finitude and human situatedness in history.

What "criticism" overlooks is humanity's immersion in history and language. Neither individuals nor cultures enjoy a God's-eye point of view on the world. Human beings always and only hold points of view from within particular histories, languages, and traditions, from within what Gadamer

---

5 Hans-Georg Gadamer, 2nd rev. edn, trans. Joel Weinsheimer and Donald G. Marshall (New York: Continuum, 2002).

calls "horizons." Not even the scientific method can free us from our particular, and limited, historical horizons. Yet it is precisely these horizons that connect us to the past, for it is the past that shapes who we are today.

Human understanding is always "from below," never "from above." Bereft of privileged perspectives, we must make do with our prejudices (preconceptions). Gadamer famously states that "the prejudices of the individual, far more than his judgments, constitute the historical reality of his being."[6] The same goes for modernity itself: "the fundamental prejudice of the Enlightenment is the prejudice against prejudice itself, which denies tradition its power."[7]

Gadamer rehabilitates tradition by arguing that prejudices are conditions of understanding: "Understanding is to be thought of less as a subjective act than as participating in an event of tradition."[8] Consciousness is not sovereign, but "historically effected." We belong to history before history belongs to us. Thinking is not autonomous, but conditioned by one's place and time. The knowing and interpreting subject is never objective, but realizing this is, for Gadamer, the first step in understanding. The second step is to translate the text into our situation so that the text can address an issue of our time. Meaning is not an objective property of the text that the interpreter discovers so much as an event in the present, a "fusion of horizons," a moment of dialogue when reader and text converse. It follows for Gadamer that to understand a text properly, according to the claim it makes on this or that situation, is necessarily to understand it in a new and different way.

Does it follow that every prejudice or interpretative approach is as legitimate as another, each equally as able to hear what the text has to say? Though he recognizes the risk of relativism, Gadamer refuses to leap to the safety of objectivity by embracing criteria of validity. Instead, he concentrates on discerning interpretations that keep the conversation about the subject matter of a text going or, even better, enhance it. The dialogue keeps going in language; language is the form in which traditions – conversations – develop through history.

The rehabilitation of tradition is also seen in the work of Thomas Kuhn, the historian and philosopher of science, whose *The Structure of Scientific Revolutions* made the scientific community rather than the scientific method the primary factor in his explanation of how science works.[9] Kuhn defines "normal science" in terms of the scientific community's commitment to a stable "paradigm" that governs long periods of research. What Kuhn says

[6] Ibid., p. 266.　　[7] Ibid., p. 270.　　[8] Ibid., p. 290.
[9] Thomas S. Kuhn, *The Structure of Scientific Revolutions*, 2nd edn (University of Chicago Press, 1970).

about "normal science" closely resembles what Gadamer says about interpretative tradition. Kuhn's paradigms function much like foundation narratives whose authority stems from the fact that the process of professional education teaches scientists to respect the paradigms/classic texts and to continue the discussion about their interpretation (for example, research). From time to time, however, so many "anomalies" fall outside the explanatory range of the paradigm that the community undergoes an epistemological crisis and searches for a new paradigm. The replacement of one paradigm by another constitutes a scientific revolution, and marks the beginning of a new tradition. On Kuhn's view, the history of science itself becomes a story of the Scripture (read "paradigm") and tradition (read "scientific community") relation. Two paradigms represent "incompatible modes of community life."[10] The net result of Kuhn's work was to construe science in terms of traditions and interpretative communities.

Stanley Fish's *Is There a Text in this Class?* argues that textual meaning is not an objective property of the text but rather a product of the interpretative strategy brought to bear on it. It is the reader, in other words, who produces meaning.[11] Fish is aware of the danger of subjectivism, but argues that relativism need not follow from his position because the readers' interpretative strategies are governed by the interpretative community to which they belong. Not just any kind of reading goes. Much like Kuhn, then, Fish argues that a given paradigm or interpretative strategy makes for what we might call "normal hermeneutics." What counts as "normal" and what counts as "factual" are a matter of social convention, a matter of holding to the assumptions and strategies that define a given interpretative community. There is no single correct way of reading texts, only ways of reading that seem normal because they are relatively stable extensions of community interests and habits. Fish situates the interpreting subject in an authoritative interpretative community.

The reader is not a free agent, but "a member of a community whose assumptions about literature determine the kind of attention he pays."[12] Fish thus transcends the subjective/objective dichotomy by making both reader and text subservient to the interpretative community: to intersubjectivity, or simply tradition. What is postmodern about Fish's proposal is his insistence that (1) texts are not the causes but the effects of interpretative traditions, (2) interpretative traditions are themselves only relatively stable, for they grow and decline, and (3) there is no community-independent

[10] Ibid., p. 94.
[11] Fish, *Is There a Text in this Class? The Authority of Interpretative Communities* (London and Cambridge, MA: Harvard University Press, 1980).
[12] Ibid., p. 11.

vantage point from which to adjudicate the conflict between interpretative traditions.

In the area of moral theory, Alasdair MacIntyre has formulated an account of "tradition-based" rationality. Like Gadamer, MacIntyre believes the Enlightenment was mistaken in pretending that rationality affords a universal or tradition-independent perspective: "to be outside of all traditions is to be a stranger to enquiry; it is to be in a state of intellectual and moral destitution."[13] MacIntyre claims that all reasoning takes place within the context of some tradition. The Enlightenment, for example, is an "Encyclopaedia" tradition, a tradition that enshrines the ideal of "traditionless reason."

For MacIntyre, a tradition is a socially embodied argument as to how best to interpret and apply some authoritative text, be it secular or religious. Traditions develop by means of bringing their formative texts to bear on new contexts. The virtue of MacIntyre's account is that it includes a proposal as to how rival traditions can be compared and evaluated. Time is a key element in the evaluation: can a tradition narrate its own history coherently? Is a tradition able to solve new problems and resolve anomalies with its own resources without losing its identity? Comparing such narrative accounts may show that one tradition is rationally superior to another. For example, the Enlightenment tradition is incapable of solving its core problem, namely, that of acknowledging "traditionless reason" to be tradition-laden, the product of a particular historical community. By contrast, a tradition may be said to be rationally justified when it is able successfully to meet the challenge from new experience and rival traditions with its own resources, and in a way that is faithful to its own authoritative texts.

With MacIntyre's account of tradition-based rationality, the postmodern reversal of the modern prejudice against prejudice, authority, and tradition is complete. The authority of tradition does not work against reason but is itself a work of reason, for rationality is always tradition-based, never tradition-independent. Yet the rehabilitation of tradition as a historically extended interpretative argument is won at the cost of surrendering claim to tradition's universal point of view. Henceforth rationality is "from below" and hermeneutical, rooted in particular situations and thus seeing only partially, as through a glass darkly.

Scripture excommunicated and become textuality: grammatology

"Script-ure," or to be precise "writing," has featured prominently in many postmodern accounts of language. "Writing" is, on one level, that

---

[13] MacIntyre, *Whose Justice? Which Rationality?* (University of Notre Dame Press, 1989), p. 367.

form of language which does not rely on the presence of a speaker. Jacques Derrida contends that Western thought from ancient to modern times has viewed writing as parasitic on speech in order to privilege the thinking, speaking subject who knows her own mind, knows the coincidence of verbal sense and thought. "Speech" stands for the unproblematic access to one's "clear and distinct ideas." Modernity is "logocentric" in its assumption that language mediates "presence" (for example, the "presence of the thing to sight as *eidos*").[14] Logocentrism is the belief that the meaning and truth of what we say can be guaranteed by some center outside language (for example, Reason) by which we gain direct access to things themselves. Derrida believes, in contrast, that "writing" is prior to speech, in the sense that we cannot even begin to think, much less speak, independently of some language or other that precedes us. "Writing" is not merely the expression of some prelinguistic thought, but rather that which conditions thought in the first place.

Language is a sign-system made up of signifiers whose meaning is a function of their difference from other signs. This differential network of signs perpetuates a system of differences that never settle on a stable extralinguistic entity. These differences do not mirror the way things are but construct it. Far from being a neutral instrument of thought, language for Derrida is rather shot-through with intellectual and cultural biases based on binary oppositions – male/female; white/black; center/margin; straight/gay – oppositions that are, moreover, arbitrary social conventions. Language therefore conditions the way we think about the world. Strictly speaking, we do not even know our own minds except through the mediation of language; even self-consciousness is linguistically mediated and so lacks "presence". Deconstruction explores the constructedness of such differential systems and exposes what a given system excludes.

Derrida's *Of Grammatology* argues that all language is "writing" in the sense that there is something in the very structure of language itself that forestalls "presence," stable reference, or context-free meaning. For in order to function as signifiers, signs must be iterable, that is, they must be able to be repeated. However, anything that is said can be recontextualized – said again in another context. Hence there is no such thing as an identical repetition, for though the signifier may be the same, the occasion of its utterance, its context, is not. It does not even make sense to ask what a signifier – a word, a text – means outside of a specific context.

Derrida's account of writing therefore problematizes and complicates the notion that authors communicate clear and distinct ideas, for authors

[14] Jacques Derrida, *Of Grammatology* (Baltimore and London: Johns Hopkins University Press, 1976), p. 12.

cannot control the process of recontextualization that necessarily accompanies reading. Derrida sees no reason why the so-called "original" context should be more privileged than another. "Grammatology" is Derrida's name for a science of writing no longer governed by the assumption that language communicates stable meanings or referents. Its focus is on the historical, cultural, and ideological conditions that govern the production and reception of discourse. When Derrida says "there is nothing outside textuality,"[15] he means that there is nothing that escapes being conditioned and contextualized by language. For many postmodern interpreters, there is no "the meaning," no "the past"; instead, there is "my interpretation" or "our interpretation" of these things.

There is also no "the book," where book is assumed to be a fixed expression of an author's thought. For every reading of the book is a recontextualization, not a recovery of some original "presence" or truth. In Derrida's view, the idea of the book is the idea of a totality, a complete system whereby material signifiers represent ideal signifieds, a system where language perfectly expresses thought. The idea of the book is thus a denial of "writing" and "difference."[16]

The watchword of deconstruction is not "to the things themselves" but "to the textual traces." Texts yield only traces, not the things themselves. "There is nothing outside textuality" means that we have always and only to do with the world via verbal fragments in which certain features of the things themselves are inevitably left out. To assert "there is nothing outside textuality" is to deny the possibility of ever achieving immediacy, philosophy's longed-for encounter with pure "presence" uncontaminated by difference, an unmediated, nonlinguistic encounter with what lies outside language.

SCRIPTURE AND TRADITION IN POSTMODERNITY

Both the rehabilitation of tradition and the textualization of the book have had important consequences for the use of the Bible in both the academy and the church. Arguably the most serious challenge that postmodernity poses to the Reformation understanding of the Scripture/tradition relation and to modern assumptions about exegesis concerns the continuing possibility of any biblical authority as well as the continuing legitimacy of the very distinction between "text" and "commentary." Are biblical texts ever self-contained repositories of meaning, or do interpretative communities *make* what they find?

[15] Ibid., p. 158.   [16] Ibid., p. 18.

The postmodern Bible: demythologizing exegesis

The transition from modern to postmodern biblical studies involves more than the substitution of literary/critical for historical/critical methods of interpretation. On the contrary, the counterpart in postmodernity to the rise of historical consciousness in modernity is the rise of *ideological* consciousness.

The mandate of modern biblical studies to serve truth and pursue objective knowledge has given way to the postmodern mandate to serve the community and pursue justice. Historical criticism brackets out the contemporary context and proceeds as if the text were isolated from the reader's cultural context and concerns, able to be methodologically mastered with the aid of critical tools. Postmodern biblical scholars, however, "share a suspicion of the claim to mastery that characterizes traditional readings of texts, including modern biblical scholarship."[17] Postmodern interpreters challenge the Enlightenment claim to universality and objective reading by showing that these critical interpretations are actually power plays that seek to impose one way of looking at things as "the" way.

To demythologize biblical exegesis is at the same time to politicize it. My way of reading seems to me natural, but that may be simply my way of legitimating as universal or scientific a habit of thought that is in fact cultural, conventional, and ultimately arbitrary. *Whose reading counts, and why?* Such is the persistent refrain of postmodern biblical interpretation: "Biblical scholars have been slow to awaken from the dream in which positivist science occupies a space apart from interests and values, to awaken to the realization that our representations of and discourse about what the text meant and how it means are inseparable from what we *want* it to mean, from how we *will* it to mean."[18] Ideology is "meaning in the service of power."[19] Ideological criticism has to do "with the ethical character of and response to the text and to those lived relations that are represented and reproduced in the act of reading."[20]

Postmodern biblical studies begin by acknowledging the "interestedness" of every text and every reading. Scripture and tradition alike are equally "ideological." So, too, is modernity. From a postmodern perspective, the Enlightenment was not so much the end of prejudice but rather the substitution of one set of prejudices for another. To read in order to recover the

---

[17] Castelli, Elizabeth A. and Stephen D. Moore, Gary A. Phillips, and Regina M. Schwartz, eds., *The Postmodern Bible* (New Haven and London: Yale University Press, 1995), p. 2.
[18] Ibid., p. 14.
[19] J. B. Thompson, *Ideology and Modern Culture* (Palo Alto: Stanford University Press, 1990), p. 7.
[20] *Postmodern Bible*, p. 275.

meaning of the original author already assumes that meaning is an affair of consciousness (rather than of language), and that an author's consciousness can be more or less recovered. Yet Derrida and others have sought to expose the "structural unconscious" of language that to some extent controls what authors can, and *cannot*, say. Ideological criticism exposes both what texts repress or do not say (and why) and what various interpretative approaches repress (and why). As such, it is a form of "resistance reading" that insists on the fundamental indeterminacy of texts and interpretations: meaning cannot be determined absolutely because meaning cannot be decontextualized.

The idea that texts convey content dies hard. Yet both Fish and Derrida, in different ways, contend that there is no content that is independent of contexts and strategies of reading interpretation. According to Stephen Moore, however, "Hypostatized Content, invariant and discoverable, is the enabling fiction of our exegetical practice. Today, it is not our biblical texts that need demythologizing so much as our ways of reading them."[21]

To demythologize our habits of biblical exegesis is at the same time to situate or historicize them. "New Historicism" names not a method but a mind-set or set of concerns that sees texts and interpreters alike as embedded and enmeshed in a vast intertext of social and cultural history. New Historicism is an approach to literature that repudiates both the tendency in New Criticism to treat texts as autonomous aesthetic objects and the tendency of historical criticism to treat the texts as evidence for "what actually happened." The focus is instead on how the way the text represents the world serves the interest of some social cause or social class: "The construction of a past that characterized the Old Historicism is being supplanted and replaced by studies of how the past is constructed, the New Historicism."[22] In place of text-centered studies, the new focus on history includes the cultural situation of the text and the cultural situation of the reader, as well as the negotiations between the two. Such concerns have led most postmoderns to abandon the once clear distinction between "what it meant" and "what it means." Indeed, most postmoderns evince an underlying skepticism about whether the past can be known. To be sure, history can be represented, but these representations are only *our* representations – representations that perhaps say more about who we are than about who they were. For New Historicists, texts are less evidence for than *traces* of the past, and the past always assumes a textualized form.

---

[21] Moore, *Literary Criticism and the Gospel: The Theoretical Challenge* (New Haven: Yale University Press, 1989), p. 66.

[22] Gina Hens-Piazza, *The New Historicism* (Minneapolis: Augsburg Fortress, 2002), p. 28.

All texts and interpretations are caught up in the politics of representation, namely, in the struggle over whose narration of the past counts, and why. New Historicists depict the relation of literature and history in terms of reciprocal influence: as social forces shape literature, so literature shapes social forces. In a nutshell: "the historicity of texts and the textuality of history". The "historicity of texts" signals an interest not in "what actually happened" (viz., the world behind the text) but rather in the way in which texts are produced, and received, within specific social, cultural, and historical conditions – conditions that at some level constitute the text. "Writing" is always enmeshed and embedded in specific sociocultural configurations. The "textuality of history" refers to the inaccessibility of an unmediated past, and thus calls attention to the ways in which the past is represented and to the question of whose purposes are served by representing it one way rather than another. The postmodern interpreter wants to know how history gets told, and whose history is related.

Postmodernity has demythologized the methods of modern biblical criticism. Deconstruction's "there is nothing outside textuality" is related to the New Historicism's "there is nothing outside contextuality." Each shares a concern to situate both the subject and the text: texts are not self-contained literary productions but rather situated within social structures that themselves are textual (i.e., constituted by the system of differences which is language). Paraphrasing Marx, we might say that the point of postmodern thought is not to interpret the text, but to *situate* it. Postmodern exegesis is always situated: always "from below," never "from above." Neither the production nor the reception of texts is ahistorical: "Texts are caught up in the social processes and contexts out of which they emerge."[23] Though only a little lower than the angels, human interpreters are mired in time and space, where the forms and shape of culture, and the meaning of texts, are continuously disputed.

"Ruled reading": the ecclesial sense

If it is interpretation "all the way down," where does one locate authority in the Scripture/tradition relation? One increasingly popular postmodern answer is to locate it not in the author's individual subjective consciousness, but in the communal consciousness of the interpreting community. What, then, does the Scripture/tradition relation look like under the conditions of postmodernity?

In a creative fusion of Wittgenstein's notion of language-games and Clifford Geertz's notion of thick description, George Lindbeck recasts the

[23] Ibid., p. 6.

Scripture/tradition relation in terms of cultural–linguistic theology. On this approach, the task of theology is to describe Christian language in the context of the Christian form of life. The church thus resembles a culture, with its own practices and idioms. Lindbeck resists the modern temptation to think of cultures or religions as having a universal essence that is then expressed in varied ways. On the contrary, one must understand these practices and idioms on their own terms rather than "explain" them in terms of some foreign conceptual framework. It follows that the best way to understand is to learn how to participate in the life and the language. Only when one knows how to use the terms and follow the practices is one then in a position to articulate the grammatical rules that govern the Christian idiolect.

On Lindbeck's view, Scripture is the paradigmatic interpretative framework that the community uses to understand the world and its own identity. However, Scripture can only be rightly understood from within the believing community. Indeed, Scripture must be understood in terms of the ancient "Rule of Faith." Faithfulness is thus a matter not of adhering to an abstract set of biblical propositions so much as continuing a particular tradition of interpretation. For the "grammatical rules" that count for Lindbeck are ultimately the rules embedded in the language of the church, not the canonical Scriptures. On Lindbeck's view, tradition is the process of socialization in which members are taught how to use Scripture Christianly. Theology, in turn, becomes a species of ethnography, whose task is to describe, much like the cultural anthropologist, the rules that govern the life and language of the Christian community.[24] Indeed, even the literal sense of Scripture is a function less of authorial intentions than it is of community habits of reading.[25]

The authority of the ecclesial community and ecclesial tradition is even more pronounced in Stanley Hauerwas' work. On his view, the Reformers erred in giving their followers the impression that the Bible could be rightly interpreted by individuals who had not first undergone training, not scholarly but saintly, in the context of the church. In order to read the Bible Christianly, one needs training in Christian virtue, and this is largely the work of the Christian community. The Reformation principle *sola scriptura*

[24] See Lindbeck, *The Nature of Christian Doctrine: Religion and Theology in a Postliberal Age* (Philadelphia: Westminster, 1984), p. 115.
[25] This, at least, is the position of the later Frei in "The 'Literal Reading' of Biblical Narrative in the Christian Tradition: Does it Stretch or Will It Break?," in Frank McConnell, ed., *The Bible and the Narrative Tradition* (New York: Oxford University Press, 1986), pp. 37–77.

is a heresy because it assumes "that the text of Scripture makes sense separate from a Church that gives it sense."[26] The historical sense here gives way to the ecclesial sense.

Hauerwas believes that it is tradition all the way down, and he explicitly mentions Stanley Fish in this regard. "Meaning" for Hauerwas is a matter of use, not the author's use, however, but the use to which one puts biblical texts for the sake of the edification of the church community. Stephen Fowl similarly argues that what defines the theological interpretation of Scripture is the end for which the community reads it, namely, communion with God and with one another.[27] Fish and Fowl alike agree that there are many legitimate interpretative ends and interests; which end one happens to pursue simply depends on the community to which one belongs. Christians read the Bible as a unified work – as canon – because that is the interest, and the rule, of their interpretative community. The Bible is Scripture in the church; in the academy it is not. Or rather, the Bible *functions* as Scripture in the church. Postmoderns are reluctant to speak in terms of natures or essences. What the Bible "is" depends on how it is used by this or that interpretative community.

"Ruled reading" is the practice of interpreting the Bible as Scripture in the interpretative tradition known as the "church." For it is in church that readers are socialized into the practices of reading the Bible for communion and edification. As to authority, it would seem to lie with tradition – the socially embodied habit of interpretative practice – not Scripture.

BEYOND POSTMODERNITY: THE RECOVERY OF THEOLOGY

Must the church accept the conditions of postmodernity and, if so, *why*? Is it interpretative community – tradition – all the way down? Why privilege the church's use of Scripture? If theology is simply a kind of ethnography, then Derrida may well be right: theology and philosophy alike would then by species of "white mythology." Are there no checks and balances with which to correct tradition or to guard against its becoming a totalitarian regime? From a theological perspective, the dangerous extremes – bibliolatry with regard to Scripture, ideology with regard to tradition – are primarily theological and spiritual in character, and only secondarily epistemological and ethical.

[26] Hauerwas, *Unleashing the Scripture: Freeing the Bible from Captivity to America* (Nashville: Abingdon, 1993), p. 155, n. 7.
[27] See Fowl, *Engaging Scripture: A Model for Theological Interpretation* (Oxford: Blackwell, 1998).

Interestingly, several genealogical analyses of modernity indicate a conspicuous absence of and atrophy of reliance on resources internal to Christian faith and life.[28] Apparently, most modern theologians, when faced with intellectual and cultural pressures, turn away from the traditional doctrinal and doxological resources and look elsewhere for help. Postmodern theologians often evidence a similar reflex. Is it indeed the case, however, that theology can do no better than exchange one philosophical master for another? Can we really recover the theological interpretation of Scripture with either the modern crutch of historical criticism or the postmodern crutch of communitarianism? Do either of these movements really recover Scripture and tradition, or do they only create pale secular shadows thereof?

According to John Webster, theology should bow its knee neither to modern nor to postmodern agendas. With regard to Scripture, neither modern nor postmodern accounts of reading can do justice to what happens when the Bible is read in Scripture in the church: "a Christian description of the Christian reading of the Bible will be the kind of description which talks of God and therefore talks of all other realities *sub specie divinitatis.*"[29] A non-reductive account of Scripture will continue to speak not only of intertextuality but of *inspiration*, not merely of undecidablity but of *clarity*, not simply of writing but of *witness*, and it will do so in properly theological terms. Similarly, with regard to tradition, Webster warns about reducing our theological language about the church to the generic language about "forms of life," "culture," or even "ecclesiality."[30] Though "community" is the darling of many postmoderns, Christian theology must describe the church in terms that go beyond the cultural and sociological, for the church is constituted by the Word and Spirit of God.

A small band of Christian theologians has begun to set to work exploring the significance of Scripture and tradition with properly dogmatic sources and resources rather than with those drawn from philosophy or cultural studies. Their discussions of Scripture and tradition are framed in terms not of modern or postmodern themes but of Christian doctrine. According to these theologians, we need to get beyond both modern *and* postmodern criticism and suspicion. Specifically, we need to reconceive the Scripture/tradition relation in terms of Trinitarian theology and in terms of the triune economy, namely, in the light of the salvific work of Father, Son,

---

[28] See, for example, M. J. Buckley, *At the Origins of Modern Atheism* (New Haven: Yale University Press, 1987); Colin Gunton, *The One, the Three, and the Many* (Cambridge University Press, 1993); John Milbank, *Theology and Social Theory: Beyond Secular Reason* (Oxford: Blackwell, 1990).

[29] Webster, *Word and Church* (Edinburgh and New York: T. & T. Clark, 2001), p. 47.

[30] Ibid., p. 85.

and Spirit. In short, *we need to view Scripture in terms of divine discourse and tradition in terms of divine deed.*

The theological recovery of tradition: the church as the work of the Spirit

The vocation of the church is to embody Scripture in new contexts. As Fowl and L. Gregory Jones rightly observe, this requires "a very different set of skills" from those required of the professional biblical scholar, skills that can only be developed by living, and reading, in community.[31] But how is the community formed? According to Reinhard Hütter, a theologically adequate description of the church and its tradition must move beyond sociology and ethnography to discuss the economy of the Holy Spirit, whose work the church is. The church does not construct its identity so much as *receive* it. The saint is a person who has not simply been socialized, but *sanctified*, into a set of new practices. Hütter believes that Lindbeck's cultural–linguistic account of the church suffers from a "pneumatological deficit"; the church is not simply an intersubjective community but a community whose practices have been formed and enabled by the Holy Spirit. Indeed, Hütter speaks of the church as "the public of the Holy Spirit" and of the Spirit as the "hypostasis" of the church.[32] Tradition is not "poetic," something the church creates, but something "pathic," something the church *suffers* as a result of the Spirit's work.

Tradition, on this theological account, is not merely human, but a way of participating in the work of God's Holy Spirit. Such is the working premise behind the recent publication of theologians associated with the Center for Catholic and Evangelical Theology, *Knowing the Triune God: The Work of the Spirit in the Practices of the Church.*[33] Knowledge of God comes from participating in the core practices of the church – baptism, the Lord's Supper, reading Scripture, communal prayer; hospitality – practices that are not simply cultural, but pneumatological. These are the public means the Spirit uses in the triune economy of salvation.

Why associate tradition with the third person of the Trinity in particular? First, to resist the modern tendency to associate "Spirit" with the private realm of inward subjectivity. Second, to acknowledge that theology and biblical interpretation are at once human practices and God's own action. On the other hand, of course, the question we are left with is, "Which church?"

---

[31] Fowl and Jones, *Reading in Communion: Scripture and Ethics in Christian Life* (Grand Rapids: Eerdmans, 1991), p. 2.
[32] Hütter, *Suffering Divine Things: Theology as Church Practice* (Grand Rapids: Eerdmans, 2000), pp. 158, 119.
[33] James J. Buckley and David S. Yeago, eds. (Grand Rapids: Eerdmans, 2001).

Hütter replies by invoking Luther's criterion of the mark of the true church, namely, the preaching of the Gospel. Yet the nagging postmodern question remains: *"Whose interpretation of the Gospel counts, and why?"*

The theological recovery of Scripture: the Word as divine discourse

Even a "spirited" tradition cannot lord it over the Word of God, for the ministry of the Spirit is precisely the ministry of the Word. Scripture is the standing testimony of the Spirit to the church concerning Jesus Christ, the one who makes the Father known and the one who accomplishes the Father's salvific will. In terms of dogmatic theology: Scripture is Christ's own witness to himself via the commissioned agency of the prophets and apostles who authored it in the power of the Holy Spirit. When one deals with Scripture one is not simply dealing with a textual object, but with a field of divine communicative action. Scripture is not merely "writing," but rather a key instrument in the communicative economy of the triune God in which the Father is revealed, the Son reveals, and the Spirit is the agent of revelation's perfection. So: whose God-talk counts, and why? The answer is: *God's*, because he is the triune Lord. Recovering Scripture theologically means acknowledging the Bible as a text of divine discourse.

The Bible is not Scripture simply because an interpretative community decides to use it as such. On the contrary, it is the divine decision to authorize, appropriate, assume, and annex these human communicative acts into the economy of revelation and reconciliation. Webster notes: "The being of the canonical texts is determined by their divine use."[34] The church acknowledges what the Bible is – divine discourse – but this acknowledgment does not make it so. The inspiration of Scripture in the past and the illumination of Scripture in the present are but twin moments of one continuous work of the Holy Spirit who, in the triune communicative economy, presents the wisdom of God in Jesus Christ.

A properly theological account of Scripture begins from the premise that God is a communicative agent, able to use language for communicative purposes.[35] Nicholas Wolterstorff suggests that God speaks by way of either deputizing or appropriating human discourse. Wolterstorff, along with a number of contemporary "speech act" philosophers of language, wants to insist that "speaking" covers a much broader range of activities than "revealing."[36] It was modern philosophers of language who tended

---

[34] Webster, *Word and Church*, p. 31.

[35] The doctrine of providence here becomes all-important. Can God do things with words? With his Spirit? Providence pertains both to the "evangelical" principle (viz., that God speaks good news in a reliable way – inspiration) and to the "catholic" principle (viz., that God leads the church to a correct understanding of the Gospel – illumination).

[36] Wolterstorff, *Divine Discourse: Philosophical Reflections on the Claim that God Speaks* (Cambridge University Press, 1995), p. 2.

to restrict the function of language to either "representing" some external state of affairs or "expressing" some subjective state. But language is far more than an epistemological tool for representing reality. As J. L. Austin argued, one can do many things with words. For, in speaking, we also perform other (illocutionary) acts: asking, asserting, warning, commanding, etc.

Given this postmodern understanding of language as doing things, it follows that a theology of Scripture need not confine itself to discussing revelation, for words do more than refer to the world. The point of speaking of divine discourse is that God does things with Scripture precisely by saying something. What does God do? Wolterstorff suggests that unless there is good reason to think otherwise, we should assume that God says, means, and does in his appropriating discourse what the human authors said, meant, and did in their original discourse.[37] Of course, what God is doing in Scripture must be determined in relation to the context of the entire canon, which forms the whole in light of which we interpret the parts. If Scripture enjoys final authority over tradition, therefore, it is because authority finally resides in the divinely authorized and appropriated discourse of the canon. Scripture, not the community, is thus the language-game whose grammar must govern the development of tradition and Christian doctrine.[38]

CONCLUSION: LIMPING TOWARD BETHLEHEM

"Where the Gospel is, and Christ, there is Bethlehem." (Luther)

Scripture and tradition are paired sources and norms for doing theology, for seeking knowledge of God and knowledge of self. How do we know God and ourselves? By attending to the story of the one true God and the one true man, the Gospel of Jesus Christ, in its canonical context. In Luther's words: "Christ is the subject matter of theology."[39] Where can we find Christ? In the Gospel. The Gospel is not simply propositional information, but narrative; not simply narrative, but promise; not simply promise, but summons. The purpose of these various evangelical illocutions is to preach and present Christ: the wisdom and salvation of God. The Scriptures are the "swaddling clothes" of Christ, the "manger" to which we come to adore him.

---

[37] Ibid., p. 236.
[38] See Kevin J. Vanhoozer, *The Drama of Doctrine: A Canonical–Linguistic Approach to Theology* (Louisville, KY: Westminster/John Knox, forthcoming).
[39] Cited in Paul Althaus, *The Theology of Martin Luther* (Philadelphia: Fortress, 1966), p. 9.

A future for *sola scriptura*?

The emergence of postmodernity coincides with what David Tracy terms the "return of the repressed." Perhaps nothing was more repressed by secular reason than the notion of divine revelation: the Word of God. Postmodernity has opened up breathing space once again to consider what is "other" to our theories. It therefore creates hearing space to hear, once again, the voice of God, the wholly "other," speaking in Scripture.

By *sola scriptura* the Reformers signaled their belief in the supreme authority of Scripture for the faith and life of the church. Both modernity and postmodernity have occasioned their respective crises of authority: whose interpretation of the way, the truth, and the life counts, and why? Those who believe in the testimony to Jesus Christ in the Scriptures, a testimony divinely authorized and appropriated, have an answer to this question. These particular texts narrate and explain God's story – what God began in the history of Israel and completed in the history of Jesus Christ – which is also the story of humanity. Scripture is a polyphonic testimony to what God has done, is doing, and will do in Christ for the salvation of the world. No other story, no work of genius, communicates that. *Sola scriptura* means that this testimony is not only irreducible, but that Scripture should enjoy epistemic and existential primacy in the life of the church.

Scripture continues to be the supreme norm for Christian faith and life, then, not as an epistemic norm that caters to modernity's craving for certainty, but as a *sapiential* norm that provides direction for one's fitting participation in the great evangelical drama of redemption. Scripture is the script to which the church constantly refers as it performs and improvises parables of the kingdom of God on the changing scenes of the world stage.

If *sola scriptura* means "the Bible alone apart from the church and tradition," it has no future. But this is not what *sola scriptura* means. *Sola scriptura* is a protest not against tradition as such but against the presumption that church tradition (interpretation) and Scripture (text) necessarily coincide. The testimony of the prophets and apostles fixed in biblical discourse thus guards against the hardening of human tradition into totalizing metanarrative. To the extent that *sola scriptura* is an indispensable tool of ideology critique, its future seems assured. Indeed, seen in this light, *sola scriptura* sounds positively postmodern to the extent that it questions whether any single human point of view captures universal truth. For the voice of God in Scripture is mediated by a polyphony of human voices.[40]

---

[40] On the importance of language as dialogic and polyphonic, see Mikhail Bakhtin, *Problems of Dostoevsky's Poetics*, trans. Caryl Emerson (Minneapolis: University of Minnesota Press, 1984) and *The Dialogic Imagination* trans. Caryl Emerson and Michael Homquist (Austin: University of Texas Press, 1981).

"Scripture" refers to this whole dialogical discourse, this unified canonical chorale.

A future for tradition?

The future of tradition similarly appears to be assured, for all forms of inquiry, indeed all forms of speech and life, are tradition-based. To read the Bible as Scripture is always to read it in a particular interpretative tradition. For the church is itself an interpretative tradition, a communally embodied, living, and active commentary on Scripture. Yet tradition, while inevitable, should never become insular or self-contained. On the one hand, tradition ought to remain open to the continuing historical effects, and corrections, of the Spirit-ministered word written. In the second place, church tradition ought to be open to having its interpretation of the Bible (not the divine discourse itself) corrected by insights from the secular world. "A church whose central activity is the interpretation of scripture is not the guardian of a timeless deposit of faith but rather the *ecclesia semper reformanda*."[41] As MacIntyre says, only traditions that allow themselves to be called into question can be deemed rational; "always reforming" here becomes the hallmark of fallibilist rationality applied to the interpretative community.

Tradition, then, is at once necessary yet corrigible. Its authority is consequently ministerial, not magisterial. Tradition's authority derives from its ministry of the Word, from its ability to direct us to the Christ attested in Scripture. For the purpose of tradition is to lead us to and then into where the Gospel is in order to meet the Christ enfolded in the Scriptures. Biblical interpreters may cast aside their modern and postmodern crutches and approach Scripture theologically. Yet ultimately we can only come limping to Bethlehem. Limping, because we are aware that our interpretative communities have not always been alert or attentive to the concerns of women, non-Europeans, much less the poor. Limping, because we have wrestled with the critical spirits of modernity and postmodernity, and have had the hip of hubris dislocated. Even our best readings, those to which Christians are most committed, remain provisional, situated this side of the eschaton. Limping, because our churches are hobbled by continuing differences, differences that temporarily belie the perspicuity of the Scriptures and the unity of the Spirit.

Limping, we nevertheless approach Bethlehem, humble and hungry pilgrims, eager to meet Christ. Yet if Scripture is directly Gospel-centered, tradition is only indirectly so, for tradition is not itself the Word of God. Tradition mediates the Gospel via catholicity, via the diverse communities

---

[41] Garrett Green, *Theology, Hermeneutics, and the Imagination* (Cambridge University Press, 2000), p. 177.

that have sought to receive and respond to Scripture across space and over time. Catholicity marks the lesson – once known, then forgotten, then re-learned in postmodernity – that it takes *many* interpreters to hear the *one* word of God in all the fullness of its glory and truth.

The future of Scripture and tradition is neither evangelical nor catholic alone but both together. The canonically bounded, polyphonic Scriptures speak in many and diverse ways of Jesus Christ (the evangelical principle). A canonically bounded, polyphonic tradition that embraces interpretative voices from East and West, ancient and modern, best corresponds to the polyphonic Scriptures themselves (the catholic principle). Honoring Scripture and tradition under the conditions of postmodernity means doing theology that is at once evangelical in its acknowledging the priority of God's communicative action, and catholic in its acknowledging God's giving the Spirit of reception to the church extended across time, space, and culture.

Further reading

Adam, A. K. M., *What is Postmodern Biblical Criticism?* (Minneapolis: Augsburg Fortress, 1995).

Buckley, James J. and David S. Yeago, eds., *Knowing the Triune God: The Work of the Spirit in the Practices of the Church* (Grand Rapids: Eerdmans, 2001) pp. 49–93.

Castelli, Elizabeth A. and Stephen D. Moore, Gary A. Phillips, and Regina M. Schwartz, eds., *The Postmodern Bible* (New Haven and London: Yale University Press, 1995).

Hens-Piazza, Gina, *The New Historicism* (Minneapolis: Augsburg Fortress, 2002).

Hütter, Reinhard, *Suffering Divine Things: Theology as Church Practice* (Grand Rapids: Eerdmans, 2000).

Vanhoozer, Kevin J. *The Drama of Doctrine: A Canonical–Linguistic Approach to Theology* (Louisville, KY: Westminster/John Knox, forthcoming).

Webster, John, *Word and Church* (Edinburgh and New York: T. & T. Clark, 2001).

Williams, D. H., *Retrieving the Tradition and Renewing Evangelicalism: A Primer for Suspicious Protestants* (Grand Rapids: Eerdmans, 1999).

Wolterstorff, Nicholas, *Divine Discourse: Philosophical Reflections on the Claim that God Speaks* (Cambridge University Press, 1995).

10 Theological method

DAN R. STIVER

Theological methodology is like one of those cases where a foreign plant is imported to provide ground cover and ends up being a persistent weed that cannot be eradicated. The more it is attacked, chopped, and hacked, the more it grows. Once, it was seen as a desirable plant, the flower of theological development. It grew because it was cultivated and highly desired. As it has grown more disputed and even out of favor, it keeps coming back and is as profuse as ever. Why is the theological garden, so to speak, in such straits?

At the fading of modernity, it has become clear in theology that methodology, or, as it is often technically called, prolegomena, was central to its assumptions. As many have pointed out, modernity generally relied on a secure foundation and then a secure method to build on to the foundation – at least that was the goal. Postmodernism is the result of repeated failure to achieve such a lofty ideal; thus the postmodern turn especially rejects such reliance on foundationalism and method. The criticism of relying on method, however, has led to the proliferation of writings on proper methodology! The result is someone like William Placher writing an excellent book, entitled *Unapologetic Theology*, on theological methodology that eschews emphasis on methodology. He reflects in the Preface, "A good many people – myself included – have urged contemporary theologians to abandon their preoccupation with methodology and get on with the business of really doing theology. I therefore confess embarrassment at being the author of a sort of extended preface to contemporary discussions about theological method. Prologomena [*sic*] to prologomena [*sic*]! Worse and worse!"[1]

The ensuing embarrassment appears to be something with which we have to live for the time being. Even though it is generally acknowledged that we are moving from modernity to whatever follows, literally "post"

---

[1] William C. Placher, *Unapologetic Theology: A Christian Voice in a Pluralistic Conversation* (Louisville: Westminster/John Knox Press, 1989), p. 7.

modernity, the problem is that we are still "on the move." What we are leaving is clearer than what we are approaching. Such trackless times call for a great deal of attention paid to navigation rather than journeying. This is a different case than where we are treading the old well-worn roads and can move quickly and lightly. It is not like driving to our accustomed workplace where we can give little thought at all to our driving; rather, it is like traveling for the first time to a new destination in a new and complex city. What are the landmarks? What route do we take? How do we know which direction is correct? In an earlier time we might have asked, can we use our traditional conveyances, or do we have to construct new ones? Like the pioneers, we generally have to do such navigation en route because we cannot anticipate all the obstacles we will confront.

The irony of our situation, however, is that postmodernity implies that we should not stress navigation as much as the journey itself. As Placher put it, we should be *doing* theology rather than talking about *how* to do it. The purpose of methodology in a postmodern context, therefore, is to be not so much a blueprint to be slavishly followed as a map to be consulted only periodically. As one sets out, in fact, the map may hardly be needed at all. At other times, it pays to stop and linger on details of the map.

My purpose in this chapter is consequently to indicate what such a map might look like and how it might be used. Thus, I will first elaborate the changed postmodern situation that calls for minimizing the importance of methodology, on the one hand, and on the other for demarcating the proper role it can and should have.

Subsequently, I will lay out a particular framework for doing theology based on an unusual connection between "postliberal theology," also known as the Yale School, and a circumspect appeal to the hermeneutical philosophy identified particularly with the thought of Hans-Georg Gadamer and Paul Ricoeur. Usually these two traditions have been seen as sharply opposed,[2] but I suggest that they can mutually enhance one another, thereby illustrating one of the marks of postmodernism, namely, the weaving together of seemingly disparate threads. The significance of Gadamer and Ricoeur is that they are significant postmodern philosophers in their own right whose ideas have been appropriated by many theologians, albeit usually in an unsystematic way. Drawing upon them will highlight the postmodern features of my approach.

---

[2] For example, Hans Frei, a major figure in postliberal theology, sees Gadamer as a subjective foundationalist in "The 'Literal Reading' of Biblical Narrative in the Christian Tradition: Does It Stretch or Will It Break?," in Frank McConnell, ed., *The Bible and the Narrative Tradition*, (New York: Oxford University Press, 1986), pp. 36–77.

POSTMODERNITY AND MINIMIZING METHODOLOGY

Ronald Thiemann, a postliberal theologian, has argued at length that theology in modernity has largely relied on a foundationalist paradigm, meaning that the basis for theology had to be nailed down before theology per se could be engaged.[3] Nancey Murphy has further shown that this reliance took place across the board in conservative and liberal theology.[4] The result was that prolegomena became of the utmost importance. In other words, if the foundation were not properly laid, then everything that followed was at risk.

Conservatives tended to move toward establishing Scripture as a bullet-proof shield against modern historical–critical challenges. Following Schleiermacher, others often looked to an impregnable religious experience that would found their theologizing. Still others relied on a philosophical system such as that of Hegel or Heidegger to ground their work.[5] Rationalists like Descartes and Spinoza prized the certainty of beliefs; empiricists in the style of Locke and Hume focused on indubitable sense experience. What is clearer now than heretofore is that rationalists and empiricists shared a common paradigm.

While one could possibly have a foundationalist "noetic structure" without founding it on such incorrigible beliefs,[6] a more attractive alternative is to understand beliefs as having a web-like structure, based on the thought of the later Ludwig Wittgenstein and W. V. O. Quine. This allows for some beliefs to be more central and solid in relation to more peripheral beliefs, akin to foundational structures, but unlike a foundational structure the logical relations do not proceed in just one way. As Wittgenstein put it, "One might almost say these foundation-walls are carried by the whole house," and again, "What stands fast does so, not because it is intrinsically obvious

---

[3] Ronald F. Thiemann, *Revelation and Theology: The Gospel as Narrated Promise* (University of Notre Dame Press, 1985).

[4] Nancey Murphy, *Beyond Liberalism and Fundamentalism: How Modern and Postmodern Philosophy Set the Theological Agenda*, Rockwell Lecture Series (Valley Forge, PA: Trinity Press International, 1996), Introduction and Part 1.

[5] Hans Frei's work shows how pervasive was the tendency from the seventeenth century forward to move from the biblical text itself to some other ground. In his estimation, too, this "eclipse of biblical narrative" was across the board. Hans W. Frei, *The Eclipse of Biblical Narrative: A Study in Eighteenth and Nineteenth Century Hermeneutics* (New Haven: Yale University Press, 1974).

[6] An example is Alvin Plantinga, "Reason and Belief in God," in Alvin Plantinga and Nicholas Wolterstorff, eds., *Faith and Rationality: Reason and Belief in Go* (University of Notre Dame Press, 1983), pp. 16–93. He offers a devastating critique of what he terms "classical foundationalism," based upon incorrigible beliefs or indubitable sense experience, but is himself a foundationalist.

or convincing; it is rather held fast by what lies around it."[7] Quine suggests that some beliefs are nearer to direct experience on the edges of the web, while others are farther removed toward the center. "Facts" themselves are not seen as incorrigible but as "theory-laden" and capable of reassessment. This is especially important in terms of the "facts" of religious experience since they are more clearly susceptible to diverse interpretation. An implication is that when a problem arises for some belief, there is no a-priori way to resolve the problem. As Quine put it: "Any statement can be held true come what may, if we make drastic enough adjustments elsewhere in the system.... Conversely, by the same token, no statement is immune to revision."[8] Usually the less central belief is revised; sometimes, however, the revision may reach to the center, much in the way that the impassibility of God, long a major divine attribute, has largely given way to affirmation of the suffering of God.

As a next step, Richard Bernstein has pointed out that the foundationalist move is only one aspect of modernity. An emphasis on proper method is also crucial. He uses the term "objectivism" to include an emphasis on both classical foundationalism and rigorous method. Thus he concludes, "By 'objectivism,' I mean the basic conviction that there is or must be some permanent, ahistorical matrix or framework to which we can ultimately appeal in determining the nature of rationality, knowledge, truth, reality, goodness, or rightness."[9]

Gadamer's *magnum opus*, *Truth and Method*, criticizes this mania for method in modernity and argues that truth is finally grasped by considered judgment that is irreducible to a strict method.[10] Even the reliance on method involves such judgments that themselves cannot be validated by method, similar to Aristotle's notion of practical wisdom where the judgment of what is just cannot be reduced to a demonstrable science. In effect, Gadamer turns Aristotle on his head since Aristotle regarded demonstration and certainty as the marks of knowledge and science in the strictest sense.[11] Gadamer is consistent with movements in philosophy of science that regard any system as grounded in what Michael Polanyi called "tacit judgments"

[7] Ludwig Wittgenstein, *On Certainty*, ed. G. E. M. Anscombe and G. H. von Wright, trans. Denis Paul and G. E. M. Anscombe (New York: Harper Torchbooks, 1969), paras. 248, 144.

[8] W. V. O. Quine, "Two Dogmas of Empiricism," in E. D. Lemke, ed., *Contemporary Analytic and Linguistic Philosophies* (Buffalo: Prometheus Books, 1983), p. 406. Originally published in 1951.

[9] Richard Bernstein, *Beyond Objectivism and Relativism: Science, Hermeneutics, and Praxis* (Philadelphia: University of Pennsylvania Press, 1985), p. 8.

[10] Hans-Georg Gadamer, *Truth and Method*, trans. Joel Weinsheimer and Donald G. Marshall, 2nd edn (New York: Crossroad, 1991).

[11] Ibid., p. 314.

that rely on explicit evidence, yet are underdetermined by such positivistic traits.[12]

Bernstein insightfully perceives that modern relativism, skepticism, and even nihilism are in many ways just the flip-side of objectivism, thus the title for his book, *Beyond Objectivism and Relativism*. When the standards for knowledge are set so high, as they have been from the roots of Western thought in Plato and Aristotle, it is difficult for anything to measure up. In many ways, the story of modern philosophy relates one failed attempt after another to attain such heights. At the outset, there was great confidence in the possibility of attaining knowledge based on the highest of standards, as evinced by Descartes, Spinoza, Leibniz, and later in subtler form by Hegel. However, more and more constraints began to be placed on the possibility of such knowledge by more skeptical thinkers such as Hume and Kant, followed by one of the most radical of all, Nietzsche. Hume and Kant still placed the standards very high; but they thought that very little could attain them. Skeptics are thus in a sense frustrated objectivists. Ironically, the last gasp of modernity's attempt to attain what Edmund Husserl termed "rigorous science"[13] came after Nietzsche: in logical positivism, in Husserl's phenomenology, and to some extent, in later structuralism in the fifties and sixties. The beginning of the twenty-first century, however, finds few who find such Herculean efforts worthwhile. The upshot is that neither objectivism nor skepticism is today regarded as inevitable.

In our postmodern situation, it also seems futile and a little foolish for theologians to have attempted to emulate the same attempts in their own province. In this sense, theology has seemed largely on the defensive in modernity because it could hardly measure up to such public standards for rigorous certainty and unchallengeable methods. Theology in modernity faced a catch-22 of either sacrificing the mystery of God to meet objectivist standards or of sacrificing the cogency of belief in God altogether to place theology in a risk-free fideistic zone of private belief. In the postmodern situation, however, no strong epistemological reason remains for theology to be so defensive. The playing field has been leveled, and, while theology is not going to be given any special favors, it is also not disqualified from playing. The challenge, on the one hand, is that no one stands in a privileged epistemological position and so relativism is a constant specter; on the other

---

[12] Michael Polanyi, *Personal Knowledge: Toward a Post-Critical Philosophy*, 2nd edn (University of Chicago Press, 1962). For further reference to the way in which contemporary philosophy of science sees science as having many of these hermeneutical aspects of religion, see Ian G. Barbour, *Religion and Science: Historical and Contemporary Issues*, rev. edn (San Francisco: HarperSanFrancisco, 1997), Part Two.

[13] Edmund Husserl, "Philosophy as Rigorous Science," *Phenomenology and the Crisis of Philosophy*, trans. Quentin Lauer (New York: Harper Torchbooks, 1965), pp. 122–47.

hand, if one drops the impossible and quixotic standards of modernity, the specter may be more easily exorcised.

The ironic consequence for theological methodology in a postmodern context is to downplay methodology. Moreover, as it is carried out in its more modest role, methodology must avoid the objectivist traps of modernity. It should not see itself as the necessary foundationalist starting point that must be settled before going on to anything else. It cannot expect such certainty, nor can it even expect agreement. In fact, it would be possible to place methodology later in the enterprise, as James McClendon has done to some extent in writing a three-volume theology that reverses the tradition by doing practical theology first, then systematic, followed by philosophical theology last.[14] Stanley Grenz exemplifies this postmodern shift in a way that I affirm by placing the usual foundation for evangelicals, Scripture, much later in the enterprise, as an aspect of the doctrine of the Holy Spirit, which he treats after themes associated with God the creator (God, creation, providence, humanity, and sin) and God the Redeemer (Christology and soteriology).[15] Karl Barth, who is seen by some as presaging postmodern approaches in many ways, is known for his opposition to apologetics by arguing that the best apologetic is a good theology, that is, the persuasiveness of theology is seen in the display of its content rather than its methodological prowess before the content is ever reached.[16] At some point, theologians should therefore be able to proceed more quickly to theology per se, as Placher saw, with more self-confidence and boldness.

However, as Placher also discerned, a need still exists for prolegomena. In a time of transition in philosophy and in a time of flux in theology, being clear about one's epistemological commitments and presuppositions continue to be desirable. The point is that methodology should be seen in this clarifying role, not as a foundation or as a proof.

Another significant implication for postmodern prolegomena is that the purpose is not to lay out the one and only step-by-step method that must be followed; rather, it is to outline the basic framework for doing theology. Thus, the actual shape and ordering of theology can, and should, vary. The church universal is best served not by attempting to write the one systematic for everyone but by distinctive theologies written in different ways

---

[14] James Wm. McClendon, Jr., *Ethics: Systematic Theology*, vol. 1 (Nashville: Abingdon Press, 1986); *Doctrine: Systematic Theology*, vol. 2 (Nashville: Abingdon Press, 1994); *Witness: Systematic Theology*, vol. 3 (Nashville: Abingdon, 2000).

[15] Stanley J. Grenz, *Theology for the Community of God* (Nashville, TN: Broadman & Holman, 1994), ch. 14.

[16] See Hans Frei's influential article about Barth's style, "Eberhard Busch's Biography of Karl Barth," in George Hunsinger and William C. Placher, eds., *Types of Christian Theology* (New Haven: Yale University Press, 1992), Appendix C.

from different perspectives. As such, theology represents an affirmation of God's mystery and majesty that is no more captured by one theology than by one canonical Gospel. For the sake of clarity, prolegomena spells out one's basic approach. This would include one's tradition and context and the major theological emphases that shape one's theology, examples of which abound in contemporary theology (for example, the social Trinity, the afore-mentioned suffering of God, liberation, the gathered church, or eschatology). It should also reveal the philosophical and other commitments that charac-terize one's approach to theology, which leads us to explore more fully the role of philosophy in relation to theological methodology.

POSTMODERN THEOLOGY AND "AD HOC" PHILOSOPHIZING

The role of philosophy is sensitive because any appeal to philosophy looks like the foundationalist dependence that characterized modernist methodology. In reaction, some see postmodernism as implying a fideistic approach to theology, removing it from the larger playing field altogether. Hans Frei, perhaps the major figure in postliberal theology, is helpful at this point in his posthumously published work on types of Christian theology.[17] He describes five types that can be plotted between two poles. At one pole, theology is an instance of a more general class, with philosophy as the nat-ural cognate discipline providing a theoretical foundation. Because of this grounding in philosophy, it is a more modernistic approach and is repre-sented by the first two of his types. At the other pole, theology tends to be a second-order description of the life of the Christian community, and the natural cognate discipline, if one is considered at all, is interpretive social science with the implication that this approach is more closely related to Christian practice. Frei sees types three to five as closer to this pole, but Frei's fifth type goes so far in this direction that it falls into fideism where Chris-tian theology only attends to itself without reference to anything outside. He sees this fideistic type as being reduced to simple repetition, the equiv-alent to "hermeneutical silence."[18] I see such fideism as ironically caught within the modernistic framework because it unnecessarily gives up on pub-lic discourse and retreats to a privatistic faith. The logic of postmodernism need not lead to fideism or subjectivism but in many ways is more open to dialogue and cross-fertilization than modernity, as we shall see.

Consequently, the third and fourth types are the ones that appear post-modern and are the ones where he sees the most promise. Here the focus

---

[17] Frei, in *Types*, pp. 1–7.   [18] Ibid., p. 6.

is on fidelity to Christian practice, but there is openness to methodical correlation (the third type) or to ad hoc connection (the fourth type) with other disciplines. While he suggests that sociology rather than philosophy may be more valuable in these types, his examples show that philosophy as well as other disciplines can be helpful as long as they are not used in a foundationalist manner. Such a nonfoundationalist approach is the way I understand philosophy as still being a conversation partner with theological methodology in the postmodern context.

Lindbeck, the other most significant figure in postliberal theology, is an example of such ad hoc connection in the way he draws upon the thought of the later Wittgenstein in philosophy and Clifford Geertz in sociology. Lindbeck's approach has been characterized as "ad hoc apologetics," stressing the way theology can appropriate the insights of other disciplines and perspectives without being based on or wedded to any one other perspective.[19]

Contrary, therefore, to what some see as its fideistic and relativistic tone, postmodern theology can freely latch on to contemporary currents while not baptizing anything. The advantage of such ad hoc philosophizing, though, is again to clarify and provide a perspective on one's theologizing, *not* to found it or determine it. This understanding may only become clear in retrospect on one's substantive theological work, so that one's methodology, as indicated above, might in some cases be most fully fleshed out toward the end, rather than the beginning.

In this spirit, I want to indicate further aspects of prolegomena with the aid of hermeneutical philosophy, pointing to the "intertextual" as well as "intratextual" nature of postmodern theology. In the pluralistic spirit of postmodernity, I do not bill hermeneutical philosophy as the only philosophical resource. In fact, in terms of self-referential coherence, it is a postmodern philosophy that implies its use only in an ad hoc fashion. I see it as a philosophical adjunct to theology that is fruitful, but other approaches are also fruitful. In this way, it differs from one of Frei's postmodern types (type three) that nevertheless requires a correlation between theology and a particular discipline. In my view, the correlation is neither necessary nor particular – but it is possible.[20] Lindbeck, as mentioned above, drew on the later Wittgenstein. Murphy and McClendon appeal to what they call the Anglo-American postmodern thought especially associated with John Austin. Murphy also heavily draws on the philosopher of science Imre Lakatos. Mark C. Taylor and Stephen Moore appeal to Jacques Derrida. In fact, some look to Ricoeur and others look to Gadamer, but few take Gadamer and Ricoeur

---

[19] William Werpehowski, "Ad hoc Apologetics," *Journal of Religion* 66 (1986), 282–301.
[20] Frei, in *Types*, pp. 5–6, 34–46.

together as exemplifying a robust postmodern philosophy. They usually are appropriated piecemeal and not holistically. I hope to show the value in seeing them more synthetically.[21]

POSTMODERN THEOLOGY AS HERMENEUTICAL

Gadamer and Ricoeur's hermeneutical philosophy offers several important advantages to theology. It has unusual affinity for theology in that its fundamental metaphor is the interpretation of rich and classic texts, which is then expanded into a full-blown philosophical view. At the center of both Gadamer and Ricoeur's thought is the central model of interpreting a text, particularly texts that involve understanding across wide horizons. Important for both are classic texts such as Scripture. Ricoeur, for example, says, "For us, the world is the ensemble of references opened up by the texts."[22] In other words, the dynamic of interpreting texts – hermeneutics – a familiar experience for theologians, becomes the paradigm for understanding all interpretation. Even more radically, human beings are understood as hermeneutical beings. Our way of being-in-the-world is irreducibly hermeneutical.[23]

The basic metaphor or model of interpreting significant texts points to the elusiveness of determinate meanings, to the surplus of meaning, and to the conflict of interpretations.[24] It points to the way in which one can offer reasons for a particular reading, say, as grounds for infant baptism or for predestination, and other equally committed Christians can offer reasons for very different readings. This does not necessarily mean either that the alternate interpreter is denigrated or that the text itself is thrown

---

[21] One of the reasons why they are not often seen in this way is the difficulty of bringing Ricoeur's work in so many areas into a whole. Even he has confessed difficulty in putting it all together! See Paul Ricoeur, "Reply to Lewis S. Mudge," in Lewis S. Mudge, ed., *Essays in Biblical Interpretation* (Philadelphia: Fortress Press, 1980), p. 41. Ricoeur has come closer, however, to doing so in his later book, *Oneself as Another*, trans. Kathleen Blamey (University of Chicago Press, 1992). Two perspectives on Ricoeur's significance for theology are Mark I. Wallace, *The Second Naiveté: Barth, Ricoeur, and the New Yale Theology*, Studies in American Biblical Hermeneutics, vol. 6 (Macon, GA: Mercer University Press, 1990); and Kevin Vanhoozer, *Biblical Narrative in the Philosophy of Paul Ricoeur: A Study in Hermeneutics and Theology* (Cambridge University Press, 1990).

[22] Paul Ricoeur, "The Model of the Text: Meaningful Action Considered as a Text," in *Hermeneutics and the Human Sciences*, ed. and trans. John B. Thompson (Cambridge University Press, 1981), p. 202.

[23] Gadamer makes this clear as well as the heritage of Martin Heidegger in *Truth and Method*, p. xxx.

[24] The latter two phrases come from well-known works by Ricoeur, *Interpretation Theory: Discourse and the Surplus of Meaning* (Fort Worth: Texas Christian University Press, 1976), and *The Conflict of Interpretations: Essays in Hermeneutics* (Evanston, IL: Northwestern University Press, 1974).

out. It allows, however, for "the full wealth of conviction." In other words, conviction can be combined with a lack of strong objectivism.

Following the paradigm of interpreting a text, Gadamer argues that, contrary to the Enlightenment ideal of presuppositionless understanding, we always bring our presuppositions, or prejudices (*Vorurteil*), to understanding, and rightly so.[25] As part of our broader contextual horizon, they can at times impede understanding, but they are also the indispensable means of being able to understand. Gadamer therefore provocatively rejects the Enlightenment "prejudice against prejudice."[26] Every act of understanding then is one of a fusion of one's own horizon with that of another. As Gadamer puts it: "It is enough to say that we understand in a different way, if we understand at all."[27] This conception does not lead to relativism in the sense that "anything goes" but is consistent with a careful concern to interpret the meaning of an ancient text. Gadamer's creative insight is that our horizon does not necessarily hinder but is the indispensable means for grasping the claim to truth in a text. This is a way of recognizing the incarnational dimension of interpretation, namely, that no reading rises above time and history but rather always originates from a particular time and place.

One mark of postmodern methodology, therefore, is greater recognition of the situated nature of the theologian. In times past, it was easy for Western, white, male Caucasians to label other theologies with a prefix such as African American theology, Latin American theology, feminist theology, Asian theology, and so on, without recognizing the white, masculine, Western flavor to their own theology. They were doing "prefix-less" theology, while everyone else was not! This is no longer possible. It is incumbent, then, upon theologians to be conscious of the tradition and perspective out of which they write – for example, my own white, North American, Baptist tradition with its heavy emphasis upon Scripture, believer's baptism, congregational church government, the priesthood of the believer, and liberty of conscience, yet with a strong ecumenical flavor.

If philosophy begins in wonder, Gadamer's philosophy begins with wonder that we indeed understand across horizons. We are not trapped in our horizons; rather, they are capable of being expanded and fused with others. A fusion does not at all mean, however, an equal synthesis between the two. In order to understand enough even to reject another view, our horizon must have fused. Fusion, therefore, does not necessarily mean agreement. It may also mean that one's own horizon ends up being largely rejected by the critical capacity to see oneself from an enlarged perspective that includes the viewpoint of the Other. This means that human beings have the capacity

---

[25] Gadamer, *Truth and Method*, pp. 265–307.   [26] Ibid., p. 270.   [27] Ibid., p. 297.

of reading a first-century Palestinian text and grasping its meaning. Rather than undermining the possibility of understanding, Gadamer's thought is an audacious celebration of it. Where the hermeneutical model holds, though, is that such understanding cannot be reduced to a rigid methodology, cannot be simple repetition, cannot be reduced to one single meaning, and cannot eliminate the human element. Ricoeur's notion of the surplus of meaning is helpful here. He calls it the "principle of plenitude," that is, a text means all that it can mean.[28] In early Separatist and Baptist history, this idea was celebrated by the alleged saying of John Robinson that "the Lord had more Light and Truth yet to break forth out of His Holy Word."[29] It represents the common spirituality that continues to return again and again to a text to find new meaning.

This notion of an incarnate self is grounded, of course, in the centrality of the Incarnation in the Christian tradition. In the larger sense, the Judeo-Christian tradition is one that emphasizes the scandal of particularity that stems from understanding God's actions in the messy arena of history and of particular people with all of their strengths, faults, and idiosyncrasies. The particularity and situatedness does not, however, isolate religion from the rest of life. A fideistic approach that attempts to segregate faith from other currents of life is, on this reading, a gnostic or docetic impossibility, contrary to the postmodern rejection of the modern "unencumbered self."

To some, postliberal theology implies such "Wittgensteinian fideism," as it is sometimes called, where the religious language-game is separable from all other games. Against this misappropriation, in my view, of Wittgenstein, human beings are immersed in a plethora of language-games that interact in numerous ways. For example, believers possess no separate language, even if they may to outsiders use religious jargon. Faith is expressed in English, Korean, and Russian that brings with it ineradicable location in those cultures. It arises in people who live in a multitude of traditions, which clearly shape the nature of their faith. Only the idea of a discarnate self could imagine that there is no issue of a fusion of horizons.

In this sense, Gadamer's notion is a corrective to Lindbeck's striking metaphor that the biblical world should absorb the modern world rather than the modern world absorbing the biblical (viz., "intratextuality").[30] Postliberals utilize this image in order to avoid the modern reliance on an external ground for faith (viz., "extratextuality") and to protect the priority of the biblical message from being swamped by the modern horizon. This

---

[28] Paul Ricoeur, "Metaphor and the Problem of Hermeneutics," *Hermeneutics*, p. 176.
[29] J. H. Shakespeare, *Baptist Congregational Pioneers* (London: Kingsgate Press, 1906), p. 165.
[30] George Lindbeck, *The Nature of Doctrine* (Philadelphia: Westminster Press, 1984), p. 118.

is a salutary emphasis and is part of the great challenge of the theologian to be faithful to the Gospel that he or she has received. Nevertheless, it is an illusion, as some in the postliberal tradition see, to think that matters are so simple.[31] What would it mean to let the biblical world absorb the modern world? Would it mean that we eat their food and wear their clothes and speak their language? And at which time would we emulate their life? Clearly, our task is to recast the theological truth of the biblical world in our world, which is a creative task that we perform with fear and trembling. Gadamer's idea of a fusion of horizons, as I pointed out above, does not mean that both horizons must be equal or that there is some mathematical synthesis. Rather, it recognizes that when we understand, we do not repeat but creatively reframe and restate. In other words, intratextuality is conditioned by *intertextuality*.

This capacity for encounter across horizons is also a counter-balance to the emphasis upon the situatedness of every theology. While one's location should be considered a strength as well as an unavoidable reality, we have an obligation to dialogue with theologies written from other perspectives. Absorption into the biblical world takes on many forms in the contemporary church because there is not just one monolithic church; nor is the biblical world itself a simple unity. Interpretations, at least, of that biblical world vary widely. Absolute agreement on all matters is neither likely nor desirable, but one's situated theology can only be strengthened by the attempt to do justice to other perspectives. For example, hopefully the European, white, Protestant theologian shares to a significant degree the passion of the Roman Catholic or orthodox theologian for the one, catholic church and the engaged sensitivity of the Latin American theologian for the concrete ways that the Gospel liberates the oppressed.

POSTMODERN THEOLOGY AS A HERMENEUTICAL ARC

In order to do justice to Gadamer's insight and to the need for critique, Ricoeur proposes a hermeneutical arc that recognizes a starting point – a first understanding – that is somewhat naive and is inherently shaped by interests and tradition.[32] This should be followed, however, by a critical

---

[31] James J. Buckley, "Postliberal Theology: A Catholic Reading," in Roger A. Badham, ed., *Introduction to Christian Theology: Contemporary North American Perspectives* (Louisville: Westminster John Knox Press, 1998), p. 97.
[32] See, for example, Ricoeur, "Model of the Text," in *Hermeneutics*, and Ricoeur, *Interpretation Theory*, pp. 71–88.

moment of suspicion and the use of whatever critical methodologies are available. Yet we should not remain in the critical moment, "the desert of criticism,"[33] but move to an appropriation that is underdetermined by methodology, which he has helpfully called a "post-critical naivete."[34] The resultant picture is actually more of a hermeneutical spiral than an arc since judgments are continually retested and reappropriated.

The implication for theology is that we begin with a text, experience, or tradition that has already grasped us, which is then critically examined and further reappropriated. In other words, we recognize that we do not start from scratch or first build a foundation but begin where we and the church are. In actuality, most begin with Scripture, which in terms of the traditional "Wesleyan quadrilateral" is amplified by tradition, reason, and experience. The incarnate, hermeneutical self that we have emphasized, however, points to a greater interaction between these sources than is traditionally recognized. Scripture never comes without interpretation by human beings shaped by tradition, experience, and reason.

The postliberals are helpful here in two ways. They indicate, first, that experience by itself lacks specificity, and, second, that experience must be taken in a social or corporate sense. More precisely, the experience of the church in its practices, not just human experience in general, is especially crucial. Frei emphasizes that theology is the self-description of faith. The hermeneutical arc may then begin with the practices of the church such as worship, prayer, ministry, and witness as much as a particular text.

The moment of reflection or criticism is the theological dimension per se. It is therefore a second-order, critical reflection on the primary texts and practices of the Christian faith. It is not a foreign element, however, in that it represents the spirit of reflective discernment for which Paul called when he urged the Thessalonians to "test everything" (1 Thessalonians 5:21, NRSV). Every critical tool and resource is called upon here, with what Ricoeur calls a "hermeneutic of suspicion."[35] Dialogue with other theologies helps us examine anew our beliefs. In biblical language, we bring prophetic criticism to beliefs and practices with the understanding that sin and idolatry infect everything, sometimes especially the life of faith, as the biblical narratives in the Hebrew Bible and the New Testament attest so clearly. The methods of criticism may be modern, or postmodern, but the practice is ancient.

---

33 Paul Ricoeur, *The Symbolism of Evil*, trans. Emerson Buchanan, Religious Perspectives, vol. 17 (New York: Harper & Row, 1967), p. 349.

34 Ibid., p. 352.

35 Paul Ricoeur, *Freud and Philosophy: An Essay on Interpretation*, trans. Denis Savage, The Terry Lectures (New Haven: Yale University Press, 1970), pp. 32–36.

The constructive or what Ricoeur calls "configurative" aspect of the systematic task brings together the different aspects of Christian beliefs and practices into rough coherence, recognizing that our thought of the supreme reality can hardly avoid a degree of brokeness.[36] "Configuration" implies the imaginative dimension of theology that is necessary to bring so much together into a unity. Usually a central metaphor or aspect of theology provides a central heuristic as eschatology and Jesus' messiahship does with Jürgen Moltmann or community and the social Trinity do with Stanley Grenz.

Another important aspect of Gadamer' and Ricoeur's thought is that they make not only the hermeneutical but also the practical turn. Both see appropriation, the third moment on Ricoeur's hermeneutical arc, as inherently involved in interpretation and consequently reject the idea that one can make the traditional clean separation between what the text meant and what it means. Rather, our idea, however dim it may be, of how the text may be appropriated is already at work in the first moment of exegesis. Ricoeur argues that actions themselves follow the model of interpreting a text. He further roots the hermeneutical human self in an ineradicable world of praxis with others.[37] This turn makes theology a practical and not simply a speculative, theoretical discipline. As Ellen Charry points out, doctrine lost its practical footing in the Enlightenment and needs to regain its pastoral function, which is manifested in a change not only in content but also in form, requiring a much more extensive use of biography and testimony as part of the theological task, as McClendon in particular has demonstrated.[38]

In Ricoeur's Gifford Lectures, he called this incarnational epistemology "attestation," which is related to his earlier reflection on the religion notion of testimony. Attestation is a testimony to the truth that involves conviction and reasons but cannot rely on Cartesian objectivism. As he puts it: "As credence without any guarantee, but also as trust greater than any suspicion, the hermeneutics of the self can claim to hold itself at an equal distance from the cogito exalted by Descartes and from the cogito that Nietzsche proclaimed forfeit."[39] Such a confession of truth is a risk and a wager that

---

[36] The modification of Ricoeur's hermeneutical arc in terms of prefiguration, configuration, and refiguration are developed in his *Time and Narrative*, trans. Kathleen Blamey and David Pellauer, 3 vols. (University of Chicago Press, 1984–1988), especially I, pp. 52–87, and II, pp. 157–79.

[37] See especially *Oneself as Another*.

[38] Ellen T. Charry, *By the Renewing of Your Minds: The Pastoral Function of Christian Doctrine* (New York: Oxford University Press, 1997); James Wm. McClendon, Jr., *Biography as Theology: How Life Stories Can Remake Today's Theology* (Nashville: Abingdon, 1974).

[39] Ricoeur, *Oneself as Another*, p. 23.

is backed up by one's life.[40] Like testimony in a trial, it can be tested and cross-examined, but it remains one's "eyewitness" report. Ricoeur says: "We must let ourselves be drawn into the [hermeneutical] circle and then must try to make the circle a spiral. We cannot eliminate from a social ethics the element of risk. We wager on a certain set of values and then try to be consistent with them; verification is therefore a question of our whole life. No one can escape this."[41]

Ricoeur especially relates such hermeneutical humility to the central focus of Christian faith and theology, the naming of God.[42] The increased recognition in postmodernity of the limitations of descriptive language to disclose reality in general, which has yielded in turn the insight that figurative language is often more disclosive than univocal language, is especially provocative when it comes to "God-talk." The awareness in the tradition at times that our language of God is an accommodation, or analogical, or even outright equivocal is sharpened in light of newer insights into the irreplaceability of metaphor and narrative.[43] Ricoeur sees that even the forms of biblical language, such as the distinctions between prophetic poetry, narrative, and parable, are all needed to mediate the world-shattering reality of God. As postmodernity's attempt to avoid objectivism need not lead to relativism, the inherently fragmentary and perilous nature of our language about God need not lead to despairing silence. The linguistic turn in postmodernity is yet another affirmation of our incarnate, finite situation along with the possibilities of nevertheless grasping in a partial and risky way a livable reality, even the mystery of God.

In Gadamer's terminology, the initial wager is related to the way we not so much play a game as are "played" by a game.[44] Although this initial "being grasped" need not be necessarily whimsical, irrational, or superficial, it needs to be tested in terms of the hermeneutical spiral. To become a conviction, it must be appropriated again in a post-critical act of holistic appropriation.

Theology is the theologian's wager that the church's testimony can stand the test of critical trial. It represents the theologian's conviction, not that he or she has the truth in a definitive, uncontestable way, but that one's theology

[40] Ricoeur speaks early of a wager in *Symbolism of Evil*, pp. 355–57.

[41] Ricoeur, *Lectures on Ideology and Utopia*, ed. George H. Taylor (New York: Columbia University Press, 1986), p. 312.

[42] Paul Ricoeur, "Naming God," in *Figuring the Sacred: Religion, Narrative, and Imagination* (Minneapolis: Fortress Press, 1995), pp. 217–35.

[43] See my *The Philosophy of Religious Language: Sign, Symbol, and Story* (Oxford: Blackwell, 1996) for a fuller treatment of the importance of the linguistic turn for theology in the twentieth century.

[44] See Gadamer, *Truth and Method*, p. 106, and the poem by Rainer Rilke that is the epigram for the book (p. v).

is worthy of being contested. Thus, along with the attempt to make one's theology systematic and comprehensive is the recognition of the partiality of its vision and the need to be placed alongside other visions and voices. Finally, the truest test of the theological methodology here envisaged is that it spring from the church's praxis, face the hermeneutic of suspicion from within and without, and in turn inspire anew a tested, developed, and even transformed praxis.

11 The Trinity

DAVID S. CUNNINGHAM

The word *Trinity* is a time-honoured shorthand for speaking about the unique claims of the Christian understanding of God. Because Christians believe that there is only one God, they have typically been classified with other monotheists, such as Jews and Muslims. But, unlike the adherents of these faiths, Christians believe that God has entered fully and directly into the created order, and has become *concretely embodied* in the world, in two ways: God became incarnate in the womb of a Jewish woman named Mary; she gave birth in Palestine some two thousand years ago, and her child was named Jesus. In addition, God has also been poured out on the world, into the communities of believers known as Israel and the church; this concrete embodiment of God is called the Holy Spirit. These two concrete manifestations of God are considered sufficiently different from the One who forever dwells in "light inaccessible" that the designation "monotheism" may simply be inadequate as a description of the Christian faith. For Christians, the one God is also three: the Father or Source, who is the origin of all things; the Son or Word, who comes forth from God and takes on human flesh; and the Spirit, the "Giver of Life," who dwells in human hearts and animates the believing community.

While certain strands of Christian faith have explicitly denied a belief in the Trinity, these have always had some difficulty accounting for the special status given to Jesus and to the Holy Spirit among most Christians. If Jesus is not understood as God incarnate, why would his teachings and his actions have any special significance? Nor would it make sense to worship and pray to Jesus, as Christians have done for centuries and continue to do today. Similarly, if the Holy Spirit is not divine, the claim that God dwells within the heart of believers, inspiring and directing them in specific ways, becomes very difficult to sustain. Nor would it make sense for the community of believers to speak of themselves as "the body of Christ" and "the vehicle for God's work in the world." Thus, despite the philosophical difficulties (and even the mathematical ones!) of asserting the simultaneous oneness and threeness of God, the claim is deeply embedded in the Christian faith.

What exactly might it mean to speak of "a postmodern theology of the Trinity"? Among the various common threads that allow us even to assemble certain theologies under the heading "postmodern," one finds the claims: (1) that the standard definitions and assumptions that have pervaded the modern era can no longer be taken for granted; (2) that the reader or interpreter plays a significant role in the making of meaning, such that we should expect to forge our own paths; and (3) that such paths will be many and various – and thus, they will not necessarily lead to the same destination.

The varieties of postmodernism are well exemplified in the first part of this volume, which explores various "types" of postmodern theology. While these types clearly do not constitute mutually isolated categories, some of them do make assumptions that are in severe tension with, and in some cases exclusive of, the assumptions of others. For example, the insistence on the priority of God's action in "radical orthodoxy" and "postliberal theology" would seem to be at odds with the atheological claims of "deconstructive a/theology." Feminist theology makes claims that might well be shunned by some postconservative theologies. Consequently, when various Trinitarian theologies employ differing understandings of postmodern theology, they will move in very different directions.

In this chapter, these variations on a postmodern theology of the Trinity will be explored in two contrapuntal "movements." First, I will take note of certain themes or elements that have arisen with special force in the postmodern era, showing how they might offer a new perspective on some of the traditional questions surrounding Trinitarian theology. Then, I will move in the opposite direction, examining how certain perennial themes within Trinitarian theology bear upon postmodernity. I will conclude with a few words on the importance of these observations for sorting out the usefulness of various postmodern approaches to Christian theology.[1]

POSTMODERN INSIGHT FOR TRINITARIAN THOUGHT

I begin with an examination of three focal points of postmodern thought that would seem to have special significance for Trinitarian theology. These three "aspects" of postmodernism are certainly not the only ones that could have been chosen, but they are broadly representative of some of its chief insights – particularly in its critique of modernist or Enlightenment assumptions. All three would, I believe, be recognized as significant by a

---

[1] Some of the themes of this chapter are developed more thoroughly in David S. Cunningham, *These Three Are One: The Practice of Trinitarian Theology* (Oxford: Blackwell, 1998).

wide variety of thinkers working within the various "types" of postmodern theology described in the first part of this volume.

Relationality

One of the distinctive features of modernity has been its enthusiasm for classifying everything into discrete categories. This tendency is perhaps most easily observed in the natural sciences, where classification and distinction have been the cornerstone of progress in our understanding of biological species, chemical elements, and physical forces. This process of discrimination and classification has been taken up with enthusiasm in the social sciences as well, and to a lesser extent in the humanities. It seemed to promise a neutral organizational scheme whereby very different objects could be analyzed, compared, and evaluated. In theology, we can see the early influence of this approach in the work of Friedrich Schleiermacher (1768–1834), who described Christianity as a particular object within the category of "religions" and further specified that it could be classified as "a monotheistic faith, belonging to the teleological type of religion."[2]

Of course, the hidden cost of such classificatory systems was that certain assumptions had to be built into them from the outset, making them not in the least bit neutral. This was true even for the natural sciences; decisions about the classification of species, for example, might be made on the basis of physical features rather than, say, habits of communication – thereby positing the claim that human beings are most closely related to apes rather than (as some have now suggested) to dolphins. Very little "objectivity" could be claimed for social–scientific constructions (as, for example, the division of the human psyche into ego, superego, and id), and less still for the humanities (as, for example, the easy division of Shakespeare's plays into comedies, histories, and tragedies; where, in the wake of the Holocaust, should one place *The Merchant of Venice?*).

This divide-and-conquer mentality exercised a negative impact on Trinitarian theology in the modern era, particularly within the academy. The entire notion of a God who is simultaneously "one" and "three" was sometimes declared inconceivable or irrational. This paradoxical God, who existed above and beyond all human categories of knowing, seemed to be quite thoroughly at odds with the spirit of the age – and particularly at odds with its penchant for rationalization and classification. Classical Trinitarian theology seemed to obscure the otherwise clear and distinct categories of

[2] Friedrich E. D. Schleiermacher, *The Christian Faith*, trans. H. R. Mackintosh (Edinburgh: T. & T. Clark, 1928), p. 52.

human and divine, transcendent and immanent, and even oneness and threeness.

More specifically, the modern approach encouraged theologians to understand God's threeness as the subdividing of God into constituent parts – like a three-person committee or a three-judge panel. This tendency was buttressed by the translation of the Latin word that had been traditionally used to refer to that of which there are three in God (*persona*) into the English word *person*, which in the modern era tended to be associated with individuality, autonomy, and even isolation from external relations. God's threeness now began to look rather like the "division of labor" so well known to the age that ushered in the Industrial Revolution. It was not too farfetched to imagine a three-personed God in which the Father created the world, then retired; the Son came along, fixed the world's problems, and exited the scene; and the Spirit was then left behind to provide long-term maintenance. This image directly contravened the ancient claim that "God's external works are undivided" – that is, that everything that God does is done by *God*, and not by one or another Trinitarian person working in relative isolation from the other two.

In contrast to the modernist penchant for division, isolation, and classification, postmodernism posits a much more interdependent approach. Individual instances are not so much sorted into discrete categories as they *set in relation* to other instances. In the modern era, the grand metaphor for the organization of knowledge had been the tree (with a single trunk, major branches, and minor branches all related in linear and hierarchical fashion). In postmodern perspective, a more appropriate metaphor is a complex *network* of relationships, in which hierarchies are much more difficult to identify and in which every element is, potentially, directly related to every other element.

This relational perspective makes it much easier to make sense of certain elements of Trinitarian theology. It has occasioned a retrieval of the medieval insight that the three "persons" of the triune God are, more fundamentally, *relations*. To speak of "Father" or "Son" is not to speak of an individual who is potentially isolated from other individuals; rather, the two terms specify *relations* that depend absolutely on *each other* for their meaning. There can be no child without a parent, but neither can there be a parent without a child: the two terms are tied together into a knot of mutual causation and interdependence.

This also calls into question any imagined hierarchy of, for example, Father over Son. As descriptions of human beings, it is true that the one called "father" must exist before the one called "son"; but here again we are misled by thinking about these entities as isolated "persons." If instead we think of them as pure *relations*, the terms "father" and "son" become fully mutual and reciprocal; the parent does not become a parent until the child is born. This calls forth a non-hierarchical understanding of the Trinity, and is of ancient origin: it underlies the Nicene Creed's claim that the Son is "eternally begotten of the Father," which rules out any suggestion that one of the divine relations existed prior to, or independently of, the others. Postmodern thought has thus helped theologians to recover the concepts of co-equality and mutual reciprocity that had been part of the original Christian conception of God's nature.

It follows, then, that when God acts upon the world, it is never merely one of the Three who acts (with the other two standing by as helpers or mere observers); rather, as the ancient claim emphasized, it is always *God* who acts, undividedly. The threefold nature of God thus specifies not a division among God's acts, but rather the source, means, and goal of those acts. (As some writers have put the matter: all of God's acts originate in the Father, are accomplished through the Son, and are perfected in the Spirit.) This helps to explain why the phrase "Creator, Redeemer, Sustainer," while certainly descriptive of the work of the Christian God, is not strictly a Trinitarian formula: God's threeness is not found in a division of labor, but in a complex structure of internal relations.

In sum, then, postmodernism's emphasis on complex relationality (in contrast to the hierarchical classificatory schemes of modernity) has made it easier for theologians to think through the fundamentally relational nature of God that is inscribed in the doctrine of the Trinity. In the process, ancient claims about the Trinity's co-equality, co-eternity, and mutual reciprocity are being recovered and reendowed with a fullness of meaning and significance that had been largely obscured in the modern era.

Difference

A second recurrent postmodern theme has been the accentuation of difference, in contrast to the modern era's search for universally applicable norms and grand overarching claims. The critique of modernity's universalizing tendencies has come from several sources. First, advances in the natural and social sciences continue to remind us of the hypothetical and provisional nature of much of our knowledge. Newtonian physics, upon which the physical sciences had depended for centuries (and which most observers had taken to be "the final truth" about the universe), was suddenly called into question by Einstein and others. As supposedly definitive paradigms are supplanted (with ever-increasing frequency) by new theoretical insights, all claims to have achieved "the final answer" are thrown into considerable doubt.[3] Second, in these waning days of the grand colonial empires, it is increasingly obvious that other cultures are not necessarily "backward" or "primitive" in comparison to European cultures, but that they have their own basis and significance – quite apart from the imperial cultures by which they had been measured throughout the colonialist age.[4] Finally, the opening up of the academy to all human beings – beyond the traditional boundaries of gender, race, class, creed, and sexual orientation – has alerted us to the fact that different people see things differently. Perspectives once deemed "universal" now appear quite parochial, given their domination by modes of thinking to which white European males had become accustomed.[5]

The universalizing tendencies of the modern era had been particularly detrimental to Trinitarian theology, on several fronts. First, the doctrine of the Trinity had traditionally been understood as arising out of the distinctiveness of Christian revelation. It is not a "natural truth" that can be recognized by careful observation of the created order; it is, rather, revealed in the historical particularity of the life, death, and resurrection of Jesus, and in the pouring out of the Spirit on the community of disciples. By contrast, the modern era has been much enamored of "natural religion" that might be demonstrated to "all rational men" (and they usually did mean *men!*) by the pure light of reason. Trinitarian claims could not be so demonstrated, and were therefore suspect.

In addition, the modern era's enthusiasm for universal claims did not sit well with the complex and articulated understanding of God expressed by the doctrine of the Trinity. If the modern era could abide a notion of "god" at all, it needed to be the god of classical theism: one, simple, omniscient, omnipresent – and incapable of suffering, division, or change. Such a god was conceivable "within the limits of reason alone," as the title of Kant's treatise notoriously suggested. More complex accounts of the divine – requiring a detailed exposition of internal and external relations, processions, and missions – were strictly out of fashion in the modern era.

---

3 A important and reasonably accessible text on the importance of "paradigm shifts" in science is Thomas S. Kuhn, *The Structure of Scientific Revolutions*, 2nd edn (University of Chicago Press, 1970).

4 Here, an influential text has been Clifford Geertz, *The Interpretation of Cultures* (New York: Basic Books, Inc., 1973), though some believe that Geertz remains too "modern" in his suggestion that observers can offer relatively neutral "thick descriptions" of cultures.

5 Here the sources are, understandably, much more diverse. Consider, for example, the new perspectives brought by women. See Carol Gilligan, *In a Different Voice: Psychological Theory and Women's Development* (Cambridge, MA: Harvard University Press, 1982) and Luce Irigaray, *je, tu, nous: Toward a Culture of Difference*, trans. Alison Martin (New York: Routledge, 1993).

The postmodern appreciation of difference has made it easier to emphasize the very specific narrative context from within which Trinitarian theology arose. Far from being the wild-eyed metaphysical speculations that some have thought them to be, the basic insights of Trinitarian theology were simply an attempt to come to grips with the concrete narratives of the Christian faith, which described a God who "became flesh and dwelt among us" (John 1:14) and who was poured out upon the disciples at Pentecost (Acts 2).

Moreover, it appears that a certain form of "difference" is built into Trinitarian theology as it was classically conceived. Christians claimed that the divine Three are not merely modalities of God or "masks" that God wears in various historical circumstances. They are of the same being or substance, but they *differ* sufficiently from one another that we can meaningfully speak of one being "sent" by another (Jesus "breathes" the Holy Spirit upon the apostles in John 20:22), or of any two having a conversation with one another (as the Garden of Gethsemane, Matthew 26 and parallels). In the postmodern era, such difference has reemerged as something for which human beings can rejoice and be thankful, rather than something that needs to be subordinated to an all-embracing desire for uniformity.

Rhetoric

This is a highly contested term in postmodern discourse. While some commentators want to describe postmodernism as "rhetorical" only in the sense of "playful" or "lacking discursive coherence," others point to continuities between postmodernism and the classical rhetorical tradition. The latter was interested in the ways that language can be used to persuade, and to bring about a change of thought and action. It was interested not merely in the logical construction of an argument, but also in the way that context, character, and disposition could contribute to an argument's success or failure – and thereby shape political deliberations, judicial proceedings, and general public opinion.

Rhetoric was highly influential in later Greek and Roman philosophy and pedagogy, and remained a focused discipline of study right through the Middle Ages;[6] but at the outset of the modern era, the rhetorical approach was accused of being inexact, unscientific, and altogether too dependent on the perceived moral and emotional states of the speaker (or writer) and audience. A leader in this anti-rhetorical charge was Peter Ramus (1515–72),

[6] For a summary of the relationship between classical rhetoric and theology, see David S. Cunningham, *Faithful Persuasion: In Aid of a Rhetoric of Christian Theology* (University of Notre Dame Press, 1991), ch. 1.

who argued for a much more precise, predictable, and monolithic mode of argumentation.[7]

The modern era thus became associated with logical and analytic forms of argument, implying that anything else was inadequate to the task. And yet, in its premodern forms, theology had very frequently operated, not according to the canons of logic, but rather in the mode of persuasion – not only in preaching, but also in arguments about doctrine and ethics. Many ancient writers had drawn close parallels between Christian theology and the rhetorical tradition, including Sts. Augustine of Hippo and Gregory of Nazianzus (arguably two of the most formative thinkers for early Christian theology). In one of Gregory's orations, for instance, he complains loudly about his opponents, who think that everything about the Christian faith is a matter of logical deduction.[8] And yet this was exactly the assumption about theology that came to dominate the modern era.

This excessive rationalism had particularly deleterious consequences for Trinitarian theology, which had always been understood in much more holistic terms than what could be easily appropriated to the canons of logical analysis. The claim was not so much that the Trinity was illogical or unreasonable, but rather that it transcended the categories of logic. Speaking about the triune God was much more akin to offering a passionate defense in the lawcourts, or to enacting a Shakespearian tragedy, than it was to solving an algebraic equation.[9] Trinitarian claims were not well suited to the narrow canons of logic; and this may have been one of the chief factors leading to the widespread marginalization of the doctrine in the modern era.

In contrast, postmodern sensibilities have recognized the situatedness of all argumentation, and are highly sceptical of the claims of logic and analytic to postulate a neutral space within which all questions can be objectively analyzed. The perceived character and dispositions of those who put forward an argument, and those who receive it, are at least as important as the argument itself. These claims are due in part to a larger twentieth-century philosophical insight, stressed by Martin Heidegger (1889–1976) and many others in his wake, about the temporality (and thus the situatedness) of all that is. But part of it is also a rather more common-sense and

---

[7] For an accessible contemporary account, see Walter J. Ong, SJ, *Ramus, Method, and the Decay of Dialogue* (1958; reprint, Cambridge, MA: Harvard University Press, 1983).

[8] St. Gregory of Nazianzus, "Oration 29: On the Son," in Frederick W. Norris, ed., *Faith Gives Fullness to Reasoning: The Five Theological Orations of Gregory Nazianzen* trans. Lionel Wickham and Frederick Williams (Leiden: E. J. Brill, 1991), pp. 245–61.

[9] Nicholas Lash makes this point – not specifically about Trinitarian doctrine, but about reading the Bible (and, by implication, about theology more generally) – in his helpful essay "Performing the Scriptures," in *Theology on the Way to Emmaus* (London: SCM Press, 1986), pp. 37–46.

ancient claim – namely, that we offer and respond to arguments within a particular context. Protests against the modern enthusiasm for a sterile and artificial formal logic were already being expressed in the nineteenth century, by such writers as John Henry Newman (1801–90), who complained of the logician who "turns rivers, full, winding, and beautiful, into navigable canals."[10]

For theologians, this has meant that treatises on Trinitarian theology no longer need to confine themselves to the canons of formal logic. An examination of Trinitarian themes in literature,[11] or an extended analogy between the Trinity and the production of a play in a theater,[12] can be just as rigorous as, and usually a good deal more persuasive than, the highly refined treatments offered by those attempting to work within the narrow confines of formal logic.

This has implications for a number of specific issues in Trinitarian theology, including the very language used to name and describe God. The traditional Trinitarian formula, usually translated into English as "Father, Son, and Holy Spirit," has sometimes been rather woodenly defended as the only possible name for God.[13] Some might assume that a postmodern approach would simply argue that "God has many names," suggesting that one description of God was just as good as another. But no rhetorician worthy of the name, whether ancient or contemporary, would be satisfied with such an account; new language is needed, but it will be meaningful only to the extent that it can display its continuities with the past. The traditional Trinitarian formula was attempting to articulate a particular point about the complex internal relationality of God. To make that point persuasively, one cannot simply repeat old formulae; but neither can one simply make up new names at will. Instead, we must attend to the particular features of a language as it is currently being used, such that the point of the traditional formula can be expressed in meaningful ways within the current cultural–linguistic context.[14] In an effort to preserve the relational claims

---

[10] John Henry Newman, *An Essay in Aid of a Grammar of Assent* (1870; reprint, University of Notre Dame Press, 1979), p. 215.

[11] I offer several of these in *These Three Are One*, chapters 4–6.

[12] As mostly famously in Hans Urs von Balthasar, *Theo-Drama: Theological Dramatic Theory*, vol. 3, *Dramatis Personae: Persons in Christ* (San Francisco: Ignatius Press, 1993), pp. 505–35.

[13] Some of the most extreme examples, and therefore the most instructive in their resolute adherence to modernist universalism, can be found among some of the essays in Alvin F. Kimel, Jr., ed., *Speaking the Christian God: The Holy Trinity and the Challenge of Feminism* (Grand Rapids: Eerdmans, 1992).

[14] I have outlined a concise form that this sort of contextual work might take in "Developing Alternative Trinitarian Formulas," *Anglican Theological Review* 80 (1998), 8–29.

of Trinitarian theology, to draw on the imagery of Bible and tradition, and to evoke new analogical resonances, I have regularly advocated the formula "Source, Wellspring, and Living Water."[15]

Another "rhetorical" insight that has been of great value in the contemporary revival of Trinitarian theology is that meaning is not a property of words alone, but is a complex interaction among the speaker (or writer), the speech (or text), and the hearer (or reader). This suggests, among other things, that assessing the "meaning of a text" is never a matter of simply pointing to the words on the page and claiming that, "obviously," they signify one thing and not another. The making of meaning is a communal and constructive affair, and is not just a matter of using a dictionary in order to decipher a great code. People have to write those dictionaries, after all; and in any case, language is always in flux.

A classic postmodern–rhetorical instance of this claim comes from the pen of the twentieth-century philosopher Ludwig Wittgenstein (1889–1951), who offers an example that is surprisingly germane to the current discussion:

> The *words* that you utter, or what you mean when you utter them, is not what matters so much as the difference they make at various points in your life. How do I know that two people mean the same when each says he believes in God? And just the same goes for belief in the Trinity. A theology which insists on the use of *certain particular* words and phrases, and outlaws others, does not make anything clearer...*Practice* gives the words their sense.[16]

So a doctrine of the Trinity, or any other Christian doctrine for that matter, cannot be simply a matter of choosing the right (eternally orthodox) words, or even of meaning or intending certain things when choosing those words. Rather, it is a matter of examining how people are motivated to act when they believe (or claim to believe) certain things. Consequently, recent Trinitarian theology has sometimes been much more intentionally focused on the *practices* that such theology motivates.[17] I will return to the matter of "practice" at the end of this chapter.

---

[15] For a complete argument in favor of this formula, see Cunningham, *These Three Are One*, ch. 2.

[16] Ludwig Wittgenstein, *Culture and Value*, ed. G. H. von Wright and Heikki Nyman, trans. Peter Winch (University of Chicago Press, 1980), p. 85.

[17] As in, for example, Leonardo Boff, *Trinity and Society*, trans. Paul Burns (Maryknoll, NY: Orbis Books, 1988); M. Douglas Meeks, *God the Economist: The Doctrine of God and Political Economy* (Minneapolis: Fortress Press, 1989); and Cunningham, *These Three Are One*, chs. 7–9.

TRINITARIAN INSIGHTS FOR POSTMODERN THOUGHT

I now wish to "turn the tables" and suggest that Trinitarian theology, in its various historical forms, has something to offer to postmodernism as well. This book has repeatedly emphasized the utter lack of convergence among various "postmodern" approaches; thus, part of the work that any postmodern theology must do is to make judgments as to which among the various competing versions of postmodernism it will employ, as resources and as foils. I want to argue that a Christian postmodern theology will need to incorporate certain key Trinitarian insights – three of which are named here.

Peace

Many of the manifestations of postmodernism display an "agonistic" structure; that is to say, they assume that conflict and even violence are necessary elements of the culture we now inhabit. In their overcoming of modern universalism, these forms of postmodernism tend to celebrate the notion that ideas are constantly at war with one another, and that certain accounts become widely accepted only by vanquishing alternative claims.

Some commentators have even argued that much postmodern discourse is "violent" at a much more fundamental level. Specifically, it postulates a world that is essentially chaotic – a world in which "things fall apart; the centre cannot hold." Whatever order there might be in the world must be imposed upon it by human beings. In this respect, postmodernism shows its continuing indebtedness to modernity; for it was the modern age, above all, that postulated the necessity of human action to bring order to the world. For example, early modern political theorists such as Thomas Hobbes described life in the "state of nature" as "nasty, brutish, and short" – and thus argued for strong nation-states to bring such chaos under control.[18]

In contrast, Christian theology postulates a world that is, at its core, well designed, well ordered, and good. It goes without saying, of course, that human beings have acted to distort and deform the goodness of the world. But the Christian account of creation does not describe God as violently overcoming the unruly chaos. Instead, God creates by sheer act of will, without any primal "substance"; the world is created "out of nothing." Furthermore, this world is repeatedly declared "good" (Genesis 1). So the Christian story does not postulate a primal act of violent overcoming, but

---

[18] For a demonstration of how the political philosophies of Hobbes (and others) operate as "secular parodies" of the Christian doctrine of creation, see William T. Cavanaugh, "The City: Beyond Secular Politics," in John Milbank, Catherine Pickstock, and Graham Ward, eds., *Radical Orthodoxy: A New Theology* (London: Routledge, 1999), pp. 182–200.

a grace-filled act of abundant and peaceable donation. For Christians, the "state of nature" is not a dire, fruitless plain, devoid of all goodness; it is, rather, a garden of abundance, given freely by God.[19]

Such giving is "natural" to God, because God is eternally in the process of giving. The Trinitarian dynamic describes a God who is always going forth – "proceeding," to use the technical term – and is therefore constantly involved in a network of internal relations that involve gift and reception. Or, to use a different metaphor: God is always in the process of "giving place," of moving out of the way so that a new divine manifestation can be recognized as "fully God."[20] The Wellspring is always coming forth from the Source ("eternally begotten of the Father," in the most common English translation of the creed), and the Living Water is always flowing out to nurture the believing community.

These acts of God are acts of pure gift, rather than occurring as a process of economic exchange (in which one party withholds something until the other has paid the necessary price). Consequently, God's internal relations, as well as God's relations with the world, are essentially peaceful and peace-making relations. They do not posit a scarcity of resources which would lead to conflict; neither do they suggest that anything is being withheld such that it would have to be taken by force.[21] Such an understanding of God lends little support to the violent and conflictual world-view that seems to be taken for granted in much postmodern discourse. In contrast to the violent nihilism that lies hidden in the heart of secular postmodernism, the Christian doctrine of God sets forth a narrative of peaceful, superabundant donation.

Personhood

I have already suggested that, in the modern era, the word *person* acquired some troublesome associations, such that its usage to describe "that of which there are three in God" has become highly problematic. Specifically, we have tended to think of a "person" as a free and autonomous entity, an independent seat of consciousness, which has no necessary relations or dependencies on anyone or anything else. Needless to say, this is not the vision that St. Augustine had in mind when he advocated the use of the word

---

[19] For a useful development of the "garden" metaphor in this regard, see Nicholas Lash, *Believing Three Ways In One God: A Reading of the Apostles' Creed* (University of Notre Dame Press, 1992), pp. 121–24.
[20] This was a central theme in Rowan Williams' 1997 Hale Lectures at Seabury-Western Theological Seminary, and in his forthcoming book on the Trinity.
[21] For a good discussion of the contrast between Christian thought and modern economic theory on matters such as scarcity and force, see D. Stephen Long, *Divine Economy: Theology and the Market* (London: Routledge, 1999).

persona to speak of the divine Three. But the modern emphases on infinite freedom (understood as lack of constraint) and on autonomy (defined as throwing off one's "tutelage" by others) have led to a highly individualistic and privatized sense of human personhood.

Nor has the "postmodern" moment fully rid itself of this tendency. Despite its attention to relationality, postmodernism has often retained a thoroughgoing devotion to the cult of the individual. In the work of some postmodernist writers, various gathered communities are held in considerable suspicion because of their potential to disrupt an individual's autonomy. And in some versions of postmodern theology, the church is described (often in rather lurid terms) as exercising an extraordinary degree of control over human freedom – as though it could compete, in the contemporary setting, with truly powerful forces of domination (such as nation-states, media conglomerates, and multinational corporations).[22] The supposedly autonomous human person is clearly under the influence and control of a wide range of cultural and political forces; but this does not seem to have stopped modern and postmodern theologians from assuming that as long as the controlling power of the church is kept at bay, all human persons will somehow be "free."

Because this individualistic understanding of personhood has achieved such widespread acceptance in our culture, some Trinitarian theologians (myself included) have argued against the continued employment of the word *person* within Trinitarian theology. The word has simply become too corrupted by the (post)modern dogmas of individualism.[23] There is, however, another way to look at the matter. One can also argue that, by strongly asserting the relational and interdependent model of personhood that is specified by the Christian doctrine of God, theology can help postmodernity extend and deepen its overcoming of Enlightenment presuppositions.

Specifically, Trinitarian theology insists that a "person" is *not* an autonomous centre of consciousness, nor a radically private entity; rather, persons are necessarily woven into the lives of other persons. They *participate* in one another's lives, whether they realize it or not. In God, the Three are all bound up in one another to such a degree that we cannot really speak of any One of them without implying something about the other Two as well. When we say that Jesus is the redeemer of the world, for example, we do not claim that the Word carried out this activity alone, as though "behind the

---

[22] For an accessible discussion of the significance of these forces vis-à-vis the cultural weakness of the church, see Michael Budde, *The (Magic) Kingdom of God: Christianity and Global Culture Industries* (Boulder, CO: Westview Press, 1997).

[23] This is the position of Nicholas Lash in *Believing Three Ways* (pp. 30–33), as well as my own position in *These Three Are One* (pp. 26–29).

back" of the Source that uttered the Word and the Spirit who was breathed out. Admittedly, we see and understand this work most clearly and explicitly when we look at the life, death, and resurrection of Jesus; therefore, we can speak of the work of redemption being "appropriated" to the Word. But it is not the exclusive work of a single divine person; here, as in all of God's work in the world, it is God who acts, and not one of the Three in isolation.

Thus, if we are to continue to speak of "God in three persons," we must simultaneously define the word *person* in a highly interdependent, relational way: to be a person is to be a relation, or perhaps a multiplicity of relations. Rather than speaking of "individuals," we might better speak of "*particular* persons." This would help shift the focus away from persons as isolated centres of consciousness, and toward persons as nodes in a network – a nexus of relations that is being specified, tentatively and temporarily, for the purposes of identification and discussion, but one that is never truly separable from the whole. In this way, the longstanding Trinitarian claim that "God is three persons" can become a powerful critique of the (post)modern tendency to understand personhood in individualistic and privatized terms.

Practice

Postmodernism regularly expresses antipathy toward broad, overarching narratives that would seek to explain the whole of reality by means of a single story or "metanarrative"; one famous definition of the "postmodern condition" emphasizes its "incredulity toward metanarratives."[24] Instead, the focus is on the local instance – on the concrete specificity of particular events. Yet postmodernism has rather famously tended to drift toward highly theoretical and abstract accounts of its subject matter; and these accounts are sometimes woven together into precisely the sort of "metanarrative" that it had so heavily criticized. Needless to say, postmodern writers vary enormously on this score; some, such as Michel Foucault, clearly seek to attend first and foremost to concrete practices. But others are well known for engaging in flights of speculative fancy and extraordinarily esoteric discussions, and some forms of postmodern theology have certainly tended in this direction.

Of course, Trinitarian theology has traditionally operated according to a particular metanarrative – an overarching story of salvation history that describes God's relationship with the created order. But this story cannot exist on its own; it only becomes meaningful when it is enacted and embodied

---

[24] Jean-François Lyotard, *The Postmodern Condition: A Report on Knowledge*, trans. Geoff Bennington and Brian Massumi (Minneapolis: University of Minnesota Press, 1984), p. xxiv.

in the local stories and the concrete practices of particular believing communities. When Christians tell the story of God, they do so from within the context of particular practices of worship, prayer, and everyday life. These practices help keep their stories from becoming the speculative and abstract sort toward which some postmodern thought has tended (its own stated preferences to the contrary notwithstanding). Christian narratives of the triune God shape, and are shaped by, the concrete practices of the church. When theologians attempt to modify these narratives in ways that drift too far from the common practices of everyday believers, they will certainly be called to account by those who do not simply *talk* about the narrative, but *live their lives* accordingly.

In other words, because Trinitarian theology is done at the service of a living, breathing community, it has to be attentive toward and accountable to the practices of that community. As I have already observed, Trinitarian thought developed in response to a very concrete, practical concern: the need to make sense of the relationships among God, Jesus, and the Spirit. It continues to be meaningful only to the extent that it is able to continue to make sense of these relationships. Like much postmodern thought, Trinitarian theology claims to be attentive to practices; but, unlike much postmodern thought, it is responsible to a particular community that will hold it accountable to that claim.

Consider, for example, the relationship between Trinitarian theology and the liturgical life of Christians. Across a wide range of denominations, the invocation of the triune God is central to the life of worship.[25] If a theologian were to describe God in ways that Christians were unable to recognize in their own worship life, that theologian would be dismissed as irrelevant. Of course, liturgical change does take place, and the relationship between theology and worship is a complex and reciprocal one. But at the very least, the Trinitarian theologian knows that her speculations are never "just gaming"; they will bear upon some of the most heartfelt concerns of a vast number of Christian believers. This necessary attention to practice continually calls Trinitarian theology back from its temptation toward speculative flights of fancy, and into the world of concrete practice.

In a sense, the practices of Christian believers – whether in the past, present, or future – serve as a test of adequacy for Trinitarian theology. Whenever it has allowed itself to become a pure abstraction, of interest only to a narrow range of highly specialized professional theologians, it has been deemed largely irrelevant. Only when it makes a difference, as

---

[25] See the thorough discussion in Bruce Marshall, *Trinity and Truth* (Cambridge University Press, 2000), pp. 24–44.

Wittgenstein says, at "various points in one's life," does the doctrine truly deserve to be described (as it frequently is) as the central core of the Christian faith.

Here, postmodern discourse has something to learn from Trinitarian thought: for in spite of its supposed attention to concrete practice, it does not operate at the service of some particular community to which it is held accountable. It must therefore find ways to discipline itself: to return, again and again, to the concrete practices from which it claims that its theories are derived. It must continue to test its theories against these practices, such that it does not drift off into the ethereal world of abstraction. This does not mean that it must be limited to "common-sense" observations (as many critics seem to argue), nor that it must be fully comprehensible by any and every possible reader. It simply means that postmodern discourse must be able to make sense of the ways that human beings live their lives, in mundane matters as well as extraordinary and dramatic ones. Interestingly enough, some of the postmodern thinkers who have best embodied this attention to everyday life have also had an interest in Christian life and thought – thinkers such as Michel de Certeau, Luce Irigaray, and Cornel West.

CONCLUSION

The time is right, it seems, for the ongoing development of a postmodern Trinitarian theology. It is surely no accident that the advent of postmodernism has coincided with an extraordinary flourishing of work on the Trinity – a doctrine that had been all but forgotten in modern academic theology. Postmodernism has focused our attention on a number of central concerns that had been neglected by theologians too fully under the sway of modernity; but, conversely, the renaissance of Trinitarian theology also has certain gifts to offer to those who live under the postmodern condition. A postmodern Christian theology can only succeed if it is able to understand and incorporate these Trinitarian insights, as well as contributing its own insights to the elucidation of Trinitarian doctrine.

Further reading

Augustine, *The Trinity*, ed. Edmund Hill (Brooklyn, NY: New City Press, 1991).

Boff, Leonardo. *Trinity and Society*, trans. Paul Burns (Maryknoll, NY: Orbis Books, 1988).

Cunningham, David S., *These Three Are One: The Practice of Trinitarian Theology* (Oxford: Blackwell, 1998).

Johnson, Elizabeth A., *She Who Is: The Mystery of God in Feminist Theological Discourse* (New York: Crossroad, 1992).

LaCugna, Catherine Mowry, *God For Us: The Trinity and Christian Life* (San Francisco: HarperCollins, 1991).

Lash, Nicholas, *Believing Three Ways In One God: A Reading of the Apostles' Creed* (University of Notre Dame Press, 1992).

Marshall, Bruce D., *Trinity and Truth* (Cambridge University Press, 2000).

Milbank, John, "The Second Difference: Toward a Trinitarianism Without Reserve," *Modern Theology* 2 (1986), 213–34.

  "Can a Gift be Given? Prolegomena to a Trinitarian Metaphysics," *Modern Theology* 11 (1995), 119–61.

Norris, Frederick W., ed., *Faith Gives Fullness to Reasoning: The Five Theological Orations of Gregory Nazianzen*, trans. Lionel Wickham and Frederick Williams (Leiden: E. J. Brill, 1991).

Rogers, Eugene F., Jr., *Sexuality and the Christian Body: Their Way Into the Triune God* (Oxford: Blackwell, 1999).

Volf, Miroslav, *After Our Likeness: The Church as the Image of the Trinity* (Grand Rapids: Eerdmans, 1998).

12 God and world

PHILIP CLAYTON

INTRODUCTION

The last years have seen a shift in the winds of culture. The approaching storm – or the dissipation of the existing storm clouds, depending on your perspective – has been widely heralded as the "postmodern shift." Postmodernity has as many interpretations as it has advocates and critics put together, which renders it impossible to begin a chapter of this sort with a pithy definition. But all (or at least most) of its descriptions exhibit two important features: a thoroughgoing critique of the "modern project" (when and what that was being a matter of deep contention), and an insistence that the solution to the problems of modernity lies not in a return to premodern questions and answers, but rather in moving beyond the modern project to something radically new and different.

Certain stereotypes notwithstanding, theologians are highly sensitive to shifts in the wind. As Walter Lowe points out in chapter 14 of this volume, Karl Barth recognized the exhaustion of the "modern" German intellectual projects (Hegel, neo-Kantianism, von Harnack) already in the opening of the twentieth century and proclaimed an anti-modernist (and in that sense, at least, postmodern) program. With no less insight, Paul Tillich put his finger on the pulse of the postwar intellectual–existential climate when he published his highly successful *The Courage to Be* (1953) and began formulating his mature systematic theology. One detects a similar cultural acuity in the death-of-God movement, in Langdon Gilkey's naming and reaping of whirlwinds, and the diverse forms of liberation theology that have left an indelible impression on theology at the turn of the millennium.

But to sense a shift in the wind is not the same as to correctly understand the significance and nature of the shift – as should be clear from recent battles over what may and may not pass as postmodern.[1] The fronts

---

[1] One need only contrast the epistemological position in Jean-François Lyotard, *The Postmodern Condition: A Report on Knowledge*, trans. Geoff Bennington and Brian Massumi (Minneapolis: University of Minnesota Press, 1984) with Nancey Murphy's *Anglo-American*

in this battle have ranged from those who take postmodernism to mean nothing more than being pleasantly free from any need to do apologetics (foundations now being terribly out of style), all the way to those who find in postmodernism the final demise of truth, assertion, or indeed any claims for constructive theory, if by that we mean a correspondence between our language and reality.[2] To say briefly what could take a chapter, I find the one response to offer too little and the other too much; surely the answer lies somewhere in between. And what is the "in between"? One can point toward it (hoping that it is indeed pointing and not hand-waving!) with a series of double negatives: postmodernism means neither the end of all constructive theorizing, nor continuing to construct detailed metaphysical systems; it means neither the destruction of any "place" from which to speak, nor giving precedence to the comfortable *loci* of modern academic theology; it means neither the equation of theological theories with the results of science nor buying into the old dichotomy between "objective" science and "subjective" religious thought; it means neither "anything goes" in theology nor "nothing goes."

Of course, like all negative theology, such a list says both too little (since it fails to give sufficient *positive* characterization of postmodern theology) and too much (since it will call forth criticism from both sides of the aisle). The goal of this section of the present volume, however, is not to offer long methodological chapters but to step *in medias res*: to demonstrate what postmodern theology might mean by actually doing it, and then to leave it to readers to infer what are and are not the important features of postmodern theology. My particular interests lying in the God–world relation, I thus turn without further ado to that subject.

THE GOD–WORLD RELATION IN A NEW KEY

To speak about the God–world relation one has to assume some things about the nature of the world. Unlike most of modern theology, postmodern theologians no longer cede the question of what the world is to science alone. Gone is the purely responsive theology that lets physics determine the nature of reality and then places God in whatever is left over (as in Kant's God of practical reasoning in the second critique). Instead, although the scientific story is carefully heeded (for one neglects it at

---

Postmodernity: Philosophical Perspectives on Science, Religion, and Ethics (Boulder, CO: Westview Press, 1997) to see how deep are the disagreements.

[2] See for example Mark C. Taylor, *Deconstructing Theology* (New York, NY: Crossroad, 1982); Mark C. Taylor, *Erring: A Postmodern A/Theology* (University of Chicago Press, 1984); Jacques Derrida, *Of Grammatology*, trans. Gayatri Chakravorty Spivak (Baltimore, MD: Johns Hopkins University Press, 1998).

her peril!), it is transformed, and perhaps radically so, when it is reread theologically.

Consider the following juxtaposition of two descriptions of the world, which under modern assumptions remained forever irreconcilable:

(1) The world consists of a purely objective "stuff" and is independent of how humans interpret or know it. It evidences a lawlike regularity at its core. Much of its regularity is mathematical in nature, being based on fundamental physical constants that are discernible throughout the observable universe. This regularity allows for predictions of incredible precision, as well as encouraging us to apply regularities found in one region of the universe to regions far beyond our horizon of observation. Thus quantum physics, the physics of the very small, developed in particle accelerators on this planet, allows us to understand processes that occurred in the first milliseconds of the universe's existence, and chemical structures discovered for substances on this planet allow us to analyze the histories of stars whose light reaches us after journeying millions of light years. Studying the universe in terms of natural laws and with the resources of mathematical physics has produced a body of knowledge unmatched, in its precision and predictive value, in any other area of human experience or study. Thus scientific knowledge is the paradigm for knowledge in general.

(2) The world is an expression of God and is permeated by the divine. All movement and action in some way expresses the divine nature and indeed *is* a part of the divine. In no place is God separate from creation, any more than "you" are separate from your body (though God is also more than the creation as a whole). The world is not mechanism but organism, not "demythologized" but "reenchanted."[3] Indeed, every emergent level in the hierarchy of reality expresses a different attribute of the divine nature: from the lawlike regularity of the physical world, through the striving and purposiveness of the biological order, to the conscious intentionality and rationality of mental experience. Finally, all is filled with spirit, so that at no point can world and God be separated. Nothing is secular; all imbibes of the presence of the divine, in whom "we live and move and have our being."

So how are these two to be brought together? At the end of the twentieth century it became the theologian's task to integrate these two perspectives. This new *locus*, the doctrine of God and world, draws from and partially

---

3 See David Ray Griffin, ed., *The Reenchantment of Science: Postmodern Proposals* (Albany: State University of New York Press, 1988).

overlaps with a number of classical theological areas – the doctrine of creation, the doctrine of God, pneumatology, anthropology, the doctrine of history – though it is identical with none. Central within the theology of God and world is the problem of divine agency: how can we attribute events to the causal activity of God when science appears to fully explain each event that occurs within the natural world? What conceptual resources might allow Christian theologians to acknowledge the power of science without reducing the divine to a "God of the [few remaining] gaps"?

PANENTHEISM AND ITS RESOURCES

Panentheism has been defined as the view that the world is within God, though God is also more than the world. Every event is located within God and expresses something of the divine nature; no event is a purely "natural" event. Thus no separation of God and these events needs to be granted; God is as intimately involved in each as you are in the beating of your heart and the movements of your hands.

Of course, different events express the divine nature in different ways. Purely physical occurrences do not reveal God's moral nature, consciousness or creativity; but they do evidence the regularity, simplicity, and predictability that are part of the divine. In their regularity they are reminiscent of the autonomic functions in our own bodies, which self-regulate rather than being steered by our conscious intentions – except that God, unlike us, is presumably aware of *everything* that occurs within Godself and, in principle, is able to change it. At a higher (emergent) level, the fecundity of evolution reveals purposiveness (though, on the standard view, not actual purpose) and incredible creativity; still, the suffering of creatures and the eventual extinction of most species does not (one hopes) reveal much of the moral nature of God. At a further emergent level, the level of consciousness, more of God appears: intentional actions express God's focal agency; altruistic acts manifest the divine character; the world of ideas gives glimpses of the realm of the eternal and necessary; and intuition and affect can reflect, albeit in a glass darkly, the unity with the divine that is the world's true nature.

A panentheism of this sort is a powerful response to the problem of divine action in an age of science. Divine action is a central problem for theology today: one cannot tell just any story about the causes of events in the natural world, and well-attested scientific explanations are not just "one story among the rest." This is not to deny that scientific theories have a preliminary status, that they are open to change, and that some of them will be falsified. Still, the fact that a given theory will possibly be revised in the future does not mean that it is on the same level as any other account of the phenomenon in the present.[4] Even postmodern theologians have to deal with the theory of relativity.

But we *can* tell multiple stories in cases where we do not have overriding scientific laws, or where the questions involved are metaphysical rather than physical in nature. The former occurs, for example, at the level of the very small: if reality is indeterminate at the quantum level, then there is no physical obstacle to telling a story of God's involvement there.[5] Likewise, there is good reason to think that the human mental life cannot ultimately be explained in a lawlike fashion, that the laws of rationality are not the same as, or reducible to, the laws of the physical world (although mental functioning clearly depends on physical regularities and a certain level of brain functioning).[6] So here, too, there is some freedom in choosing what story to tell. Perhaps you wish to tell a story of the human person as a composite of mental and physical substances *à la* Descartes, or a Marxist story of persons as the product of socioeconomic forces, or a physicalist story of the biochemical processes that determine what we naively call the "mental life." But you may also tell a story of men and women as *imago dei*, reflecting, however imperfectly, the image of their Creator.

Christian theologians are committed to avoiding deism. This means that there must be *some* place for God's action in the world. Creating and sustaining a universe is significant, I admit, but the Christian theist hopes for more. Today, stories of regular miraculous interventions have become hard to retell outside the Sunday-school classroom, except as metaphors for what we believe to be deeper spiritual truths. Situated in our particular location, children of our century, we stumble over the stories of God modifying this and that aspect of the physical world – if only because of the fact that such stories must make God responsible for *not* intervening in the Holocaust and other cases of manifest evil and suffering. At the same time, even today's scientifically informed believer *can* embrace stories of the "downward" lure of God, who offers persons possibilities for a life lived *sub specie aeternitatis*. The story that panentheist theologians want to tell is that the world is open

---

4 On the presumption of naturalism, see ch. 7 in Clayton, *God and Contemporary Science* (Edinburgh University Press and Grand Rapids: Eerdmans, 1997).

5 See Nancey Murphy, "Divine Action in the Natural Order: Buridan's Ass and Schrödinger's Cat," in Robert J. Russell, Nancey Murphy, and Arthur R. Peacocke, eds., *Chaos and Complexity: Scientific Perspectives on Divine Action* (Vatican City State: Vatican Observatory Publications, 1995), pp. 325–59.

6 See Donald Davidson's arguments for "anomalous monism" in "Mental Events," reprinted in Davidson, *Essays on Actions and Events* (Oxford: Clarendon Press, 1980), ch. 11; see also Clayton, "Neuroscience, the Person and God: An Emergentist Account," *Zygon* 35:2 (September 2000), 613–53.

"from the top" for God's activity:[7] God can influence the world as a whole because the world does not lie outside of the divine, just as (on the everyday model) one's mind or mental self can influence one's body.

Various stories could be told about how this divine influence might proceed: directly from God to human consciousness, or in some way mediated through the world as a whole.[8] But we must break off the narrative at this point. The key task was to reestablish the space for the telling of stories, against the illusion that science has said it all. This transition being made, we turn to the multiple metaphors and accounts that constitute theology in a postmodern key. In contrast to foundational theories, metaphors have some distinct features: they come in groups, multiply in overlapping fashion, and supplement rather than contradict one another. There may no longer be an antidote to metaphorical pluralism in theology (though some metaphors may emerge as more powerful and more effective than others); herein lies the burden, and the joy, of the postmodern context.

SIFTING GOD–WORLD METAPHORS

Wo/man does not live by assertion alone; various genres point in complementary ways toward the inexpressible. Among the non-assertorical genres, metaphor has played a central role in postmodern literary theory.[9] From the use of multiple metaphors it does not follow, however, that all metaphors are created equal. A panentheistic understanding of the God–world relation relies on metaphors embedded within metaphors, with the more detailed and anthropomorphic metaphors offering fuller pictures of a more fundamental intuition about God's relation to the world. (A little reflection shows that this pattern is in fact widespread in systematic theology, although postmodern theologians have acknowledged it more openly than the modern tradition did.) Failing to distinguish between the various layers of this structure, as some have, opens the proposal to unnecessary criticism.

The fundamental intuition with which panentheism begins is that the world is within the divine, though God is also more than the world. The assertion of a transcendent God, a (ground of) being who is personal and yet infinitely more than personal, makes panentheism a variety of theism. At the same time, locating the world within the divine, rather than as a

---

[7] See Arthur Peacocke, *Theology for a Scientific Age: Being and Becoming – Natural, Divine, and Human* (Minneapolis: Fortress Press, 1993).

[8] For more details see Clayton, *God and Contemporary Science* and *The Emergence of Spirit* (forthcoming).

[9] See Janet Martin Soskice, *Metaphor and Religious Language* (Oxford: Clarendon Press, 1985), and Paul Ricoeur, *The Rule of Metaphor: Multi-disciplinary Studies of the Creation of Meaning in Language*, trans. Robert Czerny (University of Toronto Press, 1977).

separate thing that God is then present to, gives panentheism a spiritual affinity to some of the Eastern traditions. For on this view the motion of a subatomic particle, the purposive behavior of a wolf, the ethical or rational actions of a human being – each directly expresses an aspect of the divine at the same time that it "belongs" to the agent in question.

The next level in the hierarchy of metaphors is embodiment. Panentheism maintains that God is not defined as pure spirit in contrast to the physical world that s/he created; God is in some sense incarnate in this world. (It will turn out that this view makes it easier to understand a doctrine like the incarnation in Christ without compromising the uniqueness of the latter.) Note that at this level the metaphor of embodiment is not yet limited to the human body; it thus encourages one to explore various forms of embodiment as possible metaphors for the God–world relation. After all, we know many types of bodies in the world, from electrons and atoms through molecules and cells to organisms and (perhaps) ecosystems and on to the "bodies" of law, corporate bodies, and bodies of doctrine. Even in cases where the precise structure of human embodiment is not present, the embodiment metaphor is illuminating. In its most general sense it expresses the carrying out of intentions through a medium that is conceptually distinct from the self though intimately linked to it. God is closer to us than we are to ourselves.

At a further level of specificity, the panentheist speaks of the world as God's body in some sense analogous to a human body. I call this the Panentheistic Analogy: the relation of God to the world parallels the relation of our minds to our bodies.[10] Within this particular metaphor, multiple metaphors can in turn be used: God is spoken of as the heart of the world, the soul of the world, the driving force or life force of the world, the mind of the world.[11] Various of these metaphors turn out to be useful for various specific purposes, for example, for explicating particular aspects of Christian doctrine, for incorporating the results of science, or for recognizing the revolutionary potential of Christian theism in new contexts.[12] In the end, it

[10] See Clayton, *God and Contemporary Science*, ch. 8.
[11] See Paul Davies, *The Mind of God: The Scientific Basis for a Rational World* (New York: Simon & Schuster, 1992).
[12] I do not, however, construe the embodiment metaphor as assuming one half of an alleged dichotomy between "organic" and "mechanistic" ways of thinking, as Sallie McFague does in *The Body of God: An Ecological Theology* (London: SCM Press, 1993). The organic model gives primacy to the biological perspective, but that model does not correctly reflect the higher-order relationship between God and the world. To recognize how the biological perspective is limited (it needs supplementing with theories from the levels of psychology and theology) allows us to see how the metaphor of the world as God's body must be corrected in the theistic case. The analogy suggests that God's relationship to the world is *like* the relationship of our minds to our bodies. Thus the structure of emergence requires that the analogy be

is a strength of a metaphor if it can both specify its areas of accuracy and find within itself grounds for whatever corrections need to be made.

In defending the Panentheistic Analogy I have focused in particular on the metaphor of God as the mind of the world. Given what we know about the relationship between higher-order mental properties in humans and their physical substratum, the mind metaphor is a powerful means of expressing traditional Christian conceptions of the God-world relationship in a manner consistent with the findings of science. (The soul conception, by contrast, faces more serious conflicts with modern science.[13]) There is an integral and bi-directional relationship between mental experience and the body's brain and central nervous system. "I" includes all the aspects of the functioning of one's body, but we identify ourselves in particular with the flow of our mental experience. When we make a decision, this occurs at the mental level of reflection, affect, or disposition; it flows from there to whatever bodily steps are involved in carrying out that decision. The analogy with God is intriguing: the mental subject of the universe has access to all occurrences in the world as input (though, of course, not by means of physical structures in the world, such as a sort of cosmic optic nerve or nervous system). And God's causal input into the world is best understood as analogous to that level of mental experience which, monitoring and responding to the various inputs from the world, makes decisions and carries out actions at a mental level that stands above, without being fully separate from, the level of physical functioning.

Of course, there are disanalogies: one does not find signs of God's central nervous system in the cosmos; and theists believe that God's existence precedes the physical universe, even if the divine experience becomes richer through the course of cosmic evolution. But to demand, as John Polkinghorne has,[14] that the universe must show a physical structure analogous to the body's central nervous system before panentheism can be taken seriously is to miss out on the level in the hierarchy of the natural world at which divine Spirit occurs. True, the body's biological system must be structured in a highly specific way if it is to give rise to mental experience and, in turn, to act on the results of a (mental) decision-making process; but this is only because the mental and the biological are contiguous levels in the hierarchy of natural emergence. In *God and Contemporary Science*

corrected in the theistic case by moving both analogs up one level: human mind is to human body as divine spirit is to consciousness in particular *and* to the world as a whole.

13 See Warren S. Brown, Nancey Murphy, and H. Newton Maloney, *Whatever Happened to the Soul?: Scientific and Theological Portraits of Human Nature* (Minneapolis: Fortress Press, 1998).

14 See John Polkinghorne, *Belief in God in an Age of Science* (New Haven, CT: Yale University Press, 1998), ch. 12.

I argued that spirit is a yet higher level in this hierarchy; spiritual properties are different from and not reducible to mental properties, although
they presuppose the life of the mind. This means that one should be looking
closely at mental/affective experience for the features that make it receptive
to the causal influence of divine spirit. In the emergentist picture, if there
is an active divine spirit – or even just an emergent spiritual level within
the one natural world – its influence will be mediated through the level of
mind and from thence to physical bodies in the world.

This is truly theology in a new key. We may shy away from magical
interventions into the physical world yet still find that world "reenchanted"
as the embodiment of the divine. The beauties of our planet and the richness
of its life forms are not distant expressions of the providence of God; they
are direct manifestations of the divine presence. When modern apologetics
has been left behind, one no longer needs to protect against the fear that
all theology is anthropomorphic projection (Feuerbach). Instead, we can
look to the structures (and contents!) of individual consciousness, and to
the growth and development of culture, for signs of divine guidance and
creativity. At these levels, if not in the biological world, the sorts of structures
that Polkinghorne calls for are richly evident. Think of the cultural means
by which individuals who are open to the divine lure can influence other
individuals. An idea of genius (Einstein's special relativity, Kant's critical
philosophy, Gandhi's nonviolent resistance) or an artistic genre (classical
harmony, the sonata form in poetry) can spread like wildfire through a large
number of minds or through human experience in general. Individual minds
integrate into groups of minds; individual actions influence other actions.
Of course, one cannot *demonstrate* that a given idea is God-breathed or that
either the church or human culture is progressing toward greater harmony
with the divine will; the previous century offers too painful a picture of
regress in the other direction for such melioristic optimism to be convincing.
Still, the "upwardly open" nature of human consciousness, infused as it is
with intimations of immortality, offers a powerful model of the integration
of mind and spirit – exactly the sort of picture that panentheism wishes to
place at the center of the God–world relation. Just as the neurophysiological
structure of the higher primates is "upwardly open" to the emergence and
causal power of the mental, so the mental or cultural world is upwardly
open to the influence of the Creator Spirit.

BEHIND THE METAPHORS

Behind the metaphors that are the daily bread of postmodern theology
lies the project of giving expression to a particular conceptual position.

Postmodernity and conceptual systems are not antithetical as long as the systems in question are not foundationalist, definitive, or context-free. A "pluralistic metaphysics"[15] need not be any of these.

There is space here only to allude to the sort of system that I would defend. Obviously, it understands the God–world relation to be as intimate ontologically as can be conceived, yet without making the world essential to the being of God. Here I follow the great twentieth-century panentheist, Charles Hartshorne, whose exposition of panentheism depends on a theory of internal relations that he derives from a detailed discussion of the theory of knowledge.[16] To know something is to be directly related to it. The more intimately we know something, the more closely linked we are to it ontologically. The way I know an external object is less intimate than the way I know a lover or friend, and both of these relations are less intimate than my internal knowledge of my own body. I am internally related to my body, immediately aware of stimuli and feelings in a way vastly different from my knowledge of the physical world. But God's relation to the world is no less intimate than my relation to my own body. Therefore we cannot speak of God's relatedness to the world using any language less strong than that of the world as God's body. But this just is the panentheistic analogy.

Joseph Bracken's notion of interlocking fields of personal presence remains an important resource for thinking the God who both contains and transcends the creation.[17] Conceptually, approaches of this sort break with theologies of pure actuality (Aristotle, St. Thomas) in favor of theologies that allow for potency in God (Schelling, Tillich, process philosophies). What is potential becomes actualized, and in this sense there is change in God as God is related to the world. Yet the process occurs within the necessary givenness of the ground of God or (to put it differently) within the primordial unchanging divine nature.

There is no way to think God's radical relatedness to the world – the fact that the world deeply matters to God – without speaking of a certain dependence relation. But this kind of dependence is fully compatible with the traditional affirmation that God did not have to create the world. Had there been no world, God would not have been essentially different, though God would have lacked certain experiences that in fact occurred (such as the experience of being aware of a prayer, an individual's existence, or an epoch

---

[15] See Clayton, *The Problem of God in Modern Thought* (Grand Rapids: Eerdmans, 2000), ch. 1.
[16] See Hartshorne, *Man's Vision of God and the Logic of Theism* (Chicago: Wilet, Clark, 1941).
[17] Joseph A. Bracken, *Society and Spirit: A Trinitarian Cosmology* (Selinsgrove, PA: Susquehanna University Press, 1991); *The Divine Matrix: Creativity as Link between East and West* (Maryknoll, NY: Orbis, 1995); *The One in the Many: A Contemporary Reconstruction of the God–World Relationship* (Grand Rapids: Eerdmans, 2001).

of cosmic history). Still, having once created a world, God must bring about an outcome that is consistent with being God *to* that world.[18] God *need* not have been dependent on any world, but, having created this universe, the fullness of God's experience – and in this sense, God Godself – is now dependent on it.

Even if God is not essentially dependent on the world, could it be that the *personhood* of God is? In one sense no: apart from the world God has an internally complex structure that Christian theologians, extrapolating upwards from the moments of salvation history recorded in the tradition, have characterized as the inner relationship of the three persons of the Trinity. But in an important sense God *is* dependent on the world. In accepting Rahner's Rule as an epistemic indicator – the principle that statements about God's eternal or "immanent" being are to be guided by God's "outward" actions in history – I am compelled to say that the revelatory and incarnational moments in the history of salvation also represent moments in God's experience. There is more in the divine experience subsequent to God's involvement in history than there would otherwise have been.

If we are to assert a genuine relation between God and world, we must speak of potentials for experience within God which become actual only through the interactions themselves.[19] Under the old metaphysics of perfection this would have been impossible, for full perfection required full actuality and potentiality was an imperfection; but when the metaphysics does not fit, it must be discarded. On this view the core of divine personhood is a combination of God's essential nature and a potential for experience. Embodiment in the world provides the vehicle for that experience.

Therefore at least two distinct positions emerge. Classical theism offers a picture of God as fully actual and creating a world separate from himself to which he is present. There can be no dependence on that world – a fact that fits nicely with the externality of the world to God. By contrast, panentheism conceives a world in which God is "embodied" and thus present with a greater degree of dependence. (Note that you can be intensely "present" to others and yet not dependent on their continued existence, whereas you are present to your body and dependent on its continued existence in a far more profound way.) In a natural fit with this closer mode of presence, panentheism speaks of a potentiality in God that is actualized in God's relations with the world. It is a contingent dependence, one that did not

---

[18] Here I follow Wolfhart Pannenberg, *Theology and the Kingdom of God*, ed. R. J. Neuhaus (Philadelphia: Fortress, 1969).

[19] See ibid., esp. ch. 4. In this work Pannenberg comes closer to process thought than in any other of his writings, e.g. "In a limited but real sense it is true to say that God does not yet fully exist" (p. 56).

have to happen; still, subsequent to the free decision to create and to be as intimately involved with the world as this, the dependence becomes basic to the divine experience.

OTHER THEOLOGICAL IMPLICATIONS

Which of the classical doctrines of the God–world relation are preserved within panentheism, and which are altered? My defense of panentheism retains the belief in the transcendence of God, in the contrast between God's necessary existence and the contingency (finitude) of the world, and in creation as a free act of God. This means that God does not require a world in order to exist. The belief that the world exists only through God's concurrence, through God's continual willing of the world again at every instance (*creatio continua*), is also retained. Indeed, it is intensified, since the age-old worry that matter might be eternal or might continue existing on its own without divine support is dissolved. On this view matter is not a separate ontological principle and does not involve a kind of existence separate from God; rather, it remains a part of the one divine unity, analogous to the way that the body of the human agent can express human agency only through the psycho-physical union which is the human person.

The immanence of God to the world is also retained within panentheism. I do not wish to be unfair to classical philosophical theism: the biblical documents as well as many of the great theologians stressed God's providential presence to each living creature and to each part of creation (the doctrine of omnipresence). It is a question not of what the tradition *intended*, but of what it was able to think, to conceive in a systematic and adequate form.[20] It is very difficult to conceive how a being who is pure spirit could be present to a world that is pure matter (or to a Cartesian combination of thinking stuff and extended stuff); how a being who must not be responsive to the world in any way lest "he" lose his perfection (as in parts of the Thomistic tradition) could interact with and respond to a world that is fundamentally interrelational; how a God who is above time and outside the process of change could really be present to a world that is ubiquitously in process. One needs some way to conceive the type of presence that one asserts of God to world. The panentheistic analogy provides the conceptual resources

---

[20] Here I have in mind the attempt to find in theologians such as Origen a solution to the problem of *how* God is present within the world. For a brilliant attempt that is, I think, in the end insufficient, see Colin Gunton, *The Triune Creator* (Edinburgh: University of Edinburgh Press and Grand Rapids: Eerdmans, 1998). By contrast, I think that there are resources in the Orthodox tradition that Western theologians have not yet appropriated as fully as they might. See John Zizioulas, *Being as Communion: Studies in Personhood and the Church* (London: Darton, Longman and Todd, 1985).

to meet this need. The relevant comparison, then, is not of the panentheistic analogy to the classic doctrine of divine omnipresence – after all, both views are characterized by a strong sense of God's presence to all things – but of the panentheistic analogy to some specific theory or analogy that classical theists might put forward to explain how this omnipresence is possible. At this point, I know of no stronger and more appropriate model than the model of mind and body.

Beyond these fundamental points, there is no reason why other central Christian doctrines would be problematic for, or would be made problematic by, panentheism. The major options within Christology all remain options here; indeed, the idea of incarnation is perhaps made easier to think by the notion of God's continual incarnation in/as the world. Room for a high Christology and a strong doctrine of the Spirit means room for a panentheistic Trinitarianism.[21] Ecclesiology remains unchanged (note that the idea of Christ's headship of the church already represents a sort of mind–body model). There can be a special presence of God to the church or manifestation of God within the church, just as the divine is differently manifest in the "worlds" of physics, biology and psychology. The theology of nature is probably strengthened by panentheism, insofar as the natural world comes to be understood as a continuing part of the being of God. Even the brief list in this article should convey some sense of the rich metaphors that now become available for offering a retheologized or "reenchanted" account of the natural world. The panentheistic analogy is also a powerful means for understanding and motivating environmental concern. By contrast, the Fall may at first seem difficult to comprehend, since the (now fallen) world must remain in some sense still within the being of God. Certainly what has to go is a notion of the purity of God that requires "him" to turn aside from all limited and sinful being. Panentheism does not grant the necessity of drawing an ontological line between God and fallen world until redemption occurs. There is room for a strong soteriology, but it occurs as a transformation of individuals and societies, not as an ontological separation and reunion (after all, a world separated from God would be nothing at all).

Moreover, we do anticipate a final eschaton when there will be no more moral separation and "no more tears" (Revelation 20). Unlike the Eastern traditions, the Christian hope never becomes total identity between God and world; infinite remains distinct in its essence from finite, necessary from contingent, creator from created. Critics of panentheism like John Polkinghorne allow for an eschatological panentheism but insist on a greater God–world separation in the present. They are right about the former, since

---

[21] See Clayton, *The Problem of God in Modern Thought*, esp. ch. 9.

in a final reconciliation in which God becomes "all in all" creation cannot be left "outside." But they are wrong to place the world "elsewhere" in the meantime: the distinction between God and a fallen world is a moral one, viz., the distinction between perfection and imperfection; it does not need supplementing through ontological distancing as well. (A mother is not "soiled" by her son's rebellious actions, and she does not need to withdraw from him in order to voice her disapproval.)

CONTRASTING PANENTHEISMS

Paraphrasing Ecclesiastes: of the inventing of new postmodernisms there is no end, and the encounter with too many postmodernisms can be wearying to the soul. One cannot legislate one postmodernism over another (indeed, would not this be a contradiction in terms?), and there are always versions of postmodernism that are more radical and less radical than one's own. Perhaps one can locate the present proposal on a rough continuum running from more extreme on the left to more conservative on the right (of course, using the adjectives "left" and "right" is completely arbitrary here). It stands to the left of those modern theological proposals that accepted the requirement of writing a prolegomenon, that is, establishing the truth of one's central premises in advance, either by appeal to scriptural truth or by finding a foundational philosophical or scientific system. I have not proceeded by constructing a chain of inferences, such that each proposition is justified as true by those that preceded it and passes on its truth to those that depend upon it. Nor have I claimed the sort of generality or timelessness typical of claims in modern theology. New knowledge of the relationship between mental and physical properties, for example, could vastly change the usefulness of the panentheistic analogy, causing us to look in completely different directions. And the specific metaphors employed will depend greatly on cultural context.

On the other hand, I have resisted two types of postmodern thinking that lie further to the left. I have not abandoned propositions or revised the ideals of constructive theology altogether. The "break" or "fissure" of language, and the breakdown of the modern confidence in reference, need not drive us to a theology that is post-propositional across the board. Theology's quest should continue to be to find models that are adequate both to its traditions and to the best of contemporary science, models that elucidate, in a coherent and rational manner, the set of beliefs associated with the Christian tradition, models that are transformative.

Nor have I abandoned the search for better formulations. The contrast with Sallie McFague's panentheism might be informative. In her book *The*

Body of God,[22] McFague wants to give equal weight to a whole string of desiderata in assessing proposed models of God. Thus the truth or conceptual coherence of a model and its consistency with the best of current science do not stand on a higher level than pragmatic criteria: its usefulness; its tendency to help overcome the oppression of the poor, nonwhites and nonmales; its fit with one or another contemporary world-view. McFague also has a very ambivalent relationship to the criterion of faithfulness to the Christian tradition.[23] In each of these areas, I would argue, the metaphorical concerns of postmodern theology are compatible with the quest for more adequate formulations (including criteria of adequacy), with talk of better and worse models, and with the process of rational evaluation that this entails.

Of course, part of the postmodern shift involves the addition of criteria such as usefulness, fruitfulness, and relevance to the contemporary context. But the result is not an unmitigated pluralism of metaphors. Not all metaphors are created equal; the question of usefulness does not trump the question of adequacy to the various publics to which theology is accountable (for example, church, academy, and society). Assessments are context-bound, questions reflect interests and assumptions; both intellectual projects and those who pursue them have a particular "location" – and yet none of these facts invalidates the pursuit of more and more valid models with improved explanatory power.

CONCLUSION

Panentheism goes beyond "seeing the face of God in his handiwork," though that metaphor remains a crucial part of Christian spirituality. It incautiously asserts a less mediated encounter with God "in, with and under" the Spirit-animated world. *God* is becoming something in and through the world and its history; thus the world adds a richness to the divine experience it would not otherwise have had.

There is no *ultimate* dependence of God on the world: the eternal divine nature does not require that there be a created, contingent world. Rather, this is the story we tell: in radical freedom God did create a world – not "outside" of Godself but as intimately linked to the divine presence as our bodies are to our minds; and God became as deeply related to that world,

---

[22] Sallie McFague, *The Body of God*, esp. ch. 3.
[23] On the one hand, she praises the tradition for stressing the symbols of interconnection, incarnation, and embodiment; on the other, she repeatedly castigates it for vilifying the body (and the gender traditionally associated with the body) and for its tendency to separate God and world.

and concerned with its fate, as we are with the fate of our own bodies. The Christian story is the story of that relationship – a relationship so radical that it culminates in a complete identification with the world's suffering: "And being found in appearance as a man, He humbled Himself and became obedient unto death, even death on a cross" (Philippians 2:8). In this sense a panentheistic understanding of the God–world relation becomes a natural partner to a strong kenotic Christology and soteriology.[24] But that is a story for another day.

[24] See Steven Knapp and Philip Clayton, "Christ as Risen: A Proposal," forthcoming.

13 The human person

JOHN WEBSTER

INTRODUCTION

The task of Christian theological anthropology is to depict evangelical (that is, Gospel-constituted) humanism. It aims to display the vision of human identity and flourishing which is ingredient within the Gospel's announcement that, in the being, action, and speech of Jesus Christ, the crucified who is now alive and present in the Spirit's power, the good purposes of God the Father for his human creation are established and their completion is promised. Christian theological anthropology offers a portrayal of the nature and destiny of humankind by explicating the Gospel's disclosure of the works and ways of the triune God.

Such claims, for all their loveliness, are culturally marginal. They are largely ignored, and occasionally repudiated, outside the sphere of the Christian confession; where they still retain profile, it is often only in crude versions. Because a Gospel-directed account of the human can thus claim almost no public self-evidence, the portrayal of an evangelical humanism of necessity involves Christian theological anthropology in a dispute about what constitutes "the humane." This chapter addresses one particular focus of the dispute: the relation of Christian theological anthropology to deconstructive postmodernism.

The way in which such a dispute is conducted depends in part upon two factors: the way in which postmodernism is construed, and the manner in which the task of Christian theology is understood. The postmodernism which is engaged here is that of "severe" or "radical" deconstructive philosophers and cultural theorists, and of those theologians for whom such theory provides the framework within which theological anthropology must be articulated. There are, as earlier chapters in this volume have shown, other uses of the term "postmodern." But it is in deconstructive postmodernism and its dependent a/theology that questions about the humane content of the Christian confession are raised with especial acuteness. This is not to presuppose that deconstructive philosophy or a/theology comprise a coherent set of doctrines or even a consistent intellectual style: looking for such is indeed "looking for perch in a trout stream."[1] Terms like "postmodern" and "deconstructive" simply identify a set of characteristic worries about or denials of the content and use of language about human "nature" and "destiny," language which is deeply embedded in the traditions of classical Christian theology and of modern culture. Whether deconstructive postmodernism is thought to constitute a decisive break from modernity depends to a large extent on how "modernity" is construed. If modernity is understood (as by Heidegger and his heirs) as a unified intellectual, cultural, and spiritual history defined by the Cartesian project of subjectivity and representation, then deconstructive anthropology can indeed be seen as innovative. On the other hand, if modernity is seen as a much more conflictual set of processes, then deconstructive anthropology may be understood not simply as a repudiation of modernity but, in important respects, as its continuation or intensification – as "late" or even "hyper" modernity.[2] What is crucial, of course, is that the terms "modern" and "postmodern" not be allowed to mesmerize: they are not statements of fact but constructions, and historians, philosophers, and theologians ought not to use them as substitutes for thought.

Three characteristics of fruitful theological engagement with deconstructive postmodernism may be suggested. First, theology will need to offer an interpretation of the bodies of thought and practice with which it engages (including its own) which is properly attentive to their complexity and variety and so avoids the slogans which lock the mind. Generalized postmodern renderings of the past sometimes reduce particular figures to mere representatives of the whole (Suarez as the ontotheologian *par excellence*) or collapse traditions of argument into simple ideas (the metaphysics of presence). Or again, wholesale rejection of deconstructionist critique of classical Christian theology overlooks the complicity of some strands of Christian theology in the culture of modernity. The safeguard against both mistakes is deference to the intricacy of the past. Second, theology needs to offer a *theological* reading of its cultural and intellectual situation, so as to avoid the resignation which comes from thinking that context is fate. There may or may not be a postmodern condition; but a responsible theology will resist making "condition" into iron necessity. Rather, theology will appeal to the categories and practices of the Christian confession to illuminate who and where we are, and, instead of passively accommodating itself to any

---

[1] C. Schrag, *The Resources of Rationality. A Response to the Postmodern Challenge* (Bloomington: Indiana University Press, 1992), p. 6.

[2] A. J. Cascardi, *The Subject of Modernity* (Cambridge University Press, 1992); A. Touraine, *Critique of Modernity* (Oxford: Blackwell, 1995).

such condition, to reach theological judgments about its context. Third, in all theological engagement with worlds of meaning outside the Christian faith, apologetics must be subordinate to and guided by biblical and dogmatic description. Biblical and dogmatic description explicates the content of the Christian Gospel out of its canonical expressions. It is an exercise of reason in which, under the tutelage of the divine self-communication, reason seeks to follow the Christian confession as it beckons to the truth of God and of all things in God. Apologetics is subordinate to and guided by this, because the defense of the Christian confession is inseparable from, and largely accomplished by, its portrayal, not by the elaboration of external conditions for its possibility. On the basis of such a conception of the theological task, how might Gospel-directed humanism be explicated in critical conversation with deconstructive anthropology?

THE DEATH OF THE SELF

In the celebrated closing paragraphs of *The Order of Things*, Foucault writes that "man is neither the oldest nor the most constant problem that has been posed for human knowledge" but "a recent invention within it," "an invention of recent date. And one perhaps nearing its end," facing its erasure "like a face drawn in the sand at the edge of the sea."[3] Though Foucault's later work (notably the aesthetics of the "care of the self" in *The History of Sexuality*) reaches a rather different set of judgments about human selfhood, this earlier text points us toward some characteristic postmodern ways of thinking about anthropology. What Foucault calls "the figure of man" is just that: a representation or invention; the appearance of this figure is recent, and is not the manifestation of a given substance but simply a false name given to a discursive product. This invention now faces its "absolute dispersion."[4] This dissolution of anthropology marks one of the primary fissures between modernity and postmodernity. Modernity (the deconstructionist argues) projects itself as an emancipation of cognitive and moral selfhood from the encompassing and founding orders of gods, societies, customs, and texts, and as the emergence of the deliberative self as that which is axiomatically real, true, and good. For postmodernism, this emancipatory myth merely masks the fact that the transcendent subject of science, ethics, or experience is a mere fictive conglomeration of fragments. As such, this myth can, perhaps, be seen as an attempt to set up bulwarks against anxiety, securing identity by rejecting selfhood as an invariable,

---

[3] M. Foucault, *The Order of Things. An Archaeology of the Human Sciences* (London: Tavistock, 1974), pp. 386f.

[4] Ibid., p. 385.

nameable, proximate presence, a ground of thought and action. And: "Is not this security of the near what is trembling today, that is, the co-belonging and co-propriety of the name of man and the name of Being...such as it is inscribed and forgotten according to the history of metaphysics, and such as it is awakened also by the destruction of ontotheology?"[5] It is precisely this "co-propriety" of anthropology and "being" which radical postmodernism thinks to dissolve: there is no human nature, no substrate to human history, just as there is no trajectory along which humankind moves.

The coinherence of subjectivity and ontotheology – the tie between the self as an enduring moral and cognitive foundation and appeal to the metaphysics of substance to explicate the nature of God and the world – is a particular target for radically deconstructive theological accounts of human selfhood. In the alliance of metaphysics and Christian theology in the West, the argument runs, God the supreme being is equally the supreme subject, the monadic, self-possessing bearer of a name. "From a monotheistic perspective," writes Mark Taylor, "to be is to be one. In order to be one, the subject cannot err and must always remain proper. By following the straight and narrow course, the self hopes to gain its most precious possession – itself."[6] Human subjectivity thus replicates divine self-possession: "The self-presence of the self-conscious subject reflects the presence of absolute subjectivity."[7] Whether Taylor is correct to claim that there is a single line of this sort from Augustine to Hegel may be doubted; it might well be argued that the claim maximizes some aspects of Christian teaching such as divine absoluteness, extracts them from their context in the overall scope of Christian doctrine, and minimizes those features of Christian teaching which serve as a corrective (such as the doctrine of Trinitarian relations, or the ethics and spirituality of dispossession). Nevertheless, the claim that Western theological anthropology rests on "the repressive logic of identity" or "the 'logic of oneness' [which] implies an economy of ownership"[8] serves as part of an account of human selfhood which "subverts the logic of identity" by viewing the self as "a function of the intersection of structures, the crossing of forces,"[9] or as a "deindividualized subject" which is "never centered in itself":[10]

> For the most part, questions about the self, and particularly questions about the self *as subject*, are deemed anathema. As there is no longer

---

[5] J. Derrida, "The Ends of Man," in *Margins* (University of Chicago Press, 1982), p. 133.
[6] M. C. Taylor, *Erring. A Postmodern A/theology* (University of Chicago Press, 1984), pp. 41f.
[7] Ibid., p. 42.   [8] Ibid., p. 130.   [9] Ibid., p. 134.
[10] Ibid., p. 139. See also R. P. Scharlemann, *The Reason of Following. Christology and the Ecstatic I* (University of Chicago Press, 1991), and C. E. Winquist, *Desiring Theology* (University of Chicago Press, 1995), pp. 99–126.

need for the unification of the diverse culture-spheres, so the problem of the self, at least as traditionally formulated, is seen to evaporate. Questions about self-identity, the unity of consciousness, and centralized and goal-directed activity have been displaced in the aftermath of the dissolution of the subject. If one cannot rid oneself of the vocabulary of self, subject, and mind, the most that can be asserted is that the self is multiplicity, heterogeneity, difference, and ceaseless becoming, bereft of origin and purpose. Such is the manifesto of postmodernity on matters of the human subject as self and mind.[11]

The question raised here for Christian anthropology is this: is there a "positive" theological anthropology (one which works from the given reality, the *positum*, of the Gospel) which nevertheless does not fall under the category of "ontotheology-to-be-deconstructed"?[12]

A THEOLOGICAL RESPONSE

To begin with, two points of orientation. First, a consideration of human nature and destiny is a necessary component of any theological account of the Christian Gospel. Because – and only because – the Christian Gospel concerns the ways and works of the triune God, it necessarily concerns the human creature whom God calls into being, saves and perfects. To detract from the significance of the human – whether by promoting the glory of God through diminishing the creature, or by deconstructive anti-humanism – is to truncate the scope of the Christian confession. A well-ordered theology resists the diminishment of humanity by attentiveness to the resources of the Christian confession of God as triune Creator, reconciler, and perfecter. Deconstructive accounts of the Christian tradition sometimes appear to neglect this point, because they are often underdetermined by the specific content of the Christian confession, which is a little too easily identified as simply a species of ontotheology. "Ontotheology" may identify some crude versions of Christian teaching; but it is simply too abstract and undifferentiated a notion to give much purchase on an authentically Christian account of the mercies of the triune God in their directedness to the well-being of humankind. Because of the content of its confession of God, Christian theology does not have to choose between God and humankind, or to abandon both; passion for God is necessarily passion for humanity.

[11] C. Schrag, *The Self after Postmodernity* (New Haven: Yale University Press, 1997), p. 8.
[12] B. D. Ingraffia, *Postmodern Theory and Biblical Theology. Vanquishing God's Shadow* (Cambridge University Press, 1995), p. 235.

Second, therefore, the context in which a theology oriented to the Christian confession pursues its interpretation of human nature and destiny is a consideration of the economy of grace. What it means to be human can only be grasped in its full scope and integrity on the basis of a depiction of the gracious work of God, Father, Son, and Spirit, in his saving self-communication with us. Three characteristics of that economy of grace are especially important here. (1) The economy of grace is a work of *grace*, the pure and uncaused turning of God to that which is not himself. This turning is not a necessity imposed on God from without; nor is it a turning evoked by something other than God. Yet in its utter spontaneity, it is a genuine turning *toward*, a spontaneity which has as its end the creation and maintenance of another reality with its own substance and dignity. It is a turning, in other words, which bestows life. And what is manifest in that turning is not a mere accidental or fleeting episode in the divine being, but its deep, constant character: to be for the creature is who God *is*. (2) The economy of grace is a work which is comprehensively true and effective. For the Christian confession, all human life and history takes place within this economy, which is definitive of what it is to be and act humanly; all human being and action are occurrences in its unfolding. The economy of grace is thus the *grand récit*, ontologically determinative of humankind. (3) In its spontaneity and comprehensiveness, the economy of grace is the enactment of the purpose of the *triune* God, and therefore the enactment of God's purpose to sustain humanity. The Trinitarian apprehension of God is thus crucial to an account of the humane character of the Gospel. This is because the personal and differentiated nature of the being of God as Father, Son, and Spirit determines the manner of God's engagement with his creatures. As the triune God, God is neither a remote causal agent nor an ultimate horizon of human history, but one who lives in fellowship with humankind, acting on our behalf, with us and, indeed, in and through us, in order that this fellowship should prosper and be brought to its completion.

The economy of grace is the history or (perhaps better) drama in which God is glorified in the creation, reconciliation and consummation of humanity. This drama provides the overarching plot out of which humankind as a whole is defined; it is also replicated in the individual drama of each human history, for to be a human person is to be a creature called to live from God's reconciling and consummating work. The drama contains three "moments" or "passages," each of which may be attributed with especial appropriateness to one of the triune persons, though not in such a way as to fragment the peace and unity of the life of God.

The first moment is the work of God the Father, Creator of heaven and earth. As creature, humankind is from, for, and with God. Humankind is *from* God, in that to be created is to be absolutely derivative, brought into being by an action which precedes the creature unconditionally. That action may be fittingly pictured as a summons or "word," a divine evocation of the creature out of nothingness into a particular kind of being. Having this nature, humankind also has an end, and so is *for* God, existing in a distinctive teleology, ordered toward relation to God. And so humankind is also *with* God, that is, created for participation in the history of covenantal fellowship between God and his creatures.

The second moment is that of God the Son's work of reconciliation. God's human creatures repudiate their absolute derivation and their ordering toward fellowship, seeking by a perverse and ultimately absurd counteract of self-creation to be human in a way other than that purposed by the creator. This perversity places the creature in absolute jeopardy, for self-making is precisely self-unmaking (in biblical terms, the wage paid by sin is death). This self-destruction also destroys fellowship between humankind and God; but it does so only from the side of the creature; the creature's repudiation of the gift of its creaturely being, form, and history does not thwart the Creator's purpose. From the side of the Creator, the fellowship stands, and is maintained against the creature's opposition. The form of that maintenance is the work of the Son of God. His taking human form, his ministry of speech and action, his destruction and being raised to new life, his glorification and rule over all things are the divine work of upholding the cause of humankind against itself. The creature's unmaking of itself is itself unmade, and fellowship maintained through the work of reconciliation.

The third moment is that of the Spirit's work of perfecting the creature. In all its objectivity and spontaneity, the divine work of reconciliation is not a merely external transaction; if it were, it would not be a restoration of mutuality and fellowship. Rather, through the presence and action of the Holy Spirit, objective reconciliation is completed through the renewal of the creature's being and the actual reintegration of humankind into the history of fellowship. Through the Spirit, humankind does not simply *observe* the economy of grace but participates in it as humankind's true history and end.

Such, in summary form, is one way of construing human nature and destiny, by portraying the economy of grace in its directedness to humankind. The question therefore is: can such an account be anything other than a unitary metaphysics of substances and presences, and therefore an imposition of coherence and identity – in short, a history of beings which must be disintegrated?

In responding to that critique, much hangs on careful theological specification of the terms "nature" and "destiny." A theological anthropology governed by the Christian confession of the triune God's works of creation, reconciliation, and perfection proposes that the nature of humanity *is* its destiny, that is, its participation in the drama of the economy of grace. To talk of human nature is to talk of a complex of events at whose center is fellowship between God and creatures. Two things follow.

First, Christian theology cannot but affirm the necessity of speaking of human "nature." To be human is to be a particular kind of being, one who has a certain kind of (extraordinarily complex, mobile and malleable but nevertheless distinct and determinate) identity. As such, to be human is not simply to be a product of discursive controversy and negotiation, or an assemblage of fragments without depth or substrate, a sort of patina on nothing in particular. Put differently: because it is appropriate to talk of humankind as having some sort of enduring identity, human being cannot be mere occurrence, or mere human poiesis; for Christian theology, there is a point in inquiring into the "ontology of this specific creature."[13]

Second, however, in its talk of human nature theology is not simply identifying something which lies *behind* the complexity and variety of human histories. Nor is it making the claim that to "have" a human nature is to be an artifact, assigned a fixed place in a taken-for-granted scheme of things. Such ways of thinking – which, it has to be conceded, have certainly found their way into some theological anthropology – are deficient because they extricate human nature from the temporal processes of the divine economy, isolating human being from the unfolding drama of fellowship with God in which humankind acquires its identity. But the corrective against this isolation is not the abandonment of an ontology of the human by espousing a non-metaphysical theology, but the development of a theological ontology whose categories are shaped by the confession of the Gospel.

Accordingly, the concept of "substance" is central to an elaboration of a theological anthropology. Deconstructive anthropology rejects such language as part of the apparatus of fixed, pre-given, nameable identities, whether of God or of the creature. Moving beyond the anthropological entailments of ontotheology means abandoning subjectivity as "self-contained presence,"[14] moving toward the "de-substantialized" self.[15] But it is worth noting that the language of substance may often serve as part of analytic, not descriptive, metaphysics (this distinction is routinely overlooked in deconstructive criticism of ontotheology). That is, its use does not prescribe the kind of being that humankind is, by, for example, placing humankind in the category of immobile presences. It identifies the subject who *is* in the history or drama of fellowship with God and the relations in which that

---

[13] K. Barth, *Church Dogmatics* vol. 3, part 2 (Edinburgh: T. & T. Clark, 1960), p. 13.
[14] Taylor, *Erring*, p. 136.   [15] Ibid., p. 135.

subject stands; and so it is entirely possible to respond to deconstructive criticism of ontotheology by developing an historical and social ontology of the human.

Theological talk of human nature and destiny does not refer to abstract, a-historical entities but to the identity acquired by subjects as they act and are acted upon in the reciprocities of relation to God and others. Unity, identity, presence, far from being barriers against the transactions of historical existence, are the unity, identity, and presence of those involved in historical action and passion. That identity both enables us to characterize human life as history (rather than mere random episode) and is itself built up through history. "Personal identity is just that identity presupposed by the unity of the character which the unity of a narrative requires."[16] In more directly theological terms: human nature is not antecedent to the economy of God's works, but precisely that which *becomes* through participation in the drama of creation, salvation, and consummation. Human being is thus in one sense a (purposed) "implicate" of the ways of God with humankind, emerging in the life and practices of covenantal fellowship. In responding to deconstructive philosophy of self, Calvin Schrag has argued that subjectivity is best understood as "self-implicature."[17] That is, selfhood is not so much a foundation for practice as that which issues from engagement in practice. In particular, communication – social and discursive transactions – is constitutive of the "domain of common praxis":[18] the "triadic intentionality of discourse (*about* something, *by* someone, *for* the other)... furnishes the proper context for a comprehension of the traces of the subject within the praxial space of discursive transactions. It is within this context that the subject emerges and establishes its presence ... The "who" of discourse is an achievement of praxis rather than a theoretically derived given, a happening, an event of participatory life within a world of nature and history."[19] There is much here that is companionable with a theological anthropology organized around the divine economy: a sense that the "presence" of humankind is a "perpetual coming-to-presence";[20] an affirmation of the "'eventful' position of the subject";[21] a sense that the self is not simply the maker of its identity but "a self authorized and constituted by the multiplicity of its responses and profiles within a public and historical world."[22]

---

[16] A. MacIntyre, *After Virtue. A Study in Moral Theory* (University of Notre Dame Press, 1984), p. 218.

[17] C. Schrag, "Subjectivity and Praxis at the End of Philosophy," in *Philosophical Papers* (Albany: State University of New York Press, 1994), p. 195; see also C. Schrag, *Communicative Praxis and the Shape of Subjectivity* (Bloomington: Indiana University Press, 1986), esp. pp. 115–76.

[18] Ibid., p. 195.   [19] Ibid., p. 197.

[20] Schrag, *Communicative Praxis*, p. 143.   [21] Ibid., p. 146.

[22] Schrag, "Subjectivity and Praxis," p. 200.

Certainly a theological portrayal of human nature and destiny will have some reservations about the residual indeterminacy of this kind of account, especially about its apparent lack of a normative or teleological framework for human becoming. Christian theological anthropology is very far from a celebration of a general principle of "becoming," still less of cultivation of the self. But the "becoming" of which human nature is an "implicate" is not anarchic; it is the shapely and ordered fulfillment of calling, filling out that to which the gracious work of the triune God appoints humankind. And so the Christian authenticity of a theological anthropology will require it to depict with clarity and persuasiveness the divine calling and appointment in which humankind has its being and destiny. The key question for human beings, as MacIntyre notes, "is not about their authorship."[23]

To sum up so far: a Christian anthropology might respond to deconstructionist critique of its account of humankind by displaying the genuinely Christian content of that account, expounding a view of human nature and destiny as neither leaden "presence" nor pure fabrication, but as participation in the unfolding of God's ways with humankind. Being and acting humanly is thus not a matter of self-possession. Mark Taylor's association of monotheism with proprietorial human selfhood, for example, misses the real force of Christian anthropological affirmations. To be human is, on a Christian account, to have one's being outside of oneself, to owe one's being to the being and activity of the triune God. True humanity is thus not possessed identity but rather life in a perpetual movement of receiving and responding to a gift. We are human as creatures of the heavenly Father in whom we have our being; as those reconciled "in Christ"; and as those led toward perfection by the Spirit. Talk of the Father's gift of life, of "Christ in us" or of living "by the Spirit" is not a mere symbolic expression or archetype of ecstatic selfhood; it is irreducible. Human being is certainly a-centric, "never centered in itself,"[24] and so free from "the circle of appropriation and possession."[25] But this does not spell the end of subjectivity, "the impropriety, expropriation, and dispossession of the subject,"[26] but rather its existence *in* (by virtue of, through the mercy of, out of the absolute generosity of) the triune God. That, of course, is why life and faith are strictly correlative, and why life in the history of God with us is the antithesis of "possessive individualism."

It is from this perspective that the common deconstructive account of established religious practices as gratification of a need for certainty and identity without contingency is to be considered. Gianni Vattimo sees

---

[23] MacIntyre, *After Virtue*, p. 216.   [24] Taylor, *Erring*, p. 139.
[25] Ibid., p. 143.   [26] Ibid., p. 138.

religions as a kind of "fundamentalism," "neurotic defenses of identity and belonging in reaction to the indefinite widening of horizons entailed by the culmination of the epoch of the world picture ... attempting to recuperate a sense of identity and belonging that are at once reassuring and punitive."[27] That there are such pathological forms of religious practice is beyond doubt; but those are just that – pathological, and to that extent a warping of authentic evangelical humanism. Moreover, Christian anthropology will be uneasy with the (fundamentally modern) assumption that human flourishing is to be equated with unrestricted emancipation. Zygmunt Bauman, for example, defines "[fundamentalist" religion (again, the target is not too specific) by its promise to deliver from "the agonies of choice."[28] The proposed remedy is an embracing of "risk-contaminated freedom,"[29] "the perpetual anxiety of being,"[30] resistance to the monopoly of monotheism: "The voice of responsibility is the birth-cry of the human individual. Its audibility is the sign of the individual's life."[31]

A Christian anthropology will need to portray how, far from suggesting an effective closure of the possibilities of historical existence, the Gospel concerns the way in which agents, by the grace of God, may flourish. In making this portrayal, a Christian anthropology must resist being caught in the dualisms which have sorely afflicted modern culture (especially its ethics and politics) and in which much deconstructive thought remains snared: between nature and history; between self and that which is not self; between givenness and choice; above all, between the freedom of God and human well-being. The portrayal may be completed by an examination of two themes which exhibit more fully the structure of what has been suggested so far: vocation and fellowship.

Vocation

[T]he Lord bids each one of us in all life's actions to look to his calling. For he knows with what great restlessness human nature flames, with what fickleness it is borne hither and thither, how its ambition longs to embrace various things at once. Therefore, lest through our stupidity and rashness everything be turned topsy-turvy, he has appointed duties for every man in his particular way of life. And that no-one may thoughtlessly transgress his limits, he has named these various kinds of livings "callings." Therefore each individual has his own kind of living assigned to him by the Lord as a sort of sentry post

---

[27] G. Vattimo, *Beyond Interpretation. The Meaning of Hermeneutics for Philosophy* (Cambridge: Polity Press, 1997), pp. 39f.
[28] Z. Bauman, *Postmodernity and its Discontents* (Oxford: Blackwell, 1997), p. 184.
[29] Ibid.   [30] Ibid., 202.   [31] Ibid.

so that he may not heedlessly wander throughout life ... It is enough if we know that the Lord's calling is in everything the beginning and foundation of well-doing.[32]

A deconstructive reading of Calvin's account of divine vocation to a way of life might construe it as a classic expression of ontotheological ethics. Is it not undergirded by anxiety about moral and social indeterminacy and disorder – "restlessness," "fickleness," the instability which "longs to embrace various things at once," which "wander[s] throughout life"? Is not such an ethic, one in which a transcendent calling has "appointed duties" and assigned different "kinds of living," in effect a way of resisting *transgression* by the establishment of limits? Is not calling – "a sort of sentry post" – a prohibition, leaving us exposed to the heavenly censor? And is not this metaphysics of duties all too readily translated into a static social order of station and rank and unprotesting acceptance of vexations as the will of God?

Perhaps. Yet it is worth asking whether to read this account of the Christian rendering of the human way of life in that fashion has to elide its Christian specificity. For who, on a Christian construal, is this "Lord" who "bids each one of us in all life's actions to look to his calling"? He is not simply obligation or commandment personified. He is, rather, the eternally gracious one whose lordship is the inexhaustible power of his mercy by which we are sustained. His bidding of us is his securing of us against waste, the dispersal of the creature into formlessness. And what is his "calling"? It is not mere designation to a location in a social or metaphysical scheme. Rather, it is to a "kind of living" characterized by both integration (what Calvin later calls "harmony") and a "path" or movement toward a "goal." "Looking to" this calling is, moreover, very far from passivity, mere occupation of a space; it is engagement "in all life's actions" in "a particular way of life." The Trinitarian setting of Calvin's sketch of calling to a human way of life is implicit; but it would not be difficult to fill it out. Created by the Father for the active life of fellowship, the creature is reconciled by the Son and renewed by the Spirit, impelled into true human living. The grace of the triune God is thus the ground, healing, and quickening of life.

To talk of human life as taking place in this way in the domain and under the impulse of the divine call is restrictive only if that call is misconstrued as pure force, a violent heteronomy. But, in refusing to think in such terms, a Christian anthropology escapes the forced option: either the "disappearance

---

[32] J. Calvin, *Institutes of the Christian Religion* (Philadelphia: Westminster Press, 1960), III.10.vi.

of man"[33] or "techniques of the self."[34] Both are inhumane; both the destruction of subjectivity and the poetic cultivation of subjectivity presuppose a nominalist anthropology, without nature and destiny. For Christian theology, by contrast, nature and destiny can be construed as "role" or – as some classical theology might have put it – as "office." Role and office are the shape of the self and its activity; like "calling" they are not mere "placing" but the form and direction bestowed upon human life through participation in a historically structured set of relations. In those relations, the human subject encounters calls, invitations, corrections and blessings which enable identity and which undergird purposive action. Thereby, "making" a human life is not "an intensification of the relation to oneself by which one constituted oneself as the subject of one's acts."[35] It is instead joyful and active consent to and performance of the task of being God's reconciled creature pointed to perfection.[36]

One corollary of this coinherence of vocation and active consent is that freedom is theologically understood in a specific way. "Calling" does not spell the end of freedom; it simply turns from the modern myth that freedom is authentic only to the extent that it is unsituated and imposes itself on resistant forces or, perhaps, on the void. Postmodern accounts of freedom as "radical carelessness"[37] follow the same trajectory of their modern precursors: both are deeply voluntarist and expressivist; both think of human being and action without backgrounds; for both, "full freedom" is "situationless."[38] On a Christian view, I am free as I become free through the loving work of God who liberates for glad participation in the calling which leads to humankind's true end.

Fellowship

"We are in the fix that we cannot say 'we.' "[39] Why? Because a "self" without shape, substance or endurance is incapable of deep, extended relations. Once the self is eviscerated of any of the commonalities and stabilities which make reciprocal relations possible and fruitful, relations become simply arbitrary encounters: shifting, transient, groundless. Accidental "relations" do

---

33 Foucault, *The Order of Things*, p. 386.
34 M. Foucault, *Ethics, Subjectivity and Truth* (London: Penguin, 1997), pp. 87–92, 281–301; M. Foucault, *The Uses of Pleasure: The History of Sexuality*, vol. 2 (London: Penguin, 1992), pp. 25–32; M. Foucault, *The Care of the Self: The History of Sexuality*, vol. 3 (London: Penguin, 1990), pp. 37–68.
35 Foucault, *The Care of the Self*, p. 41.
36 On this understanding of role, see D. Emmet, *Function, Purpose and Powers* (London: Macmillan, 1958) and *Rules, Roles and Relations* (London: Macmillan, 1966).
37 Taylor, *Erring*, p. 144.
38 C. Taylor, *Hegel and Modern Society* (Cambridge University Press, 1979), p. 157.
39 J. D. Caputo, *Against Ethics. Contributions to a Poetics of Obligation with Constant Reference to Deconstruction* (Bloomington: Indiana University Press, 1993), p. 6.

not exhibit anything permanent about humankind; at best, they simply are, they just happen. Sociality is not such as to shape or form us or require us to act for non-arbitrary reasons in certain ways; it has no roots, and it demonstrates no teleology. Hence we can neither say "we" nor act in ways that presuppose that "we" signifies anything other than a temporary alliance.

That such characterizations of sociality are hardly promising soil for ethics and politics is commonly remarked by both deconstructionist thinkers and their detractors. How might Christian anthropology pursue the discussion? If both the context and content of a theology of human flourishing is the triune economy of grace, then two things are especially important. First, being human necessarily involves those life-bestowing and life-preserving relations to God which form the heart of God's ways with humankind. Fellowship with God is fundamental to human nature and destiny. Such fellowship – because it is fellowship and not simply with a divine originator but with a purposive creator who himself reconciles and draws the creature to its true end – cannot be merely incidental or episodic; it is ontologically necessary and enduring, definitive of what it is to be human. Second, relation to the triune God is the ground of human fellowship, and of action which is ordered toward perpetuating fellowship. This second point requires a little elaboration.

"Trinity" and "sociality" are often thought together in such a way that the immanent relational life of God, which is expressed *ad extra* in God's works toward his creatures, is "imaged" in human relations. Construing the triune being of God as a model of fellowship and reconciliation, however, may transform the divine "relationality" into something resembling a socio-ethical imperative. Ethicizing the relational character of God's works can undermine the ontological basis for moral activity; human fellowship becomes largely a human work, rather than human consent to and engagement with a reality established by God. But the relations of the Trinity, internal and external, are not simply a symbol to excite our social energies; they form the depth which makes human fellowship both possible and actual. "The distinctive Christian thesis of Christian theological anthropology is that human being as relational being is rooted in the relationship of the triune God to humanity."[40]

Why is this "transcendent" ground for works of human fellowship theologically decisive? Because thereby my neighbor, the one with whom I stand in relation, is *given* to me, and forms part of the destiny which I am

[40] C Schwöbel, "Human Being as Relational Being. Twelve Theses for a Christian Anthropology," in C. Schwöbel and C. Gunton, eds., *Persons, Divine and Human* (Edinburgh: T. & T. Clark, 1991), p. 142.

to realize if I am to become the particular being which I am. My neighbor is a summons to fellowship, because in him or her I find a claim on me which is not casual or fortuitous (and thereby dispensable) but rather precedes my will and requires that I act in my neighbor's regard. Without a sense that fellowship is (God-)given, my neighbor would not present a sufficiently strong claim to disturb me out of complacency and indifference into active, initiative-taking regard. Some basic acts of human fellowship, such as mercy to strangers, fidelity, patient attentiveness to the unlovely, devotion to long-standing and largely unreciprocated care of the comatose and handicapped, require for their sustenance a perception that the neighbor is one with whom I have been set in fellowship independent of (sometimes against) my will. My neighbor *obliges* me because he or she is the presence to me of the appointment and vocation of the triune God.

Without givenness, without fellowship as more than a contingent fact, without the neighbor as a divine call, there is only my will. But if fellowship is a condition and not merely one possibility for my ironic self to entertain, then in building a common life – in culture, politics, and ethics – I resist the relationlessness of sin into which I may drift, and, remade by Christ and animated by the Spirit, I realize my nature as one created in the image of God.[41] Fellowship, in short, requires obligation, and obligation requires grounds. Modernity thought to furnish those grounds through a metaphysics of moral law, sometimes reinforced by the example and teaching of Jesus. For postmodernity, on the other hand, all that can be said is: "Obligation happens."[42] But, if obligation is poetics, just "an event that happens in the midst of a cosmic night,"[43] then I have little with which to resist wickedness, in others or in myself; and, above all, I have no ground for love.

In sum: Christian anthropology is Trinitarian and therefore practical–ethical anthropology. What it finds lacking in deconstructive anthropology is not the idea of a disposer supreme or a transcendent legislator, but rather the shapely drama of God's fellowship-establishing acts. The articulation of Christian humanism requires dogmatics, metaphysics, and ethics, all of which presuppose an historical and Gospel-derived ontology. But the enactment of that humanism requires faith, charity, and hope, for faith lets the triune God do his work; charity enables knowledge, art, and society; and hope waits for and hastens toward perfection.

---

[41] For a suggestive reflection on the Trinity and the image of God, see J. B. Elshtain, "Augustine and Diversity," in J. L. Heft, ed., *A Catholic Modernity?* (New York: Oxford University Press, 1999). pp. 95–103.

[42] Caputo, *Against Ethics*, p. 6.   [43] Ibid., p. 220.

Further reading

Caputo, John D., *Against Ethics. Contributions to a Poetics of Obligation with Constant Reference to Deconstruction* (Bloomington: Indiana University Press, 1993).

Foucault, Michel, *Ethics. Subjectivity and Truth* (London: Penguin, 1993).

The Order of Things: An Archaeology of the Human Sciences (London: Tavistock, 1974).

Gunton, Colin and Christoph Schwöbel, eds., *Persons, Divine and Human* (Edinburgh: T. & T. Clark, 1991).

Thiselton, Anthony C., *Interpreting God and the Postmodern Self. On Meaning, Manipulation and Promise* (Edinburgh: T. & T. Clark, 1995).

Schrag, Calvin, *The Self after Postmodernity* (New Haven: Yale University Press, 1997).

14 Christ and salvation

WALTER LOWE

This chapter is exploratory. It seeks to glimpse "an other Christology." I make no exclusivist claims for the project; it is one Christology among others; and, if I am correct, it is hardly a new one. The exploration is informed by the premise that those who set out in search of the tradition's "other" may discover in the process the *otherness* of the tradition.

I

"Christ and Salvation" recalls the classic theologies, which generally treat first the person and then the work of Christ. In modern theology, however, the common, even predominant, practice has been to reverse the sequence, placing some prefatory notion of salvation before the treatment of Christ. This reversal reflects the Christian community's struggle to respond to the skepticism of modern Western culture by demonstrating, in one fashion or another, a need for Christianity.

In such a situation, the need naturally comes first. The need may be portrayed in manifold ways: as need for some larger meaning in one's life, for example, or as need for deliverance from sin. Whatever the specifics, the argument generally includes four elements. The first is a broad, generally acceptable *description* of common human experience with emphasis upon certain problems or discontents: for example violence in our society, the pressures of contemporary life, the prevalence of drugs. There follows a more specific *diagnosis* of the phenomena in terms of some underlying condition, for example the search for meaning, or anxiety in the face of death. There then follow a general *recommendation* (cf. in medicine, "You need an analgesic"), and a specific *remedy* ("I suggest brand X"). "Recommendation" as used here is a general category whereas the "remedy" is a specific reality. The concepts merge in the statement, "You need to find peace in God"; but the distinction is important, for history amply testifies that an effort to direct a person toward peace-in-God is often received as recommending "peace of mind" – found perhaps in God, perhaps elsewhere.

The case becomes acute when the recommendation is "salvation" and the remedy Jesus Christ. This is "the scandal of particularity": why *this* particular remedy?[1] Liberal Christian apologists adduce a variety of explanations with varying success. Observing the liberal struggles, Christians of a more traditional bent feel confirmed in their determination not to tailor the Christian message to the dogmas of modernity.[2] But conservative presentations also tend to proceed from description through diagnosis and recommendation to remedy, as when (1) a general cultural malaise is taken as (2) evidence of troubled souls in need of (3) conversion to (4) Christ. In the modern age the salvation–Christ sequence has been indeed widespread.

But the sequence has its problems. For by the very act of prefacing one's Christology with an explanatory sequence, one establishes a framework or context to which the Christology must at all points conform. If at any point it does not so conform, the vital link between general recommendation and the specific Christian remedy – the bridge across "the scandal of particularity," across Lessing's "ugly ditch" – is lost and the project founders. A further difficulty arises from the fact that the prefatory sequence must logically include an exposition of need or lack – an exposition of the negative. On reflection, it is not self-evident that the best way to present the Christian Gospel – the good news – is to begin with the negative. If one begins by making a pact with the negative, so to speak, will that not color what comes after? Is there not the risk that, despite one's best intentions, the radical good of the Gospel will be endlessly deferred? That it will never stand forth in its own right?

II

With this issue of negativity in mind, let us turn from the modern to the classic systematic theologies.[3] One finds in their tables of contents a familiar narrative sequence that begins with God and/or revelation and then proceeds from creation on through to eschatology, "the last things." Discussion of God may include the question of God's existence, but it is characteristic of the classic format that there is no necessary preface about

[1] For a searching exploration of this issue, see Bruce Marshall, *Christology in Conflict: The Identity of a Savior in Rahner and Barth* (Oxford: Basil Blackwell, 1987).
[2] Cf. the twin crises of relevance and identity in Jürgen Moltmann, *The Crucified God* (New York: Harper & Row, 1974), p. 7.
[3] On the distinction between classical and modern approaches (which can only be relative and provisional), see Walter Lowe, "Christ and Salvation," in Peter C. Hodgson and Robert H. King, eds., *Christian Theology: An Introduction to Its Traditions and Tasks*, 2nd edn (Philadelphia: Fortress Press, 1985), pp. 222–48, esp. 222–23.

experiencing a need for God. What is virtually invariable, however, is that before either Christology or soteriology there comes an exposition of sin and the Fall. Thus, while the particulars differ, classic and modern presentations share in a pervasive practice of inserting *some* form of negativity before Christology.

Now within the classic texts one may discern a certain "economy" – a notion which takes our discussion of system and systematic theology beyond the relatively simple diachronic question of sequence. Within an economy, a negative or deficit at one point must be offset by some positive valence at another point: the metaphorics of economy are quasi-hydraulic. Freud observed that what is repressed at one point will find expression elsewhere in some fantasy, mannerism, or anxiety. Analogous observations are made in sociology and anthropology. Within Christian theology, one of the earliest accounts of salvation is the ransom theory. Humankind was lost to Satan, we had become the devil's possession; through God's mercy we were "bought back" by the suffering and death of Jesus Christ. The quid pro quo is quite explicit. But could not something similar be said of other classic theories as well? In *Cur deus homo?* (*Why the God Man?*) Anselm speaks of human rebellion as having offended God's honor, creating a liability which, since it was an offense against the infinite, could not be met by finite, human effort. Hence the specific necessity of Christ, viz. of one who would be at once both human and divine. Again it is a matter of exchange, and thus of a specific "economy" within which the particular exchange makes sense. The ransom theory, for example, implies a peculiar economy within which Satan has rights of possession despite the fact that humankind might well be placed under the heading of ill-gotten gains, acquired by deceit. Thus, while the tradition does place the person of Christ before the work, that sequence is inscribed within a larger setting which functions in its own fashion as a preface to Christology. And that preface includes an understanding of sin that is independently derived.

Now the concept of sin may be said to operate on at least three different registers. There is the familiar moral level which treats specific acts. Here one specifies the negative, spelling out just what it is that is contrary to the good. But, distinct from that, there are moments when awareness of sin merges with "the cry of the people." Then to speak of sin is to voice a comprehensive and anguished sense that there is something fundamentally wrong in the present order of things; that something which is scarcely comprehensible and profoundly destructive pervades the world we know. Third, and complexly related to the other two, there is a way in which the notion of sin becomes a sort of epistemological principle. "[F]irst take the log out of your own eye, and then you will see clearly to take the speck out of your neighbor's eye" (Matthew 7:5). If sin is a reality and if we are not exempt, then that raises severe questions about our ability to fashion an economy within which the beast would be caged. Do we in fact preside over an economy, classical or modern, within which sin can be contained or "comprehended"? If not, what justification have we for stipulating some predefined notion of sin or need as the determinative context within which the reality of Christ is to be conceived?

This is not to say that the presence of economy of any sort is reason to reject tradition out of hand. By and large, human understanding proceeds by way of economy. But it is to ask rather urgently whether the tradition thus far depicted may not need to be "supplemented" by another Christology, and whether it may not have been so supplemented in the past.

III

Elsewhere I have argued that Christian theology has had a postmodernism of its own.[4] It is generally recognized that the appearance of Barth's *Commentary on Romans* in 1919 effected a fundamental turn that was to distinguish much of twentieth-century theology from the predominantly liberal thought which went before. Gone was the ontotheological order which had grounded Western confidence in an all-encompassing reason. Gone was the triumphalist narrative of a redemptive history proceeding incrementally to its divinely appointed goal. Gone the god of theism, the benign and unintrusive guarantor of the ultimate goodness of all. And gone, too, the self-possessed human subject, assiduously generating progress out of his own interior divinity. Metaphysic, metanarrative, theism, and subjectivity: here were the usual ontotheological suspects of postmodernism already arraigned and given the third degree by Barth's own unremitting critique.

If it is indeed the case that Christian theology has had a postmodernism of its own, then it need not come to contemporary postmodernism hat in hand. It can encounter postmodernism on its own terms. The remainder of this chapter will gesture toward an other Christology by way of a specific New Testament understanding of apocalyptic and a heterodox appropriation of the Derridean concept of "presence."

In his essay on "Paul and Apocalyptic Eschatology" in *The Encyclopedia of Apocalypticism*, M. C. de Boer distinguishes two divergent patterns within

---

[4] The present paragraph is drawn from Lowe, "Prospects for a Postmodern Christian Theology: Apocalyptic Without Reserve," *Modern Theology* 15 (1999), 17–24.

the complex heritage of Jewish apocalyptic eschatology. [5] The more familiar is perhaps what de Boer labels the "forensic" pattern in which,

> [s]in is the willful rejection of the Creator God (the breaking of the first commandment), and death is punishment for this fundamental sin. God, however, has provided the law as a remedy for this situation, and a person's posture toward this law determines his or her ultimate destiny.[6]

There will be a final judgment, "conceptualized not as a cosmic war but as a courtroom" (whence the appellation "forensic"), at which time each person will receive their due punishment or reward.[7] To this pattern de Boer contrasts "cosmological" apocalyptic. In this alternative vision, "the created world has come under the dominion of evil, angelic powers in some primeval time."[8] God's people have been led into idolatry but there remains a remnant that awaits deliverance. "God will invade the world under the dominion of the evil powers and defeat them in a cosmic war."[9] It is God and God alone who can accomplish the transformation.

Now it is extraordinarily suggestive to juxtapose de Boer's recent distinction, made apropos of Jewish apocalyptic, with the typology set forth in a classic work on Christian theology, *Christus Victor: An Historical Study of the Three Main Types of the Idea of Atonement*, written in 1930 by Gustaf Aulen.[10] Aulen wrote to correct the common assumption that there are basically two options in understanding Christ's salvific work; either an "objective" doctrine according to which – to take Anselm as example – "God is the object of Christ's atoning work, and is reconciled through the satisfaction made to His justice"; or a "subjective" doctrine, exemplified by Abelard, which locates atonement "in a change taking place in men [*sic*] rather than a changed attitude on the part of God."[11] Earlier than either of these, Aulen contended, is a "classic" or "dramatic" view, the central theme of which is "a Divine conflict and victory." In this view, "Christ – Christus Victor – fights against and triumphs over the evil powers of the world, the 'tyrants' which hold humankind in bondage."[12] This account deserves the

---

5 M. C. de Boer, "Paul and Apocalyptic Eschatology" in John J. Collins, ed., *The Encyclopedia of Apocalypticism, Vol. I: The Origins of Apocalypticism in Judaism and Christianity* (New York: Continuum, 1998), pp. 345–83.

6 Ibid., p. 359.   7 Ibid.   8 Ibid., p. 358.   9 Ibid., p. 359.

10 Gustaf Aulen, *Christus Victor: An Historical Study of the Three Main Types of the Idea of Atonement*, trans. A. G. Herbert (New York: Macmillan, 1956). We may remind ourselves that, for a pattern or type to be useful or legitimate, there do not have to be actual, historical examples that are entirely pure and unambiguous. The untidiness of history need not diminish the usefulness of thoughtful typologies as a means of sorting cases and making relative distinctions.

11 Ibid., p. 2.   12 Ibid., p. 4.

title "classic" because it is, in Aulen's estimation, the predominant view in the New Testament and because "[i]t was, in fact, the ruling idea of the Atonement for the first thousand years of Christian history."[13]

One cannot miss the affinity between forensic apocalyptic and Aulen's objective type; or between cosmological apocalyptic and Aulen's classic type. Accordingly, many of Aulen's arguments for the value of the classic translate into arguments that Christian theology should take cosmological apocalyptic seriously. In the modern period the classic view was eclipsed for many of the same reasons that apocalyptic was marginalized; it seemed both mythological and dualistic.[14] In a postmodern setting, however, the "monistic and evolutionary" perspective assumed by liberal theology is no longer self-evident; the subject of the subjective view preferred by liberal modernity is no longer a sure foundation. As for the objective alternative favored by traditionalists, it rests upon one economy or another which, as economy, goes largely unexamined. Moreover, there is an ironic sense in which the "objective" type is itself "subjective." For note that, like forensic apocalyptic, it postulates a *humanly generated* negativity which must be addressed (in the Jewish apocalyptic, recurrent offenses against the first commandment). Moreover, to function as a fully realized economy, it *requires an appropriate human response* (in the Jewish, subsequent fidelity to the law). Thus even in the "objective" view, the human subject is assumed as central, even pivotal. Both "objective" and "subjective" seem constrictive vis-à-vis the classic vision in which "the Atonement is not regarded as affecting men primarily as individuals, but is set forth as a drama of a world's salvation."[15]

In the fourth section we will see how a specifically cosmological apocalyptic may provide a missing key to the theology of Paul. In the fifth, this interpretation of Paul will provide the basis for a constructive proposal about appropriating apocalyptic into Christian theology – or rather appropriating Christian theology into apocalyptic. One need not be a prophet, apocalyptic or otherwise, to know that such a proposal will raise objections. Some misgivings can be met by attending to the distinction in principle between cosmological and forensic apocalyptic, and disavowing the judgmentalism of the latter. But there are other objections which bear upon the cosmological pattern at least as much as the forensic. Cosmological apocalyptic *is* in some sense dualistic; it affirms another realm that cuts across human history and is so real as to give the key to understanding a history which is of itself virtually devoid of meaning. The more the vision attends to the higher realm, the more it is apt to be dismissed or negated for dismissing or negating the world in which we say we really live. Imagery of cosmic warfare is then regarded as proof positive of a schizoid condition inherent to apocalyptic as such. Little wonder that apocalyptic and its adherents are so consistently marginalized.

However, we are wise to think twice when those who have a stake in the reigning world-view, as the cultured despisers of apocalyptic often do, undertake to instruct us on where violence does and does not come from. Those engaged in the struggle for justice, those attuned to the cry of the poor, know the extent to which apocalyptic is not a mindless expression of violence, but a trenchant analysis of violence's roots.[16] – Moreover, a stance of considered "world-denial" is not so easily dismissed as metaphysical dualism. To cite Albert Schweitzer:

> Because it is … preoccupied with the general, the universal, modern theology is determined to find its world-accepting ethic in the teaching of Jesus. Therein lies its weakness … For the general, for the institutions of society, the rule is: affirmation of the world, in conscious opposition to the view of Jesus, on the ground that the world has affirmed itself.[17]

Today the world continues to affirm itself as factuality and power, beside which all else is made to seem wishful thinking. As Jacques Ellul has observed: "Everyone takes it for granted that fact and truth are one; and if God is no longer regarded as true in our day it is because he [*sic*] does not seem to be a fact."[18] False affirmation was for Schweitzer the canker within the liberal lives of Jesus, notwithstanding their inspirational aura. Opposing easy accommodation, he confronted his readers with a Jesus who "comes to us as One unknown, without a name, as of old, by the seaside, He came to those who knew Him not"[19] – an other Jesus.[20]

Our reflections have arrived at a point of considerable conceptual tension. But conceptual tension is a means of extending understanding. It

---

[16] See Walter Wink, *Naming the Powers: The Language of Power in the New Testament* (Philadelphia: Fortress Press, 1984); *Unmasking the Powers: The Invisible Forces that Determine Human Existence* (Philadelphia: Fortress Press, 1986); and *Engaging the Powers: Discernment and Resistance in a World of Domination* (Minneapolis: Fortress Press, 1992). Also Ched Myers, *Binding the Strong Man: A Political Reading of Mark's Story of Jesus* (Maryknoll, NY: Orbis Books, 1988).

[17] Albert Schweitzer, *The Quest of the Historical Jesus: A Critical Study of Its Progress from Reimarus to Wrede* (London: Adam & Charles Black, 1954), p. 400.

[18] Jacques Ellul, *The Presence of the Kingdom* (New York: Seabury Press, 1967), p. 37.

[19] Schweitzer, *The Quest of the Historical Jesus*, p. 401.

[20] On the scholarly debate over the extent to which Jesus' preaching and ministry were apocalyptic, see Dale C. Allison, *Jesus of Nazareth: Millenarian Prophet* (Minneapolis: Fortress Press, 1998); and Richard Hays, " 'Why Do You Stand Looking Up Toward Heaven': New Testament Eschatology at the Turn of the Millennium," *Modern Theology* 16 (2000), 115–35.

should candidly be said that the direction in which we are headed is one that no sensible person would take, perhaps, unless she were driven to it. The proposal to be offered will be strange, with a strangeness that may or may not be the strangeness of Christianity. Whether one is indeed driven to it is of necessity a judgment call. In principle it is always possible that with some further tinkering the established patterns might succeed.

Here, then, is a brief review and prospectus to summarize the considerations which might indeed drive one to despair (cf. Kierkegaard) and take the leap. (a) As regards modern Christology and Christology more generally, we have sensed problems of sequence, economy, and negativity. (b) Apocalyptic represents an alternative approach – but one which might actually intensify the difficulties! Nevertheless, the problems we observed are real, they cannot simply be ignored. Therefore (c) given the situation, it is worth trying to go *through* apocalyptic (or through the common conceptions of it) in the hope of arriving at a better result.

Specifically: (a) we have been using the relatively accessible question of *sequence* as a stalking horse for the larger issue of "inscription," which could readily lead us beyond the bounds of the present chapter. It is no accident that modern theology so tends to preface Christology with soteriological diagnosis; the procedure articulates with a variety of modern tropes (linked, for example, to the rise of modern medicine), as close study of the texts might show. Having introduced the question of sequence apropos of modern theology, we then observed that the classic presentations of systematic theology also placed a kind of soteriological preface – an account of the need for salvation which implicitly circumscribes what salvation, and the bringer of salvation, can be – before Christology. It relies, if not upon a metaphysic, then certainly upon an *economy*. In addition, we have touched upon the way in which the logic of economy requires a certain *negativity*. Without some form of need, offense or deficit, the mechanism we have described would be static or nonexistent.

(b) We have asked whether some alternative Christology/soteriology might be glimpsed by returning to Jewish and Christian apocalyptic. But apocalyptic might seem the least promising way to go. As regards sequence, apocalypticists are notorious for laying down timelines (and then readjusting them). Further, the battlefield of Armageddon seems the ultimate paroxysm of conflictual economy; and, as for the dark vision of judgment and destruction, apocalyptic gives a distinct impression of being in love with the negative.

(c) Theologians have sought to eliminate apocalyptic or to domesticate it; those are the trodden paths. But there is another way. One might ask what would be meant by an "apocalyptic without reserve."[21] Is it not possible that the common reading of the logic of cosmic victory as positing yet another economy, and an economy of a particularly nasty sort, is in fact a failure to entertain its true radicality? Is it not possible that the logic of cosmic victory is rather to *overthrow the very notion* that God's act of salvation can be so contained within *any* economy? To overthrow the instrumentalism implicit in any such economy? This proposal can already be made, I think, on the basis of our explorations thus far. That there already is sufficient warrant is important because I am about to turn to an interpretation of Paul which represents a minority position in contemporary scholarship. The interpretation is of interest because it articulates well with a number of our concerns, but undoubtedly there will be readers who will hesitate to embrace it. One may well choose to dismiss the proposed reading of Paul and the constructive proposals which will be sketched in conversation with it. If one does so choose, however, the difficulties we have observed will yet remain as a serious challenge to the general consensus.

IV

In 1997 there appeared in the Anchor Bible series a commentary on Galatians that makes important use of de Boer's distinction.[22] The author, J. Louis Martyn, finds in Paul's early reference to "the present evil age" (Galatians 1:4) evidence that Paul situates his message in a specifically apocalyptic context (97–98). Paul's "distinctly apocalyptic" phrase (97) is reinforced by subsequent references to "the fullness of time" (Galatians 4:4) and "the new creation" (Galatians 6:15).[23] Martyn's signal contribution is to read the entirety of Galatians in the light of an apocalyptic which is specifically cosmological. I intend to follow Martyn in this. At the same time, I shall press somewhat further than Martyn might. I shall stress the extent to which, even within the realm of cosmological apocalyptic, Paul seems, on the evidence of Martyn's own analysis, to be doing something "other," something quite distinctive.

Martyn notes that, whereas common apocalyptic practice is to pair "the present evil age" with a "coming age" situated in the near or distant future, Paul juxtaposes "the present evil age" with "*the new creation*." The contrast is

---

[21] The notion is developed in Lowe, "Prospects," esp. p. 23.

[22] J. Louis Martyn, *Galatians: A New Translation with Introduction and Commentary* (New York: Doubleday, 1997), see particularly p. 97, n. 51. In the present section, some of the references to Martyn's commentary appear parenthetically in the text. Translations of the Galatians text are Martyn's own; for his rendering of the entire epistle, see *Galatians*, pp. 3–10.

[23] Ibid., pp. 99, 98.

important, for whereas speaking of a "present evil age" and a "coming age" posits a sequence, speaking of "the present evil age" and "the new creation" need not; and in Paul it does not. To use terms familiar to Christology, the "coming age" is "already," and not simply "not yet." But there is more. For it is not simply that the new creation has "dawned," so to speak; it is that for Paul the crucial apocalyptic event *has already occurred* in Jesus Christ.

What, then, is the relation between "the present evil age" and "the new creation," if not that of diachronic sequence? Martyn writes that "[t]he genesis of Paul's apocalyptic – as we see it in Galatians – lies in the apostle's certainty that God has *invaded* the present evil age by sending Christ and his Spirit into it" (99, emphasis Martyn's). By placing the motif of invasion front and center, Martyn underlines the cosmological character of the apocalyptic, which, he believes, impacts one's understanding of time.

> In a significant sense, *the time of cosmic enslavement is now past, and its being past is a central motif of the entire letter.* One might suppose, then, that the "before" has come to a clean end, being replaced by the "after." The picture, however, is not so simple. The linguistic pattern in which Paul moves easily from the verb *apocalypto* ("to reveal" or "to reveal apocalyptically") to the verbs *erchomai*, "to come [on the scene]" and *expostello*, "to send [into the scene]," shows that for him the present evil age has not simply been followed by the new creation. Nor do the two exist in isolation... On the contrary, the evil age and the new creation are dynamically interrelated, as we have noted... by the motif of invasion. (99, emphases added)

Ordinarily one might think of invasion as the beginning of the end of enslavement. But no – "enslavement is now past." And, more, the very time of enslavement is past: an entire time, *an entire mode of time*, has been dethroned. That enslaving mode of time is overcome or taken up into another time, which is the time of one crucial, determinative (thus, apocalyptic) event – namely, God's decisive invasion of "this world" in Jesus Christ. It is in that sense that "the motif of invasion," or, better, the *reality* of invasion, "dynamically" interrelates the present evil age and the new creation. No longer are the "already" and "not yet" to be balanced off. The "not yet," which does have its undeniable validity, is to be interpreted – i.e. the very meaning of the "not yet" is to be understood – within the context of the "already"! *The Christ event itself* thus becomes the context within which all else is to be inscribed.

It is upon this issue of the very modality of time that Martyn focuses when he speaks of "the question Paul causes to be the crucial issue of the entire letter: *What time is it?*" (104, emphasis added). Unquestionably, the present evil age does not look like the new creation. The apocalyptic character of the Gospel "is underlined by the fact that it is not visible, demonstrable" (104). Thus it "brings about an epistemological crisis."[24] In effect, we live in an impossible contradiction – which gains voice in "the cry of the people." But what does it mean to take that contradiction seriously? It may be that one actually reduces the contradiction when one translates it into the "tension" of the "already" and the "not yet," as is suggested by a certain Christian common sense. The reasons for taking that path are abundantly apparent; but this common sense, like most, rests upon an unexamined metaphysic. It assumes a spatialization of time (in the telling phrase, a "time*line*") which invites imaginings of schematization and control. As regards praxis, the great mischief of timelines is that they underwrite a distancing of one's means from one's end – whereas Christian ethics must state the fact that (quoting Ellul):

> in the work of God the end and the means are identical. Thus when Jesus Christ is present the Kingdom has "come upon" us. This [apocalyptic] formula expresses very precisely the relation between the end and the means. Jesus Christ in his Incarnation appears as God's means, for the salvation of humankind and for the establishment of the Kingdom of God, but where Jesus Christ is, there also is this salvation and this kingdom.[25]

What time is it? It is perhaps time that we abandon the effort to situate the Christ event within a sequence that would lend it meaning. It is perhaps time that we reverse the procedure, inscribing the entirety of time/history within the Christ event. That may be the radical implication of Paul's specific, Christological appropriation of cosmological apocalyptic.[26] One way of showing this is by tracing what happens in Galatians to the forensic form of apocalyptic which reverberates through much of Western theology. Like the "objective" and "subjective" takes on atonement, it features a certain anthropocentrism. It turns upon a narrative of human rebellion, a countervalent act of divine mercy, and a "present time" in which all depends upon the believer's adherence to the way of purity and observance. As de Boer has shown, this narrative structure was readily available in the Jewish

---

[24] Ibid., 104; see also J. Louis Martyn, *Theological Issues in the Letters of Paul* (Nashville, TN: Abingdon Press, 1997), pp. 89–110.

[25] Ellul, *Presence of the Kingdom*, p. 79. The insertion of "apocalyptic" and the substitution of "humankind" for "man" are mine. We shall have more to say about the presence of Christ in the final section.

[26] We are thus engaged in a twofold process: showing that cosmological apocalyptic is present in Galatians, and attending to how the general notion of a cosmological apocalyptic is transformed by Paul's specific Christological appropriation.

tradition of Paul's time. Many believed that it could and should be adapted to Christian purposes; it was simply a matter of shifting the determinative act of divine mercy from God's giving of the Law to God's giving of Christ.

Now such a forensic apocalyptic Christology does appear in Galatians. There it associates with such binary distinctions as purity/impurity, and sacred/profane. Such a Christology does appear in Paul's epistle – but it appears as that which Paul *opposes*. It appears as the return to slavery into which the Galatian Christians are being led by "the Teachers" Paul denounces so emphatically.[27] If we take Paul's denunciation radically, and Paul certainly thinks something radical is at stake, it is not the denunciation of a particular economy, but a denunciation of any effort to contain the Christ event – to contain the invasion – within a governing sequence or economy. In Paul's cosmological apocalyptic perspective, to be guided by such terms as "pure" and "impure," "sacred" and "profane," is to remain under the sway of the God-opposed "powers." The dichotomies are chains of enthrallment. Indicative of this captivity is the fact that, even within the bounds of common human understanding, the terms do not exist in isolation. They function as elements, viz., as positive and negative valences, within a variety of specific economies by which humans think to take command of their fate, but by which, as Paul now sees in the light of Christ, they are in fact imprisoned.

Pausing to consider our own contemporary culture, we may find reason to wonder who it is that is really in love with the negative. In the early 1930s, Walter Benjamin wrote that humankind's "self-alienation has reached such a degree that it can experience its own destruction as an aesthetic pleasure of the first order."[28] The passage has its own historical context, but one finds it quoted in a revealing study of the role of style and advertising in contemporary culture. The social critic Stuart Ewen finds as early as 1932 the contention that "it was necessary now to conceive of 'obsolescence as a positive force,' a resource to be used to drive the market forward."[29] The dictionary links "consume" to "destroy" and "squander," yet in many instances "consumer" has replaced "citizen" in the lexicon of American self-understanding. Certainly the "health" of the present economic "order" is dependent upon a high level of consumption: the negative made positive. Progress, and thus history itself, becomes associated with an increasing capacity for consumption. To maintain the dynamic, particularly in the face

---

[27] Martyn, *Galatians*, p. 98, continuation of n. 52; and pp. 117–26.
[28] From the essay "The Work of Art in the Age of Mechanical Reproduction," in Walter Benjamin, *Illuminations* (New York: Schocken Books, 1969), p. 244.
[29] Stuart Ewen, *All Consuming Images: The Politics of Style in Contemporary Culture* (New York: Basic Books, 1988), p. 243.

of a mounting sense of the unsustainability of it all, and to cut through an already frenetic level of stimulation, advertising and entertainment become ever more jarring and visceral.[30] This is at least one reason why the *imagery* of apocalyptic, once expelled by the Enlightenment, reasserts itself in contemporary culture. In this condition, Benjamin's strange reference to experiencing one's "own destruction as an aesthetic pleasure of the first order" seems unsettlingly apposite.

Power as the capacity for negation, and negation as creativity, securing still greater power. This is the way in which the world affirms itself. Is this the creative power of history? Or is it evidence that, in Paul's language, history itself has become for us one of "the powers"? The latter possibility is real enough, I think, to raise the question of whether a certain confused notion of history, as simultaneously a neutral timeline and an engine of meaning, may not have become a beam in the eye of modern theology. A love of the negative, i.e. a commitment to reality/history as agon (struggle), could certainly blind one to a radical understanding of God's invasion in Jesus Christ.[31] For the Christ event is not simply an invasion incidentally launched by God. *It is the in-breaking of God's own reality.* Invasion so understood blows the circuits of a human understanding which thrives on the interplay of positive and negative. It is what one may be driven to call an "invasion by the wholly positive."

To those who have come to embrace their own captivity as ultimate reality – which, if Paul is right, means all of us – such an invasion must be first *experienced as* negative. And to human beings who tend to ground their understanding on what they themselves have made, the invasion, as God's own act unconstrained by any economy or negotiation, must seem absurd and incomprehensible. Nevertheless –and the very logic of the Gospel is, of course, "Nevertheless!"[32] – the invasion, the invading, must be understood as being in and of itself wholly positive. Otherwise it is not understood as the in-breaking of God's own reality at all. "For the Son of God, Jesus Christ, whom we proclaimed among you, Silvanus and Timothy and I, was not 'Yes' and 'No'; but in him it is always 'Yes' " (2 Corinthians 1:19). (It is the cosmological form, we should recall, that understands apocalyptic as the good Creator's reclaiming of a good creation.) So understood, the radical good of the Gospel may indeed stand forth in its own right.

---

[30] In this connection, see the extraordinary video cassette entitled "Advertising and the End of the World," written and edited by Sut Jhalli, produced by the Media Education Foundation, 1998.

[31] See the section on "The Myth of Redemptive Violence," in Wink, *Engaging the Powers*, pp. 13–17.

[32] See George S. Hendry, *The Gospel of the Incarnation* (Philadelphia: Westminster Press, 1958), p. 135. The chapter "The Living of Forgiveness" (pp. 115–47) is highly pertinent.

Certainly it is possible to dodge the awkward reality claims and portray the Christian Gospel as an inspiring, prophetic "ideal." But, as Schweitzer showed at length, that is accomplished by extracting the message from the apocalyptic world-view within which Jesus himself quite arguably inscribed it. It is the irreducible import of apocalyptic to make a reality claim. And, as Theodor Adorno cautions in a statement which serves as gloss on our entire exploration, from the analysis of "diagnosis" and "prescription" onward: "If religion is accepted for the sake of something other than its own truth content, then it undermines itself."[33] What is required is a reality which is neither economic nor ultimately agonic. What is required is a *new* reality; and that is the logic of the "new creation."

V

How is one to think such a thing? One approach would be to draw on the Derridean concept of "presence," but to do so in a way that is specifically Christological. Much of Derrida's early work is devoted to the critique of one or another form of putative "presence," understood as any reality which is taken to be autonomous, self-sufficient, and accessible in a direct, unmediated fashion. Philosophical examples are as various as the empiricist's "sense datum" and the idealist's "I."[34] Deconstruction shows how pervasive, how nearly ubiquitous, the assumption or assertion of presence is. But deconstruction also shows how pervasive the *longing for* presence is: a phenomenon which the early writings do little to explain. Is a longing so widely shared to be dismissed as sheer perversity, or might it bear some as yet undisclosed significance? Reflection along this line may have contributed to the foregrounding of religion which has emerged, rather unexpectedly, in Derrida's more recent work.[35] However it be with Derrida, it is clear that the psalms, for their part, call out for a certain presence – the manifestation of the *glory* of God: "The heavens proclaim his righteousness; and all the peoples behold his glory" (Psalms 97:6). Christian tradition associates such passages with Christ. "[A]nd we have seen his glory, the glory as of a father's only son" (John 1:14, NRSV). It affirms that in Christ one encounters God's very presence.

---

33 From Adorno, "Reason and Revelation," in Theodor W. Adorno, *Critical Models: Interventions and Catchwords* (New York: Columbia University Press, 1998), p. 139. As a brief analysis of the cultural–conceptual condition of theology in the modern period, Adorno's essay is, in my judgment, unsurpassed.

34 Jacques Derrida, *Positions* (University of Chicago Press, 1981), p. 26.

35 See for example Jacques Derrida, *The Gift of Death* (University of Chicago Press, 1995). For an interpretive overview of this development in Derrida's thought, see John D. Caputo, *The Prayers and Tears of Jacques Derrida: Religion without Religion* (Bloomington: Indiana University Press, 1997).

It also holds that the presence is "hidden" in the form of one who was rejected, reviled, and crucified. In thinking this twofold testimony to presence and hiddenness, the Derridean concept of presence may prove useful. It enables us (though Derrida himself might not encourage us) to make a distinction between something's being present, per se, and its being *present in the mode of "presence."*[36] It is the nature of what Kierkegaard calls "the aesthetic" to conflate these two; to assume that any divine presence worth bothering about will manifest itself as something obviously extraordinary. Chiding this complacent assumption, Kierkegaard's Johannes Climacus writes: "If God had taken the form, for example, of a rare, enormously large green bird, with a red beak, that perched on a tree on the embankment and perhaps even whistled in an unprecedented manner – then our party-going man would surely have had his eyes opened."[37] Christianity requires of us a capacity for that which is "only" indirect. A similar point is made when Barth, in a crucial section of the *Church Dogmatics*, absolutely insists that theology honor the distinction between "primary objectivity" and "secondary objectivity." The primary objectivity is God's knowledge of Godself, or God's "presence" to Godself, in that truly primary reality which is the Trinity. But God's presence to Godself is one thing, God's presence to finite human creatures is another. The latter occurs indirectly, by way of some other finite reality, such as Scripture or the person Jesus of Nazareth. Revelation to finite humans occurs in a finite mode, invariably.[38] But, having secured this point, Barth immediately adds a stunning affirmation. Secondary objectivity "is distinguished from the primary objectivity, *not by a lesser degree of truth,* but by its particular form suitable for us, the creature."[39]

Finite – yet not different in degree! There is a consistency between this view of revelation and what Paul proclaims as God's invasion of this world. As noted, "God's invasion" does not just belong to God, or derive from God in some incidental sense; it is God's own reality – come into the world. That is what makes it apocalyptic; that is what makes it *the* apocalypse: God's glory has shown forth – the wholly positive. But it has shown forth

---

[36] Dietrich Ritschl writes that Christ *"owns* his own mode of presence" (Ritschl, *Memory and Hope: An Inquiry Concerning the Presence of Christ* [New York: Macmillan, 1967], p. 230). See also Dietrich Bonhoeffer, *Christ the Center* (New York: Harper & Row, 1966), pp. 27–34; and Hans W. Frei, *The Identity of Jesus Christ: The Hermeneutical Bases of Dogmatic Theology* (Philadelphia: Fortress Press, 1967), pp. 33–34. Cf. Lowe, "Bonhoeffer and Deconstruction: Toward a Theology of the Crucified Logos," in Wayne Whitson Floyd, Jr. and Charles Marsh, eds., *Theology and the Practice of Responsibility: Essays on Dietrich Bonhoeffer* (Valley Forge: Trinity Press International, 1994), pp. 207–21; and Lowe, "Hans Frei and Phenomenological Hermeneutics," *Modern Theology* 8 (1992), 133–44.

[37] Søren Kierkegaard, *Concluding Unscientific Postscript to "Philosophical Fragments," Volume I: Text* (Princeton University Press, 1992), p. 245.

[38] Karl Barth, *Church Dogmatics*, vol. 2, part 1 (Edinburgh: T. & T. Clark, 1957), p. 16.

[39] Ibid. (emphases added).

in a manner of God's own choosing, in the form of one crucified. Martyn understands Paul to be saying that God's "coming onto the scene" in Jesus Christ is in a very real sense the end of religion (cf. forensic apocalyptic.)[40] Here again Paul's apocalyptic Gospel is liminal, on the edge of what can be understood. But so it may need to be if it is indeed the case that "the present evil age" is held captive by a religious delusion which is of a piece with the magical-aesthetic assumption that if God is present, it must be in the mode of a Presence. That magical–aesthetic assumption feeds the fantasy, so often operative and yet unquestioned, that if I can only *get in on* such a Presence – if I can experience it, if I can incorporate it – then I will in fact be saved: the delusion of salvation by aesthetic absorption.

That is the self-absorbed soteriology of "this world." In an individualistic culture such as our own, not to speak of the sinful condition which is our own, the great gift of Paul's cosmological apocalyptic is that with it the whole question of my particular salvation is sublated, lifted up – *aufgehoben*, if you will. More important than the question of whether I am saved or how I am saved is the apocalyptic fact that salvation *has come*. The fact that the cry of the people has been answered. Focusing on our own salvation (or wholeness) may actually prevent us, if we are among the privileged, from understanding the "cosmological" event that salvation is. *Charis*, love, is not simply a consequence of the Gospel; it bespeaks a fundamental displacement of self that is inherent in knowing the Gospel at all. It is indeed part of the good news that the story of salvation does not center upon me. The story is not anthropocentric in any of the ways we seek to make it so. It centers instead upon that which *is* the ultimate reality, the source and center of all creation: the exceeding glory of God.

At the beginning we anticipated that seeking "the other" of the tradition might lead in time to "the otherness of" the tradition. It is a strange, quixotic notion to "give glory to" a God who *is* glory (which means, in the palest possible translation, a God who is wholly positive), when thought and religion assume an economy of positive and negative, when we in our hearts have bent the knee to negative power: the power of the negative, Benjamin's aesthetic apocalypse. One religious trope is to interpret God's sheer positive as "purity" and seek to banish impurity from the realm of the sacred. As Derrida has shown, such efforts invite the return of the repressed. It is to be hoped that we ourselves will have the good sense not to advertise a postmodern Christology cleansed of all talk about (for example) atonement, exchange, and substitution. (The same would seem to hold for efforts to expunge all military metaphors.) What matters, rather, is that such language

---

40 Martyn, *Galatians*, p. 116.

be held open at the point where it presses to become the encompassing context. What matters is a vigilance which continually reinscribes its language within that "context" which exceeds all context – "let justice roll down like waters, and righteousness like an ever-flowing stream"[41] – namely God's invasion, God's triumphant *coming* in Jesus Christ. "For neither is circumcision anything nor is uncircumcision anything. What is something is the new creation" (Galatians 6:15).

What matters is that one should know in one's bowels what, even as we write and read theology, the present evil age does to humankind, the children of God. Does harm, perhaps, even to their souls. To know that, is to be caught up in the cry for justice. And it is that cry, the cry of the people, which is the proper preface to Christology.[42]

---

[41] Amos 5:24. See Martin Luther King, Jr., *A Testament of Hope: The Essential Writings and Speeches of Martin Luther King, Jr.*, ed. James Melvin Washington (San Francisco: HarperCollins, 1986), p. 282 and *passim.*

[42] In this sense, James Cone would seem justified in insisting that privileged white Christians must "become black," not only as an act of ethical solidarity, but simply in order to understand what the Gospel is talking about. See James H. Cone, *God of the Oppressed* (San Francisco: Harper & Row, 1975), *passim.*

15 Ecclesiology

STANLEY J. GRENZ

Theology is the determination, delineation, and articulation of the beliefs and values, as well as the meaning of the symbols, of a particular faith community. The task of *Christian* theology is to set forth what might be called the "mosaic of beliefs" that lies (or should lie) at the heart of the Christian community. This mosaic consists of the interlocking doctrines that together comprise the specifically Christian way of viewing the world. As a result, Christian theology is by its very nature "church dogmatics," to cite Karl Barth's famous description.

Although Christian theology has always been "church dogmatics" in this sense, the "churchly" aspect of "church dogmatics" has become even more crucial in the postmodern context. In a world characterized by the presence of a plurality of communities, each of which gives shape to the identities of its participants, the Christian community takes on a new and potentially profound theological importance as the people who embody a theological vision that sees the divine goal for humankind as that of being the bearers of the image of the God who is triune.

The goal of this chapter is to set forth an understanding of the church that is able to engage the postmodern challenge. At the heart of a postmodern Christian ecclesiology is the concept of the church as community. More specifically, the Christian church is a particular community marked by certain characteristics. The following pages outline an ecclesiology that incorporates postmodern, communitarian insights by looking at the church first as a community in general and then as a "marked" community.

One of the most crucial hallmarks of the postmodern situation is what might be termed the "turn to relationships." In contrast to what appears to have been the reigning mind-set of late modernity, there is widespread acknowledgment today that humans are fundamentally social creatures and therefore that the emptiness individuals sense can never be filled by the abundance of possessions but only in relationship with others. Viewed from a Christian perspective, the contemporary focus on relationships is not misguided. Even though the human quest for wholeness can ultimately be fulfilled only through relationship with God, belonging to God is closely linked to participation in community or, more specifically, to membership in the fellowship of Christ's disciples, the church.

THE CONCEPT OF COMMUNITY IN CONTEMPORARY THOUGHT

In recent years *community* has become a buzz-word. Like all such terms, it defies any single, agreed-upon definition. Even the new communitarian thinkers are not of one mind as to what they mean by the concept. The task of getting a handle on the idea is further complicated by the realization that people are members of several communities simultaneously[1] and therefore that community boundaries are fluid, overlapping, and even intertwined. Despite these potentially debilitating difficulties, rightly understood the concept is theologically helpful.

According to contemporary sociologists, several crucial characteristics are definitive for all functioning communities. First, a community consists of a group of people who are conscious that they share a similar frame of reference,[2] which inclines them to view the world in a similar manner, to "read" the world through similar glasses,[3] and to construct the symbolic world they inhabit using similar linguistic and symbolic building materials, even if the members of the community are not of one mind as to what their various world-constructing symbols mean. Second, operative in all communities is a group focus[4] that evokes a shared sense of group identity among the members, whose attention is thereby directed toward the group. Group identity, which is fostered in part by the belief that the participants engage in a common task, nurtures a type of solidarity among the members.[5] Moreover, rather than necessitating unanimity and uniformity of opinion among group members, group focus entails a shared interest in participating in an ongoing discussion as to what constitutes the identity of the group.[6] A third major characteristic of a community is the "person focus"

---

[1] Amitai Etzioni, "Introduction: A Matter of Balance, Rights and Responsibilities," in Amitai Etzioni, ed., *The Essential Communitarian Reader* (Lanham, MD: Rowman and Littlefield, 1998), p. xv.

[2] Ibid.

[3] Peter L. Berger, *Invitation to Sociology: A Humanistic Perspective*, Anchor Books edn (Garden City, NY: Doubleday, 1963), pp. 63–64.

[4] Arthur J. Dyke, *Rethinking Rights and Responsibilities: The Moral Bonds of Community* (Cleveland, OH: Pilgrim, 1992), p. 126.

[5] Derek L. Phillips, *Looking Backward: A Critical Appraisal of Communitarian Thought* (Princeton University Press, 1993), p. 17.

[6] Robert N. Bellah, "Community Properly Understood: A Defense of 'Democratic Communitarianism,'" in *The Essential Communitarian Reader*, p. 16.

that balances its group orientation. Insofar as its members draw their personal identity from the community, the group is a crucial factor in forming its participants.[7] This third aspect leads to what for the purposes of ecclesiology constitutes the central function of community, its role in identity formation.

Lying behind communitarian accounts of personal identity formation is the thesis that the self is dependent on the group. George Herbert Mead, to cite one important precursor, asserted that meaning is no mere individual matter but rather is interpersonal or relational, that the mind is not only individual but also a social phenomenon,[8] and hence that the self – the maturing personality or one's personal identity – is socially produced.[9] According to Mead, rather than the individual being *sui generis*, human development is a product of the process of social interaction, for the mind, critical thinking and a sense of self are facilitated by participation in the group; or, as Josiah Royce noted, humans come to self-consciousness under the persistent influence of social others.[10]

More recently, philosophers such as Alasdair MacIntyre have linked these understandings of the self with narrative theory. Like contemporary narrative thinkers, MacIntyre argues that humans are storytellers.[11] Human identity develops through the telling of a personal narrative, in accordance with which one's life "makes sense,"[12] and these personal stories are tied up with the larger group story,[13] the narrative of a community.

George Stroup provides a fuller treatment of the narrative theory of personal identity and its relationship to community.[14] Stroup theorizes that identity emerges as a person selects certain events from her past and uses them as a basis for interpreting the significance of the whole of her life. Personal identity is not created merely from the "factual data," or "chronicle," of the events of one's life, however, but requires an "interpretative scheme" that provides the "plot" through which the chronicle makes sense. The interpretative framework likewise cannot be derived from the data of one's

[7] Michael Sandel, *Liberalism and the Limits of Justice*, 2nd edn (Cambridge University Press, 1998).
[8] George Herbert Mead, *Mind, Self and Society*, ed. Charles W. Morris (1934; University of Chicago Press, 1962), pp. 118–25, 134.
[9] Ibid., pp. 144–64.
[10] Josiah Royce, *The World and the Individual* (New York: Macmillan, 1901), p. 261.
[11] Alasdair MacIntyre, *After Virtue: A Study in Moral Theory*, 2nd edn (University of Notre Dame Press, 1984), p. 216.
[12] On this point, see also, Robert N. Bellah, Richard Madsen, and William M. Sullivan, et al., *Habits of the Heart: Individualism and Commitment in American Life*, Perennial Library edition (New York: Harper & Row, 1986), p. 81.
[13] MacIntyre, *After Virtue*, pp. 216, 221.
[14] George W. Stroup, *The Promise of Narrative Theology* (Atlanta: John Knox, 1981), pp. 101–98.

own life; instead it arises from one's social context or "tradition."[15] For this reason, Stroup concludes, personal identity is never a private reality but has a communal element; it is shaped by the community in which the person is a participant. Such a community contributes to the formation of the "self" by mediating the communal narrative necessary for personal identity formation.

The identity-conferring aspect of community leads to what sociologists such as Nisbet and Perrin label a "reference group,"[16] that is, "the social group or category to which the individual 'refers,' consciously or unconsciously, in the shaping of his attitudes and beliefs and values on a given subject or in the formation of his conduct."[17] Although each person is a member of a variety of communities at any given time, only a select few function as her reference group in the full sense of the term. The community that functions (at least temporarily) as one's ultimate reference group or "community of reference" is the particular community from which she gains her fundamental identity.

The role of a group as a community of reference is connected with its ability to forge a link to both the past and the future and thereby become what Josiah Royce denotes a "community of memory" and a "community of hope."[18] A community has a history; in fact, it is in an important sense constituted by that history, a history that begins in the past and extends into the future. This "constitutive narrative" does not view time merely as a continuous flow of qualitatively meaningless sensations. Rather, in telling its story, a community punctuates the present – the day, the week, the season, the year – with a sense of the transcendent and thereby presents time as a meaningful whole.[19]

The constitutive narrative begins "in the beginning," with the primal event(s) that called the community into being, and it includes the crucial milestones that mark its subsequent trajectory.[20] More important than merely retelling past occurrences, however, reciting the constitutive past narrative places the contemporary community within the primal events that constituted their forebears as this particular community. The act of reciting reconstitutes the community in the present as the contemporary embodiment of a communal tradition that spans the years.

[15] Here Stroup is in substantial agreement with social constructionist sociologists. See, for example, Peter L. Berger, *The Sacred Canopy: Elements of a Sociological Theory of Religion* (Garden City, NY: Doubleday, 1969), p. 20.
[16] Berger, *Invitation to Sociology*, p. 118.
[17] Robert Nisbet and Robert G. Perrin, *The Social Bond*, 2nd edn (New York: Alfred A. Knopf, 1977), p. 100.
[18] Josiah Royce, *The Problem of Christianity*, 2 vols. (New York: Macmillan, 1913), II, pp. 50–51.
[19] Bellah, et. al., *Habits of the Heart*, p. 282.   [20] Ibid., 152–55.

The communal history does not end in the past, but extends into the future. As a result, a community turns the gaze of its members toward the future, anticipating the continuation of, and even the further development of the community. Not only does the community sense that it is moving toward an ideal that lies yet before it, more importantly, it expectantly looks to the ideal or "eschatological" future, when the purpose and goals – the *telos* – of the community will be fully actualized. This expectation of a glorious future serves as an ongoing admonition to its members to embody the communal vision in the present.

The community's constitutive narrative provides a transcendent vantage point for life in the here-and-now. It bestows a qualitative meaning upon time and space, and upon community members as they inhabit their world. The recited narrative offers a plausible explanation of present existence, for it provides the overarching theme through which community members can view their lives and the present moment in history as a part of a stream of time that transcends every particular "now." Likewise, it supplies a context of meaning that allows members to connect their personal aspirations with those of a larger whole and to see their efforts as contributions to that whole. In this manner, as the community retells its constitutive narrative, it functions as an "interpretive community," to borrow Royce's term.[21]

The telling of the constitutive narrative is accentuated through sacred practices that anthropologists call "rites of intensification." According to Grunlan and Mayers such rituals "bring the community together, increase group solidarity, and reinforce commitment to the beliefs of the group."[22] These "practices of commitment" define the community way of life as well as the patterns of loyalty and obligation that keep the community alive.[23] Participation in these acts solidifies the feelings of "community" sensed by the group members.[24]

COMMUNITY AND THE CHURCH

Although community language carries certain limitations, the church does form a distinct social group,[25] and it displays the basic characteristics

[21] Royce, *Problem of Christianity*, ii, p. 211.
[22] Stephen A. Grunlan and Marvin K. Mayers, *Cultural Anthropology: A Christian Perspective*, 2nd edn (Grand Rapids: Zondervan, 1988), p. 222.
[23] Bellah, et al., *Habits of the Heart*, pp. 152–54.
[24] Robert A. Nisbet, *The Sociological Tradition* (New York: Basic Books, 1966), p. 48.
[25] For an example of rejection of the conclusion that the church forms a specific society, see Kathryn Tanner, *Theories of Culture: A New Agenda for Theology* (Minneapolis: Fortress, 1997), pp. 93–102.

of a community. This observation raises the central question of ecclesiology: what is the church? Or, how is the church constituted?

The constitution of the church

One hallmark of the Enlightenment is the individualism or social atomism that has given birth to the modern social and political theory with its view of the state as the product of autonomous selves voluntarily entering into a "social contract" so as to gain certain personal advantages. Voluntarist contractualism finds its ecclesiological counterpart in the theory that sees the church as the voluntary association of individuals whose existence as believers precedes their presence in the congregation, in that the identity of each is supposedly constituted prior to their joining together to form the church. According to this model, rather than constituting its members, the church is constituted *by* believers, who are deemed to be complete "spiritual selves" prior to, and apart from their membership in the church. The church, in turn, is an aggregate of the individual Christians who "contract" with each other to form a spiritual society.[26] To provide the theological rationale for the contractual view, some thinkers appeal to the idea that the true church is the invisible company of all believers of all ages, in contrast to the visible church which is its local, institutional expression.[27]

When properly understood, a contractual ecclesiology can become a helpful embodiment of the principle of the priesthood of all believers. Nevertheless, under the impulse of individualism, the contractual view all too easily devalues the church. It readily reduces the community of Christ's disciples to little more than what Robert Bellah calls a "lifestyle enclave," a society formed by persons united by their shared interest in certain religious practices or who believe that membership in a Christian group will contribute to their individual good. For this reason, "In what sense – if any – is the church a community?" emerges as perhaps the central ecclesiological question in the postmodern context.

The sociological perspective noted above provides a helpful vantage point from which to understand the church as community. It leads to the conclusion that the church is more than the aggregate of its members, for it is a particular people imbued with a particular "constitutive narrative." The community-constituting biblical narrative that spans the ages from the primordial past to the eschatological future provides the interpretive

---

[26] Bloesch is an example of those thinkers who bemoan the "appalling neglect" of ecclesiology in evangelicalism, which he believes is due in part to the emphasis on individual decision, as evangelicals give priority to the decision of faith rather than to nurture. Donald G. Bloesch, *The Future of Evangelical Christianity* (Garden City, NY: Doubleday, 1983), p. 127.

[27] For a lucid example, see Robert P. Lightner, *Evangelical Theology* (Grand Rapids: Baker, 1986), pp. 228, 232.

framework – the narrative plot – through which its members find meaning in their personal and communal stories. Because it links the present with the entire stream of God's action, through its recital, members of the community discover the connection between their personal lives and something greater – something transcendent – namely, the work of the biblical God in history.

As a consequence of this shared narrative, believers sense a special solidarity with each other. Within the context of the church, this solidarity works its way out in the practical dimensions of fellowship, support, and nurture that its members discover through their relationships with each other as a communal people. And in this process, the church becomes what Daniel Migliore calls an "alternative community" that "gives the world reason to hope."[28] In short, as James McClendon succinctly states, the church is a community understood as "sharing together in a storied life of obedient service to and with Christ."[29]

Community and the biblical narrative

As helpful as sociological insights are in devising a Christian ecclesiology, the appropriation of sociology dare not deteriorate into a new foundationalism. Such degeneration occurs when speech about the church as community begins with some generic reality called "community" that can supposedly be discovered through objective observation of the world and then proceeds to fit the church into this purportedly universal human phenomenon, as if the community of Christ were a particular exemplar of some more general reality. This "sociological foundationalism of community" assumes the priority of sociology, treated in typical modernist form as an objective science that sets both the agenda and the methodological direction for theological reflection and construction.

The ontological connection between theology and social theory actually moves in the opposite direction. As John Milbank perceptively declared, theology is "itself a social science, and the queen of the sciences for the inhabitants of the *altera civitas*, on pilgrimage through this temporary world."[30] Theology, then, and not sociology as a scientific discipline, must emerge as the ultimate basis for speaking of the church as community. The church is a community, therefore, not so much because it reflects certain traits set forth by sociology, but because it has a special role in the divine program, at the heart of which, according to the Bible, is the establishment of community.

[28] Daniel Migliore, *Faith Seeking Understanding* (Grand Rapids: Eerdmans, 1991), p. 192.
[29] James William McClendon, Jr., *Ethics: Systematic Theology Volume 1* (Nashville, TN: Abingdon, 1986), p. 28.
[30] John Milbank, *Theology and Social Theory: Beyond Secular Reason* (Oxford: Blackwell, 1990), p. 380.

Taken as a whole, the Bible asserts that God's program is directed to the goal of bringing about community. The biblical drama begins in the primordial garden, as God notes the solitariness of the first human and concludes, "It is not good for the man to be alone" (Genesis 2:18), thereby indicating, in the words of sociologist David Lyon, that "sociality and interdependence are part of being human."[31] The divine response reaches its consummation only in the future, with the grand vision of the new heaven and new earth, in which people live together in peace, nature fulfills its purpose of providing nourishment for all earthly inhabitants (Revelation 22:1–3a), but, most glorious of all, God dwells with humans (Revelation 21:3). Consequently, God's ultimate goal is not to transpose an aggregate of individual believers to an isolated realm "beyond the blue." Rather, our human destiny is communal. Indeed, the biblical writers consistently present our eternal home in social, rather than in individual terms: it is a great city (Revelation 21:9–21), it encompasses many dwelling places or rooms (John 14:2), it is composed of a multitude of inhabitants (Revelation 7:9–10), etc.

The goal of community that lies at the heart of God's actions in history is displayed in the focal point of salvation history, the Christ event. Jesus is the exemplar human being, the revelation of who we are to be, and the design Jesus reveals focuses on living in relationship with God and with others. Further, Jesus did not come to fulfill a private vocation of discovering God for his own sake, but to be obedient to the will of his Father for the sake of humankind. Thus, in his death he took upon himself the sins of all, and he rose from the dead to mediate to us eternal life through our union with him. For this reason, as David Fergusson notes, "The individual must finally be understood in terms of his or her having an appointed place in the kingdom of God. The community under the rule of God is thus the goal of each individual life."[32]

Moreover, the work of the Holy Spirit has the establishment of community in view. The outpouring of the Spirit at Pentecost was directed toward the establishing of a new people composed of Jews and Gentiles reconciled to each other (Ephesians 2:11–22). During the present age the Spirit is bringing together a people that transcends every human division – a people from every nation and socioeconomic status, and consisting of both male and female (Galatians 3:28).

The completed work of Christ and the present work of the Spirit mean that the eschatological community that arrives in its fullness only at the

---

[31] David Lyon, *Sociology and the Human Image* (Downers Grove, IL: InterVarsity Press, 1983), p. 128.
[32] David Fergusson, *Community, Liberalism and Christian Ethics* (Cambridge University Press, 1998), p. 157.

consummation of human history is already present in a partial, yet genuine manner. Although this present reality takes several forms, its focal point is the community of the followers of Christ, the church.

Ecclesiology and human community

Not only does the biblical narrative provide the perspective from which to speak about the church as community, in the wake of the demise of foundationalism it also offers the touchstone by which Christian theology understands the truly communal dimension in any human social group. It provides the lens through which to view all human social groups – all claimants to community – from the strictly informal to the highly institutional.[33] Because all human relationships are to be measured from the perspective of the quest for true community, Christian theology understands every social group in accordance with its potential or role as a contribution to, prolepsis of, or signpost on the way toward human participation in the destiny God intends for creation.

Moreover, looking through the lens of a Christian theological ecclesiology enables us to realize that the various social groups in which people participate all fall short of the community God is fashioning. In comparison to the divine community, all human relationships are merely "splintered and tribal existence," to cite Stanley Hauerwas' description.[34] The present failure of community leads us to realize that true community always remains an eschatological ideal, an "impossible possibility," to appropriate Niebuhr's well-known phrase. This realization ought to temper our expectations as to the depth of community we will be able to experience in the here-and-now, and it ought to dissuade us from talking too glibly about our ability to construct true community in the present.[35] While we seek under the Spirit's guidance to be about the task of constructing community, we nevertheless wait expectantly for God to complete the divine work of bringing creation as a whole and the people of God in particular into the enjoyment of the fullness of community.

THE CHURCH AS A "MARKED" COMMUNITY

As the embodiment of the biblical narrative of God at work establishing community, the church is itself a community, and it constitutes the community of reference for its members. The church functions in this manner

---

[33] Nicholas Lash, *A Matter of Hope: A Theologian's Reflections on the thought of Karl Marx* (London: Darton, Longman and Todd, 1981), p. 75.

[34] Stanley Hauerwas, *A Community of Character: Toward a Constructive Christian Ethic* (University of Notre Dame Press, 1981), p. 92.

[35] Lash, *Matter of Hope*, p. 75.

as it forms a particular – or "peculiar"(1 Peter 2:9 KJV) – people, a people marked by certain characteristics.

The marks of the church

The Nicene Creed bequeathed to subsequent generations what quickly became the standard approach to the question of ecclesiology, namely, the practice of describing the church by appeal to four adjectives. Hence, the church is routinely denoted as "one, holy, catholic and apostolic."[36]

In the Middle Ages, theologians had come to predicate the four adjectives to the visible institution centered in Rome.[37] Viewed from this perspective, unity referred to the subordination of all the faithful to the same spiritual jurisdiction and teaching magisterium. Catholicity meant that the one church spread throughout the world shared the same creed, worship, and system of canon law. Holiness focused on the life of the visible community and especially on the sanctity of the means that fostered holiness, such as the sacramental system and the moral guidance of an infallible magisterium. And apostolicity referred to the legitimate succession of pastors, as well as their approval by Rome.[38]

Although the Reformers accepted the creedal marks as *notae ecclesiae,* they did not focus their attention on these four adjectives. In their estimation, such an appeal could not solve the ecclesiological problem, for describing the nature of the church as one, holy, catholic, and apostolic did not delineate where that true church was in fact to be found.[39] For the answer to this question, the Reformers turned to two other marks, which they found better suited as determinative characteristics of the true church in its visible form: word and sacrament. To cite Calvin's well-known formulation: "Wherever we see the Word of God purely preached and heard, and the sacraments administered according to Christ's institution, there, it is not to be doubted, a church of God exists."[40]

The focus on word and sacrament led to a renewed emphasis on the local church. This, in turn, set the Reformers' ecclesiology apart from the medieval Roman Catholic emphasis on the clergy, which had effectively devalued the gathered fellowship. According to J. S. Whale: "For Protestantism, the community of believers is the constitutive essence of the Church; its *sine*

---

[36] "The Constantinopolitan Creed," in *Creeds of the Churches,* ed. John H. Leith, 3rd edn (Atlanta: John Knox, 1982), p. 33.

[37] Avery Dulles, *Models of the Church,* Image Books edn (Garden City, NY: Image Books, 1978), p. 133.

[38] Ibid., pp. 133–34.

[39] Paul D. L. Avis, *The Church in the Theology of the Reformers* (Atlanta: John Knox, 1981), p. 8.

[40] John Calvin, *Institutes of the Christian Religion,* 2 vols., ed. John McNeil, trans. Ford Lewis Battles (Philadelphia: Westminster Press, 1960), 4.1.9.

262 Stanley J. Grenz

qua non. The faith, worship and life of the Church are meaningless without the *societas fidelium*, a fellowship of those who are gathered in the Spirit and united by love."[41] Linking the Reformation impulse with the results of the previous section leads to the conclusion that the church is the community gathered around word and sacrament.

The church as the community of word and sacrament

Ultimately, the church is the product of the work of the Spirit. Yet, the Spirit creates the community through word and sacrament. The Spirit creates the church by speaking through the word. By speaking in and through the biblical text the Spirit brings into being a converted people, that is, a people who forsake their old life so as to inhabit the new, eschatological world centered on Jesus Christ who is the Word. For this reason, rather than being merely the aggregate of its members, the church is a people imbued with a particular "constitutive narrative," namely, the biblical narrative of God at work bringing creation to its divinely intended goal. The church is a community of the converted, therefore, because the biblical narrative provides its participants with the interpretive framework through which they individually and corporately find their identity as those who are "in Christ" and through which they view life and the world.

The Spirit engages in the divine community-constituting work in the proclamation of the word. Although it is the Spirit's vehicle, such proclamation is ultimately an activity of the church viewed as a community of reference. As the faith community retells the biblical narrative that constitutes it as a people, it mediates to its members the interpretive framework – the narrative plot – through which they find meaning in their personal and communal stories. Through their connection with the community that is constituted by this narrative, believers find their lives linked with the work of the biblical God in history. Moreover, by proclaiming the biblical narrative of God at work in history centered in Jesus Christ, the church becomes a people focused on the Word and gathered around the word.

As was noted in the previous section, a functioning community does not only retell its constitutive narrative. Rather, in community life the "word" is accentuated through sacred practices, "rites of intensification," or "practices of commitment."[42] This observation leads to the "sacrament" side of the Reformation couplet of "word and sacrament." As many Christian thinkers since Augustine have suggested, Baptism and the Lord's Supper are visual

[41] J. S. Whale, *Christian Reunion: Historic Divisions Reconsidered* (Grand Rapids: Eerdmans, 1971), pp. 25–26.
[42] Bellah, et al., *Habits of the Heart*, pp. 152–54.

sermons; they constitute the Word of God symbolically proclaimed.[43] More particularly, these acts are visual, symbolic embodiments of the constitutive narrative of the Christian community. By linking participants with the biblical narrative, at the heart of which are the life, passion, and resurrection of Jesus and the sending of the Spirit, these acts function together with the proclamation of the word in the Spirit's identity-forming, community-building work.

Baptism and the Lord's supper are visual sermons in that they recount in a dramatic, symbolic manner the Christian declaration that "God was in Christ reconciling the world unto himself" (2 Corinthians 5:19 KJV). To this end, these practices serve as vivid memorials, recalling to mind Christ's accomplished work on behalf of humankind. Their meaning goes beyond mere memorial, however. Participation in the acts facilitates symbolic participation in the saving events that form the foundation for Christian identity as persons united with Christ. As visual sermons, the acts of commitment symbolically transport the faith community into the narrative past. Through these symbols believers reenact the story of Christ's death and resurrection, as well as their own conversion, that is, their personal death and resurrection with Christ. Thereby the Spirit vividly confirms in their hearts their identity as new persons in Christ (2 Corinthians 5:17).

The sacraments bring not only the narrative past, but also the eschatological future into view. These acts symbolically announce the promise that God will one day complete the divine creative work, but more importantly that this completion constitutes the true identity of the believer, the believing community, and even all creation. Not only do Baptism and the Lord's Supper announce this truth, through these acts believers symbolically take part in that grand event, as participants who celebrate in the midst of the brokenness of the present the glorious fullness of a future reality that is already at work in their midst and in the world by the Spirit.

In short, "sacrament" is integrally connected to "word." Baptism and the Lord's Supper comprise vivid, symbolic declarations of the Gospel narrative. Like the proclamation of the word itself, its symbolic embodiment in the sacraments connects the contemporary believing community with the biblical story that they represent. As participants symbolically experience the foundational events of Christ's death and resurrection and are gathered into the vision of God's future, their lives are linked to God's creative–salvific action, the narrative of which is the plot line of history. And this transcendent vantage point, in turn, becomes the vehicle through which the Spirit

---

43 Calvin, *Institutes of the Christian Religion*, 4.14.4.

empowers the community for the task of living as the eschatological community, founded upon their union with Christ, in the here-and-now.

The church local and universal

Viewing the church as community in this manner indicates how the church is essentially local and yet universal. The church is primarily local, for it is in the local fellowship that believers gather faithfully around word and sacrament. It is in the context of the local fellowship of believers that the biblical narrative is proclaimed and ritually embodied.

At the same time, the constitutive biblical narrative is neither the invention nor the exclusive possession of any one congregation. It is rather a shared story, a story belonging to all who in every place gather around word and sacrament, and hence a story that transcends all local congregations. Further, the proclaimed word and the administered sacraments also transcend the local gathering, for they belong to each faithful congregation of believers. The shared nature of the narrative and of its proclamation in word and sacrament not only brings together the many believers into a local congregation, therefore, it also unites each local gathering of believers with all other congregations of the faithful. For this reason, the church, which is fundamentally the particular, local congregation gathered around word and sacrament, nevertheless simultaneously transcends any one local congregation and all local congregations.

THE CHURCH AS A COMMUNITY MISSIONALLY MARKED

Despite their emphasis on word and sacrament, the Reformers agreed that the true church was to be characterized by unity, holiness, catholicity, and apostolicity. Yet they saw these four traits more as eschatological goals to be sought than as attributes that can be realized by the church on earth.[44] In this sense, the four adjectives became for the Reformers the essential marks of the true church hidden within the ecclesiastical institution, and thus the attributes of the church in its invisible fullness. Yet, ecclesiology would go astray if the "ideal" status of the marks were allowed to lead to the conclusion that they are the prerogative solely of some invisible church that is totally disjointed from the church in the world.

The creedal marks and the missional church

Their eschatological direction suggests that the creedal marks of the church ought to be seen as essentially dynamic, rather than static. Moreover,

---

[44] Avis, *Church in the Reformers*, p. 8.

rather than characterizing any one particular institution, they set forth the task shared by the people of God. The dynamic reading of the marks readily fosters a missiological ecclesiology, which arises ultimately from the mission of the triune God in the world and consequently out of an interpretation of the church's apostolicity as declaring that the church is *sent* (from *apostello* meaning "send out") into the world with the Gospel and thus is by its very nature a missionary church.[45]

Missiologist Charles van Engen takes this insight a step farther. He suggests that the marks are better read as adverbs than adjectives, so as thereby to capture the dynamic character of the church's faithfulness to her mission. In his estimation, the *notae ecclesiae* describe the missional ministry of the church as unifying, sanctifying, reconciling, and proclaiming.[46] The Faith and Our Culture work group offer an additional, helpful suggestion: the four marks ought to be placed in reverse order. Consequently, the missional church is called to be a "proclaiming, reconciling, sanctifying and unifying" community.[47] This reversal in order stands as a reminder of the directedness of the church's missional task and hence its ultimate goal.

Seen from this perspective, the four creedal marks paint a picture of a church active in mission. The church is truly apostolic not only as it stands in continuity with the apostles' doctrine, but as it is a proclaiming community, that is, as it takes seriously its calling in the divine program to be a fellowship that continually proclaims through word and sacrament the good news of God's action in Christ. In so doing, the church patterns its life after the example of Jesus, the one sent from God, as carried out by the apostles whom he sent into the world, and through the agency of the Holy Spirit sent into the church at Pentecost.

Further, the church is truly catholic, insofar as it is a reconciling community. Essentially, reconciliation involves bringing into wholesome relationships those whose differences readily occasion hostilities. The missional church engages continually in the work of being an agent of the divine reconciliation. This includes, of course, seeking fervently and untiringly to bring into the fellowship of word and sacrament – both locally and, by extension, globally – people in all their diversity. But catholicity – that is, carrying on a reconciling mission – entails also acting as an agent for the fostering of wholesome relationships among humans in every dimension of life and existence.

[45] See, for example, Melvin Tinker, "Toward an Evangelical Ecclesiology (Part One)," *Churchman* 105:1 (1991), 25.
[46] Charles van Engen, *God's Missionary People: Rethinking the Purpose of the Local Church* (Grand Rapids: Baker, 1991), p. 66.
[47] Darrell L. Guder and Lois Barrett, *Missional Church: A Vision for the Sending of the Church in North America* (Grand Rapids: Eerdmans, 1998), p. 255.

At the heart of the biblical meaning of holiness are the twin aspects of being set apart for God's use (for example, Exodus 28:41)[48] and attempting to pattern human life after the example of God (hence, Matthew 5:43–48; 1 Peter 1:15–16). The church's sanctifying mission, in turn, is both internal and external. As the *ecclesia semper reformanda*, the faith community continually reforms its own pattern of life, as it repeatedly gathers to hear the word anew and to celebrate the sacraments afresh. But it also seeks to be a people whose presence in the world results in God's name being "hallowed," in accordance with Jesus' own prayer (Matthew 6:9 KJV).

Finally, the church is one in that the mission of the church is intended to exert a unifying effect. This unifying mission begins, of course, "with the house of God" (1 Peter 4:17). The church's quest to foster unity is to be operative primarily within the local congregation (for example, Philippians 2:2) – among those who gather together around the unifying participation in word and sacrament (1 Corinthians 12:13; 10:17) – and then by extension among all congregations that share the same word and the same sacred acts. But, as John Macquarrie and others have noted, the unifying impulse of the missional church extends beyond itself. As it gathers around word and sacrament in this penultimate age, the community bears witness to, and seeks to anticipate in celebration as well as in concrete ways the Spirit's fashioning of one new humanity in Christ (Ephesians 2:15) and the eschatological day when God will dwell with the people of God in the renewed creation (Revelation 21:1–5; 22:1–5).

Theological ecclesiology and the church visible/invisible

The missional approach to the four creedal marks leads finally to the ultimate context for Christian ecclesiology, the theological. Reflection on the *notae ecclesiae* has led some theologians in recent years to the recognition that ultimately the church's character is determined by its connection with its Lord. This means that the creedal marks must be predicated first on the triune God active in and through the church, and then, by extension, on the church as the people through whom God works. Jürgen Moltmann, for example, writes: "If the church acquires its existence through the activity of Christ, then her characteristics, too, are characteristics of Christ's activity first of all. The acknowledgment of the 'one, holy, catholic and apostolic church' is acknowledgment of the uniting, sanctifying, comprehensive and commissioning lordship of Christ."[49]

---

[48] Robert G. Girdlestone, *Synonyms of the Old Testament*, 2nd repr. edn (1897; Grand Rapids: Eerdmans, 1973), p. 175.

[49] Jürgen Moltmann, *The Church in the Power of the Spirit: A Contribution to Messianic Ecclesiology*, trans. Margaret Kohl (New York: Harper & Row, 1977), p. 338.

Taking this insight a step farther suggests that, when viewed as a missional community, the church finds its central qualities in the mission of the triune God. The church's true nature as a community sent by God arises from its mandate to be the bearer of the divine mission in the world, a mission that is directed not merely toward all humankind, but toward all creation. Even more significant, however, is a further consideration. The church's identity as a community must emerge out of the identity of the God it serves and in whom its life is hidden, to allude to Luther's description of the invisible church. Denoting this theological ecclesiology provides the final link between the church in the world (i.e., the so-called "visible church") and the church in its essential nature (or the "invisible church").

At the heart of the biblical narrative is the story of the triune God bringing humankind to be the *imago dei*, that is, to be the reflection of the divine character – love (1 John 4:8,16). Because God is the triune one, the three persons-in-relationship, the *imago dei* must in some sense entail humans-in-relationship as well, i.e., humans who through their relationships reflect the divine love (1 John 4:7–8).[50] The church's mission, in turn, is related to this universal human design to be the divine image.[51] The church is to be a people who reflect in relation to each other and to all creation the character of the Creator and thereby bear witness to the divine purpose for humankind. This fundamental calling or mission to be the foretaste of the *imago dei* determines the church's proclaiming, reconciling, sanctifying, and unifying mission in the world.

The church's vocation to be the *imago dei* finds its ultimate source not in God's design for humankind, however, but in its fundamental existence "in Christ." According to the New Testament, Christ is the true image of God (2 Corinthians 4:4; Colossians 1:15; Hebrews 1:3), and through their union with Christ believers share in this designation (Romans 8:29; 1 Corinthians 15:49). Being in Christ brings the church to its true identity as the fellowship of those who participate in the life of the triune God. The facilitator of this participation is the Holy Spirit (2 Corinthians 3:18), who is the agent of the new birth – conversion – through which event believers become co-heirs with Christ in the family of God (Romans 8:14–17). By placing

---

[50] For a discussion of the implications of the social Trinity for the concept of the image of God, see, Cornelius Plantinga, Jr., "Images of God," in Mark A. Noll and David F. Wells, eds., *Christian Faith and Practice in the Modern World* (Grand Rapids: Eerdmans, 1988), pp. 59–67.

[51] For a recent exploration of this theme, see Miroslav Volf, *After Our Likeness: The Church as the Image of the Trinity* (Grand Rapids: Eerdmans, 1998). See also, Miroslav Volf, "Kirche als Gemeinschaft: Ekklesiologische Ueberlegungen aus freikirchlicher Perspective," *Evangelische Theologie* 49:1 (1989), 70–76; Kilian McDonnell, "Vatican II (1962–1964), Puebla (1979), Synod (1985): *Koinonia/Communio* as an Integral Ecclesiology," *Journal of Ecumenical Studies* 25:3 (1988), 414.

believers "in Christ," therefore, the Spirit brings them to participate in the fellowship of the eternal Son with the eternal Father (for example, Galatians 4:6). Ultimately, then, we enjoy the fullness of community as, and only as, God graciously brings us to participate together in the fountainhead of community, namely, the life of the triune God. For this reason, the communal fellowship Christians share goes beyond what is generated by a common experience or even by a common narrative. The community that is ours is nothing less than a shared participation – a participation together – in the perichoretic community of Trinitarian persons.[52]

In the end, participation in the perichoretic dance of the triune God as those who by the Spirit are in Christ is what constitutes community in the highest sense and hence marks the true church. And being a people whose life is hidden in Christ (and hence is the invisible church) even as it lives in the world (and therefore remains the visible church) is the present calling of those whose lives have been, and are being, transformed by the Spirit. Even while the community of Christ seeks under the Spirit's guidance to be about the task of enhancing community in its various forms, believers nevertheless wait expectantly for God to complete the divine work of bringing creation into the enjoyment of the fullness of fellowship as the divinely fashioned eschatological community.

Further reading

Grenz, Stanley, *Theology for the Community of God* (Grand Rapids: Eerdmans, 2000).
Hauerwas, Stanley, *A Community of Character: Toward a Constructive Christian Social Ethic* (University of Notre Dame Press, 1981).
Moltmann, Jürgen, *The Church in the Power of the Spirit: A Contribution to Messianic Ecclesiology* (Minneapolis: Fortress, 1993).
Van Gelder, Craig, *The Essence of the Church: A Community Created by the Spirit* (Grand Rapids: Baker, 2000).
Volf, Miroslav, *After Our Likeness: The Church as the Image of the Trinity* (Grand Rapids: Eerdmans, 1998).

---

[52] J. M. R. Tillard, "What Is the Church of God?" *Mid-stream* 23 (October 1984), 372–73.

16 Holy Spirit and Christian spirituality

DAVID F. FORD

The Spirit's completion of Christ's work is no longer to be seen epistemologically, as a supplement or extension to the teaching of Christ, or even as that which makes it possible to hear and receive the Word. It is, rather, a completion in terms of liberation and transformation: it is *gift*, renewal and life. It is not possible to speak of the Spirit in abstraction from the Christian form of life as a whole: Spirit is "specified" not with reference to any kind of episodic experience but in relation to the human identity of the Christian. The question "Where, or what, is the Holy Spirit?" is not answered (as it might be by Luke) by pointing to prophecy and "charismata" and saying, "Spirit is the agency productive of phenomena like this."

How then is it answered? Perhaps not at all. The theological quest which is preoccupied with identifying the *distinctive* quality or work of the Spirit has so often, as Hanson points out, produced only the most sterile abstractions. And there is at least in eastern Christian thought a sense that the "face" of the Holy Spirit is not there for us to see. If what we are speaking of is the agency which draws us to the Father by constituting us children, we are evidently speaking of an agency not simply identical with "Father" or "Son," or with a sum or amalgam of the two. That perhaps is obvious, or even trivial, but it may be that no more can be said of the Spirit's distinctiveness. The grammar of our talk about the Holy Spirit is not that proper to "God" as source, ground, terminus of vision and prayer, and so forth, nor that proper to "God" as the disturbing presence of grace and vulnerability within the world of human relationships as a particular focal story. It is the grammar of "spirituality" in the fullest sense of that emasculated word, the grammar of interplay in the human self between the given and the future, between reality as it is and the truth which encompasses it; between Good Friday and Easter. If there can be any sense in which "Spirit" is a bridge-concept, its work is not to bridge the gap between God and the world or even between the Word and the human soul, but to span the unimaginably greater gulf between suffering and hope, and to do so by creating that form of human subjectivity capable of confronting suffering without illusion but also without despair.[1]

Rowan Williams touches in this passage on key issues in any theology of the Holy Spirit and Christian spirituality: the relation of the Spirit to Jesus Christ; emphases on the Spirit as informing or transforming; the Spirit as episodic and interruptive or as forming whole lives; the difficulty of defining the Spirit in distinction from Father and Son; and the meaning of "spirituality."

But what might be "postmodern" in Williams' account? The meaning I attach to the term will emerge as this chapter develops. The signs of post-modernity in this passage might be seen both in a concept of "completion" which resists closure in the interests of continuing transformation, of living in response to gift, and also in the stress on suffering which tempts to despair.

In the rest of his essay Williams gives prominence in his treatment of the Spirit to other concerns which seem characteristically postmodern. He contrasts an unsatisfactory strand of Trinitarian theology in which the Spirit is a bridge-concept between God and the world, a mediating agency of communication, with his own preferred "rather elusive alternative"[2] which resists being given systematic shape. He criticizes Karl Barth's notion of the Spirit as "historicity" but also finds it "tantalizing and deeply suggestive."[3] It leads him, by way of a contrast of Luke with Paul and John on the Spirit, into trying to articulate the meaning of the Spirit immersed in the contingencies of history – conflict, decision, powerlessness, vulnerability, fragmentation, infinite diversity, ambiguity, suffering, and above all the cross. Yet the immersion is an involvement which differentiates, recognizes otherness, and inspires radical critique as well as new life. At the heart of it is Williams' version of a "God without being" which transforms the patristic language of substance and power by reference to Good Friday and Easter: " 'God' vanishes on the cross: Father and Son remain, in the shared, consubstantial weakness of their compassion; and the Father will raise the Son in the power of the Spirit."[4]

There is also his use of the classic image and concept of "the face," already mentioned in the opening quotation above. The face has been especially fruitful in Eastern Christianity as well as in postmodern thought, and

---

[1] Rowan Williams, "Word and Spirit," in *On Christian Theology* (Oxford: Blackwell, 2000) pp. 123–24.
[2] Ibid., p. 109.   [3] Ibid., p. 118.   [4] Ibid., p. 121.

is suggestive of how otherness, particularity, relationality, ambiguity, contingency, non-religiousness, transformation, and a refusal of both overview
and closure, can be held together:

> The face of the Spirit is – as Vladimir Lossky memorably expressed
> it – the assembly of redeemed human faces in their infinite diversity.
> Human persons grown to the fullness of their *particular* identities, but
> sharing in the common divine gift of reconciled life in faith, these are
> the Spirit's manifestation. The Son is manifest in a single,
> paradigmatic figure, the Spirit is manifest in the "translatability" of
> that into the contingent diversity of history.[5]

The "who" of the Holy Spirit recognized distributively in the faces of
others living before[6] the face of Jesus Christ will be the paradigmatic *locus*
for pneumatology and spirituality in what follows.

THE HOLY SPIRIT IN THE CONTINGENCIES OF HISTORY: FOUR APPROACHES TO THE TASK

In the light of such thinking, the subject matter for a discussion of the
Holy Spirit and Christian spirituality might be described as the renewal
and full flourishing of human life in all its diversity, seen as inseparable
from involvement with both God and the reality of history (past, present,
and future). The theological task this sets is to try to distil a wisdom of
"living in the Spirit" in holiness (understood as full life shaped by God),
in suffering, and in hope. The postmodern dimension is for this wisdom
to face the problems and traumas of modernity and to begin to do justice
both to thinkers who see themselves as postmodern, and to the diversity
and "otherness" which many forms of modernity have failed to respect.

That theological task is endless, and a relatively short treatment such
as this requires some selection of topics and approaches. Possible starting-
points include the Bible, pneumatology in the history of Christian doctrine,
one or more traditions of spirituality, a particular theologian, current understandings and practices in theology and spirituality, or a fresh analysis of
the contemporary situation and how it might best be met. Williams covers
all those,[7] and they will recur in what follows. From these many possible
approaches, I have chosen four main ways into the subject.

---

[5] Ibid., pp. 125f.
[6] Not everyone, of course, is necessarily aware of living in this relationship.
[7] Williams in the volume quoted and in other works develops, in unsystematic form, a rich
integration of theology and spirituality. Cf. especially *The Wound of Knowledge. Christian
Spirituality from the New Testament to St. John of the Cross* (London: Darton, Longman and
Todd, 1979); *Teresa of Avila* (London: Geoffrey Chapman, 1991); *Open to Judgement. Sermons*

First, I will give my interpretation of the contribution of Dietrich Bonhoeffer. There are several reasons for starting with him. I see the events of the first half of the twentieth century as the decisive catalyst in the rise of what is now called postmodernism. If there were just a single factor to be named in the widespread disillusionment with modernity it would be the impact of what Edith Wyschogrod calls that period's "man-made mass death" – the Armenian genocide, the First World War, Soviet exterminations and terror, Japanese massacres, and Nazi killings and death camps.[8] Many of those now recognized as the forerunners of contemporary Jewish postmodern thought, such as Franz Rosenzweig, Martin Buber, and Emmanuel Levinas, were formed during that period. Among Christian thinkers the mentors from that time are numerous, as the present volume makes clear. I consider that Bonhoeffer, though widely influential in many ways, has far greater potential as an inspiration for postmodern theology than has yet been recognized. His whole life (1906–45) was lived during this period, he was deeply involved in some of its key events, and his thought, expressed in many genres, grapples in a multifaceted way with many of the pivotal issues. He was impressed by the challenge of Nietzsche, who was one of the main nineteenth century "prophets" of postmodernism; and he represents an alternative, yet critically related, "theology of life," affirming the body, the natural, and "this-worldliness" while going deeper into what was most deeply allergic to Nietzsche: the cross, weakness, "the view from below." In Williams' terms, Bonhoeffer formed his mature theology through "confronting suffering without illusion but also without despair," and the theology of the Spirit and accompanying spirituality that emerged shaped practices of holiness and hope immersed in the contingencies of both ordinary living and a terrible history. With the publication of the seventeen-volume scholarly edition of his complete works,[9] Bonhoeffer is now in a position to make an unprecedented contribution to theology in the third millennium.

Second, one of the key maxims of postmodern thought is "always be open to the questioning and contribution of 'the other.'" But who is the other? In a theology of the Holy Spirit concerned with suffering and hope

---

and Addresses (London: Darton, Longman and Todd, 1994). For a more "doctrinal" approach which thoughtfully engages with the Holy Spirit from the Bible through the early church, Reformation and the twentieth century, and connects it with the wide range of issues to which it is relevant, see John McIntyre, *The Shape of Pneumatology. Studies in the Doctrine of the Holy Spirit* (Edinburgh: T. & T. Clark, 1997).

[8] Edith Wyschogrod, *Spirit in Ashes. Hegel, Heidegger and Man-Made Mass Death* (New Haven, CT: Yale University Press, 1985). Cf. her linking of the Holocaust with postmodern Jewish thought in "Hasidism, Hellenism, Holocaust," in Steven Kepnes ed., *Interpreting Judaism in a Postmodern Age* (New York and London: New York University Press, 1996), pp. 301–21.

[9] *Dietrich Bonhoeffer Werke* (Munich: Christian Kaiser Verlag, 1986–1999).

the other must primarily be those who suffer. Can any theology of the Spirit survive facing them? Bonhoeffer was exposed to a fair range of others in his life – different social classes, countries, churches (including Birmingham Quakers and Harlem Pentecostals), faiths, disciplines, fellow prisoners – and in his final years (during which his *Ethics* was written) his own persecution, marginalization, and participation in subversive activities helped give him the "view from below." Even though the Jewish "other" was not a significant part of his own life, the events of his lifetime led him into a fresh theological assessment of the Jewishness of Christianity, so that, whilst in prison at the end of his life, one of his concerns was for the "rejudaizing" of Christianity.[10] In the aftermath of that period a postmodern Christian theology concerned with suffering and hope can learn from those Jews who have grappled with philosophical and theological issues in response to a postmodernity that has the Holocaust as a pivotal event. So I will follow my retrieval of Bonhoeffer on the Holy Spirit and spirituality (much of which he includes under ethics) by suggesting a shape for Christian postmodern theology drawn from some Jewish thinkers.

Third, I will also suggest one habitable *locus communis* for a theology of the Holy Spirit as part of that theology: living before the face of Jesus Christ. He is an "other" who embodies the relationship of suffering and hope to God in the contingencies of history.

Fourth, in line with the specific concern of this chapter to link the Holy Spirit with Christian spirituality, an attractive way into the subject matter is through life-shaping practices. I will develop this approach out of Williams, Bonhoeffer, some Jewish thinkers, and others. Only a few practices will be selected – worshipping and praying, interpreting Scripture, building up a community, and acting ethically – and the treatment of them will be extremely sketchy. The aim will be to ask questions and suggest, in note form, what are some of the main items on the agenda of Christian postmodern theology in this area.

DIETRICH BONHOEFFER AS A THEOLOGIAN OF THE HOLY SPIRIT FOR POSTMODERNITY[11]

Bonhoeffer's theology of the Holy Spirit is not (partly for the sorts of reasons suggested by Williams) in the form of an explicit doctrine or

---

[10] His close friend and biographer Eberhard Bethge spent much of his time in the final years of his life before his death in 2000 on relations between Christians and Jews.

[11] Much of this section is present in expanded form in David F. Ford, "Bonhoeffer, Holiness and Ethics," in Stephen Barton, ed., *Holiness Past and Present* (Edinburgh: T. & T. Clark, 2003) pp. 361–80.

monograph. It is indirect yet pervasive. Even confining attention to a few
of his books generates a constructive and interrogative agenda for pneumatology in the coming century.

His dissertation, *Sanctorum Communio*,[12] asks about the nature of the
"holy community" of the Holy Spirit, and in particular how the social sciences relate to theology.[13] His other dissertation, *Act and Being*,[14] is perhaps
the least appreciated and discussed of his works, but it offers what is vital
for any postmodern pneumatology concerned with wisdom and truth: an
epistemology and a treatment of theological rationality.[15] The books arising
out of Bonhoeffer's years heading the seminary for the Confessing Church
at Finkenwalde are his fullest explicit treatment of "living in the Spirit," holiness, and related themes of spirituality.[16] *The Cost of Discipleship*[17] poses
the challenge of "costly grace" through its exposition of the Sermon on the
Mount; and it also has a final section on the church that includes a treatment of holiness under the heading of "The Saints."[18] *Life Together*[19] was
written in a concentrated period in 1938 after the Gestapo had dissolved
the seminary, and describes the shaping of daily Christian living before God
in community – a concentrated, practical evocation of everyday holiness.
It might stand alongside his personal testimony in *Letters and Papers from
Prison*[20] as a classic exposition of what it means to cope "in the Spirit" with
the realities of suffering without despairing.

Bonhoeffer himself saw the *Ethics* as the culmination of his theological
work, and I will draw from that some key concepts for pneumatology. Here
is his programmatic statement:

> The place which in all other ethics is occupied by the antithesis of
> "should be" and "is," idea and accomplishment, motive and

[12] Dietrich Bonhoeffer, *Sanctorum Communio. A Theological Study of the Sociology of the Church*, Dietrich Bonhoeffer Works Volume 1 (Minneapolis: Fortress Press, 1998).

[13] The latter has been a recurrent concern in Christian postmodern theologies. Richard Roberts in "Theology and Social Science" (in David F. Ford, ed., *The Modern Theologians. An Introduction to Christian Theology in the Twentieth Century* [Oxford: Blackwell, 1997]) suggests that Bonhoeffer's theological approach to the social sciences is still the best available model for how to relate the two discourses.

[14] Dietrich Bonhoeffer, *Act and Being. Transcendental Philosophy and Ontology in Systematic Theology*, Dietrich Bonhoeffer Works Volume 2 (Minneapolis: Fortress Press, 1996).

[15] Cf. Paul D. Janz, "Redeeming Modernity. Rationality, Justification, and Penultimacy in the Theology of Dietrich Bonhoeffer" (Ph.D. Dissertation, Cambridge University, 2000, unpublished).

[16] They also work out in terms of spirituality and Christian living the theological substance developed in his University of Berlin Lectures published as *Creation and Fall*, Dietrich Bonhoeffer Works Volume 3 (Minneapolis: Fortress Press, 1997).

[17] Dietrich Bonhoeffer, *The Cost of Discipleship* (London: SCM, 1959).

[18] Ibid., pp. 245ff.

[19] Dietrich Bonhoeffer, *Life Together* and *Prayerbook of the Bible*, Dietrich Bonhoeffer Works Volume 5 (Minneapolis: Fortress Press, 1996).

[20] (London: SCM, 1971).

performance, is occupied in Christian ethics by the relation of reality and realization (*Wirklichkeit und Wirklichwerden*), past and present, history and event (faith), or, to replace the equivocal concept by the unambiguous name, the relation of Jesus Christ and the Holy Spirit. The question of good becomes the question of participation in the divine reality which is revealed in Christ.[21]

This theological account of reality and the good clearly draws ethics into coincidence with spirituality as the realization of and participation in the divine reality. It also encourages one to read the rest of the *Ethics* as unfolding the implications of the *reality of Jesus Christ* being *realized through the Holy Spirit*. Read that way, Bonhoeffer provides a set of four key pneumatological ideas.

The realization of the reality of Jesus Christ versus two spheres

The first is linked to a rejection of what he sees as a fundamentally wrong form of difference, or boundary-drawing. He ranges over an array of dichotomies: God/world; holy/profane; supernatural/natural; Christian/unChristian; grace/nature; revelation/reason. His analysis has far-reaching implications not only for ethics and holiness but also for every doctrine, for basic Christian identity, for church practice, for epistemology, and for relations with all sorts of "others" – Jews, Muslims, secular people, and so on:

> Just as in Christ the reality of God entered into the reality of the world, so, too, is that which is Christian to be found only in that which is of the world, the "supernatural" only in the natural, the holy only in the profane, and the revelational only in the rational.[22]

Bonhoeffer's basic conception of reality is that God is "the ultimate reality without and within everything that is,"[23] that in Jesus Christ the reality of God comes together with, enters into, the reality of the world, and that "all concepts of reality which do not take account of Him are abstractions."[24] Some implications of this are then given:

> In Christ we are offered the possibility of partaking in the reality of God and in the reality of the world, but not in the one without the other. The reality of God discloses itself only by setting me entirely in the reality of the world, and when I encounter the reality of the world

---

[21] Bonhoeffer, *Ethics* (London: SCM, 1964), pp. 191f.
[22] Ibid., p. 198.   [23] Ibid., p. 194.   [24] Ibid.

it is always already sustained, accepted and reconciled in the reality of God. This is the inner meaning of the revelation of God in the man Jesus Christ.[25]

The first key concept is therefore that of the Holy Spirit as the gift of the possibility of participation simultaneously in the reality of God and in the reality of the world in ways which "perform" the continuing realization of the world as sustained, accepted, and reconciled through being united with God in Christ. Bonhoeffer's favorite variation on that concept of reality is through the events of Jesus Christ's incarnation, crucifixion, and resurrection, emphasizing the affirmation of the world in the incarnation, the judgment of the world in the crucifixion, and the transformation of the world in the resurrection. That "ultimate" is what defines the Holy Spirit: all of that being "realized," performed.

He describes two-sphere thinking as so ingrained that it is extremely difficult to abandon. His main therapy is to "direct our gaze to the picture of the body of Christ Himself, who became man, was crucified and rose again."[26] This corresponds to what I will propose below as an appropriate postmodern *locus communis* of "living in the Spirit": being transformed before the face of Jesus Christ.

Realization as transformative conformation to Christ

The main way Bonhoeffer conceives this realization is as formation (*Gestaltung*) or conformation (*Gleichgestaltung*) according to the form (*Gestalt*) of Jesus Christ. One summary statement is:

> formation comes only by being drawn in into the form of Jesus Christ. It comes only as formation in His likeness, as *conformation with the unique form of Him who was made man, was crucified, and rose again.*[27]

In the next paragraph the reference to key New Testament texts on being transformed in the image of Christ suggests transformation as a further key word. This is, therefore, about transformative conformation to Jesus Christ. Once again Bonhoeffer develops his thought by reference to the incarnate, crucified, and risen Jesus Christ, followed immediately by the ecclesial implication: formation "means in the first place Jesus' taking form in His church."[28] What happens before the face of Christ is transformation into a fellowship of the Holy Spirit.

[25] Ibid., p. 195.   [26] Ibid., p. 205.   [27] Ibid., p. 80.   [28] Ibid., p. 83.

Differentiation: ultimate and penultimate

Eberhard Bethge sees the concept of the ultimate and penultimate as "the most fruitful of Bonhoeffer's creative formulas" and also as being unconsciously present in his theology for a long time.[29] The last word, the ultimate, is justification, which is by grace alone and faith alone, setting life on a new foundation, that of the life, death, and resurrection of Jesus Christ. Bonhoeffer goes on to describe somewhat lyrically how faith is never alone, but, insofar as it is the true presence of Christ, is accompanied by love and hope, giving full life before God.[30] Here in the classic New Testament trio of faith, love, and hope Bonhoeffer links into what, in the history of spirituality, have perhaps been the most pervasive categories under which to discuss Christian life. It amounts to a holistic holiness in transformative conformation to the gestalt of Jesus Christ. This event is ultimate, final in two senses.

First, it is final qualitatively, "by the nature of its contents."[31] It is God's free word, not necessitated by anything in history or to be achieved by following any method. Second, it is final in temporal terms, and so always in fact is preceded by penultimate things; there is a preparation for it. These penultimate things are not such in themselves, but only through being directed toward the ultimate.

So the penultimate is an inherently relational concept, and is designed to give priority to the freedom of God while yet affirming the significance of the penultimate and in particular the freedom of humanity before God to be human and to do good. It is an original proposal on the relation of God's grace to human freedom, which has given rise to one of the most complex ongoing debates in the history of pneumatology (the Holy Spirit has often been discussed largely under the heading of "grace").

The penultimate allows for a full affirmation of the realm of the natural (of special postmodern significance in the face of Nietzschean and other attacks on Christianity as undermining, repressing, distorting, or resenting full bodily, emotional, imaginative, and intellectual human flourishing), of the right to life, and of the importance of doing good (without that being understood as justification by works). The penultimate also allows for discrimination between the natural (what is directed toward Christ) and the unnatural (such as the Nazis were doing). The ultimate and penultimate also give a dynamic, historical structure for ethics and spirituality. They are structured and normative but affirm both divine and human freedom,

---

[29] Eberhard Bethge, "The Challenge of Dietrich Bonhoeffer's Life and Theology," in Ronald Gregor Smith ed., *World Come of Age* (London: Collins, 1967), p. 72.
[30] Bonhoeffer, *Ethics*, p. 121f.   [31] Ibid., p. 123.

and insist on the continual need for ethical and political discernment in one concrete situation after another, as exemplified in the fourth concept below.

This conceptuality also has considerable potential for theological epistemology.[32] In his articulation of the ultimate and penultimate, Bonhoeffer's subtle and precise engagement with philosophy and theology culminates in a close relating of ethics and epistemology which simultaneously affirms the integrity of the world, the natural, and human freedom while keeping them radically open to the ultimate. God is both united with the world in Jesus Christ and free, other, transcendent; and this is understood historically and eschatologically. Time is therefore also built into the dynamics of transformative conformation to the living Jesus Christ, whose ultimacy blesses the penultimate that prepares the way for it. The whole structure is simultaneously Christological and pneumatological, integrating the eschatological dimension of the Holy Spirit.

Bonhoeffer here conceptualizes an integration of epistemology and transformation, and might be seen as indicating a way beyond modernity that yet avoids some pitfalls of postmodernity. His affirmation of the penultimate insists on the continuing importance of rationality and philosophical rigor, and avoids dogmatism, fideism, foundationalism, nihilism, and positivism. He also stands as a warning for theologians who, in reaction against forms of rationality and philosophy that dismiss the reality of God, take refuge in philosophies which renounce rational and ethical norms. And he radically questions epistemologies and ontologies that are closed to what is theologically ultimate.[33]

This alternative to two-sphere thinking can easily revert back if the ultimate and penultimate are taken as mutually exclusive spheres – if, for example, the radicality of the ultimate is set against a penultimate which insists on realistic compromise. In a vivid paragraph that might be read as a description of fundamental tendencies in spiritualities, Bonhoeffer contrasts these:

---

[32] Cf. Janz, "Redeeming Modernity."

[33] Janz explores the contemporary significance of Bonhoeffer by showing how the discussions in *Act and Being* have many parallels with current debates in Anglo-American philosophy, such as that between Hilary Putnam (who advocates rational normativity along anti-realist lines) and Thomas Nagel (who advocates it along realist lines). It is, he suggests, wiser to follow Bonhoeffer's example of rigorous argument with "centrist" philosophies, while also opening up room for genuine transcendence, than to be seduced by those post-structuralist, postmodern philosophies whose enmity to many of theology's enemies makes them seem attractive allies, but whose anti-rationalism, anti-subjectivity, and relativism are actually hostile to a treatment of the penultimate which allows for its orientation to the ultimate. This has many parallels in current Jewish philosophy and theology, as in Peter Ochs' engagement with C. S. Peirce in *Peirce, Pragmatism and the Logic of Scripture* (Cambridge University Press, 1999).

Radicalism hates time, and compromise hates eternity. Radicalism hates patience, and compromise hates decision. Radicalism hates wisdom, and compromise hates simplicity. Radicalism hates moderation and measure, and compromise hates the immeasurable. Radicalism hates the real, and compromise hates the word.[34]

The unity of these is, as one might expect, in Jesus Christ incarnate, crucified and risen, the gestalt of a holiness which is utterly involved in the penultimate for the sake of the ultimate. "Christian life is participation in the encounter of Christ with the world,"[35] beyond all radicalism and compromise.

The structure of responsible life

The final key concept is the structure of responsible life. Bonhoeffer sums this up in the beginning of his discussion of it:

The structure of responsible life is conditioned by two factors; life is bound to man [*Mensch*] and to God and a man's own life is free. It is the fact that life is bound to man and to God which sets life in the freedom of a man's own life. Without this bond and without this freedom there is no responsibility. Only when it has become selfless in this obligation does a life stand in the freedom of a man's truly own life and action. The obligation assumes the form of deputyship and of correspondence with reality; freedom displays itself in the self-examination of life and of action and in the venture of a concrete decision.[36]

Freedom is a pneumatological theme running through Bonhoeffer's whole theology and is a most illuminating hermeneutical key to it, as Ann Nickson has shown.[37] Here at the heart of his *Ethics* Bonhoeffer gives a concentrated set of concepts describing the gestalt of life before God. It is a substitutionary responsibility alert to the reality of world and self, and committed to the risk of free decision in specific circumstances even if that means accepting guilt. This is the culminating gestalt of the *Ethics*, taking up the other concepts that I have discussed. Representation or substitution (*Stellvertretung*) ties it to the center of Bonhoeffer's Christology, and deserves to be worked through in relation to Jesus Christ's life and resurrection as well as his death. Correspondence with (or appropriateness to) reality likewise connects to the basic Christological affirmation of the one reality of God coming together

---

[34] Bonhoeffer, *Ethics*, p. 130.   [35] Ibid., p. 133.   [36] Ibid., p. 224.
[37] Ann Louise Nickson, "Divine and Human Freedom in the Theology of Dietrich Bonhoeffer" (Ph.D. Dissertation, Cambridge University, 1998, unpublished).

with the world. Calling it a form (gestalt) indicates that it is further developing Bonhoeffer's understanding of ethics and holiness as transformative formation or conformation. And the full affirmation of divine and human freedom in all the complexities and ambiguities of history, with their demands for risky decision-taking, is the further ethical determination, "in the Spirit," of the more formal concept of the ultimate and penultimate.

The notion of the venture (*Wagnis*) of concrete decision is an appropriate keystone for this ethical spirituality. It hints at that striking feature of holiness at its liveliest: its generativity, its unpredictability, its combination of newness and rightness – rightness in relation to God, to other people, to the realities of history, and to self. Yet, as Bonhoeffer was well aware, rightness is by no means apparent as the risk is being taken, and his meditation on the acceptance of guilt is the other side of the venture of free responsibility.

A JEWISH POSTMODERN WISDOM

In order to find a shape for an explicitly postmodern theology I now turn to some Jewish postmodern thinkers.

For two thousand years Jews have been "significant others" for Christians. After the parting of the ways between Jewish and Christian communities and the development of a largely non-Jewish church, Jews and the legacy of Israel remained extraordinarily important for Christians: in the adoption of the Hebrew Scriptures as the Christian Old Testament; in polemics; in attempts to convert; in far fewer attempts to have dialogue; in persecutions; and in repeated Christian efforts to give a theological account of how the church, the biblical Israel, and the continuing Jewish people are related to God's purposes.[38] Further, among the major religious traditions Judaism has been most similar to Christianity in sharing not only a thorough involvement with Hellenic civilization, including its West Roman and East Roman (Byzantine) forms, but also an intensive engagement with the Renaissance, the Enlightenment, and other transformations of Western modernity. Jews (especially those influenced most by Western culture) have therefore been in an advantageous position to pioneer postmodern philosophical and theological wisdom. Many of them have, simultaneously, wanted to maintain strong premodern roots, been deeply affected by modernity, and faced despair at the twentieth-century "man-made mass death." They have known what it is to be the excluded "others" in their diaspora existence, to represent

---

[38] For my understanding of some aspects of this see David F. Ford, "A Messiah for the Third Millennium," *Modern Theology* 16 (2000), 75–90.

a "difference" to be eliminated, and, since the foundation of the state of Israel in 1948, to be embroiled in the complexities and moral ambiguities of exercising (or supporting or criticizing) state power in a situation of religious and political conflict. They have, of course, responded to all this in very diverse ways, but in the light of all that has been said it should be obvious good sense for any contemporary Christian theology to give priority to listening to this "other."

Here is one account of what characterizes the thought of Eugene B. Borowitz, a pioneer in American postmodern Jewish theology:

1 *An element of Jewish traditionalism*: In Borowitz's terms, this is a tendency to reaffirm Israel's Covenant with God, epitomized in the classical rabbinic community's hermeneutical, ethical, and legal rereading.

2 *An element of Jewish modernism*: In Borowitz's terms, this is a tendency to affirm the autonomy of the Jewish person within Israel's Covenant, the dignity and rights of all persons universally, and rational standards for evaluating rabbinic rereadings of the Covenant.

3 *An element of disillusionment with modernism*: In Borowitz's terms, this is a tendency to recognize the finitude or context-specificity of human reason and of humanly constructed ethics and justice.

4 *An element of textual reasoning*: In Borowitz's practice, this is a capacity to transform the modern, anti-modern, and premodern elements of Jewish postmodernism into complementary, rather than competing tendencies: generating what we might call a covenantal movement of rational *and* faithful Jewish persons, for whom the discipline of rereading the biblical and rabbinic sources of Judaism is a means of reforming the ethical and hermeneutical practices of the modern academy and modern secular society as well as of traditional Judaism.[39]

To read that, paralleling "Jewish" with "Christian" and such Jewish terms as "the classical rabbinic community" with analogous Christian ones,[40] is to begin a Christian postmodern theology with a wisdom that has (critically) retained its connections with both premodernity and modernity, has faced traumatic suffering and disillusionment, and has committed itself to postmodern practices of hope – for example, reasoning in relation to Scripture

---

[39] Peter Ochs, "The Emergence of Postmodern Jewish Theology and Philosophy," in Peter Ochs and Eugene B. Borowitz, eds., *Reviewing the Covenant. Eugene B. Borowitz and the Postmodern Renewal of Jewish Theology* (New York: State University of New York Press, 2000), pp. 29f. For a fuller, multifaceted approach to Judaism from a set of postmodern perspectives, see Steven Kepnes, ed., *Interpreting Judaism in a Postmodern Age* (London and New York: New York University Press, 1996).

[40] Which analogies fit? – This exercise leaves considerable scope for debate, not least in dialogue with Jewish thinkers.

in the interests of healing traditional religion, academic life, and modern secular society.

Drawing on such Jewish theology and philosophy,[41] as well as on Williams, Bonhoeffer, and others in the Christian tradition, suggests one way forward for postmodern[42] Christian theology. Key features include the following: being deeply rooted in premodernity (especially in Scriptures and the traditions of their interpretation through commentary, theology, and "performance" in worship and community living); avoiding the modern tendency to a superiority complex with regard to what preceded it; recognizing that there is no way of avoiding the massive transformations of modernity (which have been for better as well as for worse), and that this calls for a labor of discernment and appropriation; and, through all this, taking responsibility for serving the mending, healing, and joy of human beings and all creation. There is a further feature that postmodern emphases encourage throughout: always to engage across one's boundaries with others, paying special attention to their sufferings, joys, and wisdom in the midst of the contingencies of history and creation. In the present chapter the primary "other" is Jewish, the major discourses are theological and philosophical, and the main other doctrine is Christology. But a thorough theology of the Holy Spirit would, of course, seek its wisdom in conversation with those of other religions and traditions, in a full range of other disciplines and discourses, and in relating to all the doctrines (including a doctrine of creation which relates the Spirit to the natural world and the "co-created" world of human society and culture).

A CHRISTIAN *LOCUS COMMUNIS*

Such hospitality to others assumes a "home" – not as a prior "given" where others are entertained on one's own terms, but as a recognition that only a certain sort of home can be a place where others are genuinely

---

[41] In such varied expressions as Ochs, *Peirce, Pragmatism and the Logic of Scripture*; Kepnes, *Interpreting Judaism in a Postmodern Age*; Eugene B. Borowitz, *Renewing the Covenant: A Theology for the Postmodern Jew* (Philadelphia: Jewish Publication Society, 1991); Robert Gibbs, *Correlations in Rosenzweig and Levinas* (Princeton University Press, 1992); Susan Handelman, *Fragments of Redemption: Jewish Thought and Literary Theory in Benjamin, Scholem, and Levinas* (Bloomington: Indiana University Press, 1991). The journal *Modern Theology* has, over many years, been one of the main forums where Jewish and Christian thinkers have engaged with each other on many issues (see, for example, volume 16:3, July 2000).

[42] The term "postmodern," for all its advantages, might as well, given suitable definition, be replaced by "late modern" or even by, in the phrase of Thomas W. Ogletree, "chastened modern" in *Reviewing the Covenant*, ch. 5.

welcomed (even when they challenge domestic arrangements), or be a base from which one can go out to be the guest of others. Before discussing Christian spirituality in terms of life-shaping practices, I will sketch such a "home" theology of the Holy Spirit for Christians today.

It is a classic Christian *locus communis* [43] or "common place," which has deep resonances with postmodern Jewish, Christian, and secular concerns: living before the face of Jesus Christ.[44] In New Testament terms, this is a place of "living in the Spirit," and can be variously imagined. In all the Gospels the Spirit's presence with Jesus (paradigmatically indicated at his baptism) means that the particularities of the complex events, interactions, and communications of his life, death, and resurrection become the key reference point for "life in the Spirit." Their primary perspective is that of "facing Jesus." The Fourth Gospel culminates in Jesus breathing the Holy Spirit on his disciples, linking the Spirit as closely as possible with living before his face. In Luke–Acts this *locus communis* is the place of the outpouring of the Holy Spirit at Pentecost in the aftermath of being blessed by Jesus in his ascension – those who wait together before his ascended, absent face receive this promised blessing. One of Paul's descriptions of living in the Spirit is of being transformed "from glory to glory" before the face of Christ (2 Corinthians 3:18), where he recognizes "the light of the knowledge of the glory of God" (2 Corinthians 4:6). The theme can be traced throughout the New Testament; it also has deep roots in the Old Testament, and can be followed through the course of Christian history to the present.

The *locus communis* of life in the Spirit before the face of Jesus Christ can help us to see Bonhoeffer's four pneumatological concepts in their integration. There is no room for two spheres here: all is before this face. It is a place of transformative conformation, and the particular otherness of each face resists any "conformist" tendency to limit diversity.[45] As the place of facing the incarnate, crucified, and risen Jesus Christ, it not only allows for both ultimacy and penultimacy but could also inspire further variations on that fruitful concept. And being before this face is a classic image of freedom and responsibility together, as communities and individuals are summoned and inspired to live in response to him.

---

[43] On the role of *loci communes* during eight hundred years of Christian life and thought, see Mary Carruthers, *The Craft of Thought. Meditation, Rhetoric, and the Making of Images, 400–1200* (Cambridge University Press, 1998).

[44] For a much fuller discussion of this, especially in its philosophical, exegetical and Christological aspects, see David F. Ford, *Self and Salvation: Being Transformed* (Cambridge University Press, 1999).

[45] Cf. Williams quoting Lossky above on "the face of the Spirit" in the infinite diversity of human faces in their particular identities.

In terms of Williams' conception of the interplay between given and future, between reality and encompassing truth, between Good Friday and Easter, and between suffering and hope, this face is a sign of those being held together amidst the urgencies and agonies of life and death – of a Spirit being breathed, and a message given, that can generate fresh signs of this bridging in the ordinariness as well as in the crises of history.

What, finally, is the "form of human subjectivity" (Williams) created by the Holy Spirit?[46] To put a great deal in a nutshell: the self, or soul, that is shaped before the face of Jesus Christ is "eucharistic."[47] He or she participates with and for others in the abundance of blessing that Bonhoeffer calls "ultimate," and takes responsibility with and for others in the orientation of the penultimate toward the ultimate. It is a self that, in Paul Ricoeur's terms, is neither autonomous and centered (as in some modern conceptions) nor fragmented and dispersed (as in some postmodernism), but has its being "as another." Its very linguistic, narrative, and ethical structure and dynamics incorporate otherness in the threefold form of its own body, other people, and conscience (a "site" allowing for the ultimate otherness of God). It is a self whose truth is not usually that of certainty, yet a self that need not despair of any truth at all: rather, at its core it has the possibility of living from trust in testimony. In Christian Scripture and tradition, the Holy Spirit inspires giving and hearing testimony to Jesus Christ, an activity that is constitutive of transformed community and selfhood.[48]

In terms of the *locus communis*, "before the face of Jesus Christ" is the place where selves are formed through silent listening and through witnessing (in word, action, suffering, celebration of all sorts) to the reality they face in faith, love, and hope. What is it to be "filled with the Spirit"? – "Speak to one another in psalms and hymns and spiritual songs; sing and make music from your heart to the Lord; and in the name of the Lord Jesus Christ give thanks every day for everything to our God and Father" (Ephesians 5:19–20). This is a place of recognition, through facing others, of the "who" of the Spirit in self-distribution.

---

[46] The thoughts which follow are developed further in Ford, *Self and Salvation.*

[47] On the soul in relation to a spirituality explicitly conceived in postmodern terms, see Rowan Williams, *Lost Icons. Reflections on Cultural Bereavement* (Edinburgh: T. & T. Clark, 2000) especially ch. 4, "Lost Souls." There is a specially provocative engagement with psychoanalysis and psychotherapy. These practices (with their theories) are increasingly places where Christian and other spiritualities are being worked out, and could be fruitfully related to Bonhoeffer's concepts.

[48] This is where communication in mission and evangelism calls for consideration, incorporating a cross-centered ethic of noncoercive respect for others.

GLOBAL DEVELOPMENTS AND LIFE-SHAPING
PRACTICES: SOME NOTES

What might a Christian spirituality in line with the above theology of the Holy Spirit be like? I will give just a few hints in relation to some of the life-shaping practices that seem, in the light of Jewish and Christian wisdom in these matters, to be among those to which it is most fruitful to attend. In each case I take it for granted that there are rich possibilities for learning from both premodern and modern practices.

I also take for granted that the horizon for these practices includes a contemporary perspective that does justice to the global reality of Christianity and its interactions, dialogues, and conflicts. This chapter has offered a few pointers using the Bible, some Western Christian theologians, and some Jewish thinkers. If, however, I were choosing to discuss the Holy Spirit and spirituality with resources from the broader global scene, I would identify three urgent items for the twenty-first century agenda, which the last century raised but left very much unfinished.

First, there is the significance and continuing challenge of the Pentecostal and charismatic movement, which began at the opening of the twentieth century and, judged by numerical growth in the time since then, has become the largest religious development in world history. Part of its relevance to the theology just outlined is its genesis among black Christians in the USA and its continuing appeal in many poor countries and groups. However, in many strands of the movement there is also a renewal of the significance of the Spirit for "the natural," most obviously expressed through intensive bodily participation in worship.

Second, there are the transformations of the world and human life generated by postmodern or late modern capitalism. Its global expansion and "success" have affected every sphere of existence and has posed both crude and subtle challenges to the world's religious traditions with which they are finding it extremely difficult to cope. Such global expansion helps generate disorientation, suffering, and environmental change on a scale and of a nature that has exposed the inadequacy of resources and has strained practices of wisdom and hope.

Third, there are the particularities of gender, culture, race, class, language, age, and so on. Postmodernism has been especially acute in exploring the significance of such differences. A theology of the Holy Spirit that affirms the particular beauty before God of each human face is committed to recognizing the appropriateness of developing a huge diversity of spiritualities – but also the desirability of their continuing conversation and, in many cases, mutual confrontation.

What of the practices which constitute a spirituality that might cope with such an agenda? On each practice, I will limit myself to just two points.

Worship and prayer

One of the characteristic features of our period, often commented upon by postmodern thinkers, is its "culture of excess," in which people feel overwhelmed by images, information, stimuli, desires, possibilities, choices, relationships, and an endless diversity of world-views, values, beliefs, commitments, and alternative ways of "reading" their histories, themselves, and other people. Might worship and prayer be conceived as "practices of excess" relating to the ultimate abundance, where it is possible to develop performatively a wisdom immersed in this culture but also oriented toward being "overwhelmed" by God?[49]

The other side of this worship is the discernment of idolatries in cruder and subtler forms. It is not just the obvious temptations of wrongly ultimate orientations such as money, power, pleasure, sex, self, success, status, security, knowledge, health, family, race, nation, religion, and so on. Modernity has been painfully perceptive in exposing ways in which religion's claims to ultimacy are vulnerable to moral, intellectual, political, psychological, and other forms of critique – in theological terms often amounting to a just exposure of idolatry. Postmodernity has been even more subtly and suspiciously perceptive in its critiques of modernity itself, showing how (often precisely in the areas where it has most prided itself) it has been vulnerable to overconfident certainty and closure, to oppressively "totalizing" thinking and action, to false absolutizing, and to elimination or at best ignoring of the "other" – especially the suffering other and the female other (and, of course, the ultimate Other). But postmodernity usually stops short of discerning "true" practices of worship and prayer as responses to such idolatries. Postmodern Christian spirituality has the task of doing justice to long traditions of such discernment, including above all the role of the doctrine of the Trinity in resisting the most tempting religious idolatries (absolutizing, separately or in pairs, a transcendent, distant God, or any person or movement in history, or human subjectivity, freedom, reason, creativity, or community), while at the same time testing and embodying the wisdom of modernity and postmodernity.

---

[49] For some practical suggestions on a spirituality along these lines see David F. Ford, *The Shape of Living. Spiritual Directions for Everyday Life* (Grand Rapids: Baker Books, 1998; London: HarperCollins, 1997), especially ch. 4, "Secrets and Disciplines – Soul-Shaping."

Interpreting Scripture

Postmodernity has had strong semiotic, linguistic, hermeneutical interests. What happens when these are combined with a long tradition of
scriptural interpretation which has been sustained through many periods,
cultures, and civilizations, including learning what modernity has to teach
through historical and other forms of criticism? One answer is given in
the work of some of the Jewish thinkers referred to above, who combine
hermeneutics learned from modernity and postmodernity with innovative
continuity with rabbinic tradition.[50] Their terms for this include "textual
reasoning" and "scriptural reasoning." Christian postmodern spirituality
needs to attempt something similar. Indeed, this could well be the crucial
intellectual and imaginative requirement for generating forms of Christian
spirituality that might respond adequately to the agenda outlined above. Out
of the many efforts in this direction already made, and especially drawing
again on the Jewish experience, two lessons might be learned.

First, one of the marks of Jewish textual reasoning is that it has learnt
from Christians (and others – increasingly from Muslims) and from a broad
array of academic disciplines. This phenomenon of being deeply loyal to one
scriptural tradition while being simultaneously engaged in radical openness
with others who are likewise engaged with their Scriptures and with various
disciplines – and, of course, risking the consequences of recognizing the
need for oneself and one's own tradition to be healed or transformed – is
paradigmatic for a spirituality that genuinely faces others. It is dangerous
for all participants. But this danger might be read as a contemporary site
and trace of the otherness of God among us.

Second, this conversation with scriptural "others" is a special dimension
of an approach to the scriptural text "in the Spirit" which trusts that there
is always "more" to be given through interpretation of this text. There are
large issues about the "senses" of Scripture here, but the basic wisdom is that
various modern (scholarly, liberal, conservative, fundamentalist, and other)
reductionist attempts to restrict the conversation between the text and the
contemporary community of interpreters are questioned, and practices of
imagining and reasoning are encouraged which are inspired by comparable
practices within Scripture[51] and in its varied traditions of interpretation.

Such renewal of lively, intelligent, and imaginative scriptural interpretation can help to construct the sorts of *loci communes* which might be both

---

[50] For example, "Postcritical Scriptural Interpretation," in Kepnes, *Interpreting Judaism in a
Postmodern Age*, ch. 2, with some bibliography pp. 80–81.

[51] For example, the redactions incorporated in the Pentateuch, or Job's relation to the Wisdom
tradition, or Isaiah on creation and the Exodus, or Luke's and Matthew's reworking of Mark,
or the New Testament's many reinterpretations of the Old Testament.

habitable and hospitable places contributing to the healing of the religious communities and of the societies they inhabit.

Building communities

Postmodernity has usually been suspicious of institutions and even of communities, acutely alert to the ways in which they can be structured and legitimated in the interests of the powerful, and can be oppressive to many of their own members or to outsiders. Religious institutions and communities have usually been seen among the least satisfactory in these respects. A Christian spirituality, of course, requires a practical theology of the church, which is the task of chapter 15 in this volume. But what two guidelines might grow out of the present chapter so far?

First, spirituality needs to include a wisdom of responsibility for institutions and communities. This includes many generations of learning what makes and does not make for community flourishing, and embraces post-modernity's suspicions and critiques. But there is perhaps a special need today for wisdom about exchanges across the boundaries of institutions, communities, and cultures, and about how high-quality communication and conversation can flourish. Even when conversation happens, it is often divorced from institutional or community processes for taking decisions and changing policies or affecting behavior. An appropriate term for what is at stake is the quality of *deliberation*, that conversation aimed at decision-taking together which is neither just a bargaining on the basis of power possessed nor a confrontational argument. What might be the forms of a Christian discipline of deliberation that can cope with internal church matters as well as with responsibility toward other religious communities, educational institutions, political issues, management policies, international affairs, and so on?

Second, there is a deep convergence between, on the one hand, the role of the Holy Spirit in Christian Scripture and tradition, and, on the other, the contemporary recognition of the constitutive role of information, knowledge, and learning in society. "Information age," "knowledge economy," "learning society," have rightly become clichés. In the New Testament the Spirit is closely linked to learning and communicating Christian faith in apostleship, preaching, teaching, prophecy, prayer, worship, speaking in tongues, witnessing, knowledge, and wisdom, and these "gifts of the Spirit" are intimately related to building up the community.

The convergence is perhaps clearest in the practices of learning and teaching. Postmodernity, with its powerful, pervasive media, and massive emphasis on knowledge skills and education, has meant a crisis for all traditions (not just religious ones). Perhaps the most fundamental challenge for a Christian spirituality is to its practices of learning and teaching "in the Spirit." What shapes might postmodern catechesis take? What wisdom might help the disciplines and institutional dynamics of the postmodern university to serve wisdom better? How are good teachers and learners formed in this culture?

Acting ethically

Postmodernity has been deeply ambivalent about ethics. As Edith Wyschogrod shows, some of the main thrusts have been deeply "irresponsible" toward others to the point of nihilist reveling in "excesses" of various kinds; others have been radically concerned for their neighbors, especially the marginalized, oppressed, and suffering of all sorts.[52] This sphere has already been treated in discussing Bonhoeffer, but I will conclude with two further points.

Perhaps the main postmodern ethical concern has been about violence, and various forms of the coercive, dominating use of power. Yet it is striking how rarely the biblical possibility of "gentleness" (Greek *praütes*, and related concepts such as mercy, compassion, kindness, patience, self-control)[53] has been explored as a core notion for spirituality. It is a self-designation of Jesus: "I am gentle" (Matthew 11:29). It is a fruit of the Holy Spirit (Galatians 5:23). It is in the "headlines" for Christian conduct (for example, Matthew 5:5 in the Sermon on the Mount, and Ephesians 4:2). What would a postmodern wisdom for practices of gentleness be like?

Finally, Wyschogrod's postmodern "hagiographic" ethics gives a vital turn to my *locus communis* of living in the Spirit before the face of Jesus Christ. Her ethics draws on saints who have been altruistically responsible for others, often to the point of dying. It is an ethic of radical service, and suggests in Christian terms a closing ethical *locus*.

What if Jesus' saying about being the "servant of all" (Mark 10:44) were to be the guideline for a spirituality, and if having the "mind" of Christ as servant (cf. Philippians 2:1–13) were to be a key mark of the Spirit? The emphasis in this *locus* is less on being before the face of Christ and more on facing, with him and with others, the tasks and people that are to be served. It is an orientation to the ultimate, to the Kingdom of God, to the full flourishing of human life while immersed in the demanding contingencies of history.

---

[52] Cf. Edith Wyschogrod, *Saints and Postmodernism* (London and Chicago: University of Chicago Press, 1990).

[53] One might add notions such as meekness, docility, and humility, whose discrediting to the point of virtually being unusable in our culture tells its own story.

Service is so vital to Judaism and Christianity (as well as other traditions) that it is hard to see them being faithful to their roots without developing variations on this theme that are sensitive to postmodern suspicions of domination, oppression, and "servility." Many of those drawn upon by Wyschogrod are extremely sensitive both to those suspicions and to the degradations brought about by scorning an ethic of responsible, compassionate service of others: perhaps it is only such people who can help to recuperate a spirituality of service for postmodern living.

Two closing notes on such a Christian spirituality: in John's Gospel the culminating teaching on service in chapters 13–17 sees the transformation of service into friendship (John 15:15); and this teaching is given by Jesus as a preparation for his death. Bonhoeffer in prison summed up his spirituality in a poem "Stations on the Road to Freedom."[54] His three life-shaping practices of discipline, action, and suffering culminate in a fourth: dying. Whether premodern, modern, or postmodern, that is a "practice" which most intensively tests any spirituality's wisdom.

Further reading

Bonhoeffer, Dietrich, *Ethics* (London: SCM Press, 1964).

Chopp, Rebecca, *The Power to Speak: Feminism, Language, God* (New York: Crossroad, 1989).

Coakley, Sarah, "Why Three? Some Further Reflections on the Doctrine of the Trinity," in Sarah Coakley and David Pailin eds., *The Making and Remaking of Christian Doctrine* (Oxford: Clarendon Press, 1993).

Grey, Mary C., *Prophecy and Mysticism: The Heart of the Postmodern Self* (Edinburgh: T. & T. Clark, 1997).

Kepnes, Steven, ed., *Interpreting Judaism in a Postmodern Age* (New York and London: New York University Press, 1996).

Lash, Nicholas, *Believing Three Ways in One God. A Reading of the Apostles' Creed* (London: SCM Press, 1992).

McIntosh, Mark A., *Mystical Theology. The Integrity of Spirituality and Theology* (Oxford: Blackwell, 1998).

McIntyre, John, *The Shape of Pneumatology. Studies in the Doctrine of the Holy Spirit* (Edinburgh: T. & T. Clark, 1997).

Moltmann, Jürgen, *The Church in the Power of the Spirit* (London: SCM Press, 1975).

Ochs, Peter and Nancy Levene, eds., *Textual Reasonings. Jewish Philosophy and Text Study at the end of the Twentieth Century* (London: SCM, 2002).

Williams, Rowan, *Lost Icons* (Edinburgh: T. & T. Clark, 2000).

Wyschogrod, Edith, *Saints and Postmodernism* (London and Chicago: University of Chicago Press, 1990).

---

54 Bonhoeffer, *Letters and Papers from Prison*, pp. 370f.

Index